Ole Davidsen

The Narrative Jesus

A Semiotic Reading of Mark's Gospel

AARHUS UNIVERSITY PRESS

AARHUS UNIVERSITY PRESS
Aarhus University, Building 170
DK-8000 Aarhus C, Denmark

Denne afhandling er af det Teologiske Fakultet ved
Aarhus Universitet antaget til forsvar for den
teologiske doktorgrad.

Aarhus, 10. februar 1992
Bent Smidt Hansen
decanus

Forsvaret finder sted i Juridisk Auditorium, bygning 334,
Aarhus Universitet, fredag den 24. september 1993 kl. 13 prc.

The Narrative Jesus

To Hanne

PREFACE

Our life is aspiration and quest. On the wings of desire, borne on the unappeasable longing for knowledge and truth, we haunt the libraries whatever the season. At the outset we search high and low; later we seek with narrowing purpose until finally we are looking for the book that is never there. Then it dawns upon us that the work we are seeking with such untiring energy but cannot locate is hidden, because it has not yet been written. Bearing in mind the many magnificent monographs which exist, we at first refuse to believe this. But slowly it becomes clear to us that the missing book is the book we must write ourselves.

Is the longing then satisfied? Not completely. But in the process of the work it comes to be seen in proportion. Seldom if ever are the results as we hoped. But nevertheless they are often better than we sometimes feared. However, definitive truth and ultimate knowledge still keep us waiting.

Our libraries abound with evidence to show that from such wrestling no one prevails without a slight limping. The testimonies are published in the hope that we may nevertheless be able to recognize ourselves in each other's longings, even if only for a time.

I have written my book, but not without assistance from various quarters. First, I thank my teacher, dr. phil. Per Aage Brandt, who introduced me to the world of semiotics, and long before it became fashionable confirmed my opinion that the Christian discourse is a privileged field of research.

I am grateful to lic. theol. Aage Pilgaard and theol. dr. René Kieffer who have followed with great interest my wrestling with Mark's Gospel.

I am greatly indebted to the Faculty of Theology, Aarhus University, which awarded me a senior research scholarship for the period 1 July 1987 to 30 June 1990, and to the Institute of New Testament, Aarhus University, to which I was attached for the same period of time.

Thanks also to the translators, Christine and Frederick Crowley of Banstead, Surrey, England, who undertook to make my doctoral thesis accessible to an international public, and to cand. theol. Troels Nørager who helped with the proofreading.

Finally, I wish to express my gratitude to Aarhus University's Research Foundation for financial support in the translation and to the Danish Research Council for the Humanities for financial support in the publication of my book.

Århus, 1 June 1993

Ole Davidsen

CONTENTS

Introduction

Part One. Narrative Exegesis

Part Two. The Wonder-Worker

Part Four. The Savior

Part Five. The Christ Myth

Indices

INTRODUCTION

INTRODUCTION

A. BIBLE AND SEMIOTICS

In November 1970, ERHARDT GÜTTGEMANNS published the first number of the periodical *Linguistica Biblica*.[1] This publication may be seen as the commencement of a distinctive line of study - biblical semiotics - which has developed within exegesis in recent years.

GÜTTGEMANNS' intention was to create an inter-disciplinary scientific periodical for theologians, semioticians, linguists, philosophers of language, and students of literature. The new advances achieved by the humanities in the exploration of linguistic and textual phenomena needed to be taken account of by theology. For exegesis, this meant keeping abreast of the times.

A few years later, in 1974, another language-orientated exegetic periodical began appearing, *Semeia*.[2] In his introduction to the first number, AMOS N. WILDER explains the background to this initiative, and points out the increasing interest in *language* in all its aspects in various fields, for example linguistics, folklore, literary theory, structuralism and social anthropology. Although the prevailing exegesis to some extent is concerned about and interested in linguistic and textual phenomena, this dimension is often overshadowed by other problems. The new approaches therefore represent no radical break with tradition. But on the other hand exegesis must appreciate that developments within theory and method that have occurred in other fields within the humanities confront it with new challenges and new opportunities.[3]

Yet another periodical of this kind emerged in 1975, *Sémiotique et Bible*.[4] Compared with the other two, the perspective here is more restricted. Its concern is a semiotic exegesis on the basis of A.J. GREIMAS' formation of theory.[5] But it is true of all three that they are exegetic periodicals whose subject is the biblical texts and whose theories and methods are semiotic in a broad sense.[6]

---

[1] *Linguistica Biblica. Interdisziplinäre Zeitschrift für Theologie und Linguistik*, Bonn 1970ff.

[2] *Semeia. An Experimental Journal for Biblical Criticism*, Missoula 1974ff.

[3] Amos N. Wilder, "*Semeia*, An Experimental Journal for Biblical Criticism: An Introduction", *Semeia 1, A Structuralist Approach to the Parables*, Missoula 1974, pp. 1.

[4] Published by *Centre pour l'Analyse du Discours Religieux* under the direction of Jean Delorme, Lyon 1975ff.

[5] Or more broadly on a work that falls under the so-called "*Parisian school*", cf. J.-C. Coquet (ed.), *Sémiotique. L'École de Paris*, Paris 1982; Herman Parret and Hans-George Ruprecht (ed.), *Exigences et perspectives de la sémiotique. Recueil d'hommage pour Algirdas Julien Greimas I/II*, New York 1985.

[6] The term "semiotics" is here to be understood as on a par with terms such as psychology and sociology, i.e. as a collective term for research efforts which, in the capacity of generalizing science,

It is not unimportant that these three periodicals saw themselves as experimental from the outset. This is of course what one might expect of an inquiring science, but this self-perception is also an expression of the situation in which the initiative was taken. A fermentative process rather than a clarification process was set in motion, and the monopoly of historical exegesis meant that new initiatives appeared without institutional backing. Its self-sufficiency has had the effect that what arose was a lack of concurrence between the established problems and the new problems that presented themselves, which made dialogue difficult.

The concept of an embryonic development within a monolithic exegesis did not hold water. When the perspective is expanded and it is perceived that identification of exegesis' field with that of historical exegesis is scientifically an unjustifiable restriction of the perspective of inquiry, the situation becomes not only new but also boundless. The exegete can no longer be content quantitatively to extend the competence he has already achieved, but must, as earlier in history, set out with no guarantees into new fields in order gradually to build up expertise and to arrive at stable knowledge and serenity. The three periodicals and the studies, major or minor, that fall under the comprehensive research project of which these are merely the most obvious expression are testimony to the intention to tread new paths, to an exegesis on the move.[7]

The present study is part of the composite and comprehensive research project that the periodicals referred to and the network of researchers supporting them have designated and demarcated. The basic concept is that *Mark's Gospel is a narrative*, and as such can be made the subject of narratological analysis.

The theoretical works of A.J. GREIMAS and CLAUDE BREMOND here provide an insight into the narrative's semiotics which permits application in an exegetic perspective. In fact, it is initially the intensified comprehension of linguistic and textual phenomena that makes it possible to recognize and appreciate the gospel text as a narrative.

What is at issue, therefore, is to demonstrate and accentuate the properties of the gospel text which historical research has neglected because of its restricted

---

study the conditions for the apprehension and production of meaning. Cf. Ole Davidsen, "Der Status der Religionssemiotik als autonome Wissenschaft", *Linguistica Biblica 49*, Bonn 1981, pp. 71-84.

[7] René Kieffer, *Essais de métodologie néo-testamentaire*, Lund 1972, is a first draft of a methodological synthesis. Kieffer warns against the dangers present in exegesis' new situation, the development of "sects" and "schools" which mutually fail to appreciate one another. It is the question of exegesis' unity that arises, and therewith the question whether it is possible to prepare an elementary but adequate model within which the various methods or scientific models have their legitimate place. The problem has by no means lost its topicality, but it is uncertain whether the actual perception that characterizes Kieffer's linguistically inspired attempt is the most suitable starting point, cf. pp. 55 and 69. Within literary criticism, where the question of unity presents itself in a similar way, Peter Brask, in *Tekst og tolkning. Bidrag til den litterære semantik, Bind 1*, København 1973, pp. 59-90 (Text and interpretation. Contribution to literary semantics, Vol. 1), has put forward a significant model for the relationship between the various models. This model, cf. below Part 5, The Christ myth, pp. 331, might, with Kieffer's approach, be a possible starting point for renewed consideration of exegesis' unity.

linguistic and text-theory point of reference. The gospel text can and must be made the subject of historical research, but New Testament exegesis must include complementary augmentations if important aspects of its subject are to be fully appreciated.

B. History and Semiotics

This is not a matter of returning regressively to a pre-critical stage. The semiotic reading is not an attempt to circumvent historical criticism. If one of the constituent features of an uncritical view of the Bible is the unreflecting identification of narrative and history, it may be said that historical critical method has uncovered the discrepancy between narrative and history. By privileging history at the expense of narrative, the latter has been released for a critical investigation that does not just revert regressively to fundamentalism but rests on a clear distinction between history and narrative. Step by step, historical critical method has destroyed the gospel text as an historical account, i.e. as an account giving a coherent and simple description of actual occurrences. But it has thereby at the same time - although unintentionally - contributed to the creation of a basis for recognition of the gospel text as narrative.

From a semiotic perspective, historical criticism's assumption can be formulated as follows: from the historical fact that a series of events has been recounted, it cannot be concluded that this series of events is an historical fact. But then it must in fact be accepted that Mark's Gospel may be pure fiction or a fabrication. The remarkable fact is that this gospel is and remains itself, whether or not it is a completely veracious account of what actually took place, an only partly true description in which an historical core is encapsulated by or interwoven into secondary additions, a literary fiction from which historical facts are completely absent, or a fabrication with dispersed historical sprinklings. Irrespective of the aspect of its correspondence to historical reality, the gospel remains the same. As a linguistic entity, as a narrative, it is indifferent in its relationship to reality. It says precisely the same thing, whether historically true or false.

Semiotic exegesis, whose purpose is to establish the text's meaning by a methodological reading, can therefore quite justifiably permit itself to ignore the question of the narrative's historical truth. The narrative does not of course take its meaning from whether it is true or false, but it is this meaning which in the assertion's form can be historically true or false. From the point of view that does not understand what a narrative is, semiotic exegesis' elimination of the question of truth may appear to be an expression of uncritical scholarship, if not plain pseudo-scholarship. The historical exegete will therefore perhaps have difficulty in understanding the legitimacy of this procedure. But this is because, in such an event, the historian is on a par with the fundamentalist concerning understanding the gospel text. Both see this as a source for clarifying what actually took place, sometimes as a fully reliable source, sometimes as an only partly reliable source that must be read symptomatically.

The historian is not, however, purely and simply precluded from understanding the semiotic approach, since he himself distinguishes between the gospel text as a source of the events related (as an account) and as a source of the historical situation in which the narrative was related (as a relic). From an historical perspective, semiotic exegesis is to this extent merely a procedure employed to explain what it was that the early community proclaimed in narrative form. It is possible that the narrative's Jesus-image is fully in accordance with the Jesus-image the historian is able to reconstruct, but this is not certain. If there is discrepancy, the historian himself must ignore the narrative's claim, i.e. eliminate its own demand for truth, and he must read it symptomatically, critically, first distinguishing the historically impossible events (e.g. the resurrection) from the historically possible events (e.g. the crucifixion), and then assess whether the latter are historically probable or improbable.

The historian's reading of the gospel text as a source rests on a strategic choice. Such is the situation at least today, where other alternatives exist. The semiotician makes a different strategic choice when adopting the attitude that the gospel text is a narrative. The semiotician's choice is not, however, an attempt to evade scientific criticism; quite the opposite. The semiotic reading must be seen as a continuation and an intensification of historical criticism, drawing the full implications of the historian's perception.

The historian cannot take the gospel text at face value as an account of actual events. If he is asked to give an opinion on the gospel text as a whole, as one collective description, as one single assertion, he must reject it as unhistorical. It does not affect matters that the gospel text, despite its irrefutable nature as purpose-directed literature, nevertheless contains discursive and narrative material that may well provide historically reliable sources for interpreting what has taken place, at least in part. Neither does it alter matters that the gospel text's existence can be explained only by referring to historical events and persons (the crucifixion of Jesus of Nazareth), which at least was a reason for its appearance. The semiotician now draws the full implication by establishing that the gospel text is a narrative which as a discursive whole tells of *a narrative world*. It is in this capacity that the gospel text has functioned and continues to function.

In this context, it may be helpful to consider GOTTLOB FREGE's differentiation between meaning (*Sinn*) and "signification" (*Bedeutung*).[8] The "signification"

---

[8] Gottlob Frege, "Über Sinn und Bedeutung" (1892), Günther Patzig (ed.), *Funktion, Begriff, Bedeutung. Fünf logische Studien*, Göttingen 1969, pp. 40. Quotation-marks are used to mark his special use of the word signification; cf. Peter Brask, *Tekst og tolkning. Første del. Bidrag til den litterære semantik*, København 1973, pp. 51.

may be true or false, but not the meaning. The sentence "Odysseus was put ashore at Ithaca deeply asleep" implies a thought (*Gedanke*) or a statement that remains the same, whether or not the name "Odysseus" has a "signification". The "signification" is the object indicated by the word, the statement's truth-value. If an "Odysseus" actually exists, then the statement is true and the "signification" is *true*; if he does not exist, then the statement is false and the "signification" is *false*. Nevertheless, the meaning is the same in both cases.

From this perspective, the gospel text is one single statement with "signification" either true or false, and the historian is in no doubt that it is false. Ruled by his search for historical truth, the historian therefore ignores the text's meaning. The semiotician on the other hand is interested precisely in the text's meaning, and ignores its "signification".

FREGE says that it is desirable to have a special term for such signs as have meaning only. If, for example, they are referred to as images, then the actor's words on the stage would be images - indeed, the actor himself would be an image.[9] The opposite to such an image-language would be an object-language containing only "signification". In fact, such an object-language's "signification" would have always to be true, since one would always have what was signified at hand. In such a denotation-language the word will be the designating term and the object the designated content. The fundamentalist applauds a symbolic theory of this type. The irrevocable connection between the word and the object means that it would not be possible to explain the gospel text's existence unless everything took place as written. The historian is more critical; he knows that "signification" is either true or false. He regards the gospel text as an account which - correctly or incorrectly - represents a truth lying beyond it. Both the fundamentalist and the historian therefore equate meaning with "signification". What is "significationless" is also meaningless.

The semiotician insists on the difference between meaning and "signification", and maintains that the gospel narrative is a *discourse*, i.e. a "significationless" but meaningful figure- or connotation-language. This is how the matter must be formulated, at least by way of introduction. Only then is it possible to relate to the decisive fact that the gospel narrative is not fictional literature with no claim to truth but a special form of literature undaunted in its insistence upon its "signification". In a critical perspective, the gospel narrative can no longer be considered as the representation of a truth lying beyond it, but must be seen as a discourse which from beginning to end is engaged in convincing its reader of its own inherent truth.[10]

---

[9] Ibid. p. 48.

[10] Frege comments that in special cases only are we content to ask about the sentence's (narrative's) meaning. Usually, we also raise the question of its "signification". For those who read Homer's *Odyssey* as a work of art (fiction), it is immaterial whether the name "Odysseus" has a "signification". But if we leave "den Kunstgenuß" and raise the question of truth, then we turn to "einer wissenschaftlichen

The semiotic project within biblical exegesis must be seen as expressing the recognition of the limits of historical method. Historical criticism is a decisive precondition for the emergence of the perception that the original Christian texts are to an overwhelming degree *literature*, but at the same time it can only relate to a few aspects of this phenomenon. Literature is the "significationless" but meaningful language that must be explored for itself, for which reason exegesis must see its field as divided into two large parallel and complementary areas, the historical and the semiotic. A one-sided historical exploration of the gospel text rests upon a misunderstanding of this text's literary status and is objectively unwarrantable.

If the gospel text's status as literature is recognized, it appears as a *gospel narrative*, a *sign*, which alone has meaning. However, if one enters the universe narrated it then occurs that "significations" re-emerge. If no "signification" existed in the narrative's world, then its characters would be able to establish nothing at all. A further point is that the gospel narrative itself claims to be dealing with reality and does in fact intermingle with it, since it is read in reality. A large number of questions arise, in part for exegesis and in part for theology, after this Copernican turn, questions that can only be answered little by little. But the semiotic project rests on the critical perception that the gospel narrative has meaning only as a discourse. Only for faith can it assert itself as "signification". From this perspective, all the gospel narrative's information about "Jesus" as a person is information about a narrated actor. He is not an independently existing personage of whom the narrative tells, but a semiotic entity which exists only by virtue of the story: he is *narrative*. The narrative is a *sign* whose *linguistic* plane of expression is related to a *linguistic* plane of content. Meaning is an event in language.[11]

Historical gospel research, in so far as it is known from the form-critical school, has emphasized the gospel text's status as literature. As a literary genre, the gospel is a Christian innovation, which we encounter for the first time in Mark's Gospel. This literature is a testimony of faith. The gospel's task is to

---

Betrachtung" (ibid. p. 48). If we shift this concept in parallel to the gospel narrative, it may be said to be immaterial whether the name "Jesus" has a "signification" as long as it is read as a fictional work of art. But if the question of truth is raised, then one adopts a scientific point of view which is not interested in the narrative Jesus (on the meaning level) but in reality's historical Jesus (on the "signification" level). It appears therefore that the question of the gospel narrative's truth must be determined on a historical scientific basis. The problem is, however, that the gospel narrative, which contrary to fiction insists on its "signification", knowingly contradicts the empirical basis on which the scientific point of view's perception of truth rests. It asserts to this extent that the truth question can be raised without one therefore adopting a scientific point of view, and this is why historical scientific exploration of the gospel narrative necessarily causes a failure to appreciate it and becomes reductive; cf. further below chapter XVII.

[11] Cf. A.J. Greimas, J. Courtés, *Sémiotique. Dictionnaire raisonné de la théorie du langage*, Paris 1979, art. "Signe"; Ferdinand de Saussure, *Cours de linguistique générale*, Paris 1916, pp. 99; "Le signe linguistique unit non une chose et un nom, mais un concept et une image acoustique.", i.e. "signifié et signifiant"; Louis Hjelmslev, *Omkring sprogteoriens grundlæggelse*, København 1943 (Prolégomènes à une théorie du langage, Paris 1968), pp. 44; the sign is here set by the relation between the content and the expression.

awaken and strengthen faith in Jesus Christ, not to give a biographical account
of the historical Jesus' life.

In his account of the form-critical method's perception of the gospel,
HEINRICH ZIMMERMANN emphasizes a number of characteristics regarding the
specific nature of this literary genre; in the first place, the close association with
a preceding tradition. The evangelists are first and foremost, but not exclusively,
"Sammler, Tradenten, Redaktoren".[12] The gospel consists of joined, individual
pericopes which have existed as separate traditional items before they were
incorporated into a larger context. The gospel is therefore the result of an editor's
use of a body of material already available which refers to an anonymous
tradition and its history.

The second characteristic is a sequence structure, a superior framework,
beginning with the baptism of Jesus by John, then permitting Jesus to appear as
miracle worker and teacher, and concluding with his suffering and death. It is
characteristic that the account of Jesus' Passion is especially comprehensive.

The third characteristic is formulated by ZIMMERMANN as follows: "In Form
geschichtlicher Darstellung geschieht Verkündigung." Expressed negatively, this
formulation means that the gospel is not what it immediately appears to be, i.e.
an account of Jesus' historical life and career. In the gospel, we do not encounter
the historical Jesus. Expressed positively, it means that the gospel is a proclamation of Jesus Christ which takes the form of an historical description. It is this
which is peculiar to the gospel: the connection between proclamation and
historical description.

The last characteristic is the proclamation's topicality. It is directed towards
the present time and recorded in a concrete situation. It is, however, not the
evangelist who speaks, but through his writing he allows the elevated Lord to
speak to his community.

The question of the gospel's origin, *in casu* Mark's Gospel, lies beyond the
semiotician's horizon. This does not mean, however, that he sees the gospel text
as an innovation independent of tradition. For the semiotician, texts are not
created from the signification-maker's unique vision but on the basis of other
texts. The available text is nevertheless an innovation, an independent discourse,
sustained by the voice of one narrator. The use of traditional material is the
narrator's responsibility, since in a genuine speech act he makes its words his
own. From this viewpoint, the gospel text is one coherent and unified narrative
discourse.

In regard to the second characteristic also, the semiotic conception distinguishes itself from the historical. It is indeed revealing that ZIMMERMANN allows
the baptism of John to indicate the beginning, and the crucifixion the conclusion.

---

[12] Heinrich Zimmermann, *Neutestamentliche Methodenlehre. Darstellung der historisch-kritischen
Methode*, Stuttgart 1970, pp. 137. The quotation is from Martin Dibelius, *Die Formgeschichte des
Evangeliums*, Tübingen 1971, p. 2.

For the historian, it is these plausible events that provide the continuity-creating structure. For the semiotician, however, it is striking that, as regards Mark's Gospel, it is the anointing with the Holy Spirit at the baptism that provides the actual beginning and the resurrection that provides the actual conclusion of the chain of events recounted. On this point, ZIMMERMANN points out that the gospel is characterized by the viewpoint that Jesus' Passion is an expression of God's will, and that the structure referred to possibly derives from a previously-existing "Kerygma". But there is little kerygma in the events referred to, which are an undue reduction of the gospel narrative. What ZIMMERMANN indicates here is not the sequential structure of the gospel text but the events in the historically probable sequence in which the historian recognizes himself when considering the gospel as an historical account.

The third point is of particular importance in understanding the difference between historical and semiotic perception. Both parties will be able to call the gospel text an "historical narrative", and as such it is also the fundamental challenge of exegesis. However, this must divide itself if it is to understand this complex phenomenon. For the historian, what is at issue is a Jesus narrative constructed on certain historical events that are the subject of a mythical interpretation. The historical can, however, be recognized in spite of everything behind the veil of the proclamation. For the semiotician a Christ narrative is concerned, a myth, which by its use of proper names, place names and dates establishes an historical anchorage with a view to constituting a simulated narrative-external referent and generating the signification effect of "reality".[13] The narrated world, however, can nevertheless be discerned behind the veil of historification.

The final point ZIMMERMANN refers to also makes it possible to demonstrate a difference in concepts. The historian sees the proclamation's present as a specific historical period. The gospel addresses itself to a specific community, and is the answer to the questions asked by this community in a specific situation. The proclamation is bound up with time, place and person. On the other hand, the semiotician's interest is in the remarkable phenomenon that the narrative is no more time-rooted, place-rooted and person-rooted than to have established a quite overwhelming history of consequence. In the nature of things, therefore, he must be more preoccupied with the narrative's general and universal aspects which enable it to function in other times, in other places and for other persons, and therefore shifts attention from the communication situation to the gospel narrative's enunciation-logical structure. In investigating the relationship between enunciation and utterance, he is also in a position to explain the special characteristic of the narrative, that it is not the evangelist who speaks but the elevated Lord.

---

[13] Cf. *Sémiotique*, art. "Ancrage".

In *Offene Fragen zur Formgeschichte des Evangeliums*, ERHARDT GÜTTGE-
MANNS advanced the theory, crucial to exegesis, that the gospel form is *"eine
autosemantische Sprachform*, d.h. eine Sprachform, die in ihrem 'Sinn' nur durch
und aus sich selbst erklärt werden kann". As "Sprachform", i.e. as literature, the
gospel has no meaning by reference to or by being derived from so-called
historical facts.[14]

GÜTTGEMANNS' treatise is a theoretical confrontation with form criticism. He
himself presents no analysis of the gospel as a speech-form, but points out new
tasks for exegesis based on a new perception of the gospel text as literature. The
semiotic-exegetic project of which *Linguistica Biblica, Semeia*, and *Sémiotique
et Bible* are exponents may be said to have adopted these tasks. It is quite
characteristic that the majority of the semiotic-exegetic works available are gospel
analyses. But interest in the gospels has been so dominant because of the domin-
ance of narrative semiotics, which is itself associated with the fact that it was the
discovery of narrativity which gave serious impetus to the formation of semiotic
theory.

C. EXEGESIS AND SEMIOTICS

The crucial leap is the development from the linguist's sentence to the semiotician's discourse. The text is either merely a simple linking together of sentences,
and its meaning is then merely the result of more or less fortuitously linked
sentence-meanings, or it constitutes a *signification whole*, a meaningful speech
act containing its own organization beyond the sentence limit. It is this discursive
organization which is called narrativity, because it was first recognized through
the study of narratives.[15]

As far as exegesis is concerned, a crucial problem arises in the wake of this
insight. Either the gospel text is merely, as form criticism asserts, a simple

---

[14] Erhardt Güttgemanns, *Offene Fragen zur Formgeschichte des Evangeliums*, München 1971, p. 197.
It is the same basic concept that characterizes the literary historian Northrop Frye, who asserts that the
biblical narratives are "as distantly related to historical events as an abstract painting is to realistic
representation, and related in a similar way. The priority is given to the mythical structure or outline of
the story, not to the historical events. (...) And just as the historical books of the Old Testament are not
history, so the Gospels are not biography." The literarily orientated exegesis should therefore be founded
on the basic concept that "if anything historically true is in the Bible, it is there not because it is
historically true but for different reasons", *The Great Code. The Bible and Literature*, London 1981, pp.
40. At least since W. Wrede, *Das Messiasgeheimnis ind den Evangelien. Zugleich ein Beitrag sum
Verständnis des Markusevangeliums*, Göttingen 1901, exegesis has known the truth: "als Gesamtdarstel-
lung bietet das Evangelium keine historische Anschauung mehr vom wirklichen Leben Jesu. Nur blasse
Reste einer solchen sind in eine übergeschichtliche Glaubensausfassung übergegangen. Das Markusevangelium gehört in diesem Sinne in die Dogmengeschichte.", p. 131. But only very recently has exegesis
realized what it actually implies, that the gospel narrative, considered positively, is *literature* and not
merely, considered negatively, *non-history*.

[15] Cf. *Sémiotique*, art. "Narrativité".

linking together of pericopes, and its meaning is then merely the result of more or less fortuitously linked items of tradition, or it constitutes a signification whole, a meaningful speech act, which contains its own organization beyond the individual pericope: it is one narrative.

If semiotic exegesis could for a start be content with proclaiming the gospel to be an auto-semiotic speech form, a literary signification whole, it would soon have to begin analytical work that could at least corroborate what was still only a theoretical assumption. In other words, it would have to undertake the task of analyzing the gospel text as a gospel narrative.

Semiotic or *narrative* exegesis has mainly been inspired by A.J. GREIMAS' and CLAUDE BREMOND's theoretical studies. Within this tradition, whose acknowledged debt to VLADIMIR PROPP's pioneering work *Morphology of the Folktale* is deep, the problem of the narrative's processual organization has occupied a central position from the outset.[16] GREIMAS' investigations conclude with the definition of a canonical narrative schema which seems to be able to explain the regularity that characterizes the course of events in the folktale. He generalizes PROPP's observations, but in a deeper perspective this narrative schema seems to be a reformulation of ARISTOTLE's semiotic conception of the narrative's internal organization.

This significance of the discourse's $\mu\tilde{\upsilon}\theta o\varsigma$ is asserted in the work ΠΕΡΙ ΠΟΙΗΤΙΚΕΣ.[17] It is this course of action as a whole ($\delta\lambda o\nu$), with its beginning ($\dot{\alpha}\rho\chi\dot{\eta}$), middle ($\mu\dot{\epsilon}\sigma o\nu$) and end ($\tau\epsilon\lambda\epsilon\upsilon\tau\dot{\eta}$, 7,2f), which is the discourse's original foundation ($\dot{\alpha}\rho\chi\dot{\eta}$, 6,19). ARISTOTLE thus differentiates with clarity between the text's wholeness and extension ($\mu\dot{\epsilon}\gamma\epsilon\theta o\varsigma$, 7,2f). Another edition of Mark's Gospel which contained, for example, twice as many miracle narratives and parables, an even more detailed account of the Passion and an expanded account of the baptism and temptation, would indeed have had an extension different from that of the known version. However - and this is what matters in this context - its whole-creating mythos would have been quite the same. What is concerned, therefore, is not the elementary observation that the text, in its literal materiality as a graphic expression, must begin with the first word and end with the last word. It is the narrative content, that of which it narrates, which is organized by a form that is itself part of this content. The narrative's mythos is a form of content which establishes a connection between otherwise separate and meaningless events, and as such should therefore command the paramount attention of exegesis. The gospel narrative is only to a minor extent interested in the personage of Jesus. It concentrates on recounting *events*; its proclamation is a

---

[16] Vladimir Propp, *Morphology of the Folktale*, Austin 1968. As recognition of this work's theoretical limitations gained ground, biblical semiotic research ceased to use Propp as a direct basis for textual analysis. Cf., however, Patrice Julien de Pomerol, *Quand un évangile nous est conté. Analyse morphologique du récit de Matthieu*, Bruxelles 1980.

[17] Aristotle, *The Poetics*, The Loeb Classical Library, London 1965.

report of events that have changed the world. *The Christian gospel is a message available as a narrative whose tidings are a content which is organized by this narrative's mythos or narrative schema.*

GREIMAS regards the narrative schema as a formal framework for "le sens de la vie".[18] The beginning is a manipulation phase in which the subject is introduced into life - as a gift and a mission, one might say. The middle is the performance phase, in which through his acts the subject must fulfil himself as ordained, and the conclusion is a sanction phase, both recognition and retribution, which alone can secure the meaningfulness of its acts and institute it as a subject in accordance with being. The same elements recur in BREMOND, who distinguishes between an influence phase, an action phase, and a retribution phase.

The narrative's mythos, its narrative schema, must be seen as a whole-constituting syntactic structure (form of content) which in an existing discourse is linked to a semantic component (substance of content).[19] If one asks for the gospel narrative's mythos, therefore, one is asking not only for its form of content but for the semiotic signification structure which constitutes its syntactic and semantic whole. If it is asserted, at least in a hypothetical form, that the gospel text is a gospel narrative, then it is asserted that this discourse is organized by a whole-creating mythos which at the same time endows it with syntactic and semantic wholeness. The main task of narrative exegesis must therefore be a detailed analysis of this mythos, which may be described as the gospel narrative's *kerygmatic schema.*

It is striking, however, that the problem of the gospel narrative's kerygmatic schema is still unresolved. The majority of the available gospel analyses is concerned with other questions, in that miracle stories, parables and other relatively self-contained narrative sequences, e.g. 16,1-8, are investigated. But a number of biblical semioticians have tried to analyze the larger processes, more precisely the Passion story.[20] In an extension of classical exegesis, these scholars consider this account as a whole, and stress the connection between crucifixion and resurrection.

The Passion's special status should thus not be repudiated, but it must be emphasized that the gospel narrative is not identical with this. Neither is it merely an account of the Passion, with a detailed introduction that can in fact be ignored.[21]

---

[18] *Sémiotique*, art. "Narratif (schéma -)".

[19] The terms content form and content substance are attributable to Hjelmslev, cf. ibid. p. 46.

[20] Louis Marin, *Sémiotique de la Passion. Topiques et figures*, Paris 1971; Claude Chabrol, Louis Marin, *Le récit évangélique*, Paris 1974; Olivette Genest, *Le Christ de la Passion. Perspective structurale. Analyse de Marc 14,53-15,47, des parallèles bibliques et extra-bibliques*, Montréal 1978; Daniel and Aline Patte, *Structural Exegesis: From Theory to Practice. Exegesis of Mark 15 and 16. Hermeneutical Implications*, Philadelphia 1978; Jean Delorme, "Sémiotique du récit et récit de la Passion", *Revue des Sciences Religieuses 73*, Paris 1985, pp. 85.

[21] Martin Kähler's *dictum* that the gospels are "Passionsgeschichten mit ausführlicher Einleitung", from

A definition of the gospel narrative's kerygmatic schema can be established only through analysis of this narrative as a whole.

This task is comprehensive and difficult, but it is also pressing and indispensable. Biblical semiotic analyses of the gospel narrative will remain disjointed and vague outlines as long as this fundamental and whole-constituting signification structure has not been defined. The present study is a contribution to the resolution of this fundamental task within narrative exegesis. Considering the special position of Mark's Gospel among the synoptic gospels, the main task will be to explain more precisely this gospel narrative's kerygmatic schema.

DAN O. VIA's study "A Structural Analysis of the Markan Narrative" is the only attempt as yet to define the fundamental semiotic structure of Mark's Gospel.[22] This analysis, as an inspired pioneering work, is far from worthless, but the study as a whole contains so many flaws that a new attempt resting on a broader theoretical and analytical foundation should be undertaken. Within the history of semiotic exegesis VIA's investigation is a very early work, and in retrospect is clear evidence of the limited theoretical and analytical experience which - by its nature - characterized the first biblical semiotic attempts.

Although it must be grouped together with ethno-literature, the gospel narrative is significantly more complex than the folktales that occasioned the preparation of the first narratological theories. Exegesis cannot therefore directly transfer the results of the study of fairy-tales to the study of the gospel narrative, but must apply a different dialectic in the encounter between theory and the empirical texts.

Historical gospel research is characterized by its threefold exegetical task:

1. Interpretation of the gospels in their final form;
2. Interpretation of their previous tradition;
3. Reconstruction of Jesus' proclamation.[23]

Since semiotic exegesis investigates the gospels in their final form, this becomes directly incorporated as part of a more comprehensive exegetical

---

Der sogenannte historische Jesus und der geschichtliche, biblische Christus, Leipzig 1892, p. 33 is perhaps the most quoted phrase in the literature of gospel research. This observation, which seems to be evident if the gospel text is considered in terms of extension, must however be modified substantially if it is viewed in terms of the whole. This applies not least to Mark's Gospel. In the latter perspective, the Passion is at the middle, taking its signification from its incorporation in an overarching structure which includes beginning (baptism/anointing) and end (resurrection).

[22] Dan O. Via, *Kerygma and Comedy in the New Testament. A Structuralist Approach to Hermeneutic*, Philadelphia 1975, pp. 113. Robert C. Tannehill's article "The Gospel of Mark as Narrative Christology", *Semeia 16, Perspectives on Mark's Gospel*, Missoula 1979, pp. 57, comes immediately to mind in this context. This essay, which investigates "the narrative composition of the Gospel of Mark", is inspired by, *inter alia*, Claude Bremond's works, and contains several observations which confirm and are confirmed by this investigation's definition of the kerygmatic schema. The conformity applies in particular to the perception of the baptism event and important aspects of Jesus' role as proclaimer.

[23] Cf. Hans Conzelmann, *Grundriß der Theologie des Neuen Testaments*, München 1968, p. 116.

project. The matter is, however, more complicated than it appears. When historical exegesis interprets the gospels in their final form, it does so with a view to reconstructing and interpreting a previous tradition which serves as a basis for the reconstruction of Jesus' proclamation. The driving force in such exegesis is an interest in the historical Jesus, and in retrospect the gospel's proclamation is assessed in the light of the tradition's proclamation, which is itself assessed in the light of the reconstructed proclamation of Jesus given an historical status. Consideration of the gospel text as a source determines the task of historical exegesis and establishes its distinctive hermeneutical circle.

Semiotic exegesis considers the gospel text as a gospel narrative, and its task therefore is different:

1. Interpretation of the gospel as an occurrence-text.[24]
2. Interpretation of the gospel narrative's utterance.
3. Reconstruction of the gospel narrative's enunciation.

With this shift of interest from source to narrative, there occurs simultaneously a shift of interest from the historical Jesus to *the narrative Jesus*.

However paradoxical this may seem, it is not - irrespective of how many words and phrases from the historical Jesus' mouth may be quoted in the gospel text - this historical Jesus who speaks in the gospel narrative. Strictly speaking, it is not even the narrative Jesus who speaks. The actors spoken of, the narrative characters "John", "Jesus", "Peter", "God", etc., neither do nor say anything other than what the narrator allows them to do or say. The gospel narrative available is an occurrence-text, which as a discourse embraces an utterance that merely refers back to its enunciation.

The consequences of such a viewpoint for exegesis as a whole and for theology as well are still incalculable. But if exegesis and theology have room for critical scholarship, then this elementary semiotic fact, once it has been recognized, must be given consideration and give cause for new thought. From the aspect of research strategy, it is important that theses be given an opportunity to re-examine their own terms. Over-hasty compromise threatens to dry up the sources of knowledge.

Although experience shows that the zealous pursuit of just one viewpoint often provides an all too one-sided picture of the actual circumstances examined, the same experience indicates that only by virtue of the will and ability to pursue one specific perspective will it be possible to advance research. In any event, it is this perception which forms the basis of the present study, whose main title, "The narrative Jesus," indicates that the question of the historical Jesus is entirely absent.

---

[24] Cf. *Sémiotique*, art. "Occurrence".

The sub-title, "A semiotic reading of Mark's Gospel", indicates on the one hand the investigation's method and on the other hand its subject. The words "A ... reading ..." must be seen as expressing the investigation's limits. Only some of the problems covered by the selected semiotic theory are examined, and no exhaustive analysis of Mark's Gospel is in any way attempted. The study is, of course, not the ultimate reading, but a contribution to the comprehensive, collective and international project which consists of a semiotic exploration of Mark's Gospel and - in a wider perspective - of *Christian discourse*. On the other hand, the investigation is concerned with some of the problems, at once both dominant and fundamental, that characterize this project.

The term "reading" refers to "la construction, à la fois syntaxique et sémantique, de l'objet sémiotique rendant compte du texte-signe".[25] In its most unpretentious version, therefore, semiotic exegesis is a methodological paraphrase made on the basis of a theoretical foundation. By a series of analytical procedures, it rewrites its text with a view to establishing a meaning. This meaning is established or produced in the encounter between the biblical text and the preconception which characterizes and limits the method's cognitive perspective, its theory.

The term "theory" refers to a coherent set of hypotheses which are subject to a demand for adequateness. On the one hand, the theory is a construction derived not purely and simply from empirical observation itself but established deductively on the basis of fundamental assumptions as regards the cognitive object's nature; on the other hand, the construction of the theory serves only the one single purpose of making it possible to recognize the empirical world by application. The theory's description is therefore hypothetico-deductive, and in the confrontation between "the constructed" and the "given" it will see its adequateness confirmed or denied.[26]

From this viewpoint, the method does not attempt to expose the original or objective meaning of the biblical text, but must be seen as the application of a generalized preconception that makes possible an inter-subjective, communicable and deliberate reading. The controlled reading procedure is restricted therefore to investigation of how the biblical texts function under quite specific circumstances.

By scientific, exegetic method, then, is meant a procedure that can be presented and discussed, criticised and amended, in an inter-subjective forum, and that is arranged in such a way as to lead in principle to the same reading of a text, irrespective of who makes use of it provided the method is mastered. The fact that research remains in practice only an infinite approximation, in part because theory and method are themselves subject to change and in part because

---

[25] *Sémiotique*, art. "Lecture".

[26] Cf. *Sémiotique*, art. "Théorie".

the individual scholar necessarily works on the basis of his reception, does not affect this ideal requirement, which contra-factually must form the dialogue's starting point.

The designation of Mark's Gospel as a narrative is an initiating working hypothesis, which includes the assumption that a narrative theory will be the adequate frame of reference for an analytical reading of the empirical text. And CLAUDE BREMOND's and A.J. GREIMAS' contributions to such a narrative theory may be an expedient starting point for a New Testament exegesis whose task is, as in this study, to analyze a narrative text.

There is a difference between the perspectives of these two theorists. BREMOND has prepared a narrative theory that is predominantly a theory of narratives perceived as that class of discourses characterized by their being accounts of events and acting characters. For GREIMAS, narrative theory is a theory of narrativity perceived as a fundamental principle of organization in any discourse (narrative or non-narrative) and embedded in a general theory of signification, a general semiotics. This situation directly favours GREIMAS, since BREMOND's narratological theory, which can itself be described as semiotics, seems thereby to be sublated and integrated into a larger context, which should be chosen as a starting point.

It is, however, possible to take a different path, founded on the desire to establish a demarcated, more manageable and workable perspective of inquiry. The advantages of BREMOND's limited perspective, which is not an expression of narrow-mindedness but of demarcation, is that it has given him an opportunity to present a unified, coherent account of his narrative theory in the work *Logique du récit*.[27] In the case of Greimas, on the other hand, one has to search for the theory within various works, and keep track of the amendments they have undergone over the years.

JOSEPH COURTÉS, however, in his *Introduction à la sémiotique narrative et discursive*, gives a unified account supplemented by a copious foreword by GREIMAS, "Les acquis et les projets", that takes stock of the results achieved and problems still unresolved.[28] Although it is only a foreword, GREIMAS in fact succeeds here in presenting a concise summary of his narrative theory. In many respects this seems to be more advanced than BREMOND's, especially as regards the distinction between different representational levels (semiotic, narrative and discursive levels). However, in marking out the problem area's extension it gets no further than BREMOND, and in regard to the differentiation of sub-problems *Logique du récit* is unsurpassed.

BREMOND's unified and coherent narrative theory therefore remains the perspective of inquiry within which analysis of Mark's Gospel takes place. But

---

[27] Claude Bremond, *Logique du récit*, Paris 1973.
[28] Joseph Courtés, *Introduction à la sémiotique narrative et discursive*, Paris 1976.

it will be necessary to confine and extend this perspective. On the one hand, the investigation will raise and answer only some of the questions made possible by this narratological theory. On the other hand, perceptions from GREIMAS' theory will be included when they give rise to an opportunity for reformulating and defining BREMOND's observations.

But, in addition, this study is founded on a creative reception of these theorists' studies. It presents no new, synthetic theory, but on the other hand it is not merely an application of what is available. The semiotic exegete must himself be both semiotician and exegete, and thus participate in theoretical reflections on the basis of his analytical experience of working with the biblical texts.

The exegete must of course himself accept responsibility for such a heuristic procedure, but he is justified by objective consideration for the task. The primary interest of exegesis is not of course the establishment of semiotic theory (and certainly not its philology or history). Exegesis is looking for a general narrative theory which can be operationalized as procedure of inquiry for a semiotic or *narrative exegesis*.

D. CONTENT OF THE STUDY

The study falls into five parts or major chapters which possess a certain degree of independence, while at the same time participating step by step in the whole.

Part 1. Narrative Exegesis, is an introduction in outline to the narratological theory and method on which the investigation is built. The conversion of a *general* semiotics (in which text analysis is a means serving to shape theory) into an *applied* semiotics (where theory is given the status of an inquiry procedure on the basis of which it will be possible to analyze a given narrative) is central to exegesis. As well as introducing the fundamental narratological concepts, this part therefore contains brief directions for application of the investigation procedure which elementarily characterizes the *narrative method*.

The role concept has a special status in the investigation. The gospel narrative's image of the narrative Jesus is formed from the information which predicatively determines the proper name "Jesus". This information causes the narrative Jesus to appear in three principal roles, as *wonder worker*, as *proclaimer* and as *savior*, and these roles are the subject of closer investigation in Parts 2, 3, and 4 which form the corpus of the study.

Part 2. The Wonder Worker, is an investigation of the wonder narrative with a view to defining its narrative genre. The main purpose is to show how Jesus as a wonder worker appears in a number of thematic roles (such as healer, exorcist, shepherd) which are gathered together under the narrative role of *protector*, and also that the wonder narrative as a narrative genre must be defined as Protection. What is noteworthy is that the *salvation concept* receives its very pregnant significance from this.

The study's main concern is to define in detail Jesus' role in the overlapping salvation project which ends in the realization of the Kingdom of God, and it is probably a true observation that "si le miracle 'présuppose' le plan salvifique, ce dernier n'implique pas nécessairement le miracle".[29] It may therefore with some justification be asserted that the wonder narrative does not strictly belong to the field of investigation if the main interest concerns the overarching salvation project.

However, Jesus appears as a wonder worker in the gospel narrative, and it must therefore be asked whether there is perhaps a factual connection between the pragmatic salvation of the wonder and the overarching project. It may even be asserted that one of the tests of whether an analysis of the gospel narrative's fundamental structure is adequate is whether it is able to define Jesus as a wonder worker in relation to this. From another aspect also, study of the wonder narrative is of importance. Since W. WREDE's pioneering work on the *messianic secret*, Markan research has been dominated by such a strong interest in the narrative's cognitive problems that the question of its pragmatic dimension appears to have faded away completely. In the face of this "gnostic" trend, study of the wonder narrative is of importance in understanding the pragmatic creation aspect of the Christian message of salvation.

Part 3. The Proclaimer, is an investigation of elementary aspects of the gospel narrative's cognitive dimension. This part, in its relative independence, is concerned with the relationship between the proclaiming Jesus and the proclaimed Jesus, between the narrated proclamation, as part of the gospel narrative's utterance, and the narrating proclamation, as part of its enunciation. In a wider perspective, however, this part also serves to distinguish between different sequences of events which are indeed connected with one another but ultimately may not be intermingled. On closer examination, the gospel narrative is seen to contain two sub-narratives, one about the relationship between God and Jesus and the other about the relationship between Jesus and the disciples. The well-known similarity between the account of Jesus' baptism and the account of the transfiguration on the mountain should not, for example, conceal the crucial difference that each belongs to its own sequence of events. The main objection to DAN O. VIA's attempt to define the narrative schema of Mark's Gospel is precisely that he has not made this fundamental distinction.

Investigation of the relationship between the narrated and the narrating proclamation, including the account of the remarkable property of the gospel that it is a narrative about its own genesis as proclamation, is one of the main tasks of narrative exegesis. This study, however, is mainly concerned with the question

---

[29] Groupe d'Entrevernes, *Signes et paraboles. Sémiotique et texte évangélique*, Paris 1977, p. 196.

of the content of the proclamation. Mark's Gospel is a narrative about "Jesus Christ" (1,1), but why is it a gospel, good news?

Part 4. The Savior, deals with the content of the proclamation, with Jesus in the role of savior. Theologically, the study's main thesis is that the gospel narrative presents the narrative Jesus as the savior. It may perhaps seem both excessive and superfluous to wish to maintain this assertion, which at least in a religious context appears to be a self-evident fact. But it is noteworthy that exegesis, like the gospel text itself, avoids using the designation "savior" about Jesus.

It is characteristic of the New Testament texts as a whole that the term σωτήρ is seldom used, and then only in later texts. The explanation may be that, as a title, this was ideologically loaded because of its use within mystery and imperial cults.[30] Nevertheless, this does not explain what most people perceive: that it is *striking* that "the savior" is so seldom used. It is striking, of course, because although the title is absent the function is clear.

Now, it would be in the most literal sense merely a dispute about a word had the absence of the term σωτήρ not caused exegesis to overlook or at least severely under-illuminate the fact that the gospel narrative presents Jesus as the savior. There is good reason therefore to defend the assertion that the gospel narrative's main concern is to proclaim Jesus as the savior. In so far as the gospel narrative's christology appoints Jesus as the savior, there exists a soteriology. Indeed, this does not exist in the reflective form as found in Paul, but it is nonetheless given in the narrative's form. And narrative exegesis is able to analyze it further and explicate it.

The predominant perception has been that the synoptic tradition describes its conception of Jesus the person by giving him titles and by letting him use these titles. To the question, "Who is Jesus?", the first Christians answered with the title, "Christ", "Son of God", "Son of Man", and the like.[31] According to this conception, therefore, an investigation of the Markan narrative's christology must take the form of an analysis of its christological titles.

This study, however, is based on quite a different conception. To the question, "Who is Jesus?", the first Christians answered with a *narrative*. In this perspective, the Christ titles are designations that take their pregnant content from what the narrative says about Jesus, and consequently it is analysis of the roles of the narrative Jesus that will provide us with an insight into the christology of Mark's Gospel: Christ is the Savior.[32]

---

[30] Cf. Oscar Cullmann, *Die Christologie des Neuen Testaments*, Tübingen 1966, pp. 245.

[31] Cf. Cullmann, ibid. p. 5.

[32] Robert Tannehill's opinion is the same: "It may be possible to gain new insight into the christology of Mark by concentrating not on the titles applied to Jesus but on the narrative functions which Jesus performs within the Markan story.", cf. "The Disciples in Mark: The Function of a Narrative Role", *The Journal of Religion 57*, Chicago 1977, p. 388. Cullmann is aware that Jesus is σωτήρ, although the title occurs only rarely. He points out, as a possible explanation of the savior-title's absence, that "the savior"

The definition of the gospel narrative's soteriology coincides with the definition of its christology, which in turn coincides with the definition of its kerygmatic schema or narrative kerygma. The gospel narrative's unifying mythos is made up of a sequence of events which includes baptism/anointing (beginning), crucifixion (middle) and resurrection (end), and the task of narrative exegesis is to expound in detail the semantic and syntactic signification structures which characterize this sequence. Interest in the narrative's organizing form of content therefore leads exegesis directly into fundamental theological questions.

Part 5. The Christ myth, considers a number of primary theological subjects as an extension of the investigation's results, and leads to a discussion on the relationship between narrativity and historicity. The gospel narrative is defined as a myth which *by definition* contradicts the historian's empirical perception of reality and therefore sees its message neutralized by historical criticism. The problem presents itself in a new and unforeseen way, since it is possible to show, on the basis of the investigation, that the question of the relationship between myth and history is not initially presented by historical criticism but is a subject which permeates the gospel narrative from beginning to end.

---

could scarcely be used as a title for Jesus, since the name Jesus = Joshua = "Yahweh saves". The expression "Jesus Savior" would be a pleonasm, cf. ibid. p. 252. But Cullman's title-fixing involves that the savior function is actually disregarded in determining the Christology of the gospel narrative. Ferdinand Hahn, *Christologische Hoheitstitel. Ihre Geschichte im frühen Christentum*, Göttingen 1964, on the other hand, ignores both the title and function of savior, but does mention *in a note* that the use of σώζειν, σωτηρία and σωτήρ (i.e. the savior role) requires fundamental investigation, cf. p. 45. The paradox is therefore that the procedure proposed by Cullmann and Hahn, the study of titles, leads us away from the central role, the savior function, which gives these titles their elementary content. In this exegetic situation, one cannot accuse narrative exegesis of wanting to break down open doors.

PART ONE
NARRATIVE EXEGESIS

CHAPTER ONE

NARRATOLOGY

A. COMMUNICATION AND NARRATION

Narratology is *the theory of the narrative or the narrative discourse.*[1] The name has been formed from the Latin *narratio* signifying the act of narrating as well as the narrated, and it is reasonable to consider the narrative (for example Mark's Gospel) as a message communicated from the author (addresser or sender, e.g. "Mark") to a reader (addressee or receiver, e.g. "a community in Rome"):[2]

Addresser	→	Message/Address	→	Addressee
Author	→	Written discourse	→	Reader[3]

In extension thereof, it would then be possible to establish two sub-areas for the study of a narrative: one area consisting of the communication situation and one area consisting of that which is communicated. From this perspective, the narratological study of the narrative is then an investigation of the message, since semiotics, which is a signification theory and not a communication theory, must disregard the narrative's pragmatic context.

The message exists however as a discourse (the author's entire speech), which before it is communicated in a pragmatic sense must be seen as the result of a process that generates discourse. The act of narrating is an act of expression which before it becomes the communication of meaning is the generation of meaning.

This creative process is social in a transcendental sense and therefore itself socially articulated, since the generation of the discourse refers to a subject, alienated and decentralized by the language, which can only speak when it speaks this language and speaks to someone. Whoever speaks is irretrievably bound up with the language in the same way as the person spoken to.

---

[1] Within his theory's general economy Greimas distinguishes between semio-narrative structures, which include a deep level and a surface level, and discursive structures. A narrative analysis is here merely an examination of one level within the semiotic object, narrating or not-narrating, cf. *Sémiotique*, art. "Génératif (parcours -)". In this study the word narrative is employed in a broader sense about properties of the narrating discourse. *The narrative Jesus* is thus not only the narrative structures' actant but the Jesus depicted by the story, both narrative actant and discursive actor.

[2] On the question of the Markan narrative's pragmatic context, time, place and person, cf. Werner Georg Kümmel, *Einleitung in das Neue Testament*, Heidelberg 1970, pp. 53; Rudolf Pesch, *Das Markusevangelium, I. Teil*, Freiburg 1980, pp. 3.

[3] Cf. the communication act's functional schema in Roman Jakobson, "Closing Statement: Linguistics and Poetics", in Thomas A. Sebeok (ed.), *Style in Language*, New York 1960, pp. 350.

Sociologist of religion PETER L. BERGER plainly declares:

Whatever else it may be, religion is a humanly constructed universe of meaning, and this construction is undertaken by linguistic means.[4]

He here in fact formulates the fundamental assumption of semiotics of religion and states, at the same time, its central position in the science of religion.[5]

From the perspective of narrative exegesis, this assumption can be reformulated: Christianity is, as a cultural universe of meaning created by man, fundamentally established through the construction of narratives: i.e. *the Christian universe of meaning is a narrated world.*

This perspective can be further specified, in that Mark's Gospel is seen as such a narratively constructed universe of meaning.

In his attempt to explain this duality, namely that culture on the one hand is a human product whereas human beings are on the other hand a product of culture, BERGER introduces the terms externalization, objectification and internalization, which can be employed advantageously to establish an understanding of the narrative as a cultural product.

Man does not have a given relationship to his world, but he must continuously establish, change and preserve his relationship to it: man's being is fundamentally unstable. As an acting subject, man can develop only in change or preservation of this being and thus sees himself primarily as alienated and decentralized, since he is always already intentionally enrolled in a world. Subject and world cannot be separated without both disappearing.

Man's being is not something self-contained to be subsequently expressed and materialized in the surrounding world, but something created through the constant development of his activity in the world in which he finds himself and through which he sees himself defined. Externalization is thus the transition to the act that is aimed at changing or preserving man and his world.

Objectification means that the result of the acts, e.g. a product, but generally the changed or preserved world, obtains a status of reality which meets its producer as a factuality external to, detached from and alien to himself, whereas internalization indicates the process by which the objectified world is readmitted to the subject in such a way that this world's structures become determinative for the subjective structures.

Externalization is a making external, a process resulting in an externality, objectification. Internalization is a making internal, a process resulting in an internality which additionally indicates a subjectification:

---

[4] Peter L. Berger, *The Social Reality of Religion*, Harmondsworth 1973, p. 177.

[5] From the perspective of religious science, it is appropriate to speak of semiotics of religion on the same footing as psychology and sociology of religion, cf. Introduction, note 6.

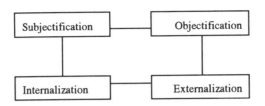

The subject intervenes in what is always already objectified; the world asserts itself in what is always already subjectified.

From this perspective, Mark's Gospel can be regarded as the result of an externalization process that *in and through* the language produces a narrating discourse which immediately detaches itself from its producer and emerges objectified and alien as a narrative *sui generis*. When the producer, who indeed does not create *ex nihilo* but intervenes modifyingly in the already existing narrated universes of meaning, has concluded his act, the narrative remains and asserts itself as long as it can find a reader. But the author is already himself the first reader. Internalization is then the reading and identification process through which the constantly destabilized but meaning-seeking subject assimilates the narrative's structures in such a way that they become determinative for the subjective structures.

But if the narrative's producer himself becomes the reader, who is then in fact the narrator in this process? It is the objectified narrator who asserts himself in the discourse, even where he tries to conceal his presence by not representing himself in what is narrated. It was this objectified narrator-role the author had to adopt in order to be able to narrate. Analogously, the discourse provides an objectified reader-role, a viewpoint any reader must adopt if the intended internalization and subjectification are to be able to take place.[6]

From this perspective, the narrative act or the *narration* is not a communicative but a creative and constructive process which is described as an enunciation and is logically presupposed by the existence of the discourse. Addresser and addressee are no longer real persons but linguistically objectified actants which as such are generally referred to as enunciator/enunciatee and can be defined only through an analysis of the discourse, which like the realization of a virtual language carries traces of its enunciation.[7]

The difficulty of distinguishing the enunciation's difficulties from the communication's complex of problems arises largely because the generation of

---

[6] Mark's Gospel is an open text in the sense that the model reader must take an active part in the interpretative reading. It is, however, at the same time a closed text, since it tries to produce its own model reader, to create his interpretative competence. This does not contradict the fact that even Mark - though aiming at eliciting a sort of obedient cooperation - in the last instance is randomly open to every pragmatic incident. But he who believes that Mark presents Jesus as one of the bad guys, is really a bad reader. Cf. Umberto Eco, *The Role of the Reader*, London 1981.

[7] Cf. Tzvetan Todorov (ed.), *Langages 17, L'Énonciation*, Paris 1970; *Sémiotique*, art. "Énonciation".

meaningful speech is fundamentally a social phenomenon, since the speaker can as it were only reach himself, i.e. reach an understanding of himself in the world, through dialogue. The inner speech that flows along more or less incessantly even as we sleep is a dialogue, in so far as it is always orientated towards a recipient: the enunciation articulates the speaker - λογοποιός - into enunciator and enunciatee.

The narratological study of the narrative, which is the study of the objectivized, narrating discourse, thus falls into two sub-sections: the study of the enunciation or *narration* whose actants are in this context described as *narrator/narratee*, and the study of the enunciate (utterance) or the *narrate* whose narrated persons are described as narrative subjects:[8]

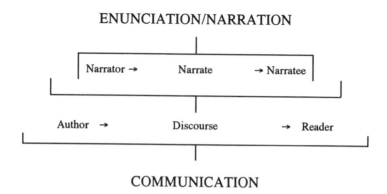

ENUNCIATION/NARRATION

COMMUNICATION

By the story-teller, or Mark, therefore is meant the narrator, unless otherwise stated. Similarly, the reader is to be understood as the implicit narratee whom the narrative has established. The main interest, however, concerns the narrate, i.e. the narrated world in which the narrative subjects are involved.

B. Narrativity and Narrative

The empirical object of narrative semiotics is the narrative, whereas its theoretical object is the narrativity, i.e. the abstract and general forms of

---

[8] Greimas employs narrator/narratee to describe the discourse's explicit destinator/destinatee. Its implicit destinator/destinatee is described as enunciator/enunciatee, cf. *Sémiotique*, art. "Destinateur/Destinataire" In this study, narrator/narratee is used about the narrative's enunciator/enunciatee, a practice followed by Bas van Iersel, *Reading Mark*, Edinburgh 1989, pp. 4. David Rhoads, Donald Michie, *Mark as Story. An Introduction to the Narrative of a Gospel*, Philadelphia 1982, distinguish between "the content of a narrative, its *story*" and "the form of a narrative, its *rhetoric*" (p. 4) corresponding to narrate and narration; between "author/actual reader" (pp. 35) corresponding to author/reader, and between "narrator/implied reader" (pp. 137) corresponding to narrator/narratee.

organization to which any series of associated acts must be subjected if the narrative is to be understood.

1. The Narrativity

The issue here is the intelligibility of the narrative itself, its *narrative rationality*. In general semiotics, the analysis of the narrative serves the preparation of the theory which is the true objective. In an exegetic perspective, however, where applied semiotics are concerned, the theory is a means of exploring the narrative.

An occurrent narrative, e.g. Mark's Gospel, will at various levels of generalization be characteristic of a culture, an epoch, a literary genre, a narrator's style, or an individual narrative. Every narrative is unique, but is at the same time subject to general, narrative constraints that fundamentally condition its intelligibility. It thus appears as the specific realization of a logically presupposed narrative system. On this basis, one may anticipate that an analytical reading founded upon a theory of narrativity will be awarded a fundamental role within text-orientated exegesis. Narrativity is the transcendental organizing principle that controls the production and reading of the narrative. Narrativity can then no longer be considered merely an immanent property of the discourse.

As a component of enunciation, narrativization is a performance that presupposes a narrative competence. Not only does the ability to narrativize - an ability that must be assumed to control the signification-producing and signification-perceiving subject rather than the reverse - assert itself among professional narrators, but every subject acquires its reality by virtue of this semiotizing signification practice. The act of thinking (the inner dialogue where speech precedes thought) is constantly taking place in any normally functioning person, although it is often concealed to the outsider. This process is substantially an act of language aimed at the production of relatively independent narrative sequences in which this person himself is - necessarily - the structuring point of departure. Quite elementarily, this concerns an incessant interpretation process, which even in the most minute detail asks about the meaning of life and thus about the person's identity, his being.

2. The Narrate

CLAUDE BREMOND has given the following definition of the narrative/the narrate:

> Tout récit consiste en un discours intégrant une succession d'événements d'intéret humain dans l'unité d'une même action.[9]

---

[9] Claude Bremond, "La logique des possibles narratifs", *Communications 8, L'analyse structurale du récit*, Paris 1966, p. 62.

Most important in this definition is the emphasis on the human aspect, i.e. that the events have significance only in relation to a human project. It is people (or at least anthropomorphized existences) who exercise and undergo the acts which institute the events; it is persons who ask about the meaning of these acts and their results.

The order of events immediately suggests a chronological sequence, but the chronology is secondary to the movement of the narrative which changes one situation into another. Events do not become coherent by virtue of their contemporaneity but by being related to one and the same process of change which affects one and the same person. The events that take place have importance to the person and his existential project. They receive their meaning in the light of the person's attempt to realize himself according to his own life project. In themselves they mean nothing, but as the surrounding world of a person who is seeking a meaningful existence they receive existential significance. The narrative subject thus becomes the natural starting point for the establishment of a theory of the narrate's organization, its narrativity.

The persons or actors appearing on the stage of the narrated, in the world of the narrate, seem able to act only in a limited number of narrative roles that comprise a limited number of narrative processes. These processes or narrative sequences can be classified into various fields that emerge through an increasing differentiation of the narrative subject perceived as actant, i.e. an entity that carries out or undergoes the act and thereby participates in the act process.

The actant may be defined as a subject-predicate relationship in which the narrative process predicates the narrative subject. The narrative concerns the actor's destiny and fate. To narrate is to tell of a genesis, to take a position on a possible process of change, now to affirm it, now to deny it. But no genesis, no process of change or preservation, can be recounted without reference to a fixed point - the narrative subject - which in spite of all the vicissitudes it undergoes nevertheless remains identical with itself by virtue of its proper name.

1. The starting point of the differentiation of the narrative processes is the passion, where the subject as the sufferer, the patient, i.e. as a *subject of being*, passively undergoes a *process of change or preservation*. As a reified subject of a process in which it participates passively, the narrative subject is merely an unresisting thing. This field can be referred to as the *ontic field of being*.

2. If the subject of being's coming into existence is valorized it obtains status as a personage, and the change itemizes itself into *progression* (BREMOND: amélioration) and *degression* (dégradation), the preservation into *protection* (protection) and *repression* (frustration).[10] These four processes form the value field or the *ontological field of being*.

---

[10] The use of progression and degression rather than amelioration and degradation is for stylistic reasons. The use of repression, however, is because the term frustration is objectively inappropriate, because it does not describe the process but the subject's reaction thereto.

3. The narrative subject itself, however, can act on the basis of its competence (which includes not only its knowledge of what and how it is to act but summarizes the entire complex of presuppositions that define the act's starting point), referring back to two sets of processes of influence:

a) Cognitive processes, which include *information/dissimulation, distraction/admonition, denial/confirmation* and *veridiction/simulation* (révélation/induction en erreur)

b) Affective processes, which in part concern the subject of being's current perception of its present condition, *satisfaction/dissatisfaction*, and in part concerns its current perception of a future condition: induction/evocation of *hope* or *fear*.

The processes of *persuasion/dissuasion* and *trap-setting* also belong to the field of influence.

4. Competence establishes the subject of being as a virtual subject of doing that can change into action-form or performance. The act constitutes a process with the character of a project sequence. Depending upon whether the subject of doing acts voluntarily (intentionally) or involuntarily, the project differs from the pseudo-project. In association with the project's realization, processes are encountered for *assistance* (help) and *resistance*, and strategic processes for initiating means, obtaining assistance or ending resistance. What is concerned here is the central *field of doing* or *field of action*.

5. The question of the narrative subject's worthiness or unworthiness refers finally to processes for the acquisition of *merit* that give a right to reward, and the acquisition of *undeservedness* (blameworthiness, culpability) which gives the possibility of punishment. This field is referred to as the *retribution* field.[11]

The above fields describe briefly the concept of the narrative subject which marks out the narrative theory's limits. The processes referred to, which will be presented in detail in the context of the analysis, constitute the core itself of this narratology.

If one is to distinguish between progression and degression, the subject of being will be considered, now in the role of the favoured (beneficiary), now in the role of the disfavoured (victim). It is, however, only a human or anthromorphized being which, whether in its own eyes or in the eyes of others, will be able to undertake these roles. Is not such anthropocentrism an unnecessary curtailment of the narrative perspective?

The question must be answered in the negative, since, on the contrary, anthropocentrism is a constituting property of narrativity. The simple process is significant only when it performs a function in the sequence of events, i.e. when it serves or injures the goal-directed action project. But such a project exists only in the case where a human subject is inscribed in a value system.

---

[11] Cf. Claude Bremond, *Logique du récit*, pp. 313.

BREMOND gives an illustrative example: why, for instance, are expansion/contraction not functional processes in the sequence of events when this holds for the processes of progression/degression? Because expansion/contraction as a simple fact is in itself entirely without significance to the impersonal subject - e.g. an iron bar - which these processes change. It can assume significance only in relation to three finalities linked to three persons:

a) the iron bar itself, if the narrative personifies it; but in that case the process of expansion (or contraction) will be functionally translated into progression or degression of the iron bar's lot, its fate in the world;

b) a person present in the sequence of events and taken up by the phenomenon. It may be an engineer who hopes for or dreads this expansion, since it plays a role in the successful completion of his task. In this case also, the expansion is translated functionally into progression or degression of the personal subject's lot;

c) a person outside the narrated sequence of events - the narrator or narratee - and whom the phenomenon concerns. This may be a physicist who listens to his assistant making a report on an experiment. This latter finality outside the sequence of events indicates the information's *raison d'être*. As an answer of a kind to the narratee's question to the narrator: why do you tell me this? this finality is always present in every narrative. Examination of this, however, has a place in the analysis of the narration.[12]

A narrative analysis which rests on the assumption that the gospel narrative constitutes a signification whole which contains its own narrative organization must, then, have the task of laying bare this organization. It must analyze ahead the action unity which gives the gospel narrative its narrative unity. Should this prove to include several relatively independent sequences of events, it must also demonstrate them and give an account of their mutual connection. This can be done only through a definition of the gospel narrative's primary action unity from which every other unity obtains its reason of being. Like every other action unity, this primary action unity must be indissolubly linked to the narrative's main character.

The procedure must then in principle consist in the advance analysis of all the narrative processes concerned in the gospel narrative. These processes' mutual lines of connection must then be defined with a view to establishing the narrative's process hierarchy. The various processes come within various process levels, each with its own finality, but must at the same time be mutually connected relative to a superior finality. One of these levels must be designated as the basic level, and the main objective of this study is indeed to identify and define the action unity in relation to which every other process in the gospel narrative receives its reason of being.

---

[12] Claude Bremond, ibidem, pp. 328.

On the basis of narrative theory, to be introduced and developed in detail in the context of the analysis, the task then becomes to identify and define the processes in which the actor Jesus is involved, in order thereby to identify and define the roles that constitute *the narrative Jesus*. The object of such a methodical reading is to reveal the *narrative rationality* of the gospel narrative's message.

CHAPTER TWO

TEXT AND NARRATIVE

A. THE GOSPEL TEXT

The textual basis of this study is the reconstructed Greek text KATA MAPKON which methodically is given the status of a basic text.[1] An examination of Mark's Gospel is therefore an examination of this empirically existing text, i.e. this occurrence-text.

The empirical object of the examination has itself been established by text-critical research, which shows that the scientific perception of the surrounding world is a creative appropriation whose subjective element is dissolved in the inter-subjective or social status of theory and method. We cannot content ourselves by referring to empirical objects as if they were simply objectively existing entities; our empirical objects have themselves come into being through our classifying and forming intervention.

The relativity of scientific endeavour, which may seem to threaten its validity, represents a constituent feature that without affecting its legitimacy places science on a line with other cultural practices (e.g. art and religion) through which man creatively acquires his reality. It has its validity by virtue of its self-defining procedures which establish it as prescribed practice.

Textual criticism's continuous revisions thus change nothing relative to the fact that the edition of the text currently valid exists as the optimal reconstruction, the methodically established basis. In the nature of things the reconstructed text appears as *the true text*, and the Markan occurrence-text is referred to as the *gospel text*.

The term "fragment" refers to a broken-off piece of a whole. If the gospel text is precisely identified as Mark 1,1-16,8, this may be defined as an unbroken whole. Viewed as an occurrence-text, there is nothing fragmentary about this. The gospel text is characterized by *philological unity*; it has a beginning ('Aρχὴ ...) and an end (... γαρ.), and everything between stands where it is meant to stand. Nothing is missing. There is not too much. This is the starting point of textual analysis.[2]

---

[1] E. Nestle, K. Aland: *Novum Testamentum Graece*, 26th edition, 7th revised impression, Stuttgart 1983.

[2] The reconstructed Markan text ends with 16,8, as evidenced by Codex Sinaiticus and Codex Vaticanus, cf. Kurt Aland, "Bemerkungen zum Schluss des Markusevangeliums", E. Earle Ellis, Max Wilcox (ed.), *Neotestamentica et Semitica. Studies in Honour of Matthew Black*, Edinburgh 1969, pp. 157; "Der Schluss des Markusevangeliums", M. Sabbe (ed.), *L'Évangile selon Marc. Tradition et rédaction*, Gembloux 1974, pp. 435.

1. The Textual Units: Basic Sequences

The first step in the analysis consists in a segmentation of the text, i.e. a preliminary division of the text into more manageable entities. The parts resulting there from can be further divided into sections until a line is reached that forms the basis for identification of the *basic sequences*.

Further division of these is possible, but merely causes the emergence of sub-sequences. Sections and parts now in turn appear as structures of basic sequences.

There is wide agreement that segmentation of Mark's Gospel gives the basic sequences set out in the survey below.[3] This list is more or less identical with the section division to be found in *Novum Testamentum Graece*, where the basic sequences marked * are however sub-divided. The headings that have the nature of summarized paraphrases serve primarily a mnemonic purpose, but at the same time give an initial overview of the narrative's thematics. The criteria for this segmentation seem primarily to be based upon spatial (here/elsewhere), temporal (before/after) and actorial (us/them) opposites of the type:

They went to Capernaum; and when the sabbath came, he entered the Synagogue and taught ... As soon as they left the synagogue, they entered the house of Simon and Andrew ... (1,21.29);

A leper came to him ... When he returned to Capernaum after some days ... (1,40; 2,1);

Again he began to teach beside the sea. Such a very large crowd gathered around him ... When he was alone, those who were around him along with the twelve asked him about the parables. (4,1.10).

Changes in location, time, and person serve to mark the boundaries between the basic sequences.

2. The Macro-sequences

Whereas there is broad agreement on the definition of the basic sequences, there is some disagreement as regards the identification of the macro-sequences (joining of basic sequences) to be found between the basic line and the narrative as a whole.

Four classical commentaries on Mark's Gospel by 1) ERNST LOHMEYER, 2) VINCENT TAYLOR, 3) WALTER GRUNDMANN and 4) EDUARD SCHWEIZER suggest the following main divisions:[4]

---

[3] Cf. Index of Sequences, pp. 377.

[4] Ernst Lohmeyer, *Das Evangelium des Markus*, Göttingen (1937) 1967; Vincent Taylor, *The Gospel According to Mark*, London (1952) 1959, cf. pp. 107; Walter Grundmann, *Das Evangelium nach Markus*,

1)	1,1	-	3,6	3,7	-	6,29	6,30	-	8,26	8,27 - 10,52
2)	1,1-13	1,14 - 3,6		3,7 - 6,13			6,14	-	8,26	8,27 - 10,52
3)	1,1-13	A	B	C	D	E		F		8,27 - 10,52
4)	1,1-13	1,14 - 3,6		3,7 - 6,6a		6,6b - 8,21		8,22	-	10,52

1)	11,1 - 13,37	14,1 - 16,8
2)	11,1 - 13,37	14,1 - 16,8
3)	11,1 - 13,37	14,1 - 16,8
4)	11,1	-	16,8

A = 1,14-45; B = 2,1-3,6; C = 3,7-4,34; D = 4,35-5,43; E = 6,1-44; F = 6,45-8,26.

There is no reason to go further into these suggestions regarding a division into textual macro-sequences.[5] As an aid to grasping the text they may be equally good individually, but by virtue of their dissimilarity from one another they may serve as a starting point for discussion directed towards comprehension of the narrative's unity.

The fact is that the divisions referred to rest on the assumption that all basic sequences belong to the same text. This is not of course to contest the assertion of the gospel text's philological or textual unity. The problem is to be found elsewhere, and emerges only when it is realized that the complication of division into macro-sequences is because the textual units - the basic sequences - are not on a line with one another as regards content. The story's narrative units that constitute the basic component of its narrative and thus content-related organiz-ation by no means always coincide with the textual units. In one case these refer to several narrative levels and in another to one such line, which is to be considered merely as a specification of a main level. The textual division is and remains pre-analytic and serves narrative exegesis only in establishing a surveyable and manageable text.

The division into basic sequences forms the foundation in the form-critical method as known from RUDOLF BULTMANN's *Die Geschichte der synoptischen Tradition.*[6] The basic sequences are first classified according to whether they are dominated by speech and thereby profile Jesus as proclaimer (discursive material)

Berlin 1971; Eduard Schweizer, *Das Evangelium nach Markus*, Göttingen 1978. Rudolf Pesch, *Das Markusevangelium*, Freiburg 1980, follows Lohmeyer.

[5] On the matter in general, cf. F.G. Lang, "Kompositionsanalyse des Markusevangeliums", *Zeitschrift für Theologie und Kirche*, 74. Jahrgang, Tübingen 1977, pp. 1.

[6] Rudolf Bultmann, *Die Geschichte der synoptischen Tradition*, Göttingen (1921) 1970.

or by narrative and thereby profile Jesus as proclaimed (narrative material). But no formal, categorical division is concerned, since narrative is given in the discursive material (cf., for example, 12,1ff) and discourse in the narrative material (cf., for example 14,1ff).

Within these main areas, various textual forms are to be distinguished. With regard to the discursive material, the following formes are found: "Apophthegmata" (apophthegm, apothegm), which is subdivided into "Streit- und Schulgespräche" and "Biographische Apophthegmata", and "Herrenworte" which is subdivided into "Logien (Jesus als Weisheitslehrer)", "Prophetische und apokalyptische Worte", "Gesetzesworte und Gemeinderegeln", "Ich-worte", and "Gleichnisse und Verwandtes". The narrative material is divided into "Wundergeschichten" and "Geschichtserzählung und Legende"; and it is this area that is of primary interest to the narratologist. BULTMANN includes the following in the narrative material:

1,1-13; 1,21-31; 1,40-45; 2,1-12; 4,37-41; 5,1-43; 6,34-52; 7,32-37; 8,1-9; 8,22-30; 8,27-30; 9,2-8; 9,14-27; 10,46-52; 11,1-10; 11,12-14.20; 14,1-16,8;

and the history narrative and legend include:

1,1-8	Activity of John the Baptist
1,9-11	Baptism and anointment
1,12-13	Temptation
8,27-30	Peter's confession
9,2-8	The transfiguration
11,1-10	Entry into Jerusalem
14,1-15,47	The Passion
16,1-8	The empty tomb

BULTMANN means by "legend" a narrating item of tradition that is not in fact a miracle story, neither is it historical, but is of a religious-homiletic nature. Miraculous incidents may occur, but not necessarily (cf. 14,22-25). The legend differs from the miracle story primarily in that it does not constitute a unity in itself but acquires its point only by virtue of its association with a larger context. This context may be the religious hero's life, and in that case a biographical legend is concerned. But it may also be given with the community's belief and cult, and then a belief legend or cult legend is concerned. As regards the relationship between historical narrative and legend, BULTMANN points out that, although many of the synoptic traditional items are purely legendary, it is not possible to distinguish history-narrating items from legendary items because "die Geschichtserzählung so sehr unter der Herrschaft der Legende steht". The main emphasis is on "Legende" and "Erzählung" and not on "Geschichte".[7]

If one looks more closely at the narrative material characterized as legend, it becomes obvious that "Peter's confession" and "the transfiguration" are not on a par with the other text sections. However important it may be in another context, Peter's confession cannot be juxtaposed with the baptismal, death and resurrection events in which Jesus is the main figure. And however much the transfiguration may remind one of the baptismal event, it is aimed at the disciples and not at Jesus. It is also clear that the Baptist's activities lead to Jesus' baptism and the temptation associated therewith, and that the entry into Jerusalem is the introduction to the Passion. Three macro-sequences can therefore be identified in this narrative material: 1,1-13, which constitutes a beginning; 11,1-10 and 14,1-15,47, which form a middle part; and 16,1-8, which sets an ending.

These textual macro-sequences may be identified as the gospel text's fundamental narrative material, and a division of the entire text into main sections will then on this basis appear as follows:

1.   1,1-13   Jesus' baptism/anointing
2.   1,14-15,47   Jesus' death
3.   16,1-8   Jesus' resurrection

The difference between this and the above commentators' divisions is that this division has been made on the basis of just one criterion, the changes in the relationship between God and Jesus, whereas their divisions result from the blending of different criteria, which may not have been intentional but which arises as a result of the implicit assumption that the basic sequences tell of events that merely follow one another and are therefore to be found on the same action level. The gospel text's *content* is not however organized into textual units but into hierarchically arranged narrative units that emerge only when one moves from text to narrative.

B. THE GOSPEL NARRATIVE

Perceived as a narrating discourse, the gospel text manifests a narrative whole which is referred to as the gospel narrative. This is supported by a consistent narration which refers to a single narrator, who transforms all applied traditional material by infusing it with his own enunciation. This creative overwriting produces an autonomous narrative that disengages itself from its substantial presuppositions even where traditional items appear to have been taken over

---

[7] Ibidem, p. 261.

without alteration. Narrative exegesis does not therefore distinguish tradition and redaction, but considers the gospel narrative as sustained by just one narrator.

The gospel narrative as an enunciate is similarly coherent. The sequence of events is unbroken; the "Jesus" introduced at the beginning is the same as we encounter at the end. One narrative is concerned, and it establishes a narrative universe that can be read without reference to the historical events that may have occasioned its appearance. The gospel narrative does not receive its meaning by referring to extra-textual matters. If the science of history should succeed in proving that nothing in Mark's Gospel corresponds to factual historical events the perception of its value as a source might perhaps change, but not its narrative status.

This follows from a consideration of the gospel texts as discourse, but does not mean purely and simply an ahistorical approach. Mark's Gospel is a narrative that has come into being at a certain historical time, which is why knowledge of contemporary culture may be a precondition for understanding the text. The gospel text itself has nevertheless absolute priority. The information it contains about persons and events is information about *narrated* or *narrative* persons and events, and the entire quantity of information is considered by the narrator as sufficient to convey the narrative's message.

A narrative, however extensive and detailed it may be, cannot say everything a reader may wish to know. It is therefore always open to supplementary interpretation. But it is important that the quantity of information the narrator reveals has primary status and must be considered sufficient. No information is lacking. Everything that must be said is said, and the significance of each item of information is governed by the total quantity of information, *the narrative context*, in which it is included. This may here be spoken of as the gospel narrative's *semiotic unity*.

The identification of the analysis' subject - the gospel narrative according to Mark - is in the nature of a demarcation, in that it is considered in isolation from its New Testament context (and any narrower contexts, e.g. the synoptic question, or wider contexts, for example the relationship to the Old Testament). Such a demarcation involves a *closure* that opens for a possible, coherent reading. The closure is in this case of a dual nature: on the one hand outwardly, as already referred to, but also inwardly, in that the gospel narrative's micro-narratives, for example the miracle stories, are not themselves considered in isolation from the macro-narrative's context.

The isolated consideration of the gospel narrative may remind one of redaction criticism's interest in the individual gospel scripture, but as already pointed out no distinction is made here between redaction and tradition. Consideration of the micro-narratives as subordinate to the macro-narrative gives a reading of these which will differ from that obtained when they are perceived as independent traditional items linked to an extra-textual context. The difference between a narrative and a form-critical analysis is plain here, although they work with the same material.

This methodically conditioned closure must be distinguished from the closure which is due to the gospel narrative's semiotic, i.e. semantic and syntactic, unity. The semantic closure which may be envisaged can already be recognized at a pre-analytical stage by virtue of the marked redundance which characterizes the gospel narrative. The number of miracle stories is a striking example here. If one imagines this number as doubled, nothing fundamentally new would be added to the narrative's basic semantics.

The syntactic closure is also immediately recognizable. If Jesus' death and resurrection are not irreversible events which institute a new reality, there is no Christian message (cf. Rom 6,10; Heb 7,27 et al.).

The methodically founded closure and the gospel narrative's inherent closure thus justify one another, and make it legitimate to speak of Mark's Gospel as a specific subject of analysis.

1. The Narrative Units

It seems unavoidable that scientific work must consist in explaining the unrestricted by way of the restricted. The concern of VLADIMIR PROPP, who found himself confronted with a corpus of Russian folktales which represent an - in principle - infinite number of narratives, was to determine the constant features that made it legitimate to consider these tales as belonging to one and the same genre.

His investigations caused him to conclude that the narrative was constructed of *functions*, and that it was therefore possible to study the narrative on the basis of the persons' functions. PROPP understood "function" to mean "an act of a character, defined from the point of view of its significance for the course of the action".[8]

Although the number of characters appearing was extraordinarily large, the number of functions was shown to be very small. PROPP's observations led to the establishment of four assertions:

1)   Functions of characters serve as stable, constant elements in a tale, independent of how and by whom they are fulfilled. They constitute the fundamental components of a tale.
2)   The number of functions known to the fairy tale is limited.
3)   The sequence of functions is always identical.
4)   All fairy tales are of one type in regard to their structure.[9]

---

[8] Vladimir Propp, *Morphology of the Folktale*, Austin 1968, p. 21.
[9] Ibidem, pp. 21.

As is clear from items 2) and 4) these assertions have a limited range of validity, in that they are aimed at certain types of tale, the so-called magic tales. His work has nevertheless been an invaluable source of inspiration for scholars who have tried to prepare a general theory of the narrative. PROPP's observations are indeed a mixture of general and specific discoveries. This is clearly to be seen if one attempts to generalize his perceptions and give them a hypothetical form.

According to PROPP, it is reasonable to assume that the narrative consists of a limited number of functions organized in sequences, that a narrative is a syntagmatic sequence of functions that may be perceived as the specific realization of a presupposed paradigmatic system of functions. Narratives with identical sequences of function belong to the same type, but all different types belong in turn to one and the same general system of functions. The objective of a general narratology must then be to determine the narrative's system of functions and the rules applicable to their linking together into sequences.

CLAUDE BREMOND's main work, *Logique du récit*, presents such a general narratology or narrative semiotics. He adheres to PROPP's function concept: it is functions, acts and events that, grouped in sequences, produce the narrative. But the total function sequence is now seen as composed of functions which are necessarily included in elementary sequences, so that the narrative's global function sequence appears as composed of these elementary sequences. The sequence of functions consists of linked sub-sequences which are themselves constructed of functions.

The elementary sequence contains three functions, corresponding to the three necessary elements in the development of each *narrative process*. In his article, "La logique des possibles narratifs", BREMOND defines these elements as follows:

1) a function, "qui ouvre la possibilité du processus sous forme de conduite à tenir ou d'événement à prevoir";

2) a function, "qui réalise cette virtualité sous forme de conduite ou d'événement en acte";

3) a function, "qui clôt le processus sous forme de résultat atteint".[10]

In *Logique du récit*, the three elements are defined merely by "virtualité, passage à l'acte, achèvement".[11]

To avoid misunderstanding, it should be emphasized that the first element is not the act or event which establishes the possibility of the act, but merely that the act is possible, virtual; that the second element, the actual transition to action,

---

[10] Claude Bremond, "La logique des possibles narratifs", *Communications 8*, Paris 1966.
[11] Claude Bremond, *Logique du récit*, Paris 1973, p. 131.

does not realize the virtual objective but actualizes it; and that the third element is the same act as the accomplished realization of the original possibility.[12]

In contrast to PROPP, for whom the sequence of functions appeared as a regularity, BREMOND emphasizes that one function does not follow from another. After each function an alternative is given: the possibility of action may be utilized, but the mere possibility does not mean that a person therefore initiates the act. Similarly, the transition to action does not necessarily mean that this act achieves its objective. The efforts may prove to be in vain, the act is not accomplished according to its intention. In a forward-looking perspective the process is thus open; whatever will occur cannot be predicted with certainty. Retrospectively, however, the matter looks different. It is clear in retrospect that the act's accomplishment is presupposed by its initiation, which itself presupposes its possibility.

The act may be seen as a doing which as its result causes something to be. Doing is a realization of a being which it serves. Doing is a means, whereas being is an objective. In the light of this teleology, the three elements of the narrative basic-syntagm can be determined, on the one hand as regards doing:

1)   Virtual doing
2)   Actualized doing
3)   Realized doing

and on the other hand as regards being:

1)   Virtual being
2)   Actualized being
3)   Realized being.

There will be ample opportunity later to look more closely at the modality problems associated with this structure, abbreviated to VAR.

BREMOND differs from PROPP in another aspect also. Where the latter was inclined to focus on the act as a purely objective matter, BREMOND emphasizes the important fact that an act's function cannot be determined without considering the persons involved therein. The act, or the narrative process, involves persons, in part those performing the act, in part those subject to the act.

The function then appears as a subject-predicate relation in which the person is the subject and the process the predicate. If the act is linked to a subject in this way, the person acting, the act and the result of the act cannot be separated, but appear as a narrative role.

---

[12] The opening and closing functions are described below as manipulation and sanction.

2. The Role Concept

If not only the execution of the act but also its result is to relate to a subject, the first two *narrative roles* which can be distinguished become the agent and the patient, or the subject of doing and the subject of being.[13]

Every act or event, every narrative process, refers in principle to a subject of doing which performs the act and it is usually not associated with difficulties of identifying the subject of doing and the subject of being of the processes. In the story of the healing of Simon's mother-in-law (1,29-31), which will be discussed in detail below, it is clearly Jesus who is the subject of doing (the healer) and the mother-in-law who is the subject of being (the healed).

The subsequent basic sequence, the summary in 1,32-34, says that Jesus healed many suffering from various diseases. The verb θεραπεύω defines Jesus as θεραπευτής, and it may then be said that the performance inherent in the verb *to heal* is summarized in the healer *role*.

The role consists of a somewhat fixed and therefore largely predictable action programme performed by a competent subject of doing with a view to achieving a prescribed result. The role may therefore be defined as the structural relationship between:

the person acting - the act - the result of the act.

The lexeme θεραπεύω refers to a class of lexemes comprising all the forms derived from the root: θεραπαινίς, θεραπεία, θεράπευμα, θεραπευτής, θεραπευτικός, θεραπεύω et al. Within such a class, interest is centred around the group of lexemes indicating the role's three components: the act is expressed by a verb; the person acting by a noun which will most often be formed by the use of a suffix that refers to the performer of the activity expressed in the corresponding verb, for example -της; whereas the result of the act perceived as a product is a noun which is frequently formed with a suffix that indicates concepts such as -ια (-εια) and -μα. The presence in the text of the verb θεραπεύω thus refers to the following group of role lexemes:

θεραπευτής - θεραπεύω - θεραπεία

and the role is referred to as θεραπευτής/healer after the person acting. The role of *healer* is not a narrative role but a *thematic role*, which belongs to the narrative's discursive level. A distinction can be made between an actor level of

---

[13] Bremond employs the terms agent and patient; Greimas prefers *sujet de faire* and *sujet d'état*, cf. *Sémiotique*, art. "Programme narratif". It is unclear whether Greimas merely understands by *sujet d'état* a subject of state or a definite subject of being, cf. ibidem art. "État" and "Être", but for a narrative analysis which, like the present one, insists on the significance of events to the persons involved, the subject of doing's complementary role is a subject of being.

a specific nature, where for example a person, the actor Jesus, heals another person, the actor Peter's mother-in-law, and an actant level of an abstract nature, where a subject of doing changes the subject of being's fate. A distinction is thus made between actor roles and actant roles, and the investigation rests on the assumption that it is the narrative actant roles which govern the discursive or thematic actor roles.

It should be stressed that the thematic role's structural unity means that the presence of just one role lexeme in the discourse (for example θεραπεύω) is sufficient to acknowledge the presence of the role (*in casu* θεραπευτής). The narrative's image of Jesus has been produced by the predication of an empty proper name with thematic roles which constitute the discursive Jesus. The narrative Jesus, in a narrow sense of the word, is constituted by the connection between a subject actant and different narrative roles. But as already pointed out, the designation, the narrative Jesus, is chiefly employed in the wider sense, where it refers to the story's Jesus, defined both narratively and discursively.

It will often be found that the text does not itself, by the use of role lexemes, explicate the role or roles concerned. Thus, in the story of the healing of Peter's mother-in-law, neither the lexeme to heal nor any synonym for this appears. The difficulty here is not to acknowledge that Jesus acts in the role of one who makes a sick person well but in describing this role. In such cases one should employ the descriptions that the narrative employs - explicitly or implicitly - for similar acts, e.g. healer and not e.g. doctor, physician, wonder-worker or miracle-monger.

In cases where the text contains a role lexeme, it is by no means taken for granted that the entire lexeme group is encountered. Thus, θεραπεία is not to be found in the Markan narrative, but for example in Lk 9,11 (E.T. cure), where it appears in connection with the verb ἰάομαι referring to the role ἰατρός, which raises the question of role synonymity. The lexeme θεραπευτής on the other hand is found nowhere in the New Testament; that it to say, it is not found explicitly but is manifested implicitly only by virtue of the presence of θεραπεύω.

The roles refer to the narrative processes, acts and events which constitute the narrative. As concerns the narrative roles, a fundamental distinction is made between doing roles and being roles, which are then specified.

For exegesis the narrative theory is a means, and it is therefore most appropriate to present the specification of the narrative processes and roles in the form of a presentation of the method of narrative exegesis.

CHAPTER THREE

NARRATIVE METHOD

The term "narrative method" refers to the special way of reading employed in the investigation of the gospel narrative. The approach of narrative exegesis is an analytical procedure including a number of analytical operations which are the application of the theoretically substantiated inquiry horizon.

It is not the intention here to submit a complete check-list but to arrive at the basic features of the investigative method by analyzing the clear and simple basic sequence, 1,29-31, the healing of Peter's/Simon's mother-in-law:

> As soon as they left the synagogue, they entered the house of Simon and Andrew, with James and John. Now Simon's mother-in-law was in bed with a fever, and they told him about her at once. He came and took her by the hand and lifted her up. Then the fever left her, and she began to serve them.[1]

A. NARRATIVE PROPOSITIONS

The first operation is the basic sequence's division into presentic, narrative propositions. Since this often refers back anaphorically to one or more preceding basic sequences, it is frequently necessary to include information therefrom for the formulation of these propositions.

For example, in the English translation "they" refers back to 1,21-28, where a different "they" refers back to 1,16-20, where Simon, Andrew, James and John are introduced. It will also often be necessary to formulate propositions about events that are mentioned only implicitly. For example, having left the synagogue (ἐξελθόντες) presupposes that one goes out of the synagogue. The following presentic narrative propositions can then be identified:

1) Jesus, Simon, Andrew, James and John go out of the synagogue;
2) Jesus and his disciples go into Simon and Andrew's house;
3) Simon's mother-in-law is lying in bed with a fever;
4) The disciples tell Jesus that the mother-in-law is sick;
5) Jesus goes to the sick person;

---

[1] Texts from the Bible are rendered in English in accordance with *The New Oxford Annotated Bible with the Apocryphal/Deuterocanonical Books*, Oxford 1991.

6)   Jesus takes the sick person by the hand and lifts her up;
7)   The fever leaves the sick person;
8)   The healed person serves Jesus and the disciples.

If the formulated propositions are compared with the text referred to, it will be seen that the anaphoric elements (e.g. "they" and "her") have been replaced by the persons to which they refer (the anaphora are however permitted within the proposition itself). The presentic formulation cancels the grammatical tenses to the benefit of a kind of non-tense, but the propositions' sequence retains the text's temporalization which interprets every logically presupposed narrative process as preceding and every logically presupposing narrative process as subsequent. It is on the basis of this temporalization, which rests upon the dichotomy of anteriority/posteriority and not upon simple chronology, that the logic of the narrative processes can be determined.[2]

Yet another feature must be pointed out: once introduced into the propositions by the proper name or the thematic role explicitly given by the narrative, the persons can be anaphorically represented by the implicit, thematic roles this contains.

"Jesus, Simon, Andrew, James and John" in proposition 1) can thus be replaced by the reduced form, "Jesus and his disciples", in proposition 2) on the basis of the preassumption that the important point, i.e. that Simon, Andrew, James and John are observers of the healing, is closely linked to their role as disciples. Similarly, the "mother-in-law" in proposition 4) can be replaced with "the sick person" in proposition 5), since it is by virtue of this passive, thematic role that she is relevant.

The presentic narrative proposition has emerged through an objectification of the text, a procedure consisting in an elimination of the material which is not relevant to the analysis envisaged (the eliminated material can of course be taken into consideration in a different context) and in a reformulation of what is relevant thereto. By not allowing the narration's actants, the narrator and the narratee, to be represented in the basic sequence, this already appears from the narrator's side as strongly objectified. In order further to concentrate attention on the narrate, it is expedient to allow the objectification to follow by an *anonymization*, i.e. an elimination of any *anthroponyms* (proper names), *toponyms* (place names) and *chrononyms* (indications of time).[3]

The anonymized text can then be given:

1)   The teacher and his disciples go out of the synagogue;
2)   The teacher and his disciples go into the house of some of the disciples;

[2] Cf. *Sémiotique*, art. "Localisation spatio-temporelle".
[3] Cf. *Sémiotique*, art. "Onomastique".

3)   A disciple's mother-in-law is lying in bed with a fever;
4)   The disciples tell the teacher/healer that the mother-in-law is sick;
5)   The teacher/healer goes to the sick person;
6)   The teacher/healer takes the sick person by the hand and lifts her;
7)   The fever leaves the sick person;
8)   The healed person serves the teacher/healer and the disciples.

As can be seen, the anonymization involves a dehistorification, the text loses its historical anchorage. Nevertheless, the narrative-constituting events remain the same. If on the one hand the proper names contribute to the formation of signification by evoking an external referent, then it is on the other hand evident that these proper names are persons only by virtue of the properties ascribed to them via what is narrated.

The anonymous narrative constitutes the substance of the discourse, even for the gospel narrative as a whole. In a generative perspective this anonymous corpus of signification is a material which is overwritten with historifying markers, which are in turn an expression of a secondary transformation.[4] The anonymization procedure serves to clarify that the narrative Jesus of the story is defined by the anonymous narrative context, not by an external historical context.

B. THE PIVOTAL POINT

The next step is to define the narrative proposition which thematizes the narrative pivotal point. This refers to the act on the basis of which the other acts retrospectively appear as presuppositions and consequences. In this case, the narrative pivotal point is thematized in proposition 6). The central narrative proposition which identifies the main narrative process can then be subjected to an analysis, the persons involved being identified either by a proper name or a thematic role employed as a personal designation: here, Jesus the healer and the sick person.

The subject of doing and the subject of being are identified, and the proposition is defined as transitive (subject of doing $\neq$ subject of being) or reflexive (subject of doing $=$ subject of being). The narrative focuses on the healing, and in accordance with this the proposition can be defined as transitive: Jesus is the subject of doing, the sick person the subject of being.

---

[4] This secondary treatment should not be confused with a redaction of the material from an available Jesus tradition. It is possible that the oldest Jesus transmission "ist 'Perikopen'-Überlieferung, also Überlieferung einzelner Szenen und einzelner Aussprüche, die zum grössten Teile ohne feste chronologische und topographische Markierung innerhalb der Gemeinde überliefert worden sind", as asserted by Karl Ludwig Schmidt, *Der Rahmen der Geschichte Jesu*, Berlin 1919, p. v. But the anonymous text lacks not only chronological and topographical information but also personal names. It does not therefore belong to the Jesus tradition but forms part of the library of thematic and narrative roles which characterize a cultural tradition.

Processes may appear to which no definite subject of doing has been assigned. In most cases, however, the narrative identifies a definite subject of doing that is characterized according to whether in the light of the consequences it is acting voluntarily (intended) or involuntarily (unintended). Here, Jesus acts voluntarily.

The pragmatic narrative process (cf. $\pi\rho\hat{\alpha}\gamma\mu\alpha$: the done, the deed; $\pi\rho\acute{\alpha}\sigma\sigma\omega$: carry out, effect, execute, act, do), which concerns the direct influence upon being is defined as virtual, actualized or realized. Here the healing has been accomplished, realized. The lifting up ($\dot{\epsilon}\gamma\epsilon\acute{\iota}\rho\omega$) means much more than the change from a horizontal to a vertical position of the body (cf. Jas 5,15); it is the healing itself.

The narrative process is then defined on the basis of the change/preservation dichotomy. The fever indicates sickness, which can be considered on two different but connected levels. One immediately fastens on the fact that the mother-in-law's situation changes. She is initially sick but becomes well by way of the process, and it must therefore be correct to define the healing as a process of change. In this sense the sickness is seen as the result of a preceding and completed process of change characterized by the transition from well to sick. But the analytic value of distinguishing between process phases according to the VAR structure becomes clear when, as in this case, it promotes the perception that the sickness can also be seen as the indication of a process of change taking place which has been actualized as such but not yet realized.

The narrative has nothing more specific to say about what is wrong with the sick person. It could be mild influenza if one considers that this would be sufficient reason to trouble the Master. But even in this case, where the sickness is not immediately life-threatening, it is nevertheless taking place, i.e. an actualized process of change, which will end in the result of every sickness, death, unless it is combatted. Jesus combats the sickness, whose death-seeking process is revoked before it succeeds in realizing its objective. To be healed is to regain one's health and well-being, and the healing must here be defined as a preservation process. It will then be seen that the process of change defined above forms part of a subordinate hierarchic relationship to this preservation process in which it is embedded.

The process of change is now specified on the basis of progression/degression; the doing role on the basis of progressor/degressor. The preservation process is specified on the basis of protection/repression (withholding, retention); the doing role on the basis of protector/repressor. Quite independently of the sick person's own perception of the situation, the process of change can be defined more specifically as a progression process in which Jesus adopts the role of progressor (life-builder). There is of course no doubt here that the healing is for the benefit of the mother-in-law. Similarly, the preservation process can be defined more specifically as a protection process where Jesus adopts the role of protector (life-preserver).

It is then possible to give an elementary definition of narration:

1) The narrator (No) attempts to impart to the narratee (Ne) the conception of a state of being and/or a course of action (virtual, actualized or realized state/process).

2) The subject of being for this state/process is No, Ne or a third person A.

3) The responsible subject of doing for this state/process is No, Ne, the third person A or a fourth person B.[5]

The message is a narrate which concerns a principal subject of being and a principal subject of doing. Narrative in a stricter sense is concerned only when the subject of being and the subject of doing are neither the narrator (Mark) nor the narratee (the reader) but an objectified third person A (for example, the sick person) or a fourth person B (for example, the healer). The narrate most often concerns not only one but several states/processes, and the model then serves to distinguish the states/processes from one another, which must then be defined in their relationships of mutual dependence.

Even in the face of the gospel narrative's complex narrate, exegesis must elementarily inquire about the principal state/process which is the content of the joyful message, about the principal subject of being who benefits therefrom, and about the principal subject of doing who is responsible for the main action.

C. The Subject of Being

The next operation consists of defining the subject of being's narrative process. This can be given a canonical form, in that the suffering subject can be distinguished by three modes of existence.

The starting point is the subject of being's initial situation (I), which is characterized by non-being (e.g. sickness). In this situation it is a virtual subject of being, in that the intended state (e.g. health) is defined by being-able-to-be and by being-able-not-to-be.

If the process is not started, the subject of being remains in the initial situation (non-being). If it starts, however, this passes to the mode of existence of actualized subject of being (the intermediate situation II, where the intended being is to be found as becoming). If the process does not reach its objective, the

---

[5] The model is a generalized version of Bremond's model of the narrated information process, cf. *Logique du récit*, p. 261, and as such can be employed to analyze both the narrated and the narrating narration.

subject of being remains in the initial situation (non-being), but if it is accomplished according to intention it will pass to the mode of existence of realized subject of being and then find itself in the final situation (III; being):

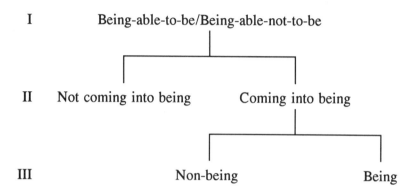

In the light of the healing process, the narrative proposition 3) primarily thematizes the mother-in-law's initial situation. But on the basis of this proposition's information alone there is not as yet a basis for identifying her as virtually favoured, since the sickness may, of course, be incurable. Only with hindsight, in the light of the act's successful accomplishment, can she be identified at this stage of development as a possible subject of being for a process of change: from sick to well.

The act of healing itself lies in Jesus' taking the sick person by the hand and lifting her up. Had she fallen back onto the bed the healing would not have succeeded, but here it is expressly stated in propositions 7) and 8) that the fever left her and that she served them. However brief the time interval between the treatment and its result, a distinction must be made between two modes of existence: the sick person is first an actualized subject of being during the treatment, and then a realized subject of being. The comment that she served them indicates the realization of full recovery, in that the mother-in-law has achieved the final state of being fit and well.

Seen as a preservation process, the starting point of the healing is an initial situation defined by being (living) which is threatened by a degressive becoming (the on-going sickness process) moving towards the final situation of non-being (death). The realized healing means the ending of this degressive becoming in favour of a protected being.

The subject of being must then be specified in detail. It is first defined in the initial situation, where the subject of being is either favoured by a satisfactory state owing to a preceding or on-going progression; or disfavoured by (victim of) an unsatisfactory state owing to a preceding or on-going degression.

Peter's mother-in-law, or more generally the sick person (thematic role of being), is the victim of a degression process which can be viewed either as completed (but in that event a chronic sickness is concerned) or as on-going.

The subject of being's role in the initial situation must then be defined. If it is favoured, i.e. characterized by an abundance of being (for example, life), it will then be a virtual or actualized victim of a virtual or actualized degression process (for example, a process of death).

If it is disfavoured, i.e. characterized by a lack of being (for example, sickness), it will then be pointed out as a virtual or actualized beneficiary by a virtual or actualized progression process (healing process).

With regard to a possible different process, the sick person is pointed out as a virtual or actualized beneficiary by a virtual or actualized progression process, which means that here the healing is perceived as a process of change.

In the event of preservation, the subject of being is either favoured by protection, which at one moment consists in the ending of a virtual degression process (in fact a modal transformation from possibility to impossibility), and at the next moment consists in the interruption of an on-going degression process.

The other possibility is that the subject of being is a victim of repression, which at one moment consist of the ending of a virtual progression process and at the next moment consists of the interruption of an on-going progression process.

In the example analyzed, the sick person is in the initial situation of virtually favoured by virtual protection, which will consist of the ending of the on-going sickness process. Finally, the subject of being's role in the final situation is defined. The healthy person, or to be more precise the healed person (thematic role of being), has been realized favourably by virtue of a realized change/preservation. What is therefore concerned is to determine whether the subject of being assumes the role of favoured or victim, and then to follow the role in the various modes of existence.

D. THE SUBJECT OF DOING

The specification of the subject of doing's narrative process takes its starting point in this possibility. If it is possible it is at the same time unnecessary (avoidable or uncertain), since the subject of doing can both act and refrain from acting. The starting point is therefore characterized by being-able-to-do/being-able-not-to-do. Equipped with this freedom of action, the subject of doing will then either pass on to action (doing) or refrain from action (not doing).

If it passes on to action, it will either achieve realization of the intended objective (being) or have exercised its efforts in vain; nothing came of it (i.e. non-being):

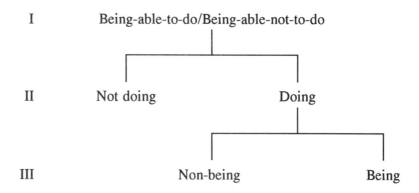

I   Being-able-to-do/Being-able-not-to-do

II   Not doing   Doing

III   Non-being   Being

The acting subject can thus be distinguished in three modes of existence: in the project phase (I) it is virtual, in the performance phase (II) actualized, and in the result phase (III) a realized subject of doing. The specification is then expanded, in that these three elements are separately considered in more detail.

In the project phase, when the narrative subject recognizes itself in the role as a possible acting subject, the subject of doing can be characterized according to the influence that determines its decision to refrain from or pass on to action. In the performance phase, it can then be described on the basis of the assistance or resistance the project realization encounters. Finally, in the result phase, it can be described according to whether the result is successful or unsuccessful, and on the basis of the consequences resulting therefrom.

The role of virtual subject of doing exists when the narrative states that the necessary conditions for the exercise of doing are objectively present. If, therefore, the narrative states that 1) a subject of being is a victim of an unsatisfactory state of being and/or threatened by an on-going degression process and that 2) by passing on to action a virtual subject of doing would be able to make an attempt to improve (progress) this state of lacking or to protect against this degression process, then the roles of virtual progressor and/or virtual protector will be established.The role of actualized subject of doing exists in the passing over to action. The action programme initiated, which serves as a means of achieving the anticipated objective, is specified as progression or protection.

The narrative proposition 6), "Jesus takes the sick person by the hand and lifts her up", thematizes the initiation of the action programme, which serves as a means to achieve the healing as an objective. The verbs κρατέω and ἐγείρω can be further analyzed, in that they are considered as role lexemes, which refer to two thematic roles: κρατῶν (the possession-taking, dominant, conquering) and ἐγείρων (the lifting up, resuscitating). These roles become significant when one makes a comparison with the usage of these verbs in Mt 12,11, where Jesus asks the rhetorical question: "Suppose one of you has only one sheep and it falls into a pit on the sabbath; will you not lay hold of it (κρατέω) and lift it out (ἐγείρω)?". The sheep which is the victim of an on-going degression process that ends in death cannot get out of the pit by its own effort. It can be saved only by outside help, in that this degression process is neutralized.[6]

This opens up another specification possibility. The action programme will often include the ending of resistance or the obtaining of assistance. The opposition is either impersonal (not attributed to a certain subject of doing) or personal; it is owing to either another person (transitive) or to the person himself (reflexive). Similarly, the assistance is impersonal/personal and transitive/reflexive.

On the one hand Jesus is the subject of being's assistance-giver. On the other hand he is in a polemical confrontation with the impersonal but personifiable opponent: sickness, which must be combatted. The sickness has taken possession of the subject of being, who is held in captivity and must be wrenched away in overcoming an opposition. The use of the aggressive verb κρατέω refers to this combat aspect and thematizes the acting subject's strength, power, and supremacy (κράτος). As regards ἐγείρω, it is clear that the lifting up involves the restoration of the subject of being's integrity.

The definition of the role of realized subject of doing is finally effected on the basis of whether the result is successful or unsuccessful. Here, the successful result is thematized in proposition 7), and its consequence, as an opening up of new possibilities for the subject of being, in proposition 8).

The narrative analysis procedure is described here only in outline. Strictly, the analysis operations referred to concern only that which constitutes the narrative's basis, i.e. the narrate's pragmatic dimension, which includes the direct changing or preservation of being. The indirect situation, which includes the cognitive (and affective) dimension, whose content is the pragmatic dimension which precedes it as well as the underlying modality problems, has not been included, or only touched upon. However limited the perspective may be relative to the theory's overall inquiry horizon, the analysis procedure presented may nevertheless be said to form the foundation of narrative exegesis, and may as such serve as an anchorage for the following investigations of the gospel narrative.

---

[6] The victim of an on-going degression process is a Christian arch role, often represented by the pit (βόθυνος; or the cistern, well, φρέαρ, Lk 14,5) cf., e.g. Anselm of Canterbury, *Hvorfor Gud blev menneske* (Why God became Man), København 1978, pp. 69.

PART TWO
THE WONDER-WORKER

CHAPTER FOUR

STORY AND NARRATIVE

Wonder-working encompasses two dimensions between which, although they are linked, a distinction must be made. Acts 2,22 says:

> (...) Jesus of Nazareth, a man attested (ἀποδείκνυμι) to you by God with deeds of power (δύναμις), wonders (τέρας), and signs (σημεῖον) that God did through him among you, (...)

According to this account, wonder-working has an informative or cognitive function, in that relative to the persons who witness but do not themselves participate in the miracle itself it serves to identify Jesus as the one sent by God.

The miracle is a sign in the sense of an index, which on the basis of a directly perceptible event (the miracle) allows the recipient to perceive or at least to notice something concerning another event which is not visibly present in the same way (the mission and its content).[1]

But the miracle's cognitive sign-function, which is by no means absent in Mark's Gospel, although the word "sign" (σημεῖον) in 8,11ff has a negative meaning, is only one aspect of the matter. The miracle itself comes within the pragmatic dimension which precedes the cognitive. It is a change or preservation of being that constitutes the basis of the narrative, including the wonder narrative, and the circulating information is relevant only in so far as it is related to a pragmatic project.

The wonder-worker thus sees himself as entered into a dual act, partly as pragmatic subject of doing who intervenes in being and partly as a cognitive subject of doing who, voluntary or involuntary, informs about himself and his task.[2]

The wonder-work's pragmatic dimension will be the subject of a closer examination in the following analysis with a view to defining the wonder-worker's pragmatic role and the wonder narrative's genre.

---

[1] The wonder work's sign-function, which is expressed most clearly in the Gospel of John, has been made the subject of a semiotic investigation by Trond Skard Dokka, *Å gjenkjenne den ukjente. Om menneskers mulighet for å kjenne Gud - en studie basert på Johannes-evangeliets tegnstoff* (To Recognize the Unknown. On Man's Possibility of Knowing God - A Study Based on the Sign Material in the Gospel of John), Oslo 1989.

[2] The question of the wonder-work's epiphanic nature and revelatory purpose, including the question of the command for secrecy and the disciples' failure to understand, belongs to the cognitive dimension, which is disregarded here; cf. Aage Pilgaard, *Jesus som undergører i Markusevangeliet* (Jesus as Wonder-Worker in the Gospel of Mark), København 1983.

A. THE MIRACLE STORY

The genre concept of narrative exegesis may be illustrated profitably against the background of form criticism's genre concept. RUDOLF BULTMANN defines the following basic sequences as miracle stories ("Wundergeschichten"):

1,21ff; 1,29ff; 1,40ff; 2,1ff; 4,37ff; 5,1ff; 5,21ff; 6,34ff; 6,45ff; 7,32ff; 8,1ff; 8,22ff; 9,14ff; 10,46ff and 11,12ff.

There are two other basic sequences which tell of a miracle, 3,1ff and 7,24ff, but these are not told in the miracle-story style, writes BULTMANN, "da das Wunder ganz der apophthegmatischen Pointe dienstbar gemacht ist". These basic sequences are not therefore miracle stories in a form-critical sense. 2,1ff, on the other hand, is defined as "eine eigentliche Wundergeschichte" because it was developed into an apophthegm only secondarily.[3]

It is basic sequences, text items, that are identified with regard to genre. Form criticism defines the miracle story as a *text-form*. As genre ("Gattung"), the miracle story, like every other form-critical genre, is a *text-genre*. In his form-critical investigation, *Urchristliche Wundergeschichten*, GERD THEIßEN has attempted to develop further the classical form-critical method by analyzing the synoptic genre *miracle story*. In this connection, he distinguishes clearly three aspects of form-critical questioning: a synchronic aspect, a diachronic aspect and a functional aspect.

As "*Form*geschichte" the method contains a *synchronic* element, in that it analyzes genres and thus classifies the various texts under this category, disregarding their mutual chronological and tradition historical lines of connection.

As "Form*geschichte*", however, it is characterized by a *diachronic* element, in that it inquires about a text's origin and development. The tradition historical element comes to the fore here, and thereby the question of the text's oral prehistory. The basic assumption is that it will be possible in the light of the social transmission situation (for example, service to God, mission, teaching), the text's "Sitz im Leben" and the transmission trends involved therein to reconstruct the text's oral prehistory.

The question of the text's "Sitz im Leben" involves, however, not only a diachronic but also a *functional* aspect, since what is concerned is the text's function in social life and thus the text as a *sociological* function of this life. What is required is to clarify, "warum Menschen zu einer bestimmten literarischen Form greifen und sie zur Entfaltung bringen".[4]

---

[3] Rudolf Bultmann, *Die Geschichte der synoptischen Tradition*, Göttingen (1921) 1970, p. 223.

[4] Gerd Theißen, *Urchristliche Wundergeschichten. Ein Beitrag zur formgeschichtlichen Erforschung der synoptischen Evangelien*, Göttingen 1974, pp. 11.

Against this background, THEIßEN sets himself the task of developing these coherent views by analyzing the miracle stories, which are synchronically considered as structured, literary forms, diachronically as reproduced narratives, and functionally as symbolic acts.

It is form criticism's synchronic aspect which establishes the common problems that make a meaningful discussion with narrative exegesis possible.

THEIßEN's identification of miracle stories differs from BULTMANN's at various points. First, he disregards 11,12-14 (Fig tree cursed). He then includes 3,1ff and 7,24ff as miracle stories, and finally he includes the epiphanies 1,9ff (Jesus' baptism) and 9,2ff (The transfiguration); but neither 15,33ff nor 16,1ff.

The lack of clarity that characterizes both the classical and the newer form-critical definition of the miracle story is significant. It clearly shows how the method's form-concept obstructs the perception of the gospel text's content. THEIßEN feels it unreasonable to disregard 3,1ff and 7,24ff, but from a form-critical aspect it is correct to exclude them. At the very moment he includes these basic sequences in his investigation of the miracle story he abandons the form-critical method. By including them he reveals that his interest is not really concerned with the miracle story as a text-form but the miracle story as a narrative form, i.e. as a *wonder narrative*.

The lack of clarity which characterizes THEIßEN's investigation is largely because, in his loyalty to form criticism, he confuses text and narrative. By turning his interest towards all the basic sequences which thematize a miraculous act (including 1,9ff and 9,2ff) - that is, even those which are not miracle stories in a form-critical sense - he also tries to expand the miracle concept of form criticism. But, as will be shown later, such an expansion only confuses the issue. Although it is, of course, possible to speak of a miraculous act in general, it is in the nature of things most expedient to separate the miraculous acts for which Jesus is the subject of doing (which excludes 1,9ff and 9,2ff), and then to separate the specific miraculous act that does not serve a person in need (11,12ff). This results in a uniform group of stories that can be made the subject of a comparative and generalizing investigation.

B. The Wonder Narrative

Form criticism's concern is the synoptic miracle-story text-genre. The present investigation is, on the other hand, interested in the wonder narratives of Mark's Gospel, the narrative sequences or basic syntagms in which Jesus appears in the role of wonder-worker. Attention is therefore concentrated on the following basic sequences in the narrative material:

A)	1,21-28	Exorcism in the synagogue at Capernaum
B)	1,29-3	Healing Simon's mother-in-law

C)	1,39-45	Cleansing of a leper
D)	2,1-12	Healing a paralytic
E)	3,1-6	Healing a man with a withered hand
F)	4,35-41	Wind and sea calmed
G)	5,1-20	The Gerasene demoniac
H)	5,21-24	Jairus' daughter a)
I)	5,25-34	The woman suffering from haemorrhages
J)	5,35-43	Jairus' daughter raised b)
K)	6,30-44	Five thousand fed
L)	6,45-52	Walking on the water
M)	7,24-30	The Syrophoenician woman
N)	7,31-37	Healing of a deaf mute
O)	8,1-9	Four thousand fed
P)	8,22-26	A blind man healed (Bethsaida)
Q)	9,14-29	Epileptic child healed
R)	10,46-52	Healing a blind man (Jericho)

The wonder-narrative is not a text genre but a narrative genre whose centre is Jesus as wonder-worker. The classification of the gospel's wonder narratives will then appear as a result of an articulation of the general thematic role of *wonder-worker* in thematic variants: exorcist, healer, rescuer, feeder, and the like. With this change of perspective from text to narrative all information on Jesus as wonder-worker contained in the gospel narrative becomes relevant. The investigation's corpus must therefore be expanded to include the following basic sequences:

1,32-34	Summary: healings and exorcisms
2,15-17	Eating with sinners and tax collectors
3,7-12	Summary: healings and exorcisms
3,13-19	The Twelve chosen
3,20-21	Family reaction
3,22-30	Conversation about Beelzebul
3,31-35	The real family
6,1-6A	Rejection at home
6,6B-13	Commissioning and instruction of the Twelve
6,53-56	Summary: many healings
8,10-13	Demand for a sign
8,14-21	Yeast of the Pharisees
9,38-41	The unknown exorcist
13,21-23	False messiahs and prophets

These will not be analyzed as such but function as a collection of information on Jesus as wonder-worker, which can be included anywhere in the analysis.

CHAPTER FIVE

THE ROLES OF THE WONDER NARRATIVE

A. GENRE AND ROLE-CONFIGURATION

The term *narrative genre* refers to a relatively independent narrative sequence, a unit of action, a basic syntagm characterized by a definite configuration of narrative roles. The narrative process which characterizes the basic syntagm is a process of change or preservation directed towards being or non-being.

These four elementary narrative processes now give an opportunity to distinguish four abstract genres: Progression, Protection, Degression and Repression:[1]

	BEING	NON-BEING
CHANGE	Progression	Degression
PRESERVATION	Protection	Repression

Invested with certain thematic roles, the narrative genre appears concretized as a *discursive configuration* that can now stand alone and can now be included as a micro-narrative in larger narrative sequences, which then contextualize it and give it a function as an episode in an overlapping macro-narrative.

The wonder narrative is just such an embedded discursive genre, which can, however, initially be defined without regard to its place and function in the overlapping gospel narrative.

Bremond has emphasized a special property of the general narrative roles of progressor, protector, degressor and repressor: these are included in "une série de rapports fixes avec la constellation des rôles qui leur sont associés".[2] Such a constellation of roles is here described by the term *role-configuration*.

---

[1] In C. Hugh Holman (ed.), *A Handbook to literature*, New York 1972, the article *Comedy* reads: "As compared with tragedy, comedy is a lighter form of drama which aims primarily to amuse and which ends happily.". Although belonging to dramaturgy, the comedy/tragedy pair of concepts is frequently employed to designate narrative genres, which is confusing and may give rise to methodically unclear comparisons, for example between classical Greek comedy and Pauline theology, cf. Dan O. Via, *Kerygma and Comedy in the New Testament*, Philadelphia 1975, pp. 39. The designations Progression/ Protection and Degression/Repression may replace the far too ambiguous terms of comedy and tragedy. In Christian discourses, the two main genres may be referred to as eu-angelium and dys-angelium.

[2] Claude Bremond, *Logique du récit*, Paris 1973, p. 282.

The basic genre of Progression can then be said to be constituted by a role-configuration that includes the roles of *progressor* (subject of doing) and *favoured by progression, beneficiary* (subject of being):

PROGRESSOR	BENEFICIARY

The active role of progressor involves the presence of the complementary passive role, beneficiary: there is no progression that does not try to promote a subject of being's fate. This relationship is constitutive, but other, facultative relationships can be included in the role-configuration.

The constitutive roles in the basic genre of Degression are similarly:

DEGRESSOR	VICTIM

The role-configuration that characterizes the basic genre of Protection is more complex. In addition to the core relationship of protector/beneficiary this includes a polemic correlate, since the act of protection presupposes a virtual or actualized degression process that sets the role of *disfavoured by degression, victim*. If this process incarnates itself in a subject of doing the role of *degressor* is present, and another core relationship is obtained: degressor/victim of degression:

DEGRESSOR	VICTIM	BENEFICIARY	PROTECTOR

The constitutive roles in the Repression basic genre, whose repression process presupposes a virtual or actualized progression process that is impeded, become similarly:

PROGRESSOR	BENEFICIARY	VICTIM	REPRESSOR

The role-configuration includes a constellation of constitutive roles that subjugate and interpret all facultative roles associated therewith in the light of the genre-specifying narrative process. The persons who appear in a wonder narrative can thus be defined on the basis of the narrative roles they occupy in this genre's role-configuration.

The analysis of 1,29-31, the healing of Simon's mother-in-law, has already brought to light an important perception: as regards genre, the wonder narrative must be defined as Protection. It is true that a progression process can be distinguished here (sickness → healing), which is, moreover, the most conspicuous, but a closer look shows that it is merely a sub-process in an overarching protection sequence (life ← death).

The wonder narratives may therefore be expected to be characterized by a role-configuration that includes minimally a dual-defined subject of being: partly disfavoured by an on-going degression, partly favoured by protection. Since wonder narratives are more specifically perceived as those in which Jesus appears as wonder-worker, the role of protector may further be considered as constitutive. On the contrary, the degressor role is not assumed in all instances; the on-going degression process, which is genre-constituting, is not always attributed to a responsible subject of doing (cf. sickness as an impersonal process). In the narrative discourse, however, there is often a tendency towards personification.

B. THE DISCURSIVE ROLE-CONFIGURATION

As opposed to the narrative actant roles, the discursive actor roles articulate the abstract signification in a semantically concrete form. Narrative exegesis' next step consists in searching the selected text-corpus with a view to listing and grouping the subject of doing's/the protector's thematic roles.

1. The Thematic Protector-Roles

Attention is concentrated on the verbs that express the action process. On this basis, the pertinent role lexemes are defined according to the structure:

the acting - the act - the result of the act

corresponding to:

$$\pi o\iota\eta\tau\acute{\eta}\varsigma - \pi o\iota\acute{\epsilon}\omega - \pi o\acute{\iota}\eta\mu\alpha,$$

which results in the following list:

a. Main Corpus

A)   1,21-28 Exorcism in the synagogue at Capernaum.
       ἐκβάλλων - ἐκβάλλω - ἐκβολή

B)   1,29-31 Healing of Simon's mother-in-law.
       θεραπευτής - θεραπεύω - θεραπεία
       ἐγείρων - ἐγείρω - ἔγερσις

C)   1,39-45 Cleansing of a leper.
       βοηθός - βοηθέω - βοήθεια
       καθαρτής - καθαρίζω - καθαρισμός

D)   2,1-12 Healing a paralytic.
      θεραπευτής - θεραπεύω - θεραπεία
      ἐγείρων - ἐγείρω - ἔγερσις

E)   3,1-6 Healing a man with a withered hand.
      θεραπευτής - θεραπεύω - θεραπεία
      ἀγαθοποιός - ἀγαθοποιέω - ἀγαθοποιία
      σωτήρ - σῴζω - σωτηρία
      ἀποκαταστάτης - ἀποκαθίστημι - ἀποκατάστασις

F)   4,35-41 Wind and sea calmed.
      ἐπιτιμητής - ἐπιτιμάω - ἐπιτιμία

G)   5,1-20 The Gerasene demoniac.
      ἐκβάλλων - ἐκβάλλω - ἐκβολή

H)   5,21-24 Jairus' daughter raised.
      σωτήρ - σῴζω - σωτηρία

I)   5,25-34 The woman suffering from haemorrhages.
      σωτήρ - σῴζω - σωτηρία
      ἰατρός - ἰάομαι - ἴασις/ἴαμα
      ὑγιάζων - ὑγιάζω - ὑγίεια

J)   5,35-43 Jairus' daughter raised.
      ἐγείρων - ἐγείρω - ἔγερσις

K)   6,30-44 Five thousand fed.
      ποιμήν - ποιμαίνω - ---
      χορτάζων - χορτάζω - ---

L)   6,45-52 Walking on the water.
      (ἐπιτιμητής - ἐπιτιμάω - ἐπιτιμία)

M)   7,24-30 The Syrophoenician woman.
      ἐκβάλλων - ἐκβάλλω - ἐκβολή

N)   7,31-37 Healing of a deaf mute.
      θεραπευτής - θεραπεύω - θεραπεία
      λυτήρ - λύω - λύσις

O)   8,1-9 Four thousand fed.
      χορτάζων - χορτάζω - ---

P)   8,22-26 A blind man healed (Bethsaida).
      ἀποκαταστάτης - ἀποκαθίστημι - ἀποκατάστασις

Q) 9,14-29 Epileptic child healed.
βοηθός - βοηθέω - βοήθεια
ἐκβάλλων - ἐκβάλλω - ἐκβολή
ἐγείρων - ἐγείρω - ἔγερσις

R) 10,46-52 Healing a blind man (Jericho).
σωτήρ - σῴζω - σωτηρία.

b. Supplementary Corpus

In the supplementary corpus thematic roles already known appear: θεραπευτής (1,32ff; 3,7ff and 6,1ff), ἐκβάλλων (1,32ff; 3,7ff and 3,22ff), σωτήρ (6,53ff), ὑγιάζων and ἰατρός (2,15ff), as well as some new roles.

In 6,1ff, the lexeme δύναμις is used to describe Jesus' doing. The English translation literally renders this as "deed of power", but in general such an act is named "wonder-work", which literally however corresponds to θαυματουργία, which together with θαυματουργός and θαυματουργέω forms a lexeme group. In the narrative of the crossing of the Jordan, LXX, Josh 3, Yahweh thus appears as a thaumaturge, but for one reason or another θαῦμα (in the sense of wonder) and its derivatives are not used in the New Testament, although Jesus amazes the people, makes them wonder (θαυμάζω, 5,20; cf. Mt 8,27). Whatever the reason for this - perhaps θαυματουργός had a negative ring because it was associated with degression/repression, was considered to be ψευδουργός, i.e. delusion and conjuring, or as magic (μάγος - μαγεύω - μαγεία, cf. Acts 8,9ff; 13,6ff) - the result remains that no designation is to be found in the New Testament of Jesus as wonder-worker. In 1 Cor 12,29, where a number of thematic roles are listed - apostle, prophet, teacher - δύναμις appears to be used for wonder-worker, but perhaps this strange use of the word must be seen as an expression of the linguistic difficulty that arises with the exclusion of θαυματουργός.

It is similarly difficult to define a lexeme group on the basis of δύναμις because the central verb in the lexeme class is δύναμαι, which is not an action verb but a modal verb governing doing, as in 6,5:

$$\text{"... οὐκ ἐδύνατο ἐκεῖ ποιῆσαι οὐδεμίαν δύναμιν, ..."}$$

where ποιέω/δύναμις together indicate the act. The word's semantic essence is ability, strength, power and might, and it should rightly be translated by act of strength or deed of power, but the term "wonder-work" has been adopted into the ordinary language and should be retained. In accordance with the tacit practice hitherto, the role of wonder-worker may be referred to, whose lexemes must be given in English as:

wonder-worker - wonder-working - wonder-work.

What this role indicates above all is that the existing doing presupposes a special competence, an extraordinary ability, without identifying the specific features of the act (cf. 14,62; Lk 1,49). No equal-sign can thus be placed between protector and wonder-worker, but the wonder narrative's main act is doubly defined: it is a protection act carried out by virtue of an extraordinary ability, a miraculous power.

A special area is constituted by the paradoxical roles in 3,22ff cf. διαρπάζω; δέω):

$$ἄρπαξ - ἀρπάζω - ἀρπαγή$$
$$δεσμεύων - δεσμεύω - δεσμός$$

Whoever robs unlawfully, misappropriates another's property, inflicts a degression on this person. Here, however, there is a legitimate recapturing of robbed booty, a release of what has been captured. There is nothing in itself paradoxical in Jesus' binding the strong (ἰσχυρός; stresses Jesus' strength, he is the strongest). But it is remarkable that the narrative employs the dysphorically connotated verb, δέω, which is included in a paradigmatic relationship to the euphorically connotated λύω (cf. 7,31ff) to refer to a protective act. It focuses upon the struggle aspect rather than the protection aspect.

c. Role-Groups

The thematic roles to be found in the main corpus having been selected, the basic sequences A)-R), can be divided into groups:

A healer group comprising:

$$θεραπευτής - θεραπεύω - θεραπεία$$
$$ἰατρός - ἰάομαι - ἴασις/ἴαμα$$
$$ὑγιάζων - ὑγιάζω - ὑγίεια$$
$$καθαρτής - καθαρίζω - καθαρισμός$$
$$σωτήρ - σῴζω - σωτηρία;$$

an exorcist group:[3]

$$ἐκβάλλων - ἐκβάλλω - ἐκβολή;$$

---

[3] Cf. the role ἐξορκιστής - ἐξορκίζω - --- in Acts 19,13.

and a shepherd group:

$$\pi o \iota \mu \acute{\eta} \nu - \pi o \iota \mu \alpha \acute{\iota} \nu \omega - ---$$
$$\sigma \upsilon \nu \alpha \gamma \acute{\omega} \nu - \sigma \upsilon \nu \acute{\alpha} \gamma \omega - \sigma \upsilon \nu \alpha \gamma \omega \gamma \acute{\eta}$$
$$\chi o \rho \tau \acute{\alpha} \zeta \omega \nu - \chi o \rho \tau \acute{\alpha} \zeta \omega - ---.$$

The relatively low degree of abstraction is characteristic of these roles. It is true that healer, exorcist and shepherd are general terms, but they are more specific than the other roles which comprise three sub-groups:

a)
$$\beta o \eta \theta \acute{o} \varsigma - \beta o \eta \theta \acute{\epsilon} \omega - \beta o \acute{\eta} \theta \epsilon \iota \alpha$$
$$\grave{\alpha} \gamma \alpha \theta o \pi o \iota \acute{o} \varsigma - \grave{\alpha} \gamma \alpha \theta o \pi o \iota \acute{\epsilon} \omega - \grave{\alpha} \gamma \alpha \theta o \pi o \iota \acute{\iota} \alpha$$

b)
$$\grave{\epsilon} \gamma \epsilon \acute{\iota} \rho \omega \nu - \grave{\epsilon} \gamma \epsilon \acute{\iota} \rho \omega - \acute{\epsilon} \gamma \epsilon \rho \sigma \iota \varsigma$$
$$\grave{\alpha} \pi o \kappa \alpha \tau \alpha \sigma \tau \acute{\alpha} \tau \eta \varsigma - \grave{\alpha} \pi o \kappa \alpha \theta \acute{\iota} \sigma \tau \eta \mu \iota - \grave{\alpha} \pi o \kappa \alpha \tau \acute{\alpha} \sigma \tau \alpha \sigma \iota \varsigma$$
$$\lambda \upsilon \tau \acute{\eta} \rho - \lambda \acute{\upsilon} \omega - \lambda \acute{\upsilon} \sigma \iota \varsigma$$

c)
$$\grave{\epsilon} \pi \iota \tau \iota \mu \eta \tau \acute{\eta} \varsigma - \grave{\epsilon} \pi \iota \tau \iota \mu \acute{\alpha} \omega - \grave{\epsilon} \pi \iota \tau \iota \mu \acute{\iota} \alpha$$

The role ἐπιτιμητής is distinctive in that it focuses on the aspect of struggle. Only to a certain extent the same may be said about the role of ἐκβάλλων (exorcist), since this simultaneously involves the aspect of protection.

The Healer
The roles θεραπευτής, ἰατρός and ὑγιάζων are parasynonyms; they contain - despite any difference between them - a common semantic core, and can all mean healer. The role καθαρτής refers to a special kind of healing, cleansing, and may as such be considered as a specifying healer-role. But there is reason to point out at the same time that the use of the verb καθαρίζω to refer to a healing act is employed in a restricted sense, in that the basic meaning of cleansing is expiation. On the other hand, it appears that roles such as θεραπευτής, ἰατρός and ὑγιάζων can receive an extended area of signification in that they are re-categorized by their context, giving them further meaning. This is particularly clear in 2,17, where ἰατρός is re-categorized by a further retribution context.

The role σωτήρ, which appears here in connection with healing, is in fact an abstract role that is almost identical with the protector role. The verb σῴζω has the basic signification of preserve, protect, deliver, free from affliction and danger: to save is to save someone from something that is threatening. The main usage is medical: to heal a sick person; the physician is σωτήρ, and σωτηρία becomes a parasynonym for ὑγίεια. But it can be used for rescue from any danger, including mortal danger, cf. 3,4; 15,32; σωτηρία is thus opposed to ἀπώλεια, annihilation, destruction, damnation, perdition. In the New Testament, the word's further religious signification is otherwise dominant, where it involves saving the people from their sins (cf. Mt 1,21), i.e. their culpability.

When roles are aligned and have the same degree of abstraction, such as θεραπευτής, ἰατρός, ὑγιάζων, and σωτήρ in the sense of healer, they are said to be parasynonymous. Taking this abstraction level as a base, the role καθαρτής in its stricter sense can then be referred to as a hyposynonym, whereas the role σωτήρ in its broader sense of savior and protector can be referred to as a hyperosynonym. Every θεραπευτής is σωτήρ, but not vice versa; every καθαρτής is θεραπευτής, but not vice versa.

The Exorcist

It must be considered, of course, whether exorcism falls under healing, or whether it constitutes a sub-genre of its own. Formulations of the type: "And he cured many (...) and cast out many demons (...).", 1,34; "They cast out many demons, and anointed with oil many who were sick and cured them.", 6,13, shows that the gospel narrative itself distinguishes between healer and exorcist (and between "the sick (κακῶς ἔχοντες) and the possessed (δαιμονιζόμενοι)", 1,32).

But in Mt and Lk mixed constructions appear of the type: "Then they brought to him a demoniac (δαιμονιζόμενος) who was blind and mute, and he cured (θεραπεύω) him", Mt 12,22. "And those who were troubled with unclean spirits were cured.", Lk 6,18. Here, the role of exorcist is merely a special healer-role on a line with the role of καθαρτής. But it is not significant whether one distinguishes between two forms of healing, partly of somatic and partly of psychically sick persons, or employs healing as opposed to exorcism. The decisive point is to insist that the roles of healer and exorcist in all their possible differences are closely associated.

The Shepherd

The role ποιμήν appears in a figurative sense by virtue of a metaphorization. Instead of a people without a leader, Jesus speaks of a flock of sheep without a shepherd. The substitution that has taken place presupposes a paradigmatic correlation which rests upon the similitude of the relations contained therein: leader relates to people, in the same way as shepherd relates to sheep:

Leader : People :: Shepherd : Sheep.

It is the underlying, common actantial structure that seems to make this metaphorization possible. In both cases the protector role (the shepherd tends sheep; cf. 13,6ff), and the asymmetrical relationship between the protecting and the protected is clear.

The role συναγών established on the basis of 14,27 (διασκορπίζω) and Lk 11,23 (συνάγω vs. σκορπίζω), defined by way of μετά (the protagonist's synagonists) and κατά (the antagonist's synagonists), should be included here.

The role χορτάζων may be considered as a hyposynonym of ποιμήν, in so far as the shepherd's duty includes feeding or securing forage for the sheep. But since it appears in a general, independent role, a feeding or satiety miracle may be referred to here. The actualized degression process that is stopped is hunger (πεῖνα), which in its radical version is known as famine (λιμός, for example 13,8).

The contrast between πεινάω (to hunger) and χορτάζεσθαι (to be replete; fullness) may be considered as a figurative concretization of the abstract contrast ὑστερεῖσθαι (to suffer a lack; ὑστέρημα, lack; want) and περισσεύειν (to have abundance; περισσεία, abundance; cf. Phil 4,12).

The role may, therefore, appear in a recat⌐gorized, perhaps metaphorized, version, as in the well-known Beatitude: "Blessed are you who are hungry (πεινάω) now, for you will be filled (χορτάζομαι)", Lk 6,21.

Subgroup a)
The role βοηθός is an abstract, thematic role that can be directly identified as a narrative role. Assuming that intentional help is concerned, the role may be said to contain the following features: the helper is hierarchically superior to whoever is helped, and is defined as helper on the basis of the needy person's situation, in that he appears as provider of assistance relative to the subject of being's project, cf. Heb 2,18; 13,6 and 2 Cor 6,2.

The role ἀγαθοποιός is paradigmatically contrasted with the role κακοποιός (ἀγαθός vs. κακός), the corresponding verbs of which in 3,4 are parallelized with σῴζω ψυχὴν and ἀποκτείνω: "Is it lawful to do good on the sabbath, to save life or to kill?". A given doing (cf. ποιέω) then fundamentally appears as either good or evil/bad, i.e. either as progression (protection) or degression (repression).

The value perspective concerned refers to the narrative's fundamental axiology, which distinguishes between that which should be and that which should not be. On the basis of its perception of what true being is, i.e. on the basis of its ontology, the narrative can thus distinguish between the good progressive or protective processes that realize or protect being and the evil/bad degressive or repressive processes that realize or uphold non-being.

A distinction can thus be made between life-building or being-edifying (cf. to save life) and life-annihilating or being-destroying processes (to kill; cf. ἀπόλλυμι, Lk 9,55*), corresponding to the contrast οἰκοδομέω vs. καταλύω, or creation vs. destruction.

Subgroup b)

The role ἐγείρων refers to the verb ἐγείρω, which is included in a structural context with the verbs πίπτω, ἵστημι and κατάκειμαι/κεῖμαι:

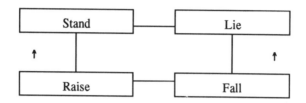

Referring to the body's position in space, stand/lie indicates the contrast between verticality and horizontality, or merely the contrast between up (high) and down (low) without in itself indicating any value articulation. But when the state of being stand/lie appears as a result of the transitive processes raise/fall (as regards the fall, perhaps because of a reflexive but unintended act), the value articulation clearly emerges. The point of departure is the subject of being's body control, which elementarily characterizes its integrity. In this perspective, the fall may be seen as the result of a neutralization of the preservation process that keeps the body upright. In the same perspective, the raising up is the re-establishment of the subject of being's integrity (cf. the crippled woman in Lk 13,10ff). The fall refers to a degressive process, whereas the raising up refers to a progressive process, in that the fall involves a loss of being, a degradation (cf. ταπεινός, ταπεινόω), whereas the raising up involves a gain, an elevation (cf. ὕψος, ὑψόω).

The role ἐγείρων thus refers to a subject of doing that intervenes to neutralize the effect of the fall, which is the act's starting point. To the extent that the fall is due to a degressor, the raising up becomes included in a polemic relationship to the being-destroying forces.

The role ἀποκαταστάτης refers to the verb ἀποκαθίστημι, which means the re-establishment of a former state and thus clearly emerges as a protector role.

The role λυτήρ is paradigmatically contrasted with the role δεσμεύων, as λύω is contrasted with δέω/δεσμεύω; cf. Mt 16,19; 18,18. The loosened is tied (cf. 3,27; Rev 20,3) and the tied is loosened (cf. Lk 13, 12ff). What is concerned is liberation/release; cf. the lexeme group λυτρωτής, λυτρόω, λύτρωσις (and also ἄφεσις), and capture (cf. αἰχμαλωτεύω; φυλακίζω and also παραδίδωμι). This role thematizes at the same time the subject of being's impotence and the subject of doing's polemic struggle-situation.

Subgroup c)

The verb ἐπιτιμάω means to blame, reprimand, scold, reproach, talk strictly to, threaten in order to stop a virtual or on-going act that is considered to be an infringement, an offense. A process of influence is concerned that interferes in and changes a virtual or actualized subject of doing's self-knowledge and thus his motivation to act.

The role ἐπιτιμητής is thus closely associated with the role ἐπιτακτήρ (the commander; ἐπιτάσσω, ἐπιταγή; cf. 1,27; 9,25). Exercising his authority (ἐξ-ουσία, cf. 1,22.27) the commander sets the limits: something is prescribed because it promotes the realization of being (impedes the realization of non-being), anything else is prohibited because it impedes the realization of being (promotes the realization of non-being). These two roles, ἐπιτιμητής and ἐπιτακτήρ, that focus on the struggle aspect are more precisely related to the antagonistic subject of doing, e.g. the unclean spirits in 1,27, wind and sea in 4,41 (cf. also 6,45ff where these roles appear to be involved). Jesus' authority and strength is emphasized by the unclean spirits, wind, and sea obeying and subjecting themselves (ὑπακούω) to him.

d. Summary

This investigation of the wonder narrative is restricted. The wonder-work's cognitive function is disregarded in favour of a more specific analysis of its pragmatic dimension. The intention is to show and define aspects of the matter that are otherwise easily overlooked or underexposed.

The role of wonder-worker has a pragmatic dimension that includes a number of thematic roles organized by the narrative roles that constitute the narrative genre of Protection. The gospel narrative's information on Jesus as wonder-worker defines him pragmatically as protector, a role that cannot be identified by the designation of wonder-worker.

The relationship between the protector and the person in need is asymmetric, the former being superior to the latter, who would be lost if no help was forthcoming. But this hierarchic relationship, known, for example, from the relationship between physician and patient, does not in itself validate protection as wonder-work. Only when an extraordinary ability is being employed does wonder-working exist. If the main emphasis is on the wonder-work's cognitive function - as evidence of revelation - the person in need who experiences the act becomes the epiphany's hostage, and it is overlooked that the protection, however anticipatory it may be in a dominant perspective, has its own objective at this moment.

As pointed out above, it is the thematic, although rather abstract, role σωτήρ that is most nearly identical with the narrative role of protector: to save is to save (protection/protector) someone (victim/beneficiary) from something that threatens (degression/degressor). Pragmatically, the wonder narrative defines Jesus as σωτήρ, savior. Conversely, the protector role gives the term salvation its pregnant content. Although the salvation act more often than not contains a progression, it is the overlapping protection that defines this.

The degression process may be virtual or on-going. In the latter case, help may consist in stopping the process at a moment when it has as yet caused no damage, or when damage has taken place but is prevented from becoming worse. But real protection is concerned only when the damage that has occurred is re-established (cf. ἀποκατάστασις), when the victim is raised up again (cf. ἔγερσις) and reinstated in his former integrity. This insight proves to be of decisive importance to the understanding of the dominant salvation project, which is aimed at the realization of the kingdom of God. The tension between the wonder-worker's salvation in strength and the overlapping act of salvation in powerlessness will be discussed later.[4]

2. The Thematic Victim-Roles

The next step in narrative exegesis is to search the chosen text-corpus with a view to listing and grouping the subject of being's/the victim's thematic roles.

First, the subject of being's initial state (the victim situation) is considered, and attention is concentrated on the verbs expressing the state. On this basis, the pertinent role lexemes are defined according to the structure:

the sufferer - the state of suffering - the suffering;

corresponding to:

πάσχων - πάσχω - πάθημα.

a. Main Corpus

A)   1,21-28 Exorcism in the synagogue at Capernaum.
δαιμονιζόμενος - δαιμονίζομαι - ---

B)   1,29-31 Healing Simon's mother-in-law.
κατακείμενος - κατάκειμαι - ---
πυρέσσων - πυρέσσω - πυρετός

C)   1,39-45 Cleansing of a leper.
λεπρός - λεπράω - λέπρα
ἀκάθαρτος - --- - ἀκαθαρσία

D)   2,1-12 Healing a paralytic.
παραλυτικός - παραλύομαι - παράλυσις

---

[4] Chapter X, B.1.

E) 3,1-6 Healing a man with a withered hand.
ξηρός - --- - ξηρότης

F) 4,35-41 Wind and sea calmed.
ἀπολλυμένος - ἀπόλλυμαι - ἀπώλεια

G) 5,1-20 The Gerasene demoniac.
δαιμονιζόμενος - δαιμονιζόμαι - ---

H) 5,21-24 Jairus' daughter raised α).
ἐσχάτως ἔχων - ἐσχάτως ἔχειν - ἐσχάτως ἔχειν

I) 5,25-34 The woman suffering from haemorrhages.
αἱμορροῶν - αἱμορροέω - ῥύσις αἵματος

J) 5,35-43 Jairus' daughter β).
ἐσχάτως ἔχων - ἐσχάτως ἔχειν - ἐσχάτως ἔχειν

K) 6,30-44 The feeding of the five thousand.
διασκορπιζόμενος - διασκορπίζομαι - ---
πεινῶν - πεινάω - πεῖνα

L) 6,45-52 Walking on the water.
ἀπολλυμένος - ἀπόλλυμαι - ἀπώλεια

M) 7,24-30 The Syrophoenician woman.
δαιμονιζόμενος - δαιμονίζομαι - ---
πεινῶν - πεινάω - πεῖνα

N) 7,31-37 Healing of a deaf mute.
κωφός - --- - κωφότης
μογιλάλος - μογιλαλέω - μογιλάλη
δεσμώτης - δεσμεύομαι - δεσμοί

O) 8,1-9 Feeding of the four thousand.
πεινῶν - πεινάω - πεῖνα
ἐκλυόμενος - ἐκλύομαι - ἐκλύσις

P) 8,22-26 A blind man healed (Bethsaida).
τυφλός - τυφλοῦμαι - τυφλότης

Q) 9,14-29 Epileptic child healed.
δαιμονιζόμενος - δαιμονίζομαι - ---
ἄλαλος - --- - ---

R) 10,46-52 Healing a blind man (Jericho).
τυφλός - τυφλοῦμαι - τυφλότης

b. Supplementary Corpus

The already-known thematic role of being δαιμονιζόμενος (1,32ff; 3,7ff; 3,13ff; 3,22ff; 6,6bff and 9,38ff) appears in the supplementary corpus, but otherwise only new, general roles relating to sickness appear. The general aspect emerges in the lack of specification. There are references to "various diseases" (νόσος), 1,34, "all who had diseases" (suffering, afflictions; μάστιξ), 3,10. Most general is the role κακῶς ἔχων (to be unwell; 1,32; 2,17 and 6,55), followed by ἄρρωστος (sick, weak; cf. ἀρρωστέω, ἀρρώστημα; 6,5 and 6,13), and finally there is ἀσθενής (feeble, weak; cf. ἀσθενέω, ἀσθένεια; 6,56).

c. Role-Groups

The total inventory of thematic roles of being can then be divided into the following groups:

A sickness group, which includes:

a) Specific sicknesses:

λεπρός - λεπράω - λέπρα
παραλυτικός - παραλύομαι - παράλυσις
ξηρός - ---- - ξηρότης
αἱμορροῶν - αἱμορροέω - ῥύσις αἵματος
κωφός - ---- - κωφότης
μογιλάλος - μογιλαλέω - μογιλάλη
ἄλαλος - ---- - ----
τυφλός - τυφλοῦμαι - τυφλότης

b) General sicknesses:

πυρέσσων - πυρέσσω - πυρετός
κατακείμενος - κατάκειμαι - ----
ἐσχάτως ἔχων - ἐσχάτως ἔχειν - ἐσχάτως ἔχειν
κακῶς ἔχων - κακῶς ἔχειν - κακῶς ἔχειν
νοσῶν - νοσέω - νόσος
μαστιγούμενος - μαστιγοῦμαι - μάστιξ
ἄρρωστος - ἀρρωστέω - ἀρρώστημα
ἀσθενής - ἀσθενέω - ἀσθένεια

A possessed group, which includes:

$$\delta\alpha\iota\mu\text{ov}\iota\zeta\acute{o}\mu\varepsilon\text{vos} - \delta\alpha\iota\mu\text{ov}\acute{\iota}\zeta\text{o}\mu\alpha\iota - \text{---}$$

A flock group, which includes:

$$\delta\iota\alpha\sigma\kappa\text{op}\pi\iota\zeta\acute{o}\mu\varepsilon\text{vos} - \delta\iota\alpha\sigma\kappa\text{op}\pi\acute{\iota}\zeta\text{o}\mu\alpha\iota - \text{---}$$
$$\pi\varepsilon\iota\nu\hat{\omega}\nu - \pi\varepsilon\iota\nu\acute{\alpha}\omega - \pi\varepsilon\hat{\iota}\nu\alpha$$
$$\dot{\varepsilon}\kappa\lambda\upsilon\acute{o}\mu\varepsilon\text{vos} - \dot{\varepsilon}\kappa\lambda\acute{\upsilon}\text{o}\mu\alpha\iota - \dot{\varepsilon}\kappa\lambda\upsilon\sigma\iota\varsigma$$

And a varia-group, which includes:

$$\dot{\alpha}\pi\text{o}\lambda\lambda\upsilon\mu\acute{\varepsilon}\text{vos} - \dot{\alpha}\pi\acute{o}\lambda\lambda\upsilon\mu\alpha\iota - \dot{\alpha}\pi\acute{\omega}\lambda\varepsilon\iota\alpha$$
$$\delta\varepsilon\sigma\mu\acute{\omega}\tau\eta\varsigma - \delta\varepsilon\sigma\mu\varepsilon\acute{\upsilon}\text{o}\mu\alpha\iota - \delta\varepsilon\sigma\mu\text{o}\acute{\iota}$$

The Sick

Among the specific sicknesses, two stand out: leprosy and haemorrhage. These sicknesses have a dual aspect, in that they constitute in part a physical disease and in part validate the sick person as unclean. The leper is unclean (ἀκάθαρτος, cf. Lev 13-14), and is as such outside the social community, an isolation that involves the leper's social death. It is not therefore surprising that the healing of a leper may be equivalent to resurrection from the dead.

The narrative of the prophet Elisha's healing of the leper Naaman tells how the king of Aram sends his army commander Naaman to the king of Israel with a letter in which he asks him to rid Naaman of his leprosy. But the king of Israel sees this request as a provocation, since the king of Aram places him in an awkward position by asking for the impossible. "Am I God", he exclaims, "to give death or life (LXX, θανατόω καὶ ζωοποιέω), that this man sends word to me to cure a man of his leprosy?" (2 Kings 5,7).[5] Part of the story is that the prophet Elisha effects a cure, making Naaman bathe (λούω), i.e. immerse himself (βαπτίζω; 5,14), seven times in the Jordan so that his flesh "was restored" (ἐπιστρέφω), i.e. returned to its previous state of health, and he became clean (καθαρίζω; pragmatic dimension); and that Naaman recognizes (cognitive dimension): "Now I know that there is no God in all the earth except in Israel", 5,16. According to Job 18,13, leprosy is "the firstborn of Death"; and in Num 12,12 the leper Miriam is compared with "one stillborn child, whose flesh is half consumed when it comes out of its mother's womb." The woman suffering from a discharge of blood is likewise unclean, cf. Lev 15,19.25f.29.30.

The other specific sicknesses are paralysis (which includes withering), deafness, dumbness (which includes speech impediment) and blindness, which

---

[5] Cf. Jn 5,21; Rom 4,17; 1 Cor 15,22.45; 2 Cor 3,6; 1 Pet 3,18.

correspond to the catalogue of sicknesses to be found in Isa 35,5f: "Then the eyes of the blind shall be opened, and the ears of the deaf unstopped; then the lame shall leap like a deer, and the tongue of the speechless sing for joy;". If one compares with Lk 7,22; Mt 11,5: the blind walk, the lepers are cleansed, the deaf hear, the dead are raised, the absence of "the dumb speak" may perhaps be noted in the latter texts, and the presence of "the lepers are cleansed" and "the dead are raised". The texts nevertheless cover the same things (cf. also Isa 26,19), since the point is not that the Messiah acts exclusively as a nose, ear and throat specialist, as an ophthalmologist, as a dermatologist, etc., but it is he who heals all sicknesses.

The ordinary sicknesses include fever, since this is merely an indication of some form of sickness; the role κατακείμενος refers to the involuntary sickbed. The most neutral role is νοσῶν, whereas the role of μαστιγούμενος (strictly speaking, he who is scourged) seems to refer to an acting subject that torments, perhaps chastises or punishes. The roles ἄρρωστος and ἀσθενής, whose terms as far as both are concerned have been formed with *alfa privativum*, indicate a condition of want: the feeble are without energy (cf. ῥώννυμι, ῥώμη), the weak are without strength (cf. σθένω, σθένος). One thinks here first of the body's constitution, but this involves a social powerlessness resulting in distancing from the community.

The role of κακῶς ἔχων refers in part to the sick person's subjective perception (to feel unwell) and in part to the sickness' objective aspect (to suffer). Here a value perspective clearly emerges that determines the condition of sickness as non-being according to the narrative's ontology. The sickness should not be, according to the narrative's axiology (cf. the promises referred to above), and its presence is therefore in itself evidence that the world is in a deficient state of being.

The sickness as an on-going degression process will result in death, unless it is neutralized. In this perspective, the role of ἐσχάτως ἔχων is a role aspectualizing the process by indicating its imminent termination, in this case the end of life and the occurrence of death. The further the sickness advances the more difficult it becomes to neutralize it and the greater is the subject of being's distress and need for help.

The Possessed

The role δαιμονιζόμενος indicates that the subject of being is possessed by a demon (δαίμων, 1,34; 3,15.22; 6,13; 7,26.29f; 9,38), i.e. a spirit (πνεῦμα, 9,20) which can be defined more precisely as unclean (πνεῦμα ἀκάθαρτον, 1,23.26f; 3,11.30; 5,2.8.13; 6,7; 7,25; 9,25; or evil (πνεῦμα πονηρόν), for example Lk 7,21; 8,2)), perhaps as deaf and dumb, 9,25.

In 3,22-30, the Beelzebul speech, it is said that "Beelzebul", identified with "Satan" later in the text, is the ruler of the demons. The demons, the unclean spirits, are thus perceived as Satan's representatives dispatched with power to practice unclean or evil, i.e. being-destructive acts (cf. Mt 6,13; 13,19). The binding of "the strong man" (ἰσχυρός), which presupposes that the one who binds him is stronger (cf. 1,12ff; Lk 11,22), is itself the presupposition that whatever is bound (cf. 7,35; Lk 13,16) can be loosened.

A polemic struggle-aspect is concerned here. The struggle is between the being-destructive and the being-edifying powers, between Satan and God. The existing world is under the control of Satan (cf. βασιλεία, 3,24; cf. Jn 12,31), but the kingdom of God has come near (1,15), a process of change has begun. Equipped with the Holy Spirit, Jesus is able to take up the struggle.[6]

The flock
The roles in the flock group, which corresponds to the shepherd group, are the hungry (πεινῶν), and in extension thereof the weakened (ἐκλυόμενος). The symbolic strength of these roles is that natural, organic processes can be used as an image of longing for the fulfilment of other needs.

A flock without a shepherd is scattered (cf. 14,27), but the scattering of the flock is synonymous with its destruction. The scattering refers to an on-going degressive process (cf. Mt 9,36), perhaps initiated by an antagonistic subject of doing (cf. Lk 11,23), the scattered (διασκορπιζόμενος) are the victim.

Varia
The two last roles, δεσμώτης and ἀπολλυμένος, indicate in part that the subject of being has been involuntarily retained in the victim position and in part that it is in a situation of imminent danger tending towards destruction.

d. Summary
It was shown earlier that the wonder-worker role cannot in itself be defined as a protector role. Among the thematic protector roles it is the role of σωτήρ which in its wider sense is most nearly identical with the narrative role of protector.

The central saying in 2,17 reads: "Those who are well have no need of a physician, but those who are sick", i.e. the sick person has a need (χρείαν ἔχω) to be cured (cf. Lk 9,11).

The term χρείαν ἔχω means to be in distress, cf. 2,25. Χρεία means necessity, need (for the sick, medical help is a need, a necessity). Moreover, it can mean lack of, need for (the sick person lacks or needs medical help); but also longing for (indicating, for example, the sick person's subjective perception of the situation). Finally, it can mean wish or plea, in that the person in distress (for example, the sick person) expresses his need for help.

---

[6] Cf. Chapter XI, C.2.

It is then correspondingly possible to define a general, thematic victim-role, χρείαν ἔχων, the person in distress:

$$χρείαν ἔχων - χρείαν ἔχω - χρεία$$

(cf. δεόμενος (the person in need, in distress), δεόμαι (require, need; beg for, cf. Lk 5,12; 9,38); cf. ὑστέρημα, ἀνάγκη, κίνδυνος (cf. Lk 8.23) and further θλῖψις), which is obligatory to the wonder narrative.

3. The Paradigm of Thematic Roles

The thematic roles defined hitherto cover only two parts of the field in the protection narrative genre, the protector's doing roles and the victim's being roles. It remains to consider the degressor's doing roles and the beneficiary's being roles.

This can best be done by paradigmatically contrasting respectively victim/ beneficiary and degressor/progressor, with inclusion of the roles' concepts, i.e. the action result and the suffering, alone. The most significant opposing pairs are given here:

hunger (πεῖνα)	vs.	(κόρος) satiety
weakness (ἀσθένεια)	vs.	(ἰσχύς) strength
infirmity (ἀρρώστια)	vs.	(ὑγίεια) health
destruction (κατάλυσις)	vs.	(ἀποκατάστασις) restoration
annihilation (ἀπώλεια)	vs.	(σωτηρία) salvation
malefaction (κακοποιία)	vs.	(ἀγαθοποιία) benefaction
fall (πτῶμα)	vs.	(ἔγερσις) rise
opposition (ἐναντίωμα)	vs.	(βοήθεια) help[7]

It is in the nature of things that protection involves a reversibility. The subject of being's initial state, characterized for example by health, is risked in an on-going degression process whose intermediate state, for example the state of sickness, can be neutralized to re-establish the initial state. In a vertical understanding, the transition from the initial state of being (over, up, high) to the intermediate state, which is orientated towards the final state of non-being

---

[7] Κόρος, (κορέννυμι cf. Acts 27,30 and 1 Cor 4,8, cf. χορτάζω) κατάλυσις (cf. 13,2; 14,48) πτῶμα (cf. πτῶσις, Lk 2,34), and ἐναντίωμα is not found in the corpus studied.

(below, down, low), is considered as a fall. The restitution, re-establishment of the initial state, similarly becomes a raising (ἔγερσις as parasynonym of ἀνάστασις, cf., for example Lk 2,34).

In its attempt to preserve and maintain its initial state, the subject of being is confronted with a resistance that actively asserts itself as a malefaction aimed at annihilation and destruction. The protection is a help, a redeeming benefaction that ends the on-going degression process and heals that which may have been broken. The following thematic roles provide a possibility of distinguishing between various wonder narratives according to their thematics:

	DEGRESSOR	VICTIM	BENEFICIARY	PROTECTOR
A)	Possessor	Possessed	Liberated	Liberator
B)	-	Sick	Healed	Healer
C)	-	Life-threatened	Rescued	Rescuer
D)	-	Hungry	Satiated	Feeder

Besides exorcisms (A) and healings (B), rescue miracles (C) and feeding miracles (D) can thus be distinguished.

The demons and the unclean spirits are Satan's henchmen, and possession means that the possessed is the victim of an on-going degression. If the basic sequences which characterize possession more specifically are considered, 5,1ff and 9,14ff, it becomes clear that this degression process tends towards death and annihilation.

The possessed in the country of the Gerasenes is found in the tombs, as if he were already dead (5,2f). His behaviour of bruising himself with stones (5,5) is self-destructive, and when the evil spirits have flown into the swine they throw themselves into the sea and drown. In 9,22, it is clearly stated that the spirit's intention is to take the boy's life (ἀπόλλυμι). Life and death are concerned, which is indeed further thematized in 9,26, where Jesus appears in the role of ἐγείρων (cf. κρατέω, ἐγείρω, ἀνίστημι; cf. 1,31; 2,11; 5,41), which makes the act reminiscent of a resurrection from the dead.[8]

The underlying contrast between the state of being of the victim and of the beneficiary is the contrast:

death (θάνατος, ἀποθνήσκω) vs. (ζωή, ζάω; ψυχή) life

---

[8] Cf. Rudolf Pesch, *Das Markusevangelium*, 2. *Teil*, Freiburg 1980, p. 94.

corresponding to the contrast between degression and protection (cf. 3,4):

"to kill" (ἀποκτείνω) vs. (σῷζω ψυχήν) "to save life"

This is of course most apparent in the gospel narrative's only report of a resurrection from the dead, 5,21ff. The daughter is at the point of death, and Jairus begs Jesus to lay his hands upon her so that she may be made well (σῷζω) and live (ζάω). At a certain time Jairus receives a message that she has died, and the professional mourners have already begun to weep and wail. Against this stands Jesus' dictum: "The child is not dead but sleeping.".

The question is whether this is a resurrection from the dead or a healing. Jesus' question: "Why do you make a commotion and weep?" may be understood in two ways. The lament presupposes death, and when Jesus indirectly points out that there is no reason to lament this may mean that death has not yet occurred: the child is sleeping. But there is also the possibility that the lament is meaningless even if death has in fact occurred, because death no longer marks an irreparable loss because resurrection from the dead is no longer impossible. That the child is sleeping means, then, that death is not irreversible but inscribed in a cycle of the type:

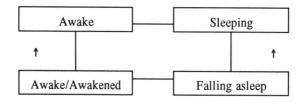

which is isomorphous with:

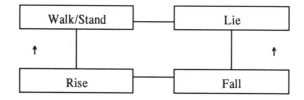

(note the transitive act: "He took her by the hand and said to her 'Talitha cum,' which means, 'Little girl, get up!'"), and

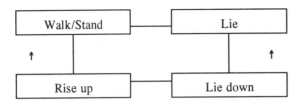

(note the reflexive act: "And immediately the girl got up and began to walk about (she was twelve years of age).").

Irrespective of whether the wonder-work is understood as a healing or a resurrection from the dead, what is concerned is protection. The initial state of life is threatened by an on-going degression process which is about to reach, or is thought to have reached, its objective: death. When it is maintained, despite the possible ending of the degression process, that protection is concerned, this is because the wonder-work as resurrection from the dead brings the deceased back into the normal state of life. By the wonder-work, Jairus' wish that his daughter be saved so that she can live the life she was leading before she fell sick is fulfilled. The crucial point here is that resurrection to eternal life is not concerned.

As a sign that the daughter has become quite well, Jesus tells the parents to give her something to eat. Consuming food is the most elementary form of sustaining life, and hunger (cf. the feeding miracles) is the first sign of its destruction. The antithesis, hunger versus satiety, is a weak version of the antithesis, sickness versus health (cf. healing and exorcism), which is itself a weak version of the antithesis, death versus life. (cf. the imminent mortal danger in the rescue miracles):

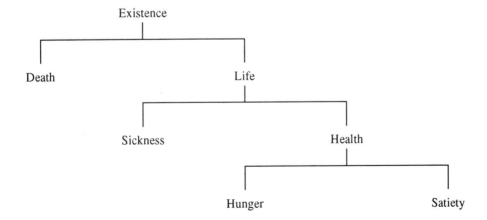

Considering that the antithesis between life and death is the fundamental conflict in the wonder narrative, the role of the distressed is too weak to denote the victim role.[9] The role, which is the adequate counterpart to the protector role σωτήρ, is the lost:

$$\dot{\alpha}\pi o\lambda\lambda\acute{\nu}\mu\epsilon\nu o\varsigma - \dot{\alpha}\pi\acute{o}\lambda\lambda\nu\mu\alpha\iota - \dot{\alpha}\pi\acute{\omega}\lambda\epsilon\iota\alpha.$$

This role denotes the calamity of the degression process, i.e. that the victim is annihilated unless the savior intervenes.

---

[9] Cf. Geert Hallbäck, *Strukturalisme og eksegese* (Structuralism and Exegesis), København 1983, p. 134: "det er over for den i sygdommen potentielt tilstedeværende Død hans [Jesu] helbredelse sætter ind og i stedet genopretter Livet" (it is against the Death potentially present in the disease that his (Jesus') healing intervenes and instead restores Life).

CHAPTER SIX

ACTOR AND ROLE

A. The Wonder Narrative's Actors

An actor may be individual (Jesus, Peter) or collective (the disciples, the crowd). Its peculiarity or individuation is often marked by the assignment of a proper name, although this is not an indispensable condition of its existence. A thematic role often serves as a designation for the actor (a paralytic, the sick person, etc.).

Although a proper name may have an etymological meaning (for example Jesus/Joshua: "Yahweh is salvation", cf. Mt 1,21; Peter: rock), its function does not depend on a descriptive content but is semantically empty. The actor appears in the narrative with a certain identity by virtue of the content attributed via its roles. For the analysis, therefore, it is important to distinguish between when a thematic role is employed as designating a person or actor and when it is employed as a description of an actor. Thus the thematic role of "disciple" is regularly employed to designate a collective of persons without the thematic role that specifically validates them in a given situation therefore being defined. After sending out the twelve (6,7ff) these are still Jesus' disciples, but as apostles they appear to the people as preachers and wonder-workers and not as disciples. So an actor can appear in several different roles. But a person or a personified entity must be the bearer of at least one narrative role in order to be called an actor.

In the wonder narrative's setting, those actors appear primarily who directly form part of the wonder act: the pragmatic subject of doing and the pragmatic subject of being. The wonder-worker, which here means the protector, is the same universal actor: Jesus of Nazareth. Where the degressor is actorialized he appears as demon or demonic forces (wind and sea), pointing towards Satan. In the exorcisms and healing wonders, the victims/beneficiaries are individual actors who appear here only: "a man with an unclean spirit" (1,23), "Simon's mother-in-law" (1,30), "a leper" (1,40), "a paralyzed man" (2,3), "a man who had a withered hand" (3,1), "a man ... with an unclean spirit" (5,2), Jairus' "little daughter" (5,23), "a woman who had been suffering from haemorrhages for twelve years" (5,25), a "little daughter" who "had an unclean spirit" (7,25), "a deaf man who had an impediment in his speech" (7,32), "a blind man" (8,22), a son who "has a spirit that makes him unable to speak" (9,17), "Bartimaeus son of Timaeus, a blind beggar" (10,46). In the feeding and rescue wonders, the actor is collective and appears in other contexts: "a great crowd" (6,34; 8,1), the disciples (4,35ff; 6,45ff).

In the wonder act's pragmatic dimension the starting point is a general, thematic role of being: the person in need, χρείαν ἔχων, which may be itemized into four role-variants: the possessed, the sick, the life-threatened and the starving. One role-variant, such as the sick, can perhaps be further itemized into hypotactic role-variants: the blind, the paralysed, the deaf, etc. What will then be observed is that the subject of being in the exorcisms and healings has been singled out by its pragmatic role of being, whereas in the rescuing and feeding wonders this is singled out by roles: disciple, crowd - which do not in themselves identify the collective subject as in need.

The wonder narrative has been defined by the narrative genre of Protection, which includes the constitutive narrative roles:

Degressor - Victim/Beneficiary - Protector.

If one understands by an actant whoever carries out or undergoes the act, any actant can be seen, now as subject of doing, now as subject of being. In a value perspective, this purely formal definition makes it possible to distinguish between four forms of doing actants: degressor, repressor, protector and progressor; and four forms of subjects of being: victim of degression, victim of repression, favoured by protection and favoured by progression. In a given situation, a given actant sees himself as defined by one of these forms, which are also referred to as narrative roles. In the same way as the actor is defined by his thematic role, the actant is defined by his narrative role.

The wonder narrative's narrative roles or actants are articulated in the gospel narrative and specified in thematic roles which, at a superior level of generalization, include the following roles:

$$\dot{\alpha}\pi o\lambda\lambda\acute{\upsilon}\omega\nu - \dot{\alpha}\pi o\lambda\lambda\acute{\upsilon}\mu\varepsilon\nu o\varsigma/\sigma\omega\zeta\acute{o}\mu\varepsilon\nu o\varsigma - \sigma\omega\tau\acute{\eta}\rho.$$

The gospel narrative's actorialization of these actants means, first, that they are linked to three different actors. The role $\dot{\alpha}\pi o\lambda\lambda\acute{\upsilon}\omega\nu$ falls under the actor Satan (cf. Rev 9,11), whereas the role $\sigma\omega\tau\acute{\eta}\rho$ falls under the actor Jesus. The role $\dot{\alpha}\pi o\lambda\lambda\acute{\upsilon}\mu\varepsilon\nu o\varsigma/\sigma\omega\zeta\acute{o}\mu\varepsilon\nu o\varsigma$ falls under various actors, now individual, now collective, who are either anonymous or named. These three roles thus refer to three actants, the degressor, the victim/beneficiary and the protector, which is represented by a single actor (Protector = Jesus, who however refers to God), one or more representatives of a collective actor (Degressor = a demon/demons which refer to Satan) and a number of actors (Victim/Beneficiary = people in need).

An actant who has been defined in a superior act by a narrative role may be defined in an associated but inferior act by a different role. The person in need thus appears in the role of subject of doing when he seeks out Jesus and asks for help. The actant may submit to a number of roles, which moreover may be attended to by different actors. In the narrative of Jairus and his daughter, it is not the suffering daughter who seeks out Jesus for help but Jairus. In such cases, the two actors are considered as belonging to one and the same actant.

B. CRITICISM OF THEIßEN'S CHARACTER ROLES

Where a genre analysis is concerned, THEIßEN comments in his examination of the miracle story, the individual characters are not crucial, but "entscheidend ist ihre Rolle in der Erzählung".[1] This opinion is shared by narrative exegesis, and it may therefore be informative to compare and discuss the two investigations.[2]

THEIßEN defines seven roles, referred to here as *character roles*: Miracle-Worker (M), the Sick Person (S), Demon (D; if he appears as an acting character in the story), Companion (C), Crowd (c), Opponent (O) and Disciples (d):

B/C	M	S	D	C	c	O	d
Q	+	+	+	+	+	+	+
H,J	+	+		+	+		+
D	+	+		+	+	+	
A,G	+	+	+		+		
E	+	+			+	+	
I,R	+	+			+		+
N,P	+	+		+	+		
C	+	+			+		
B	+	+					+
K,O	+				+		+
M	+	+		+			
F,L	+						+

The table reproduces his definition of the character-distribution in the basic sequences here described (cf. pp. 59; B = Basic sequence; C = Character role).

---

[1] Gerd Theißen, *Urchristliche Wundergeschichten*, Göttingen 1974, p. 14.

[2] Cf. also Hendrikus Boers' and Paul Achtemeier's criticism of Theißen in *Semeia 11, Early Christian Miracle Stories*, Missoula 1978, pp. 1.

It will first be noted that the miracle-worker is the only character who appears in all basic sequences, and second that all characters only appear simultaneously in one basic sequence, Q) Epileptic child healed, 9,14-29.

There are, however, a number of ambiguities in THEIßEN's terminology and analysis. The objection that must be directed against his definitions is that these character roles refer, now to roles, but of a different type, and now to actors, and that the role system that must be presupposed, if these character roles are to be mutually linked and form a unity, is never defined precisely.

The Miracle-Worker

The "Miracle-worker" character role refers to the actor "Jesus of Nazareth", but is unspecified as a role. As pointed out, it is the pragmatic role of σωτήρ/protector that is fundamental.

The Demon

The character role of "Demon" can be immediately recognized as the degressor. THEIßEN, however, wishes to speak of this character role only when the demon appears as an acting character in the miracle story (cf. A, G and Q). One might consider, he writes, whether the list of character roles should include nature. If, however, one imagines this as an acting person, then one must perceive it as demonic.[3]

One may imagine this, but the important thing must be the perception which characterizes the gospel narrative. In 4,35ff, which THEIßEN himself has in mind, the sea and the wind are actors, which quite clearly appear as degressor. Jesus appears here (4,39) in the role of ἐπιτιμητής, a role that is to be found again in other places in the gospel narrative, always in connection with the struggle against the demonic forces (cf. 1,25; 3,12; 8,30.33 and 9,25); that is, also in the basic sequences A, G and Q where the demon appears according to THEIßEN.

If the demon in the form of sea and wind does not appear as an acting person in 4,35ff, who then is Jesus talking to and commanding?

That the miracle story in 4,35ff is not defined as an exorcism is only because nature is not considered as a victim, and that the victim - here the disciples - is not possessed.

There should be no doubt, however, that an actor is present who represents the degressor, and this degressor is to be found in all the miracle stories, even when it appears to be an impersonal process, as demonic.

---

[3] Theißen, ibidem, p. 53.

The Sick Person

"The sick person" character role includes both the sick and the possessed. To this extent, the role designation is imprecise. But the objection here is that this character role is not on a level with protector and degressor, since it is merely a variant of the victim/beneficiary role. One may well assemble into one group all the actors who are sick or possessed, but this is only because they occupy the same narrative role. Within the universe of the wonder narrative, however, the victim/beneficiary role is not restricted to the sick and the possessed but includes the hungry and the life-threatened, the crowd and the disciples. One could now perhaps imagine that THEIßEN's character roles of "the sick", "the crowd" and "the disciples" were merely sub-divisions of the victim/beneficiary role. The problem is, however, that, whereas the actors who are sick or possessed appear only in the victim/beneficiary role and can therefore be designated according to their thematic role, there are other actors - the crowd and the disciples - who may appear in the wonder narrative's setting without occupying the victim/beneficiary role. THEIßEN's character roles "the crowd" and "the disciples" are not therefore roles but designations of actors who may appear in various roles, including the victim/beneficiary role.

The Disciples

In the case of "the disciples", THEIßEN complicates the matter by employing a thematic role as actor designation. There is, of course, good reason to separate the disciples from all other actors, but for this very reason it is also much more important to clarify their particular roles in the wonder narrative. As can be seen from the above table of the character distribution in the basic sequences designated by A)-R), according to THEIßEN the disciples appear in only 10 out of the possible 18. According to the table, they are, for example, supposed to be absent in A) Exorcism in the synagogue at Capernaum, 1,21-28.

But the disciples are by no means absent. In 1,29, "As soon as *they* left the synagogue", "they" refers to Jesus and the disciples, and "synagogue" to the synagogue at Capernaum in 1,21ff. The change of person in 1,21, "*they* went to Capernaum; and when the sabbath came, *he* entered the synagogue and taught", does not mean that the disciples remained outside, but merely marks a shift in the *focus* of the narrative.

A similar change occurs in 1,38f: "Let *us* go on to the neighbouring towns, so that *I* may proclaim the message there also; for that is what *I* came out to do."; and "*he* went throughout Galilee, proclaiming the message in their synagogues (...)".

In the light of 1,35ff (6,46, 14,32ff), where it is explicitly said that Jesus is alone, it must in fact be assumed that the disciples are at Jesus' side unless otherwise stated. It is in this context not unimportant to note that nothing is said about Jesus' activities in this period during which the disciples were sent out. The story of the Baptist's execution, 6,14-29, is told between the dispatch in 6,7-13 and the return home in 6,30.[4]

According to this opinion, the disciples (how many is unimportant in this context) are present and attending on Jesus as a practising wonder-worker in all the basic sequences referred to.

In that they participate neither actively nor passively in the wonder process itself, it is initially possible to ignore them. It is not of course asserted that the disciples' presence is a necessary precondition for Jesus to be able to practise his wonder-working; what is here pointed out is that the wonders he carries out in the narrative are all attended by the disciples, who appear in a particularly privileged form as audience. For the wonder itself the wonder-worker's presence is necessary, but the disciples' is facultative. It is not therefore possible to operate with the role of disciple on a line with the role of wonder-worker. THEIßEN confuses role and character or actor designation.

The role of disciple ($\mu\alpha\theta\eta\tau\dot\eta\varsigma$) which - and this is confusing - is most often occupied by the actor disciple corresponds to the role of teacher ($\delta\iota\delta\dot\alpha\sigma\kappa\alpha\lambda\sigma\varsigma$). But these thematic roles are not tied to the wonder but appear in many other contexts in the gospel narrative.

However, if "the twelve" (all or some; cf. proper names in 3,16ff) always attend Jesus' performance of the wonder, it is perhaps in the very role of disciples, i.e. as pupils, that they receive instruction or teaching from their teacher. There is much to support that this is the case. In general it may be said that the sending out in 6,7ff implicitly involves preceding instruction, but there are also explicit elements of disciple-teaching in several wonder narratives: 4,35ff; 6,30ff; 6,45ff; 8,1ff; 8,14ff; 9,14ff.

The cognitive-didactic function of the wonder must, however, be distinguished from the pragmatic function. As concerns the latter, only those characters are relevant who actively or passively, directly or indirectly, participate in the wonder process itself.

During the healing of Peter's mother-in-law, the disciples appear as companions (which THEIßEN overlooks) and have a function in the wonder process, since they point out to Jesus that the mother-in-law is sick. It is true that the actor disciple appears here, but in the role of assistant or helper-protector. In F) Wind and sea calmed, 4,35ff the actor disciple also appears, but in the role of victim/beneficiary. The fact is that the actor disciple appears in several different roles, which cannot be subsumed under the character role of "the disciples".

---

[4] Cf. Joanna Dewey: "Even in those passages in which the disciples are not explicitly present, they may be assumed to be there since the disciples accompany Jesus continuously from 1:16 to 14:50 except for 6:12-29.", "Point of view and the Disciples in Mark", Kent Harold Richards (ed.), *Society of Biblical Literature 1982 Seminar Papers*, Chico 1982, p. 102.

The Crowd

The character role of "the crowd" is also problematic. It refers to a group of characters, ὁ ὄχλος, who are either designated as such (4,36; 5,21.24.27. 31; 6,34; 6,45; 7,33; 8,1.2.6; 9,14.15.17.25; 10,46; 2,13; 3,9.20.32) or are merely present (cf. 1,27 ἅπαντες; 2,2; 10,48 πολλοί; 5,20 πάντες). The lexeme ὄχλος does not in itself state any specifying narrative or thematic role, but is a collective actor including a collection of individual actors whose being and doing (V, A or R) is shared. This actor, who can be defined more specifically as a paradigmatic, collective actor in that he forms a whole referring to a more comprehensive collective that is hierarchically superior (the people, cf. 14,2, or the whole world, cf. 14,9), appears in the feeding wonders in the role of victim/beneficiary, but appears in the role of disciple as well: "And he began to teach them (διδάσκω) many things." (6,34). Jesus appears in the role of teacher (διδάσκαλος), and the crowd thereby adopts the complementary role of disciple (μαθητής), cf. 4,1; 7,14; 8,34; 10,1; 12,38, but also, for example, 3,32.

The difference between the actor crowd and the actor disciples is that the latter, who are sometimes merely part of the crowd (cf. for example 8,34), receive special teaching, and therefore appear as specially privileged disciples. The disciples are thus present at the feeding wonders, whereas the crowd is absent at the rescue wonders (cf. for example 4,36; 6,45; 7,17). It applies to both actors that they are often present and attend Jesus' wonder-works without participating in the wonder process themselves. As universal actors they are *cognitive* subjects whose roles fall under the wonder's cognitive-didactic function, which remains secondary compared with their pragmatic function. The experience that the *observers* (the crowd and the disciples) undergo has a content, the wonder itself.

The Companion

In the setting of the wonder narrative, various actors appear who have in common that they help the needy by fulfilling a number of conditions that must be accomplished before the wonder can take place. A general feature of the wonder narrative is that the needy person must himself turn to Jesus and induce him to exercise his wonder-working. If the sick person cannot do this himself, others must help, and THEIßEN subsumes these helpers under the character role of "the companion".

He points to the four men who carry the paralytic to Jesus (D, 2,1ff), the father Jairus (H, J, 5,21ff), the Gentile mother (M, 7,24ff), those who came to him with a deaf person (N, 7,31ff), those who lead a blind man to him (P, 8,22ff) and the father of the epileptic boy (Q, 9,14ff). But one should then also point to the disciples in 1,29ff and those who bring the sick and possessed to Jesus in 1,32 and 6,53ff.

The needy person must himself contribute to the realization of the wonder. First, Jesus must be sought out, then contacted, and finally convinced that an opportunity is given him to perform the wonder. The leper (1,40ff), for example, seeks out Jesus and begs him to help. Jesus is moved ("moved with pity") and starts acting. Compared with the main act for which Jesus is a subject of doing, seeking him out and entreating are two help-acts for which the needy person himself is the subject of doing. In the role of seeker and beseecher the needy person is his own giver of assistance or help-protector.

These roles may, however, be carried out by an actor other than the needy person himself, and the relevant character then becomes the giver of assistance. The character role of "companion" thus falls under the wonder's pragmatic dimension, but the narrative is not interested in the destiny and fate of this functionary. Closely associated as they are with the needy person (cf. parents/child; mother-in-law/son-in-law), they form a collective actant whose doing is attended to by an actor other than the needy person himself. In some cases, the needy person himself appears as subject of doing; in other cases this doing is attended to by other actors. The roles of "the seeker" and "the beseecher" are, like the role of victim/beneficiary under which they fall, obligatory in the wonder narrative. The fact that these roles are attended to by actors other than the needy person himself is, however, a facultative matter, and the role of "companion" cannot therefore be given a constitutive role in the wonder narrative. Wherever the companion actors appear, merely a special actorialization of the wonder narrative is given. Certain roles are made independent and appear in the form of actors separated from but in solidarity with the subject of being.

The Opponent

According to THEIßEN, this character role appears in the basic sequences D, 2,1-12; E, 3,1-6 and Q, 9,14-29, but it is the two former in particular that invoke interest. It concerns "some of the scribes" (2,6), the Pharisees (3,6) and "some scribes" (9,14). In the setting where the wonder act takes place actors other than those occupying the role of degressor, victim/beneficiary and protector often appear. These facultative actors, however, will see themselves semiotized by the protection role configuration.

A given actor who sees himself voluntarily or involuntarily framed by a project will either act or fail to act. The actor's doing will either promote or hinder the realization of the project, and he then appears either as actant (protagonist) or antactant (antagonist). The actor's not doing will correspondingly be seen as semiotized, since the passivity is seen, now as opposition, now as assistance, and he will then appear either as negantactant (passive protagonist) or negactant (passive antagonist):

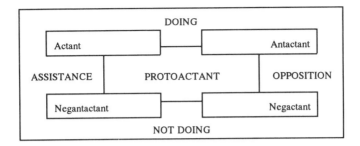

In the light of the protection project, actant and negantactant then appear as helpers (assisters/helping-protector); actant and negactant as opponents (opponent/helping-degressor).[5]

The decisive point is thus that any doing and action to be found within the frame of the action - which in fact means any character to be found in the wonder act's setting - sees itself as semiotized as actant in the situation; either as Actant (helper), Antactant (opponent), Negantactant (passive helper, i.e. someone who fails to show opposition) or Negactant (passive opponent who fails to help).

In 1,29ff; 1,32ff; 2,1ff; 5,21ff; 6,53ff; 7,24ff; 7,31ff; 8,22ff; 9,14ff, companions act as helpers. It is, however, also possible for a character who appears in one of the obligatory roles to play different roles in the course of the narrative: in 1,39ff; 4,35ff; 5,25ff; 10,46ff the needy person is thus his own helper. In 1,21ff; 5,1ff the demons are opponents, since they attempt to suppress a possible course of protection; in 2,1ff; 3,1ff; 3,22ff, the scribes and Pharisees are opponents; in 3,20f; 3,31ff; 6,1ff, his neighbours and his native town; in 5,21ff "some people ... from the leader's house".

In the wonder narrative's setting, actors other than those who incarnate the constitutive narrative roles thus appear. If these constitutive roles are seen as the core of the configuration, the facultative roles can be distinguished in roles of the first and second degrees. The realization of a project can thus encounter obstacles, which may incarnate themselves in an *opponent*, or be allowed to proceed, which may incarnate itself in an *assister*. In relation to the favoured one, the opponent appears as repressor, the assister as helping progressor.

The opponent is a facultative narrative role, which cannot be identified with the specific collective actor referred to as the Jewish leaders (here represented by the Pharisees and the scribes), although he perhaps appears in this role only. In the wonder's pragmatic dimension, representatives of the Jewish leaders appear in 2,1ff and 3,1ff as opponents, since they intimidate Jesus to cause him to abstain from action. As repressor, they then appear in the wonder project's perspective as helping degressors.

---

[5] Cf. *Sémiotique*, art. "Actant" and "Protoactant", and *Logique du récit*, pp. 282. As to the model, cf. Excursus: The Semiotic Basic Model, p. 102.

But an additional point is that these wonders are merely episodes in a cognitive project-course, which concerns the proclamation of the coming of the kingdom of God and Jesus' mission in the realization thereof, cf. the teaching in 2,10 and 3,4. The Jewish leaders thus also - and especially - appear as opponents relative to Jesus as teacher, since they attempt to protect and communicate their own conception of the nature of the situation by disputing Jesus' pragmatic and cognitive doing (cf., for example, 3,2ff etc.).

C. CRITICISM OF THEIßEN'S FIELD ROLES

Within the wonder narrative the analysis has distinguished between three constitutive actants, i.e. degressor, victim/beneficiary and protector. Accordingly, in his paradigmatic motif analysis THEIßEN distinguishes between three perspectives: the demonic, the human and the divine (the wonder-worker's) sphere.[6] But before he comes this far he sets out a model to explain the character structure within the representative basic sequence, 9,14ff, which alone manifests all seven character roles. This character structure contains two poles: the miracle-worker (M) and the demon (D). The former belongs to the divine sphere, the latter to the anti-divine sphere. These are the actual opposing players ("Gegenspieler"), whereas all other characters are "intermediate players" ("Zwischenspieler"). On the side of the sick person (S) is the father, on the side of the miracle-worker are the disciples (d); between these is the public divided into those who reject (the scribes, O) and those who accept (the crowd, c). Graphically represented:

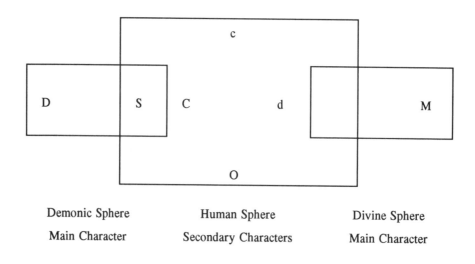

| Demonic Sphere | Human Sphere | Divine Sphere |
| Main Character | Secondary Characters | Main Character |

[6] Theißen, ibidem pp. 83.

This tripartite character-field, which, according to THEIßEN, is characteristic of all the miracle stories, may be occupied by different characters. The individual characters have no fixed position within this field, but the disciples can for example become the approving audience, and opposing players can become intermediate players. The field structure remains the same; the characters change. The sections of the field do not refer to specific characters but to "roles" (THEIßEN's quotes), which can be taken over by different persons. The miracle-worker's field alone is constantly occupied by the same person, while the person of the opposing player is variable. All characters who form the intermediate field can enter into this role, and the intermediate field becomes correspondingly smaller.[7] It is these roles in quotes which are here described as *field roles*.

The three spheres appear to correspond to the three constitutive narrative roles. But against the background of the narrative analysis presented above, it can be maintained that, in his model, THEIßEN confuses different levels, which is why it becomes inadequate and misleading. This becomes clear when it is further considered how these field roles (roles in quotes) are in fact to be perceived and what connection there is between these and the seven character roles.

As already shown, the seven character roles are actor designations rather than actual roles, and the roles occupied by these actors are not to be found on the same level. The problem is that THEIßEN does not succeed in determining the wonder narrative's paradigmatic role system but operates with character roles that have in fact emerged only by way of an intuitively based selection of actors and actor groups. This fundamental defect becomes fatal when he draws further conclusions and gathers his observations into a hypothetical model that aims to explain the structural basis of the classification of miracle stories into various thematic types. Guided by the concept that all seven character roles should be able to occupy the place of the opposing player, he sets out the following model:

OPPOSING PLAYER	MIRACLE-WORKER	EXAMPLE
Demon	M	9,14ff
Sick Person	M	5,25ff
Companion	M	7,24ff
Opponent	M	3,1ff
Crowd	M	6,34ff
Disciples	M	4,35ff
Miracle-Worker	-	9,2ff

---

[7] Theißen, ibidem pp. 54.

Since the inventory includes seven character-roles and each character may occupy the opposing player position, writes THEIßEN, then "sieben Themen von Wundergeschichten" are obtained: 1) where the demon is opposing player, *exorcism* is concerned; 2) where the sick person is opposing player, *healing* is concerned; 3) where the opponent occupies this position, a so called *rule* miracle ("Normenwunder") is concerned; 4) in the case of the crowd he speaks of a *gift* miracle; and 5) in the case of the disciples of a *rescue* miracle.[8]

As far as the remaining two themes are concerned, a few problems arise. Where the miracle-worker is in the opposing player position the *epiphany* exists, which thus becomes a sixth theme. This is, however, as THEIßEN comments, a borderline case. The final possibility, where the companion is opposing player, should now give the seventh theme, but 7,24ff, as he himself states, is an *exorcism* (although the demon does not occupy the opposing player position, which it should preferably do), and thus falls under the first theme. The seven miracle-story themes announced became only six; something is wrong.

THEIßEN introduces a new element when he permits the miracle-worker to occupy the opposing player position. He writes: "In den Epiphanien wird sogar der Wundertäter selbst 'Gegenspieler': an ihm wird wunderbar gehandelt. Er ist der Adressat des Wunders.".[9] He refers to the Transfiguration on the mountain, 9,2ff. The quotes around "Gegenspieler" nevertheless reveal that something is uncertain. The emphasis here is on the miracle-worker as a subject of being. However miraculous the Transfiguration on the mountain may be, this is not a miracle story in the same sense as the other basic sequences in which Jesus is the subject of doing. In 9,2ff, where Jesus is considered by THEIßEN as a subject of being ("an ihm wird wunderbar gehandelt. Er ist der Adressat des Wunders"), he in no way himself appears in the role of miracle-worker. It is therefore quite misleading to say that the miracle-worker himself becomes "Gegenspieler"; the quotes do not remedy this misunderstanding. "Ein Grenzfall sind die Epiphanien", writes THEIßEN, but they in fact have nothing to do with the context of the miracle stories.[10] Only five themes now remain.

Where the opponent occupies the opposing player position, THEIßEN claims that a rule miracle is at issue, but in 3,1ff, to which he refers, a healing is found that shows the unfounded aspect of operating with the rule miracle theme. In this case, the problem is clearly associated with the difficulty that in the basic sequence 3,1-6, Jesus appears in different roles that makes it possible to consider it now as a controversy dialogue, now as a miracle story.

This awkward situation is clear evidence of a basic flaw in form criticism: it confuses text forms and narrative forms. When THEIßEN indicates the opponent

---

[8] Theißen, ibidem p. 55.

[9] Theißen, ibidem pp. 54.

[10] Theißen, ibidem, p. 55.

and companion as opposing players he is operating at the text-forms level, in that he follows the individual basic sequences' point of focus (in sympathy with BULTMANN).

However, the genre definition that he tries to establish concerns narrative forms. His attempt to classify thus rests upon two incompatible criteria, and he cannot extricate himself from this situation by using quotes and speaking of borderline cases. Four themes then remain that alone may be relevant to the wonder narrative: exorcism, healing, gift or feeding wonder, and rescue wonder.

Another problem is the term "Gegenspieler", which can be understood in at least three different ways.

First, the above graphic model, in which a demonic sphere is opposed to a divine sphere, gives reason to perceive the relation between the two opposing players as a contrast of the antagonist-versus-protagonist, degressor-versus-protector type. But since THEIßEN believes that all the characters referred to must be able to occupy the opposing player position, this perception makes no logical sense (nevertheless, it seems to be this perception that makes THEIßEN select the demon in 9,14ff as opposing player, although this basic sequence is quite clearly dominated by the relationship between the father and Jesus).

It is possible to perceive, in the main player, the miracle-worker as subject of doing and the opposing player as the complementary subject of being, i.e. the beneficiary of the miracle-work; but this cannot be the case, since the demon should be able to occupy this position (nevertheless, this appears to be the perception that causes THEIßEN to select Jesus as opposing player in 9,2ff).

Finally, "Gegenspieler" may be seen as the character who together with the miracle-worker is the main actor in the basic sequence, i.e. the character in focus. In 7,24ff, the companion, i.e. the mother, is the opposing player and not the possessed daughter, which raises the question of whether it is in fact a miracle story in a form-critical sense. THEIßEN insists however that a sub-type within exorcism is concerned. But in that case the possessed daughter is in focus and not the mother. As can be seen, THEIßEN tries to ride two horses at the same time: as a faithful form-critic he wants to define the miracle story as a text genre (the mother is in focus), but at the same time his real interest is in the wonder narrative (the daughter is in focus).

The basic sequences with which THEIßEN works are merely different textual manifestations of the wonder-narrative's narrative and discursive genre which fall under the gospel story's narratively-structured content and not under the gospel text's form.

D. CRITICISM OF THEIßEN'S MOTIF ANALYSIS

1. The Miracle Story

According to THEIßEN, the *miracle-story* genre includes an inventory of motifs against the background of which one can (ideally) consider the individual miracle story as *a combination of motifs*.[11] He refers to the following:

1. The coming of the miracle-worker. Cf. 1,21.29 et al.
2. The appearance of the crowd. The crowd is met, 1,21; 3,1; 9,14, brought along, 5,24; 10,46, or is attracted, 1,45; 2,1f; 5,14; 6,30ff; 7,32.
3. The appearance of the distressed person. Cf. 1,23; 1,40; 2,1 et al.
4. The appearance of representatives. Cf. 5,21ff; 7,34ff.
5. The appearance of embassies. Cf. 5,35; 7,24ff
6. The appearance of opponents. Cf. 2,1ff; 3,1ff; 9,14.
    (Motifs 3-6 form a motif group)
7. Reasons given for the coming of people seeking help. Jesus is sought out because one has heard of him, cf. 5,27; 7,25; 10,47; cf. 3,8.

These seven motifs form an *introduction*. As can be seen, the primary point here is to locate the performing character in a specific setting. Then follows:

8. Description of the distress. It may be sickness, possession, mortal danger or hunger. For sickness, the duration of the situation of need, 5,25f; 9,21, and unsuccessful attempts at healing, 5,26; 9,14ff, may be emphasized. Cf. also the helplessness in 5,4; that Jesus does not arrive until the fourth night-watch, 6,48; and that the crowd has already been with Jesus for three days with nothing to eat, 8,2.
    Finally, the finality of the degression process may be emphasized: the sickness becomes worse, 5,26; the demon wishes to take the boy's life, 9,22; the boat is about to be swamped, about to sink, 4,37; Jairus' daughter is at the point of death, 5,23.
9. Difficulties in the approach. Although he who seeks help is introduced onto the scene, contact with the miracle-worker does not follow from this. There are often obstacles in the way, the crowd (2,4; 5,24), the disciples (9,14ff), the companions (10,48), or Jesus himself (7,27).
10. Falling to the knees. Cf. 1,40; 5,6; 5,22; 7,26.
11. Cries for help. Cf. 10,47.
12. Pleas and expressions of trust. Cf. 4,38; 9,22; 10,48 and 1,40; 5,23.28.
    (9-12 form the "Approaching the miracle-worker" motif group)

---

[11] Theißen, ibidem, pp. 57. The Marcan material only is referred to here.

13. Misunderstanding. Cf. 5,39; 6,37; 6,49; cf. 2 Kings 5,5-7.
14. Scepticism and mockery. Cf. 5,35.40; 9,22; cf. 2 Kings 5,11.
15. Criticism from opponents. Cf. 2,5ff; 3,1ff.
16. Resistance and submission of the demon. Cf. 1,23; 5,7.
    (13-16 form the "Withdrawal" motif group)
17. Pneumatic excitement. Cf. σπλαγχνίζομαι (1,41; 6,34; 8,2; ὀργίζομαι, 1.41 varia lectio), ἐμβριμάομαι (1,43), συλλυπέομαι (3,5) and στενάζω (7,34; cf. also 9,19).
18. Assurance (consolation). Cf. 2,5; 5,34.36; 6,50; 7,29; 9,23; 10,49.52.
19. Argument. Cf. 2,9; 3,4; 3,24.
20. The withdrawal of the miracle-worker. Cf. 4,38; 6,48; 7,27; cf. also 1,35.45; 5,19ff; 6,32 and 9,19.
    (17-20 form "The miracle-worker's attitude" motif group.)

Motifs 8-20 form the miracle story's exposition, and as such give an introduction to the situation which is the starting point or *beginning* of the miracle act itself as a narrative pivotal point. Then follows:

21. Setting the scene. Before the miracle itself there are certain preparations. The sick person must be brought within reach, 3,3; 9,19; 10,49. The disciples are sent across the sea, 4,35; 6,45. The public is excluded, 5,40 (5,43); 7,33 (7,36); 8,23 (8,26); (9,25).
22. Touch. Cf. 1,31; 1,41; 3,10; 5,27; 5,41; 6,56; 7,33; 8,23; 10,13.16 (cf. 1 Kings 17,21; 2 Kings 4,34). As regards the touching, THEIßEN states that it is always assumed "daß dabei wunderbare Lebenskraft auf den Kranken ausstrahlt", cf. 5,30.[12]
23. Healing substances. Cf. 8,22ff.
24. Miracle-working word. The word acts either as a word of power (command, threat, invocation; 1,25; 4,39; 9,26) through its cryptic content (5,41; 7,34) or indirectly, since a command follows and thus makes the miracle occur (8,6f).
25. Prayer. Cf. 9,29; (7,34).
    (22-25 form the "Miracle" motif group)
26. Recognition of the miracle. The miracle can be confirmed without its miraculous nature being emphasized, 1,42; 3,5; 4,39b; 6,51; 7,30; 8,25. But the suddenness is often emphasized, 1,42; 2,12; 5,29; 5,42; 7,35; 10,52, or the violent departure of the demon, 1,26; 9,26.

Motifs 21-26 form the miracle story's *middle*, the centre surrounding the miracle itself.

---

[12] Theißen, ibidem p. 71.

Then follows:

27.   Demonstration. Usually the miracle is not merely established but demon-
      strated by a new act. The healed person serves (1,31), carries his bed
      (2,12), can walk and follow (5,42; 10,52), gets something to eat (5,43).
      The unclean spirits enter a herd of swine which throw themselves into the
      sea and drown (5,13). In the feeding miracle, the abundance is emphasized
      (6,43f; 8,8f).
      (The motif refers to the reaction of the opposing player).
28.   Dismissal. Cf. 1,44; 5,19; 5,34; (7,29); 8,9; 6,45; 10,52.
29.   Command to secrecy. Cf. 1,34; 1,44; 3,12; 5,42; 7,36 (cf. 8,30; 9,9); cf.
      5,19; 8,26.
      (28-29 form a motif group referring to the miracle-worker's reaction)
30.   Wonder. Cf. θαυμάζω (5,20), ἐξίσταμαι (2,12; 5,42; 6,51), ἔκστασις
      (5,42), φοβοῦμαι (4,41; 5,15 (10,32; 16,8)), φόβος (4,41), θαμβοῦμαι
      (1,27; 10,24 (10,32)); ἐκπλήσσομαι (1,22; 6,2; 7,37; 11,18), (ἐκθαυμάζω,
      12,17), (ἐκθαμβοῦμαι, 9,15 (16,5)) and (ἔκφοβος, 9,6).
31.   Acclamation. Cf. 1,27; 2,12; 4,41; 7,37.
32.   Rejection. 3,6; 5,17; 6,3.
33.   The spread of the news. Cf. 1,28; 1,45; 5,14.20; 7,37.
      (30-33 form a motif group referring to the intermediate player's reaction).

Motifs 27-33 form the miracle story's *ending*.

2. The Wonder Narrative

It is illuminating to consider THEIßEN's motif inventory against the background
of an objectified basic sequence, for example the narrative about Jairus' daughter,
5,21-24; 35-43 (the embedded narrative, 5,25-34, is disregarded here), which can
be reproduced by the following narrative propositions:

1.   Jesus goes over to the other shore
2.   A large crowd of people gathers around Jesus
3.   The leader of the synagogue, Jairus, arrives
4.   Jairus catches sight of Jesus
5.   Jairus falls down at Jesus' feet
6.   Jairus entreats Jesus
     1. Jairus daughter is on the point of death
     2. Jesus goes to the daughter
     3. Jesus lays hands on the daughter
     4. The daughter is healed and lives

7. Jesus goes with Jairus
8. A large crowd follows Jesus
9. There is a throng around Jesus
10. People from the leader of the synagogue's house come and say
    1. Jairus' daughter is dead
    2. Jairus is troubling the Master
11. Jesus overhears what is said
12. Jesus speaks to Jairus
    1. Jairus is not afraid
    2. Jairus believes
13. The crowd stays behind
14. Peter, James and John follow Jesus
15. Jesus and his disciples arrive at Jairus' house
16. Jesus sees
    A crowd weeping and wailing loudly
17. Jesus speaks to the crowd
    1. The crowd is noisy and weeping
    2. The child is not dead but sleeping
18. The crowd laughs at Jesus
19. Jesus puts the crowd outside
20. Jesus takes with him the child's father and mother and his companions
21. Jesus goes in where the child is
22. Jesus takes the child by the hand
23. Jesus speaks to the child
    The little girl gets up
24. The girl gets up
25. The girl walks about
26. The girl is twelve years of age
27. Those present are overcome with amazement
28. Jesus issues a ban
    No one is to know
        Cf. 22.-29.
29. Jesus issues a command
    The parents give the child something to eat

If one compares this series of propositions with THEIßEN's motif inventory, it becomes clear that the motifs are almost identical with the acts that constitute the propositions.

The proposition, "Jesus goes over to the other shore", corresponds to the motif "The miracle-worker's arrival"; the proposition, "A large crowd of people gathers around Jesus", corresponds to the motif "The appearance of the crowd";

the proposition, "The leader of the synagogue, Jairus, arrives" corresponds to the motif "The appearance of representatives".[13]

THEIßEN's motifs "sind durch Vergleich und Abstraktion gebildete Einheiten".[14] He follows the classical form-critical method: compares all the genre texts and extracts those recurrent elements which are narratively relevant. Against this background, it is then possible to perceive the miracle story as a combination of motifs.

If narrative analysis were to compare the objectified basic sequences A)-R) and generalize the recurrent narrative propositions it would arrive at a similar result. The difference between the two procedures does not emerge until the question relates to a joining of the motifs/propositions.

THEIßEN's motif-inventory, and not least his grouping into expositional (beginning), central (middle) and final (ending) motifs indicates a rounded course of events, a syntagmatic motif-composition. But the motifs are viewed as pearls on a string; they are seen as belonging to one and the same level, whereas in fact several connected, narrative processes are concerned.

Narrative analysis formulates the basic sequence in presentic narrative propositions in order to define the wonder narrative as a narrative unity which as a basic syntagm is organized around a main action in relation to which any other action receives its *raison d'être*.

Narrative analysis cannot content itself with reeling off the succession of actions in the basic sequence but must inquire about their mutual narrative connection. It is beyond the scope of this study to pursue this question of the process of the wonder narrative. It is nevertheless relevant briefly to include this perspective, since it casts light on the wonder narrative, which is not a textual basic sequence but a narrative basic syntagm.

As a narrative unity, a basic syntagm, the wonder narrative must be defined on the basis of the constituting pragmatic action or narrative process from which every other narrative process (including the cognitive ones) takes its reason of being. The point of departure must therefore be taken in the structure of the basic syntagm:

      1)   Virtual wonder
      2)   Actualized wonder
      3)   Realized wonder.

---

[13] The following motifs correspond to the other propositions: 4/4; 5/10; 6/12; 6.1/8; 7/1; 8/2; 9/9; 10/5.14; 11/(17); 12/18; 13/21; 14/1; 15/1; 16.1/13; 17.1/13; 17.2/18; 18/14; 19/21; 20/21; 21/21; 22/22; 23/24; 24/26; 25/27; 26/27; 27/30; 28/29; 29/27. There is nothing remarkable in that the motif of the wonder-worker's coming can appear several times when the scene in fact changes in the course of the narrative. Also to be noted here is an essential defect in Theißen's motif-definition: the disciples are always present when Jesus carries out wonder-works.

[14] Theißen, ibidem, p. 17.

If the syntagm is defined more specifically as protection, it will be linked with another, degressive basic syntagm:

Virtual degression

⇓

Actualized degression   = Virtual protection

⇓

⇓   Actualized protection

⇓

Non-realized degression   = Realized protection

The most elementary wonder-narrative might read as follows: "Jesus cured many who were sick with various diseases", cf. 1,34. Although Mark's narration is often very concise, he nevertheless has more to say. However, all other information contained in the gospel narrative about Jesus as wonder-worker is mere detail compared to this complex sequence.

A somewhat more expanded wonder narrative might read: "That evening, at sundown, they brought to him all who were sick or possessed with demons. And the whole city was gathered around the door. And he cured many who were sick with various diseases, and cast out many demons; ...", 1,32f. Or: " ... he had cured many, so that all who had diseases pressed upon him to touch him.", 3,10. Or: "..., they laid the sick in the market places, and begged him that they might touch even the fringe of his cloak; and all who touched it were healed.", 6,56. The summaries 1,32ff; 3,7ff and 6,53ff are basic sequences that are not miracle stories although they contain wonder narratives.

The wonder narrative's pragmatic basic syntagm *does not* gather and organize independent motifs but constitutes the action unity that falls into beginning (virtual wonder-work; presupposition; motifs 8-20, cf. 5,21-24.35-39), middle (actualized wonder-work; narrative pivotal point; motifs 21-26, cf. 5,40-42a) and ending (realized wonder-work; result; motifs 27-33, cf. 5,42b-43). Summarized or expanded, the wonder narrative has the same constituent mythos.

THE SEMIOTIC BASIC MODEL

The graphic model shows the "semiotic square" or semiotic basic model employed in this study:

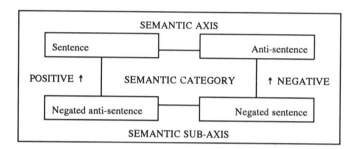

The term *sentence* means whatever is set (assumed, postulated), for example *Full*. The opposite, termed *anti-sentence*, here *Empty*, is arrived at by a privative negation. The terms on the semantic axis are terminals, while the terms on the semantic sub-axis are liminals, unstable relatives, which are processually orientated (↑) towards the terminals. The *negated sentence* refers to a (degressive) process, emptying, which tends towards anti-sentence, but may categorically be maintained in its relative stability as *Half empty*. Similarly, *negated anti-sentence* refers to a (progressive) process, filling, which tends towards sentence, but may categorically be maintained as *Half full*. Whether a bottle (or time, cf. 1,15) is half empty or half full thus depends upon whether it is about to be emptied (the negative deixis) or filled (the positive deixis).

The semiotic square or the elementary structure of signification has been the subject of various interpretations, cf. A.J. GREIMAS, *Sémantique structurale. Recherche de méthode*, Paris 1966, p. 18; *Sémiotique*, art. "Carré sémiotique"; FRÉDÉRIC NEF (ed.), *Structures élémentaires de la signification*, Bruxelles 1976. It is the privative or monistic understanding, however, that characterizes the articulation of modalities, cf. below, which in a narrative perspective appears to be the most adequate.

PART THREE
THE PROCLAIMER

THE PROCLAIMER HIERARCHY

The semiotic study of the narrative has been defined as a study of the objectivized, narrating discourse. Semiotic investigations fall into two sub-fields: 1) study of the enunciation or narration; 2) study of the utterance or narrate. In addition it has been emphasized that the present investigation is mainly concerned with the narrate, i.e. the narrated world. The two main types of investigation which can thus be envisaged, and which may in general be said to relate to one another in the same way as tradition history relates to redaction criticism, are however so closely connected that they can scarcely be carried out in a pure form. It is rather a matter of a heuristic and practically based perspective in which the narrate is the centre and the narration the periphery, or vice versa.

There are two contexts in which the question of the relationship between narration and narrate are presented with special insistence: where the discourse begins and where it ends. Here the two classical problems of Markan research are to be recognized: the question of the gospel text's uncertain beginning in 1,1 and its obscure ending in 16,8. Clarification of these questions requires, as will be demonstrated below, analysis of the relationship between the gospel narrative's enunciation and utterance.

The proclamation is in this context the central point of intersection, since the gospel narrative tells not only about Jesus' proclamation but is itself the proclamation of Jesus Christ. The task then is to give a more explicit account of the relationship between the *narrated proclamation* and the *narrating proclamation*.

In the context of these problems, it is important to note that the gospel narrative is not only a story of Jesus' words and deeds. It is also a detailed story about its own origin as a proclaiming narrative: had the disciples not come to believe that the crucified Jesus of Nazareth was truly the Son of God who was raised on the third day, no narrative would have existed, no proclamation sounded.

A. THE THEMATIC PROCLAIMER ROLES

The narrated characters have been given linguistic ability and may therefore break into speech at any moment, often in the form of a quoted dialogue or enunciation framed by references to a situation, anaphoric resumptions and narrator comments of the type:

1,14   Now after John was arrested, Jesus came to Galilee,
        proclaiming the good news of God and saying;
4,1   Again he began to teach beside the sea;
4,9   And he said;
4,33   With many such parables he spoke the word to them, as
        they were able to hear it;
8,27   on the way he asked his disciples;
8,28   And they answered him;
9,31   for he was teaching his disciples, saying to them, etc.

Within this framework a series of verbs are used, sometimes with supplementing definitions that describe Jesus' discourse.

One group of verbs, whose function is primarily to call attention to the speech
act itself, is descriptive only to the extent that comments are added. This applies
to λέγω, λαλέω, φημί and ἐπερωτάω, ἀποκρίνομαι, which are neutral, in so far
as they disclose nothing about the content or mood of the discourse. Only an
adverbial definition of the type ἐν παραβολαῖς (3,28; 12,1) or παρρησίᾳ (8,32)
qualifies this.

Other verbs indicate that in certain situations Jesus blesses (εὐλογέω), thanks
(εὐχαριστέω) or prays (προσεύχομαι); calls (καλέω) and calls to him (προσκα-
λέω, φωνέω); threatens, forbids, reproves (ἐπιτιμάω), commands (ἐπιτάσσω),
permits (ἐπιτρέπω), forbids, warns (διαστέλλω), commands (παραγγέλλω) and
urges (ἀναγκάζω). The verbs that generally describe Jesus' discourse are
κηρύσσω and διδάσκω: Jesus speaks in his capacity of *proclaimer* and *teacher*.

The verb κηρύσσω is used for Jesus only in 1,14 and 1,38f. The verb διδάσκω
is used much more extensively: 1,21f; 2,13; 4,1f; 6,2; 6,6; 6,34; 8,31; 9,31;
10,1; 11,17; (12,14); 12,35; (12,38); (14,49).

The very existence of two different general expressions for Jesus' discourse
raises the question of whether there is a difference in content between to proclaim
and to teach.

According to 1,38f, Jesus came to *proclaim*, it is his mission, and he
proclaims in all the synagogues in the towns of Galilee. According to 1,21; 6,2.6
he *teaches* in synagogues and villages; according to 11,17; 12,35 and 14,49 he
teaches in Jerusalem in the temple. On this basis, proclaiming and teaching must
be seen as parasynonyms.[1]

This impression is confirmed by 6,12.30, which says first that the disciples,
sent out as apostles, went out and *proclaimed*, that people should repent (cf.
1,14), and then says that they returned and told Jesus that they had *taught* people
(cf. Lk 20,1, Mt 11,1). In the gospel narrative the imaginable difference between

---

[1] I.e. as lexemes with an approximate identity that can be substituted for one another in certain
contexts, although not in all; cf. *Sémiotique*, art. "Parasynonymie".

the two enunciation acts is not relevant, but the emphasis is on the parasynonymity, since to proclaim and to teach serve the same purpose.[2]

At first, therefore, two thematic proclaimer roles may be distinguished, the teacher and the proclaimer:

$$διδάσκαλος - διδάσκω -διδαχή$$
$$κῆρυξ - κηρύσσω -κήρυγμα.$$

But the use of εὐαγγέλιον (1,14), ἄγγελος (1,2) and προφήτης (6,4; cf. also 6,15; 8,28, (11,32); (14,65)) gives an opportunity to distinguish three further roles:

$$εὐαγγελιστής - εὐαγγελίζω -εὐαγγέλιον$$
$$ἄγγελος - ἀγγέλλω -ἀγγελία$$
$$προφήτης - προφητεύω -προφητεία.$$

The thematic proclaimer roles are concretizations of the narration (for example διδάσκω) and its narrator (διδάσκαλος) and narrate (διδαχή).

B. THE HIERARCHY OF NARRATION

1. Prophetic Narration

The thematic proclaimer role can have a new representation of the type:

NARRATOR	NARRATEE	NARRATE
Prophet	-	Prophecy

indicating its emissive aspect: the narration is directed towards an implicit narratee.

It is, however, just as important that the prophet has been called and sent out by a superior authority (No1, Yahweh; cf. among numerous examples, Isa 6), which means that he has been a narratee himself (Ne1) in a preceding narration:

NARRATOR	NARRATEE	NARRATE
Yahweh	Isaiah	Yahweh's words

---

[2] Employed intransitively, the two verbs can be substituted for one another. As transitive verbs they exclude one another by virtue of the object; one can proclaim the gospel, but not learn the gospel or proclaim a teaching.

that *establishes* him as narrator (No2) for another narratee (Ne2). Two hierarchally connected enunciation structures exist:

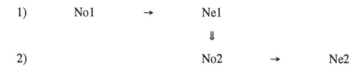

1)   No1   →   Ne1

                            ⇓

2)   No2   →   Ne2

in that Ne1 and No2 are roles handled by the same person who acts as cognitive
intermediary for No1 and Ne2.

Yet another enunciation actant can thus be introduced: the *discursivator*, i.e.
the authority that has given the narrator access to knowledge and truth. The
religious narrator never speaks in his own name, but is the mouthpiece of the
authority that has established him as narrator. When a given enunciation level is
considered, discursivator is thus seen as the authority that has established the
transmitter of the discourse as narrator. Isa 6 thus has the following investment
of the prophetic narration:

DISCURSIVATOR	NARRATOR	NARRATEE
Yahweh	Isaiah	People

It forms part of the picture of prophetic narration that the discursivator must
reflexively have established himself as such.

2. Kerygmatic Narration

The lexemes that form the thematic proclaimer roles are all employed in the New
Testament writings, and it becomes apparent that they can be combined by the
use of lexemes from the various inventories: Jesus is a teacher (διδάσκαλος) who
proclaims (κηρύσσω) the gospel (εὐαγγέλιον).[3] The wide-spread parasynonymity

---

[3] Cf., for example the use of the angelic, evangelic and kerygmatic role lexemes. In Mark there is
ἄγγελος, εὐαγγέλιον and κηρύσσω. The lexemes ἀγγελία (1 Jn 1,5; 3,11), ἀγγέλλω (Jn 4,5; 20,18),
εὐαγγελιστής (Acts 21,8; Eph 4,11; 2 Tim 4,5) and κῆρυξ (1 Tim 2,7; 2 Pet 2,5) are not used in the
synoptic gospels. Common to these are ἄγγελος (Mt 11,10; Mk 1,2; Lk 7,27) and κηρύσσω. Mark has
εὐαγγέλιον, but not εὐαγγελίζω and κήρυγμα (16,9 is disregarded here). Lk has εὐαγγελίζω and
κήρυγμα (although only in 11,32 about the prophet Jonah), but not εὐαγγέλιον (although in Acts 15,7
and 20,24). Mt has εὐαγγέλιον (and this only together with κηρύσσω), εὐαγγελίζω (11,5) and κήρυγμα
(although only in 12,41 about the prophet Jonah). It can thus be observed that the synoptic gospels
preferably use εὐαγγέλιον, κηρύσσω and εὐαγγελίζω. Mark combines κηρύσσω and εὐαγγέλιον; Mt also,
but on one occasion also εὐαγγελίζω is found, which is exclusively used by Lk. The latter lexeme,
however, states implicitly that the utterance is the gospel, and the terms "κηρύσσω τὸ εὐαγγέλιον" and
"εὐαγγελίζω" must thus be considered as synonymous (cf. Rev 14,6; 1 Cor 15,1; 2 Cor 11,7 and Gal
1,11, where εὐαγγελίζω is used with explicit εὐαγγέλιον; and Gal 1,8, where the verb is combined with
ἄγγελος).

must be attributed to the fact that in all cases a narration is concerned in which a narrator proclaims a message of salvation in the name of the discursivator God.

In Mark's Gospel the teacher role dominates. Even in 6,1ff, where Jesus indirectly describes himself as a prophet, it says that he taught in the synagogue. He is addressed as teacher, and his utterances are referred to as teaching. The privileged narratee of this narration is the pupil or disciple, and it is the unravelling of the teacher/disciple relationship that can give an insight into the gospel story's narration hierarchy. The disciple role is supplementary to the teacher role, and it is thus possible to distinguish an emissive didactic:

$$\delta\iota\delta\acute{\alpha}\sigma\kappa\alpha\lambda o\varsigma - \delta\iota\delta\acute{\alpha}\sigma\kappa\omega - \delta\iota\delta\alpha\chi\acute{\eta}$$

and a receptive didactic proclaimer role:

$$\mu\alpha\theta\eta\tau\acute{\eta}\varsigma - \mu\alpha\nu\theta\acute{\alpha}\nu\omega - \mu\acute{\alpha}\theta\eta\mu\alpha/\mu\acute{\alpha}\theta\eta\sigma\iota\varsigma.[4]$$

The calling and sending out of the disciples (1,16ff; 3,13ff; 6,7ff) show that they are called by Jesus in his capacity as narrator (No1) and appointed as narratees (Ne1) before they are sent out as narrators (No2) to proclaim for a new narratee (Ne2):

1)	No1	→	Ne1
	Jesus		Disciples
		⇓	
2)	No2	→	Ne2
	Apostles		People

It should be noted here that a *disciple* is a *narratee*, whereas an *apostle* is a *narrator*. In the first place, it can be seen from 6,12 "So they went out ($\dot{\epsilon}\xi\acute{\epsilon}\rho\chi o\mu\alpha\iota$) and proclaimed that all should repent" that the teaching of the disciples is done with a view to their conducting a proclaimer mission. They are trained as apostles, sent out as proclaimers.

Jesus also has such a mission; he has come out ($\dot{\epsilon}\xi\acute{\epsilon}\rho\chi o\mu\alpha\iota$, 1,38) to fulfil a predicatory duty (cf. 6,12 with 1,14f). The question is whether he has been called and sent out. As regards the sending out there is direct information in 9,37: "and whoever welcomes me welcomes not me but the one who sent me ($\dot{\alpha}\pi o\sigma\tau\acute{\epsilon}\lambda\lambda\omega$)". Jesus is God's apostle. As regards the calling, the matter is less clear, but the story about Jesus' baptism (cf. in detail below) contains a rudimentary (elliptical)

---

[4] Cf. Friedrich Normann, *Christos Didaskalos. Die Vorstellung von Christos als Lehrer in der christlichen Literatur des ersten und zweiten Jahrhunderts*, Münster 1967, pp. 21.

calling-story in which he is established as narrator. It is God who is the discursivator for Jesus' proclamation, which also emerges in the expression τὸ εὐαγγέλιον τοῦ θεοῦ (1,14), i.e. the gospel from God.

The following narration hierarchy is given:

1)	No1	→	Ne1		
	God		Jesus		
			⇓		
2)			No2	→	Ne2
			Jesus		The disciples
					⇓
3)				No3	→
				The apostles	

No3	→	Ne3
The apostles		All nations (13,10)

As will be seen, what is concerned is the communication between God (No1) and humankind (Ne3) through intermediaries, religious narrators (No2 and No3). Such an enunciation structure in which the divine powers are discursivators may generally be described as prophetic narration. In this case, where the Christian narrative is specifically concerned, one may speak of an evangelic or *kerygmatic narration*.

The kerygmatic narration hierarchy is closed. There is no discursivator for God; no narratee for "all nations" who as narratees see themselves as nominated and appointed as possible disciples (cf. Mt 28,19). If a person from "all nations" appears in the role of narrator, he is given the status of apostle.[5]

The above narration hierarchy belongs to the gospel story's narrated enunciation. Standing opposite to this is the narrating enunciation for which Mark is the narrator, and the reader (cf. 13,14) is the narratee. The reader sees himself as nominated by the narrative as one among "all nations". Mark, in turn, sees himself appointed as apostle. Since he does not perform in the narrated world, he appears as an apostle who, as narrator, must have been instituted by one of the twelve. The narration is thus itself a kerygmatic enunciation, and it therefore becomes pressing to obtain a detailed explanation of the relationship between the narrating proclamation (τὸ εὐαγγέλιον Ἰησοῦ Χριστοῦ, 1,1) and the narrated proclamation (τὸ εὐαγγέλιον τοῦ θεοῦ, 1,14).

---

[5] Cf. Rom 1,1. In the case where the term apostle is reserved for persons thought to have been in personal contact with Jesus, one or more enunciation levels are inserted between apostles and "All nations", cf. the ecclesiastical conception of apostolic succession.

CHAPTER EIGHT

THE GOSPEL OF GOD

Explicit information on Jesus' proclamation is to be found in the summary 1,14f:

> Now after John was arrested, Jesus came to Galilee, proclaiming the good news of God, and saying, 'The time is fulfilled, and the kingdom of God is come near; repent, and believe in the good news.'[1]

In the capacity of proclaimer of the gospel of God, the narrative's Jesus of Nazareth in Galilee (1,9) must have been called and sent out by God. Immediately after - but *only after* - baptism/anointing and temptation he appears as the proclaimer of God. Anointed with the Holy Spirit (1,10), he has been sent with good news to proclaim liberty to the captives (cf. Isa 61,1).[2]

A. THE NARRATIVE PROCLAIMER ROLES A)

As pointed out earlier, two dimensions are distinguished within the narrative: the *pragmatic* dimension, in which reality is realized (cf. πράσσω, πρᾶγμα, πρᾶξις; also ἐργάζομαι, ἔργον) by significant behaviour, a practice that appears to the observer as concrete and tangible events, for example the realization of the kingdom of God; and the *cognitive* dimension, where this pragmatic dimension in its capacity of *narrative-internal referent* is represented in a communication, for example the proclamation of the kingdom of God, which implies a complex of problems of knowledge and belief.[3]

It is quite crucial that the cognitive dimension presupposes the pragmatic dimension, and not vice versa. The information communicated in the narrative

---

[1] There is no other information on the content of Jesus' preaching. Walter Schmithals states: "Wenn in der Grundschrift immerfort berichtet wird, Jesus habe das Volk gelehrt, ohne dass doch Predigten Jesu mitgeteilt worden, so liegt am Tage, dass die Erzählungen der Grundschrift als solche die Lehre Jesu enthalten und dass diese Lehre demzufolge den Christus Jesus selbst zu ihrem Gegenstand hat.", *Einleitung in die drei ersten Evangelien*, Berlin 1985, p. 415. But as, *inter alia*, the messianic secret bears witness to, Jesus can accurately not proclaim the gospel of Jesus Christ. Between Jesus' proclaiming of God's gospel and the gospel narrative's proclaiming of the gospel of Jesus Christ there is not a public proclamation to the people but an esoteric (cf. 4,11.34) teaching of the disciples that relates to events (crucifixion and resurrection) that have not yet taken place; cf. Hejne Simonsen, "Messiashemmeligheden og Markusevangeliets struktur" (The Messianic Secret and the Structure of the Gospel of Mark), *Svensk Exegetisk Årsbok 37-38*, Lund 1973, p. 120.

[2] Cf. Rudolf Pesch, *Das Markusevangelium, I. Teil*, Freiburg 1980, p. 101.

[3] Cf. *Sémiotique*, art. "Pragmatique" and "Cognitif".

by cognitive subjects of doing - proclaimers - has a content that is pertinent to the extent that it concerns the subject of being's pragmatic or narrative existence. The information has a pragmatic objective; it is relevant because it informs about the subject of being's existential situation. The knowledge communicated concerns the subject of being's pragmatic life-situation, which also includes the pragmatic modal states.

1. Information

a. Information and Dissimulation

A subject of being which according to the narrative finds itself in a given state of being, descriptive or modal (for example the state which exists in that the kingdom of God has come near), may either be aware or unaware of this, i.e. either realize that a certain state of being is concerned, since his attention was drawn thereto, or be unknowing that something is on the tapis.[4] The proclamation is then initially an *information process* that aims at giving the subject of being knowledge of this new situation. He can, however, be kept in ignorance if this information is withheld, for example because of a command to secrecy.[5]

In the first case information is concerned, a saying, a diction; in the second case it is dissimulation, a non-saying, a non-diction (strategic silence). In that Inf refers to the informing, the two diction-positions can be noted (example: X = "The kingdom of God has come near"):

A)   Inf says that X is the case;

B)   Inf does not say that X is the case.

Two further positions can be derived therefrom:

C)   Inf says that X is not the case;

D)   Inf does not say that X is not the case;[6]

---

[4] Cf. *Logique du récit*, pp. 147.

[5] The paradoxical form of proclamation, the parable discourse, in which one both speaks and keeps silent, cf. 4,11ff, shows clearly that the proclaiming must be seen in relation to the strategic silence. 4,1-34 is not discussed in detail in this study, cf. for example, Bent Noack, *Markusevangeliets lignelseskapitel* (The Parable Chapter in the Gospel of Mark), København 1965; Frank Kermode, *The Genesis of Secrecy. On the Interpretation of Narrative*, Cambridge 1979; Jean Delorme, "La communication parabolique d'après Marc 4", *Sémiotique et bible 48*, Lyon 1987, pp. 1.

[6] In utterance C) the informing party is a person who denies a previously given item of information. Utterance D) concerns, for example, the situation in which the dissimulating party, knowing that X is not the case, withholds this information from the person who thinks he knows that X is the case. The dissimulating party here not only allows the dissimulated party to remain in ignorance but under a delusion, either to injure him (by himself benefiting from the situation) or to protect him (as when a

and the four positions can be indicated by the following model:

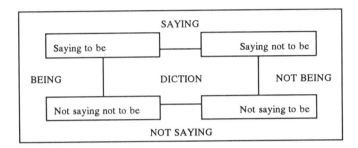

The diction system includes two dictions (saying) and two non-dictions (non-saying). The two dictions and the two non-dictions are positive (being; X is the case) and negative (not being; X is not the case) respectively, which gives:

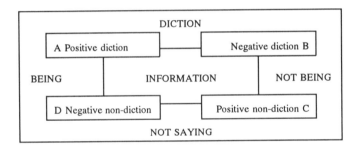

The informative doing in the form of the saying is *emissive* and corresponds to a *receptive* hearing (passive) or listening (active). The emissive entity, i.e. the informing, is referred to as *enunciator/narrator*; the receptive entity, i.e. the informed, is referred to as *enunciatee/narratee*.

b. Informator and Dissimulator

A subject of being may be informed without the narrative's explaining how or by whom. But if the narrative selects a responsible subject of doing for an item of information effected this will adopt the narrative role of *informator*.

Similarly, the cognitive subject of doing that withholds the information will adopt the role of *dissimulator*. The cognitive doing and not doing can also be specified according to whether it is voluntary or involuntary, reflexive or

---

doctor keeps silent about the fatality of the sickness process).

transitive.[7] In his capacity as the proclaimer of the gospel of God, Jesus thus adopts the narrative role as voluntary, transitive informator.

The content of what is narrated (saying) or suppressed (non-saying) is a *mise en scène* of actors (subjects of doing or subjects of being) and is as an utterance directed to a recipient who is assumed to be ignorant of the roles concerned in the given scenario. This utterance or message is thus *a narrative, a narrate*; here primarily: "The time is fulfilled and the kingdom of God has come near".

The informative doing can be considered to be a process of change causing a transition from one cognitive state to another, from ignorance to knowledge:

Initial state $\Rightarrow$ Final state

not knowing X   knowing X

If the information serves the narratee, this process of change can be more specifically defined as progressive; if it harms him, however, it is degressive. The dissimulation is similarly a preservation process, now a repression, now a protection.

Where the information process has the nature of argument and struggle, i.e. where two opposing information processes collide polemically (cf. the controversy dialogues), the informator appears, now in the role of the affirmer who attempts to strengthen the information's power of conviction, now in the role of the denier who attempts to weaken the information's power of conviction.

Such a polemic aspect, however, will probably always assert itself. The transition from:

"The narratee does not know that the kingdom of God has come near"
to:
"The narratee knows that the kingdom of God has come near"

is not a simple transition from ignorance to knowledge but from false knowledge:

"The narratee knows that the kingdom of God has not come near"

to true knowledge:

"The narratee knows that the kingdom of God has come near".

Doubly informed, from two different narrators who mutually negate one another, the subject of being must adopt a position towards the information available.

---

[7] Cf. *Logique du récit*, pp. 259.

2. Veridiction

a. The Veridictory Modalities

The information a proclaimer spreads may be false. Perhaps misinformation is concerned, a message that is by no means the truth. What is true is determined by the narrative, which thereby validates the circulating information on the basis of the veridictory modalities (cf. τὴν ἀλήθειαν λέγω; ἀληθεύω).[8]

If X = "The time is fulfilled and the kingdom of God has come near" (cf. the information diagram above) is the case in the reality established by the narrative, then A) and D) can be verified and B) and C) falsified:

A)	Verifiable positive diction	=	Veridiction
B)	Falsifiable positive non-diction	=	Dissimulation
C)	Falsifiable negative diction	=	Negated veridiction
D)	Verifiable negative non-diction	=	Negated dissimulation

corresponding to:

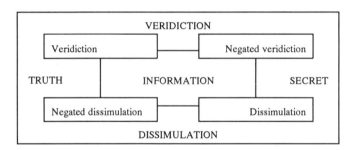

As a disclosure of that which is the case, i.e. that which has become the case by virtue of an accomplished (perfective, cf. πεπλήρωται, ἤγγικεν) process of change, the veridiction has the status of revelation (cf. γνωρίζω; δηλόω; φανερόω, φανέρωσις; ἀποκαλύπτω, ἀποκάλυψις). Where that which is the case

---

[8] Cf. *Sémiotique*, art. "Véridiction" and "Véridictoires (modalités -)"; A.J. Greimas, "Les actants, les acteurs et les figures", *Du sens II. Essais Sémiotiques*, Paris 1983, pp. 49. Greimas has constructed these modalities on the basis of the *être/paraître* discrepancy; here the model is differentiated and founded upon the act of communication.

is hidden (cf. κρύπτω, κρυπτός, ἀποκρύπτω, ἀπόκρυφος; καλύπτω), suppressed (σιγάω), there is a secret (μυστήριον; cf. 4,22; cf. e.g. Rom 16,25).

If X is not the case in the narrative's reality, then A) and D) can be falsified and B) and C) verified:

A)   Falsifiable positive diction   =   Simulation

B)   Verifiable positive non-diction   =   Falsidiction

C)   Verifiable negative diction   =   Negated simulation

D)   Falsifiable negative non-diction   =   Negated falsidiction

corresponding to:

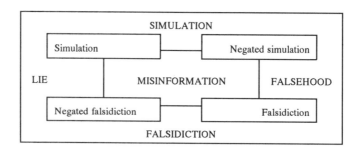

One observes that both truth and lie (veridiction and simulation), like secrecy and falseness (dissimulation and falsidiction), have the same form, positive diction and positive non-diction respectively.[9] It can also be seen that these four dictions are positive. The four negative dictions are simple negations of the positive, and thus presuppose them as an operational basis (to say or to suppress that something is not the case thus presupposes a preceding assertion).

b. Revealator and Deceptor

When the question of the information's veridictory status is included, it becomes possible to distinguish the true information, the *veridiction*, from the lie, the *simulation*. The subject of doing responsible for the veridiction adopts the role of veridictor (ἀληθεύων - ἀληθεύω - ἀλήθεια) or *revealator*, whereas the subject of doing responsible for the simulation adopts the role of simulator or *deceptor*.[10]

---

[9] It has not been possible to avoid the double use of the term dissimulation which has now a wider (vs. information), now a narrower (vs. falsidiction), meaning.

[10] Cf. ψεύστης - ψευστέω/ψεύδω - ψεῦδος; cf. ψευδάγγελος, -απόστολος, ψευδοδιδάσκαλος, -κῆρυξ, -λόγος, -μάρτυς, -προφήτης, -χριστος; πλάνος - πλανάω - πλάνη; ἀπατῶν - ἀπατάω - ἀπάτη. Cf.

If he is in good faith, the voluntary informator adopts the role of voluntary revealator; but if he makes a mistake and in fact simulates, he adopts the role of involuntary deceptor. Thus, it must be said of the evangelist Mark that he adopts the role of voluntary revealator. But if he is misled he adopts the role of involuntary deceptor. Jesus also adopts the role of voluntary revealator, a role which the narrative confirms, but which some of the actors who appear negate. Designated as a liar, the Jewish leaders must express an opinion on whether Jesus acts against his better knowledge (and in this case tells a downright lie) or whether he is enveloped in an illusion (cf. the accusation against him that he is out of his mind, possessed by Beelzebul, 3,21f).

If he speaks against his better knowledge, and if he acts in bad faith, the voluntary informator adopts the role of voluntary deceptor; but if he is enveloped in self-delusion and is in fact telling the truth, believing that he is simulating, he adopts the role of involuntary revealator. The soldiers who give Jesus a purple cloak and a crown of thorns, and salute him: "Hail, King of the Jews!", 15,16f, have perhaps no real intention to deceive, but their behaviour can nevertheless be compared with simulation, in that they act as if Jesus were a king. The entire enthronement scene is to this extent an intentional deceit in which the soldiers disclose a truth, though they believe they are simulating. Involuntarily, they salute the Christ King.[11]

Logique du récit, pp. 263.

[11] As regards this "dramatic irony", cf. Robert C. Tannehill, "The Gospel of Mark as Narrative Christology", *Semeia 16*, Missoula 1979, pp. 78.

B. Content of the Proclamation

1. God's Transition to Action

The thematic proclaimer role relates to the narrative narrator role. Jesus appears in the role of narrator, and the proclamation must be more specifically defined on the basis of the model of narration:

1)   The narrator attempts to convey to the narratee the concept of a virtual, actualized, or realized state of being and/or process.

2)   The subject of being for this state/process is the narratee, the narrator, or a third person A.

3)   The subject of doing responsible for this state/process is the narratee, the narrator, the third person A, or a fourth person B.

The proclamation must have a *content* which is indeed a narrate, and here interest is primarily concentrated on "πεπλήρωται ὁ καιρὸς καὶ ἤγγικεν ἡ βασιλεία τοῦ θεοῦ" (1,15a).

1) *State/process.* The expression πεπλήρωται ὁ καιρός, the time is fulfilled, the time has come, the measure is full, should be understood as aspectual rather than temporal. What is concerned is not that a predetermined chronological date has arrived but that a process has been accomplished, since *empty - half-full - full* corresponds to *beginning - middle - ending* (VAR). A sub-process has been completed which opens to a new course of action.

For the narratee, Jesus' proclamation presupposes a more or less clear expectation implying the hope that God will pass to action in order to realize his kingdom. At that moment, when God passes to action, a sub-process is concluded which makes a change from virtuality to actualization and establishes a new horizon of expectation.

The kingdom of God (ἡ βασιλεία τοῦ θεοῦ) is a state of being which, from being virtual, has now become actualized, i.e. is being realized. The kingdom of God has come near (ἤγγικεν), since a transition to action has taken place. Here also the aspectualization is decisive, not the temporality. The kingdom of God (KG) is not a situation that either exists or does not exist, is either absent or present, but is a state of being *that is to be realized through action*. A narrative process is concerned, a basic syntagm stretching over not only most of the gospel narrative but extending beyond it:

A1: KG virtual ⇒ A2: KG actualized ⇒ A3: KG realized

The transition from a virtual to an actualized kingdom of God may itself be understood as an hierarchically embedded process (B) with the same articulation.

Similarly, the transition from an actualized to a realized kingdom of God may be considered to be such a process (C):[12]

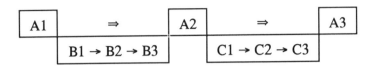

The expression "the time is fulfilled" refers to the completion of a process (B3), whereas "the kingdom of God has come near" refers on the one hand to the actualization phase (A2) and states on the other hand that the realizing action has begun (C2). A1 is an initial state of being where the kingdom of God is absent (non-X); A3 is the final state of being where the kingdom of God is present (X). A2 is a transitional phase, a grey zone, where the kingdom of God is both present and absent, and neither present nor absent. *It is within this liminal field on the threshold between possibility and reality that the gospel narrative's main events unfold.*

A narrative process aimed at the realization of a given state of being exists either as V, A, or R. Often the narrative will concern a complex hierarchy of narrative processes that exist in different phases, but if one looks at the superior process (A1, A2, A3), Jesus proclaims that the kingdom of God is actualized, i.e. is being realized.

An especially illustrative example of such a complex narrative process is given by the motif of *birth*. The narrative of Isaac's birth plays a central role in the Genesis stories about Abraham. It is sufficient here to consider basic features of a process that ends in his birth. The following information is relevant:

a)   Sarah is barren (Gen 11,30)
b)   God makes Sarah fertile (21,1)
c)   Sarah is made pregnant by Abraham (21,2)
d)   Sarah gives birth to the son Isaac (21,2)

A crucial concept is that it is God who opens and closes the womb (cf. 20,18). Sarah's barrenness thus indicates a state of fatal preservation (repression); motherhood is impossible. Through a factitive (causative) process of change, God makes Sarah fertile. What was previously impossible has now become possible, motherhood exists virtually (A1). But God has thereby played his part. Abraham and Sarah are themselves responsible for the embrace that is to ensure conception. The transition from fertile to pregnant, from virtual to actualized motherhood

---

[12] Cf. *Logique du récit*, p. 132, fig. 2.

(A2), is handled by an independent process (B). The pregnancy, however, is no guarantee of the birth of a fully developed foetus. There is a process (C) between conception and birth, a progressive becoming aimed at being, but which can be interrupted either voluntarily or involuntarily. The birth itself finally marks realized motherhood (A3). Motherhood is impossible for the barren Sarah; motherhood is virtual for the fertile Sarah. For the pregnant Sarah, motherhood is actualized, she is already/not yet a mother; for the Sarah who has borne her child, motherhood is realized. If one considers the child, that which has come into the world, which is realized in the course of events, it is characterized to begin with by being wished for, but as an impossible existence. God's factitive intervention which opens the womb gives the child a virtual existence, whereas the conception gives it an actualized existence. The birth finally marks the consummation as realized existence.

Definition of the process for the realization of the kingdom of God is crucial to an understanding of the gospel narrative's *eschatology*. Realization of the kingdom of God is a *future* event, however imminent it may be. In the same way, the realized motherhood is a future event, however far in her pregnancy the woman may be. But the process has commenced, the kingdom of God is coming into existence and therefore qualifies the present. To Sarah, the main contrast has been established between the impossible motherhood's epoch and the realized motherhood's epoch. The intermediate time, however, can be articulated in transitional phases. The beginning is the factitive act that makes motherhood possible. Then follows an intermediate period until fertilization exists. Then follows the period of pregnancy, with its special signs of the developing stages of the process (the first signs of life; the first premonitory pains), and finally comes the birth that concludes the course of events.

Despite chronology, the narrative process is recognized by virtue of its aspectual articulation: beginning/inchoateness, middle/durativeness and ending/terminativeness.[13] How long it is before Yahweh opens Sarah's womb is immaterial - provided it happens before the vital process is concluded. How long it is before Sarah conceives is likewise immaterial, but conception indicates that motherhood has come a step nearer. It is true that the pregnancy runs a certain time, but this is the time it takes for the fertilized egg to run through the process of development. It is not therefore *epochs* (eons; periods of time) but *process phases* that should have the attention of exegesis.[14]

The proclamation of the kingdom of God is given a presentic dimension because the pragmatic process of creation has already begun - God has passed to action - and because Jesus of Nazareth, selected and equipped by God, is the subject of doing responsible for that part of the process lying between baptism/

---

[13] Cf. *Sémiotique*, art. "Aspectualization".

[14] In accordance with the gospel narrative's own reticence concerning chronometries, cf. 13.32.

anointing and resurrection. The realization of the kingdom of God is not a process to be implemented only some time in the future, but an event that is already being realized, But only in the future will this process of creation be completed.[15]

2) *Subject of being*. The subject of being for the state/process referred to is anyone who is appointed as narratee by the proclamation. The message is not aimed at a third person A but is directed at the second person. Whoever hears the message, hears a message that does not apply to another but to himself. It is indeed characteristic that the being which is narrated concerns the narratee's being. Thereby he sees himself as portrayed. In this way the narrative determines the recipient, who sees himself as interpreted and semiotized by the narrated roles.

The word εὐαγγέλιον means a good or joyful message. When a message is qualified as joyful, good, it must mean that the content of the message, whatever it may be, is positive in the light of the recipient's situation. A joyful message is a proclamation that appoints the recipient as a favoured subject of being. But here also one must distinguish between what has occurred and what will occur. A completed process of change has in fact taken place when the subject of being's status changes from virtual to actualized beneficiary. The realization has moved a step nearer; a new phase (temporally: a new epoch) has begun. However, the intermediate state thereby established should not be confused with the final state of being intended.[16]

---

[15] Cf. Vincent Taylor: "the main emphasis lies upon the Kingdom as future", *The Gospel According to St. Mark*, London 1959, p. 114. Of course, the kingdom of God, or rather kingship/rule, as emphasized by, *inter alia*, Rudolf Bultmann, emerges in Jesus' wonder-works, but it should be stressed here that the presentic dimension in Mark's Gospel gets its value from the futuristic eschatology; cf. *Theologie des Neuen Testaments*, Tübingen (1958) 1968, pp. 2. As emphasized by Rudolf Pesch, it applies to Mark that "die Gottesherrschaft ist das ewige Leben", *Das Markusevangelium, 1. Teil*, p. 107; for eternal life, cf. Part 4, The Savior. But the awakening of Jairus' daughter is not an arising to eternal life. An overemphasis of the presentic dimension can easily lead to failure to appreciate the death's significance to the realization of the final salvation. Pesch, however, is not entirely unambiguous. When he writes, for example, about the kingdom of God: "Sie ist so nahe gerückt, daß kein Zeitzwischenraum mehr bleibt; die Wartezeit ist abgelaufen, der καιρός ausgefüllt.", ibidem, p. 102, he seems to agree with a presentic perception which is clearly contrary to the gospel narrative's information. The waiting time that has ended is the time when it was expected that God was to pass over to action and set the process in motion. However strong the expectation (cf. 13,30), the definitive realization of the kingdom of God has been eschatologically postponed. Cf. also Heinrich Baarlink's sober presentation in *Die Eschatologie der synoptischen Evangelien*, Stuttgart 1986, pp. 30; and Aage Pilgaard, "Gudsrigebegrebet i Markusevangeliet" (The Concept of Kingdom of God in the Gospel of Mark), Dansk Teologisk Tidsskrift 43. årg, København 1980, pp. 20.

[16] Willi Marxsen takes as his point of reference the *"opinio communis"*, "daß es sich hier [1,14f] um einen Sammelbericht handelt, dessen Formulierung auf den Evangelisten zurückgeht", *Der Evangelist Markus. Studien zur Redaktionsgeschichte des Evangeliums*, Göttingen 1959, p. 88. Since it is the redactor Mark who speaks, 1,14f is pronounced *after* Jesus' death and resurrection, so that the gospel of God and the gospel of Jesus Christ become identical: "Soweit Jesus (...) selbst Inhalt des Evangeliums ist, ist τοῦ θεοῦ in 1,14 eine christologische Aussage. Jesus ist das Evangelium Gottes" (p. 88). Marxsen thus reads the narrated enunciation as a narrating enunciation; that the kingdom of God has come near means that the Parousia is just around the corner. The call for repentance and belief does not therefore apply to the narrated persons in the narrate but to the narratee: "der Evangelist stellt dieses Wort nicht

3) *Subject of doing*. Grammatically, the expression τὸ εὐαγγέλιον τοῦ θεοῦ can be considered, now as an objective genitive, the gospel about God, now as a subjective genitive, the gospel from God.[17] As regards content, however, a both/and is concerned, since Jesus' proclamation does not only have its source in God but tells that God has passed to action. An event has taken place for which God is the subject of doing responsible. God has taken on the task of realizing his realm, his kingdom, and the process(es) to effect this change have already begun (by virtue of the anointing of Jesus).

To summarize, then, it can be said that Jesus' proclamation is the narrative about a process taking place which is aimed at realizing the kingdom of God. The subject of being for this proclamation is anyone who thereby sees himself appointed as narratee, and the subject of doing responsible for the reality-changing process is God (not the narrator himself but the fourth person B). But two questions have not as yet been clarified: 1) Is the actor Jesus entirely defined on the basis of the proclaimer role, or has he as pragmatic subject of doing an integrated task to resolve within the project to realize the kingdom of God? 2) Has the subject of being been given only a passive role as beneficiary, or is this itself the subject of doing responsible for a task to be realized? For the time being, however, these questions must be left unanswered.

2. The Consummation

In relation to the here-and-now of the narration, the gospel story tells not only about what has occurred but also about what is to occur. The overarching course of events that ends in the final coming of the kingdom of God is not consummated in the narrated world but only in the narrator's and the reader's world.

---

an den Anfang der Verkündigung des historischen Jesus, sondern an den Anfang der Verkündigung des Auferstandenen" (p. 89). Marxsen appreciates the metaphoric tension between the narrated and the narrating proclamation, but by virtue of his redaction-critical viewpoint he ends in an aporia. He may be right that it is not the historical Jesus who speaks but the redactor. But as a redaction-critic Marxsen never realizes that it is Mark as narrator who sustains the entire narrative, and that this narrative is split into narrate and narration. He fails thereby to appreciate the gospel story's narrative articulation, that there are limits to what the *narrative* Jesus can proclaim at the moment when he is still only an actualized Christ who is neither dead nor resurrected. Marxsen does not see that the kingdom of God (the Parousia) after the baptism/anointing merely exists as a *possibility* whose realization depends upon death on the cross and resurrection, whereas the kingdom of God (the Parousia) after death on the cross/resurrection exists as an eschatological *inevitability*. Classical exegesis' lack of knowledge of the narrative processes' modalization makes it unable to comprehend the gospel narrative's dynamic articulation. Thus Werner H. Kelber's assertion: "The time is fulfilled because the Kingdom has in fact made its arrival. Both the singular eschatological force of the initial time saying, and the conjunction of this time saying with a Kingdom saying suggests an interpretation of 1:15a in terms of present arrival and realized fulfilment: the eschatological time has been fulfilled and the Kingdom of God has arrived.", *The Kingdom in Mark. A New Place and a New Time*, Philadelphia 1974, p. 10, may be seen as an expression of this ineptitude. Kelber emphasizes that Mark is the only New Testament theologian who allows Jesus to make "the bold assertion: 'fulfilled has been the Time!'" (p. 9), but he does not see that here Jesus speaks of the end of the process (age or waiting time) which is followed by God's transition to action.

[17] Cf. Vincent Taylor, ibidem, p. 166.

In the narrated world, Jesus proclaims that the kingdom of God has come near (1,15), but emphasizes its final coming as a future eschatological event. Sometime in the listener's future the Son of Man will come in the glory of his Father and with the holy angels, and then the kingdom of God will have come with power (8,38; 9,1).

In Chapter 13, which may be considered as a farewell speech to the disciples, Jesus discloses what is to happen between resurrection and parousia. After a time of tribulation, which is not the end (τέλος) but only the beginning (ἀρχή; 13,5f) of the birth pangs (ὠδίν), more affliction will come culminating in a cosmic catastrophe: the sun darkens, the moon ceases to shine and the stars fall down, i.e. the heavens and the earth (Gen 1,1) come to an end (παρέρχομαι; 13,24.31), and then the Son of Man will come in clouds with great power and glory (13,26). It is stressed that the existing generation will not pass away (παρέρχομαι) until all these things have taken place (13,30).

The transition from the existing age (cf. Mt 12,32: ὁ αἰὼν οὗτος) to the age to come (10,30, ὁ αἰὼν ὁ ἐρχόμενος; Mt 12,32: ὁ αἰὼν ὁ μέλλων), i.e. to the kingdom of God, will occur by way of a catastrophe that allows this world to fall back into the chaos that reigned before God created it (cf. 13,19). The final coming of the kingdom of God, i.e. the realization of the kingdom of God, is the creation of a new age: *the kingdom of God is this new world.*

God's transition to action marks a pivotal point which separates between what was and what is. Considered as an independent process (B), this transition has caused a change in the subject of being's situation from the initial state non-X to the final state X. The progression is merely a first step within the overarching process (A) leading to the realization of the kingdom of God.

But as will be described in detail later this progression process must be understood within the framework of a superior protection process. An analysis of the proclamation's content, which is the message of the realization of the kingdom of God, must therefore take its point of reference in the situation in which the subject of being finds itself *before* God passes to action, i.e. before the baptism/anointing of Jesus. The degression process contained in the Protection is therefore initially isolated and considered as a simple, i.e. uncompounded, Degression:

DEGRESSOR	VICTIM

The initial situation is that the existing world is a state of being X which is orientated towards the state of being non-X. As victim, the world has entered into an on-going degression process directed towards destruction. The creation, what has been created in a broad sense, sees itself as threatened by destruction.

If what has been created is referred to as cosmos and the uncreated or over-thrown is referred to as chaos, then cosmos is orientated towards chaos. Narrative exegesis now has an opportunity to characterize this situation more specifically through an analysis of the modalization that characterizes the narrative process.

a. Factitive Processes and Modal States

The narrative is constituted of processes and states. The processes serve to preserve or change the states and thus refer to doing. The states indicate what is the case for a given subject at a given place at a given time, and refer in turn to being.

However, a distinction must be made between two kinds of process: there are the *operative* processes that aim at change or preservation of being, and the *factitive* processes that concern change or preservation of the modalization of being or doing.[18]

The factitive processes serve to preserve or change modal states that refer to the modal being of the subjects of doing and being. The operative processes take place within a modally established space; the factitive processes establish the modal spaces or worlds.

A given factitive doing establishes a modal state, a world which it will then be possible to change by, or preserve against, actions that imply a new modal transformation. If the subject of being's initially established modal state modalizes a state of being, desired by the same subject of being, as being impossible to achieve (cf. Sarah whose womb is closed), then a factitive change can consist in making this state of being possible (Yahweh opens Sarah's womb; which should not be confused with divine conception).

From a general viewpoint, a given modal state, a given world, is thus only one *possible world*.

b. Dynamic Modalities of Being

In a given, possible world, which is the narrative subject's world, this will be the subject of being for processes (V, A or R) that are either possible and evitable (avoidable), impossible or inevitable (unavoidable). The narrative subject's being has been modalized by the *dynamic* (cf. δύναμαι, δύναμις) modalities of being:[19]

---

[18] Cf. *Sémiotique*, art. "Factitivité"; A.J. Greimas, "Pour une théorie des modalités", *Du sens II*, Paris 1983, pp. 67.

[19] In contrast to, for example, having-to-be called alethic modalities and having-to-do called deontic modalities, Greimas names neither being-able-to-be nor being-able-to-do. The term dynamic modalities is suggested here, and a distinction is made between the dynamic modalities of being and of doing. Accordingly, this study does not distinguish between alethic and deontic modalities, but between deontic modalities of being and of doing.

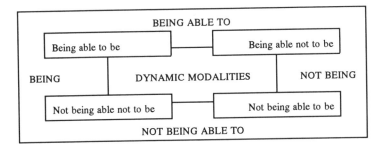

corresponding to:

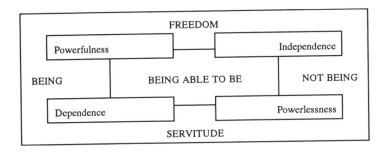

According to this modal category, a *non-realized being* can exist in four different dynamic ways:

- it may be *impossible* (ἀδύνατος), i.e. the subject of being is powerless, fixed in its initial state by virtue of a fatal course of preservation (repression or protection);

- it may be *inevitable*, i.e. the subject of being is dependent, it will enter the final state by virtue of a fatal course of change (degression or progression);

- it may be *possible* (δυνατός), i.e. the subject of being is powerful, the initial state can be changed (progression or degression);

- it may be *evitable*, i.e. the subject of being is independent, the initial state can be preserved (protection or repression).

"For mortals it is impossible (ἀδύνατος), but not for God; for God all things are (δυνατός) possible." reads 10,27. Quite independently of its context, this saying states that the difference between God and human beings is a fundamental difference in being able to. God knows only freedom, power and independence, the possible and the avoidable, whereas humankind's being able to has limits. Humankind thus finds itself placed in a world which is modalized in such a way that it appears at one and the same time as a latitude (being-able-to; freedom) and as a prison (not-being-able-to; lack of freedom, bondage).

c. The World as Victim to a Fatal Process of Degression

The narrative analysis of a subject's narrative process (virtualized, actualized, realized subject) involves an analysis of the associated modality problems. The modal situation in which the subject of being finds itself is considered as either satisfactory or unsatisfactory, either as a result of a preceding process of progression or degression. Narrative analysis must try to define the factitive process that has caused the existing dynamic modalization, and its first analytic operation must be to define the modal initial state.

From a given moment that marks a sudden change the created world sees itself modalized as a cosmos unable to continue to exist. The world is condemned to destruction ($\kappa\alpha\tau\acute{\alpha}\lambda\nu\sigma\iota\varsigma$), all will be thrown down (13,2; $\kappa\alpha\tau\alpha\lambda\acute{\nu}\omega$). The subject of being for this fatal process is humanity or humankind, which as virtual/actualized victim can only wait for the subject of doing responsible for the process of destruction itself to commence or accomplish the destruction already begun. The cosmic collapse is not due to fatigue in or corrosion of the supporting constructions but must be seen as God's punishment of sinful humankind. It is God who initiates the throwing down, he is the subject of doing responsible for the annihilation process, which is itself, however, founded in creation's revolt against the creator. As responsible subject of doing, humankind itself has an integrated role in this cosmic drama.

There is thus a modal space in which humankind is the subject of being for virtual or on-going degressive processes that cannot be neutralized. Annihilation is the fatal, degressive process *par excellence*; viewed as a state of being, nothingness is unavoidable and furthermore irreversible. According to the narrative, this modalized, narrative space exists as an objective fact.

The narrative subjects which are defined by this world may have a realistic or unrealistic understanding of its nature, but the narrative supremely decides what is reality. A world that is modalized in such a way that destruction is inevitable and definitive is ruled by Death, it is the realm of Death. The word $\beta\alpha\sigma\iota\lambda\epsilon\acute{\iota}\alpha$, kingdom, rule, refers indeed to a possible world whose subordinate members see themselves as set in a *modalized space*.

Powerlessness/dependence is relative. What is impossible for one subject of doing may be possible for another. In the final instance, everything is indeed possible for God. When the modal status of a future state of being is thus defined as inevitable (unavoidable), it means that the on-going course of change cannot be interrupted by a subject of being that undergoes the transitive process, since this subject is cut out of the game as an operative subject of doing. There is one world in which humankind is first a virtualized, then an actualized, and finally a realized victim of a fatal degression process which ends in annihilation.

In this world produced, nothingness as a state of being will be defined by fatal preservation that is irreversible. Opposed to nothingness or Nothing is not the existing world but the kingdom of God which represents the true Being. The initial situation is, then, that the realization of Nothing, which already/not yet exists, is inevitable (unavoidable), whereas the realization of the kingdom of God is impossible.

The narrative analysis can be carried further, in that exegesis inquires about the factitive process that has caused an existing world's modal nature. If the narrative has nothing specific to say about this, one must examine whether it is possible, on the basis of other explicit information, to reconstruct an answer. If this approach is not practicable, other related texts' view of this matter must be examined. In the context of an examination of the Adam-Christ typology's narrative basis, an opportunity to discuss this question in detail will be given later.[20]

d. The Favoured World

From the moment when God passes to action and selects Jesus of Nazareth as his Son, the initial world of suffering humankind is remodalized. What was impossible, i.e. the realization of the kingdom of God, has now become possible (cf. the narrative of Abraham and Sarah). According to the narrative, it is an objective fact that world's nature has become different by virtue of a factitive course of change, a modal transformation.

The subject of being was initially a virtual, actualized, or realized victim of a *fatal* degression process. Because of a process of change that has not yet been defined, it finally becomes a virtual, actualized, or realized victim of a *possible* or *avoidable* degression process.

The transition from the unavoidable to the avoidable means that the degression process can be neutralized and that the subject of being thus adopts the role of virtual beneficiary of a virtual protection process:

BENEFICIARY	PROTECTOR

It is important to observe that the possibility of protection is not a matter of course. The operative protection process is preceded by a factitive process

---

through which the subject of being's world is changed, not pragmatically but modally:

Initial state	⇒	Final state
Protection impossible		Protection possible

When Jesus proclaims that the kingdom of God has come near, he proclaims that God has passed to action, that a factitive process of change *has taken place*, and that protection (salvation) is possible. He proclaims: a) that the subject of being is no longer a victim of a fatal (unavoidable) annihilation but merely a virtual victim of an evitable (avoidable) annihilation; b) that the subject of being is a virtual beneficiary by virtue of an on-going protection process (A2) and already the real beneficiary of a realized, factitive progression (B3; modal transformation).

In the protection narrative genre, it follows that the subject of being will initially be doubly defined, on the one hand as a virtual or actualized victim and on the other hand as a virtual beneficiary. It will, however, often be important for exegesis to ask about the factitive process or processes that have established the sphere of possibility in which the narrative has its beginning. It is thus decisive to the understanding of Jesus' proclamation of the gospel of God that the world has been remodalized. *By the anointing of Jesus in the context of baptism, the impossible has become possible.*

e. Cosmology and Ontology

Annihilation must be seen in the light of creation. A series of possibilities should be considered:

1)   By God's hand the created world is characterized by a fatal preservation process (protection), and cannot therefore be annihilated.

2)   By God's hand the created world is characterized by a fatal process of change (degression), and cannot therefore be preserved.

The concept of a fatal progression process or repression process is excluded, since what is created is self-sufficient in having been created. But there is reason to consider the following:

3)   By God's hand the created world is characterized by evitable
     annihilation, i.e. possible preservation and evitable preserva-
     tion, i.e. possible annihilation.

Protection, maintenance of what is created, is either inevitable 1), impossible 2),
or possible 3); degression, annihilation of what is created, is either inevitable 2),
impossible 1), or possible 3).

Since the work of creation is threatened by annihilation at a given moment,
the first possibility 1) makes no sense. One must therefore decide on a
deterministic reading 2) in which annihilation is seen as an inherent necessity in
what is created or an *indeterministic* reading 3) in which annihilation is
considered as an inherent possibility in what is created. In the first case 2),
created humankind has no role other than to be the victim of a virtual or on-going
degression process. But in the other case 3) humankind plays an integrated role
in the cosmic course of events, since only an act on the part of Man (Adam) will
be able to effect the factitive transition from possible to unavoidable annihilation.

The gospel narrative is largely silent as regards the difference between what
exists and the new world. But the concept of an eternal life in the age to come
(10,30) must mean that this new age must itself be eternal (cf. 2 Pet 1,11) and
thus represent a *definitive cosmos* characterized by fatal preservation: annihilation
will be impossible in this world (cf. l)).

In contrast to the new imperishable (ἄφθαρτος) world stands the old
perishable (φθαρτός) world, which as such represents a *provisional cosmos*. In
contrast to these two worlds there stands, then, a *definitive chaos* characterized
by fatal preservation (repression), since no re-creation is possible, and a
provisional chaos where re-creation is unavoidable, i.e. characterized by fatal
progression. Paradigmatically, the following cosmological state of being can be
distinguished within the gospel story's narrative universe:

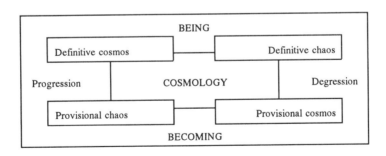

(cf. 3,29; Mt 25,31ff: eternal life versus eternal fire, eternal punishment; 2 Thess
1,9)

There is an overarching narrative process for which the realization of the kingdom of God is the final objective; i.e. a process in relation to which any other narrative process sees itself as defined. This course of events must be linked to a principal subject of doing (God) and a principal subject of being (humankind), which remains itself from beginning to end. The relationship between creation and re-creation can be recognized only because these two events belong to one and the same process of change, which is itself recognizable only by virtue of its aspectual articulation: beginning (inchoateness), middle (durativeness) and ending (terminativeness). It is true that the beginning of time and the ending of time are connected, but only in that they are related to one and same process, which in turn appears as the syntagmatization of a paradigmatic structure of signification.

If a course of events can be said to be concluded only when it has reached the objective for which it was initiated, then God's creation is completed only by virtue of the establishment of the kingdom of God. Retrospectively, the kingdom of God appears to be the creator's objective, the intended state of being that according to the gospel narrative's ontology represents true being.[21]

The narrative's cosmology (its implicit theory of the created) is congruent with its narrative ontology:[22]

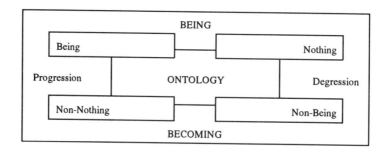

in that the mutual relationship between the cosmological and ontological terms are homologous: Definitive cosmos ≅ Being; Definitive chaos ≅ Nothing; Provisional chaos ≅ Non-Nothing; Provisional cosmos ≅ Non-Being.

This world, the existing world of the listener, then sees itself identified by the proclamation as an ontic state of being characterized by anomie (Non-Being), since it is not in accordance with its purpose. Hunger, sickness and death (cf. the wonder narrative) bear witness to this. However, this state of being is an

---

[21] Cf. Mt 25,34: "the kingdom prepared (ἑτοιμάζω) for you from the foundation of the world (ἀπὸ καταβολῆς κόσμου)"; Mt 13,35: "I will proclaim what has been hidden from the foundation of the world".

[22] Cf. below C.4.

intermediate state, a state of becoming, more specifically a degressively determined state of becoming that is fatally orientated towards Nothing. Against this background, the proclamation of the coming of the kingdom of God is initially the proclamation of a possible salvation from this threatening annihilation, which is now no longer unavoidable. It is true that heaven and earth will pass away, but this chaos is merely a transition to the creation of the kingdom of God (definitive cosmos). In the same way as Jesus himself must endure death to obtain eternal life, this world must suffer a chaos in order to rise again as the kingdom of God. Matthew 19,28 speaks very accurately about a rebirth ($\pi\alpha\lambda\iota\gamma\gamma\epsilon\nu\epsilon\sigma\iota\alpha$) which corresponds to the reference to tumultuous tribulations as birth pangs (13,8). The gospel narrative is otherwise silent as regards the specific circumstances.

He for whom the existing world is orientated towards a definitive annihilation will be able to consider whether the on-going disintegration process is not yet concluded because of protection. The on-going process may be perceived as obstructed or delayed so that this - without being abolished - does not reach its definitive objective.

A kind of balance is thus possible in which disintegration corresponds to building-up, as when generations die out but succeed in reproducing themselves before this (with Adam, death entered the world, but Eve became the mother of all living, Gen 3,20). Such a deferred eschatology in which God sustains the created by postponing the definitive annihilation thus already has the character of a salvation project (cf. God's covenant with Noah, Gen 8,20 - 9,17). If the subject of being experiences especially violent examples of the devastation of destructive forces (earthquake, war, starvation or the like), it may interpret these events as a sign of abolition of this balance. Annihilation no longer encounters resistance, and will therefore soon realize its definitive objective. The subject of being is then stricken by a negative, apocalyptic expectation, and will desperately seek a possible way out.

C. The Narrative Proclaimer Roles B)

1. Persuasion

Proclamation is not only a simple conveyance of knowledge but a *process of influence* directed against the narratee in his capacity of virtual subject of doing. The proclamation "The time is fulfilled, and the kingdom of God has come near" is indeed followed immediately by a double imperative: "repent and believe in the good news" (1,15).

In the role of *influencer* or *manipulator* ($\pi\epsilon\iota\theta\omega\nu$ - $\pi\epsilon\iota\theta\omega$ - $\pi\epsilon\iota\sigma\mu\omega\nu\dot{\eta}$), the proclaimer exercises influence upon a recipient with the intention of provoking a reaction from him. Fundamentally, the influence consists either in inducing a virtual subject of doing to pass to action, *persuasion*, or to induce him to refrain from action, *dissuasion*; and like any other subject of doing the influencer can act voluntarily or involuntarily, reflexively or transitively.[23]

The influencer may intervene in various elements of the decision process through which the person influenced must pass:

a)   a first element, where the virtual subject of doing must take a decision on whether the opportunity is given (or is not given) to take on the task. What is concerned here is the dynamic modalization;

b)   a second element, where the subject conceives its action-promoting or action-preventing motives. What is concerned here is the bulistic (wanting to) and deontic (having to) modalization, cf. below;

c)   a third element, where the subject considers whether the means necessary for carrying out the task are available or not. What is concerned here is *savoir-faire*, competence to know how and why, to know the way by which the objective can be reached, to know about method.

The action as *performance* presupposes a *competence*, i.e. all the conditions and presuppositions, which make possible the execution of action. As one can see, this competence is an organized whole of modalities: being-able-to-do, wanting-to-do, having-to-do and knowing-how-to-do (*savoir faire*).[24]

Establishing competence is in itself a factitive doing, which is referred to on the one hand as *manipulation* (using the word in a non-derogatory sense about a person's influence on other people with a view to making them perform a certain

---

[23] Cf. *Logique du récit*, pp. 242.

[24] Cf. *Sémiotique*, art. "Compétence" and "Performance".

action), and on the other hand as *influence*.[25] But one should distinguish the more heavy-handed (dynamic) manipulation that consists of restricting or extending the acting person's latitude from the cognitive-affective influence aimed at conceiving of motives and action strategies.

Analysis of the beginning of the process thus includes an investigation of influence and competence. By revealing the competence, the narrative explains the action; but by revealing the influence it explains the competence.

In recounting, therefore, that people from the whole Judean countryside and all the people of Jerusalem were going out to John the Baptist and were baptized by him in the river Jordan, confessing their sins (1,5), it may be said that these subjects of doing have passed to action, because they a) believe that the opportunity is given to take on this task (it is possible to obtain forgiveness of sins); b) wish and find it correct to obtain forgiveness of sins; and c) know how this objective can be reached, i.e. through John the Baptist at the River Jordan. The motives for action can in turn be understood only as a result of a process of influence, the Baptist's proclamation of the baptism of repentance for the forgiveness of sins (1,4).[26]

Jesus preaches "The gospel of God", he informs that "The time is fulfilled and the kingdom of God has come near". But he also tries to persuade the narratee to "believe in the good news", to believe ($\pi\iota\sigma\tau\epsilon\acute{u}\omega$) this message. The call to repent ($\mu\epsilon\tau\alpha\nuo\acute{\epsilon}\omega$, $\mu\epsilon\tau\acute{\alpha}\nuo\iota\alpha$, cf. $\nuo\acute{\epsilon}\omega$, $\nuo\hat{u}\varsigma$) is indeed aimed at the narratee as a pragmatic subject of doing, but what is primarily concerned is a change in the latter's competence controlling the transition to pragmatic action.

Repentance is then fundamentally a cognitive-affective change in the subject of being's sentiments, which stands or falls with belief in the gospel.

2. The Believer

During the process of influence, the informing narrator exercises a persuasive doing aimed at making the informed narratee think or believe that this or that is the case, here that "The time is fulfilled, and the kingdom of God has come near.".

The narratee, however, is not just a passive, recipient body who allows himself unhindered to be convinced of anything, but a competent subject who exercises an *interpretative* doing, which ends in an epistemic judgment concerning the circumstances - processes and states - presented to him by way of information. It is momentous that the veridiction and the simulation have the same form, i.e. that lying is a possibility. For this reason the narratee will never

---

[25] Cf. *Sémiotique*, art. "Manipulation"; Greimas prefers the term *manipulation*; Bremond the term *influence*.

[26] It should perhaps be emphasized that the analysis does not consist in "identifying oneself" with the narrated persons but in making more explicit the narrative rationality of the gospel story.

be able to endorse the truth of the information on the basis of the communicative act itself. This communication does not exist where the possibility of lying has been abolished, and therefore realization of the process of influence presupposes an implicit or explicit *fiduciary* contract, an implied or declared relationship of trust between the parties involved.[27] Even if the narratee is informed and to this extent knowing, he cannot know whether Jesus is telling the truth, whether the kingdom of God has really come near, but it must be believed.

a. The Epistemic Modalities

The unknowing, i.e. the non-informed subject of being, has good reason to refrain from adopting an attitude towards the case concerned. The informed subject of being, however, will think and believe on the basis of his preassumptions that he finds himself in the state of being X or non-X; - or would be uncertain about where he finds himself, since the concessive and conceding doubt (perhaps, probably, presumably) and the deprecatory and rejecting doubt (scarcely, probably not) hold each other in check.

The subject of being that hears Jesus' proclamation of the gospel of God may thus either arrive at the conviction that a new modal state exists (believing-to-be, i.e. the narratee believes that the kingdom of God has come near, that salvation is a possibility) or think that everything is as it was before (believing-not-to-be). Or there may be doubt about what is really the case (not-believing-not-to-be/not-believing-to-be):[28]

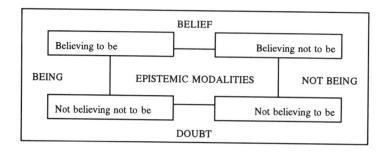

---

[27] Cf. *Sémiotique*, art. "Fiduciaire (contrat, relation -)".

[28] Cf. *Sémiotique*, art. "Épistémiques (modalités -)"; A.J. Greimas, "Le contrat de véridiction", *Du sens II*, Paris 1983, pp. 103, and "Le savoir et le croire: un seul univers cognitif", ibidem pp. 115. It is suggested here that the four epistemic positions be interpreted as follows:

A)   Ne believes that X is the case; i.e. Ne believes that X is not-able-not-to-be the case, it is necessary, given; Ne is certain that X.

C)   Ne believes that X is not the case; i.e. Ne believes that X is not-able-to-be the case, it is impossible; Ne is certain that non-X.

B)   Ne does not believe that X is the case; i.e. Ne believes that X is able-not-to-be the case, it is unnecessary, not given; Ne is uncertain whether non-X.

D)   Ne does not believe that X is not the case; i.e. Ne believes that X is able-to-be the case, it is possible; Ne is uncertain whether X.

The subject of being who thinks that he finds himself in the state of being X (salvation is possible) or in the state of being non-X (salvation is not possible) may lose his conviction.

The subject of being may be *distracted,* someone or something diverts his attention (for example "the cares of the world, and the lure of wealth, and the desire for other things", cf. 4,19); he perhaps *forgets* what matters. On the other hand there is the *reminder* (*remembrance,* cf. 8,18), which as a counteraction thereto serves to recall, preserve and retain the awareness that the subject of being had about his state of being (cf. μιμνήσκω, μνημονεύω, ὑπομιμνήσκω, ἀναμιμνήσκω/ἀνάμνησις, for example Lk 22,19; 1 Cor 11,25; cf. κατέχω, τηρέω et al.; cf. also καθεύδω - διεγείρω - γρηγορέω).

The subject of being may be exposed to a *denial* that is aimed at making him change his mind from X to non-X or vice versa. This initiative may be at variance with an *affirmation* (of the first opinion) and a *counter-denial* (of the denial). Cf., for example the mutual rebuke (ἐπιτιμάω) in 8,32f. And finally the subject of being can be made to lose his composure by an initiative, which seeks to raise doubts in his mind (cf. Gen 3,1, "Did God say, ..."). The narrative subject may thus assume, reject, preserve, or abandon an opinion.[29]

b. The Clear-Sighted and the Blind

It is now possible to introduce the question of the truth of conviction. If the narrator says that X is the case ("Protection is possible"/"God has passed to action"), and X is in fact the case in the narrated reality, then a *successful veridiction* exists if the narratee believes that X is the case, and he then appears in the role of the sighted (ὁ βλέπων) or *clear-sighted.* In the opposite case an *unsuccessful veridiction* is concerned, and the narratee appears in the role of the blind (ὁ τυφλός).[30]

If the narrator says that X is the case, but X is not in fact the case in the narrated reality, then a *successful simulation* exists if the narratee believes that X is the case (blindness, τυφλότης). In the opposite case, an *unsuccessful simulation* (clear-sightedness, βλέμμα) is concerned.

The subject of being who has not yet heard Jesus' proclamation of the gospel of God believes himself to be in the modal state of non-X, where protection is impossible, although in reality he is in the modal state of X, where protection is possible. This is then a realized victim of an unintended simulation and a virtual victim of a dissimulation. But he is at the same time virtual beneficiary of a veridiction, i.e. the proclamation.

---

[29] Cf. *Logique du récit,* pp. 148.

[30] Cf. 8,22ff and 10,46ff which encircle the central disciple-teaching.

If he rejects the truth (believing-not-to-be X), he simultaneously confirms the lie (preservation of believing-to-be non-X); preservation may be specified here as a repression of the process of truth that has not reached its objective. In this blind subject's own self-knowledge, protection against the lie is of course concerned. If the clear-sighted accepts the truth (believing-to-be X), then he rejects the lie at the same time (believing-not-to-be non-X). The veridiction process then emerges as a process of change, specifically as progression.

A subject that finds himself in an untruth will then either maintain this state while rejecting the truth (repression) or change this by accepting the truth (progression).

Similarly, a subject that initially finds himself in the truth could maintain this by rejecting the lie (protection) or change it by accepting the lie (degression).

Believing-to-be X and believing-to-be non-X have the same form, likewise veridiction and simulation. In a value-perspective, however, the narrative will select one as belief, another as disbelief, corresponding to the roles of the *believer* (πιστός - πιστεύω - πίστις) and the *disbeliever* (ἄπιστος - ἀπιστέω - ἀπιστία).

As already referred to, the influence consists in persuading a subject either to act or to fail to act. An active aspect of the subject of being's role thus asserts itself, since he allows himself to be considered as a virtual subject of doing at any time. If the narratee is convinced that protection is impossible, he sees no reason to accept the task, the programme of action that involves repentance. If, however, he believes in the possibility of protection, he also sees therein an opportunity to pass to action.

Let it be assumed that the opportunity is in fact given. Exposed to a veridiction, the narratee will then either think that the opportunity is given to him (confirmatory clear-sightedness) or is not given to him (negating blindness). Exposed to a negated veridiction, the narratee will correspondingly think that either the opportunity is given to him (negating clear-sightedness) or is not given to him (confirmatory blindness).

Let it be assumed then that the opportunity is in fact not given. Exposed to a simulation, the narratee will then either think that the opportunity is given to him (confirmatory blindness) or is not given to him (negating clear-sightedness). Exposed to a negating simulation, the narratee will correspondingly either think that the opportunity is given to him (negating blindness) or is not given to him (confirmatory blindness).

Negation of the veridiction leads into the negated veridiction; negation of the negated veridiction then leads back to the veridiction. A corresponding movement applies to simulation.

But these two loops are at the same time connected by virtue of the relation non-X/X (opportunity not given/opportunity given). The negated veridiction establishes simulation; the negated simulation establishes veridiction:

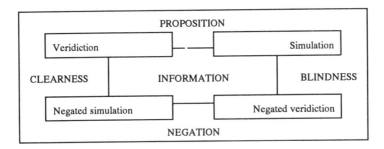

It may seem somewhat disingenuous to refer to the two epistemic roles, the believer and the disbeliever, as the *clear-sighted* and the *blind*, since it is of course only in retrospect that they appear as such. As long as it is a question of belief they are both equally blind, and the designations refer solely to a superior authority, which knows the truth in the narrated world. But regarded from the side of the proclaimer, this distinction corresponding to the difference between trust and distrust or obedience/disobedience (cf. πείθομαι, πεποίθητις; πειθαρχέω; ἀπειθέω, ἀπείθεια) is meaningful.

The problem for the narratee is that he finds himself in a dilemma: if he fails to act he will thereby either reveal his wisdom (φρόνησις, σοφία, γνῶσις) or his folly (ἀφροσύνη, μωρία, ἀγνωσία); if he acts he will thereby similarly reveal either his wisdom or his folly. If the opportunity is given but he fails to act, or if the opportunity is not given but he passes to action, he reveals himself as a fool (ἄφρων, μωρός). The narratee does not know, *cannot know*, whether this is a trap that the narrator - intentionally or unintentionally - has set.

If an episteme (ἐπιστήμη: information, insight, understanding, knowledge) is understood as information on the nature of the world objectively acceptable in a society, it becomes clear that the narratee has not only to choose between two equal opportunities but must choose between an opportunity, which is confirmed by the prevailing episteme (protection is impossible) and an opportunity, which is rejected by this (protection is possible). Doubly interpellated, he is thus up against an opposition within himself, which must be overcome. Against this background, his faith in the possibility of protection emerges immediately as stupidity, and his passage to action as discreditable, shameful. But in God's eyes the same act by which he displays his faith must appear as a glorifying act confirming the alternative episteme, which is then verified by the resurrection of Jesus.[31]

---

[31] Or perhaps rather the meeting with the resurrected one (cf. 14,28; 16,7). It is worth noting that the gospel narrative shows the improbability of its own message. It is not only the modern reader who experiences the conflict; the resistance is given from the outset. The difference between the narrate's and the narration's narratee consists fundamentally in that the meeting with the resurrected one will be able to verify the proclamation to the former (cf. Jn 20,24ff), whereas the latter is thrown on the delayed

3. The Good News

Based on the information in 1,14f, it seems impossible to define the narratee more specifically. Proclamation address an appeal to a general or implicit recipient, a role that will be assigned to anyone interpellated by the announcement. This narratee role can, however, be characterized in more detail by a reconstruction that builds on the knowledge of the narrative roles which must be assumed in the proclamation situation.

God's message is a gospel, good news, and thus thematizes a value-per-spective. Besides the cognitive or epistemic dimension of faith (the mind as the seat of thought), which concerns the dynamic mode of the proclamation's content, the affective dimension of faith appears (the mind, the heart, as the seat of affection, mood), which concerns the subject's *passion*.[32]

In the capacity of subject of being, the narratee fundamentally perceives his actual state of being (descriptive or modal) as satisfying or unsatisfying (cf. χορτάζω vs. πεινάω; πλήρης vs. κενός; περισσεύω vs. ὑστερέω). The satisfying state is desired, whereas the unsatisfying state is feared.

If the subject of being considers his initial state, i.e. his existing state of being, as satisfying (X), he will consider a possible final state as unsatisfying (non-X). In this situation, he will desire protection and fear degression (the healthy person desires the preservation of life and fears sickness and death).

But if the subject of being finds the initial state unsatisfying (non-X), imperfect, he will desire a possible final state as satisfying (X). In this situation, he will desire progression and fear repression (the sick person desires healing and fears processes that may obstruct this).

a. The Bulistic Modalities of Being

Desire and fear, satisfaction and dissatisfaction, refer to the subject of being's own value-interest, his existential involvement, that is to be found articulated according to the *bulistic* modal category (cf. βούλομαι, wanting, wishing ≅ θέλω):[33]

---

parousia.

[32] The word "passion" is ambiguous; it means passion, intense feeling, inclination, but also suffering, agony and death. The word πάθος/πάθημα has the same ambivalence, and means on the one hand suffering, now bodily pain, now what one is encountering, fate, and on the other hand state of the spirit, zeal, affect, for example love and hate. The Passion is the story of Jesus' suffering and death, his pain and his fate. As regards his sentiments or states of mind the narrative gives little information, but the Gethsemane incident, for example, contains information on this (cf. 14,34: "I am deeply grieved, even to death"). It is the states of mind that clearly cannot be separated from the subject's fate, which for semiotics refers to the subject's passion. These express how the subject relates to its own situation, its being, and it must be stressed that the term "passion" thus includes both the positive (e.g. joy/love/desire) and the negative (e.g. sorrow/hate/fear) affects. Passion relates to the subject's existential relationship to being, i.e. its modal existence. Cf. A.J. Greimas, J. Courtés, *Sémiotique. Dictionnaire raisonné de la théorie du langage, Tome 2*, Paris 1986, art. "Passion"; A.J. Greimas, "De la modalisation de l'être", *Du sens II*, Paris 1983, pp. 93.

[33] Cf. *Sémiotique*, art. "Vouloir" and "Modalité".

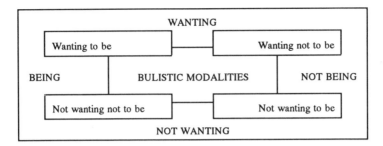

corresponding to

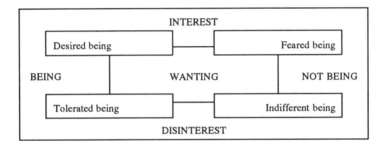

Viewed in relation to a future state of being (resulting from realization or deactualization), a process of change or preservation is experienced either as progression/repression or as degression/protection, and the final state is seen either as satisfactory or unsatisfactory. If the state of being is seen as satisfactory, the subject of being sees itself as *favoured* (*beneficiary*); in the opposite case, as *disfavoured* (*victim*).[34]

The bulistic modalities concern the subject of being's own subjective evaluation of the value of the state of being. In an interpretative acquisition of its reality, the narrative subject evaluates his fate, the destiny of his existence, and appears as such in the role of narrator of his own story since this interpretation and the view or perception resulting therefrom is narratively organized.

The subject of being's own interpretation of his state of being and the perception of his existence resulting therefrom may, however, be incorrect, and it is the narrative that supremely decides whether the interpretation is true or false, whether it *in reality*, the reality established by the narrative, is favoured or disfavoured.

The good news presupposes that the narratee experiences his actual state of being as defective. It is spoken to the starving, the sick, the possessed, the lost,

---

[34] Cf. *Logique du récit*, pp. 153.

i.e. a subject of being that is victim of degression and/or repression. The proclaimer thus interprets or semiotizes the narratee's existence, in that he defines the existential roles of this. But it is not certain that the narratee shares the proclaimer's value concept. He perhaps gives more weight to the existing state of being's relative abundance in the light of an inevitable annihilation ("Let us eat and drink, for tomorrow we die", 1 Cor 15,32). Or he is in two minds: desires the coming of the kingdom of God but nevertheless clings to this life (cf., for example, Rom 7,4ff or Mk 14,32ff).

As regards the subject of being that perceives himself as victim of an on-going degression process and as such is oppressed by anxiety and sorrow, the proclamation of God's passage to action, which establishes this as already/not yet favoured, is good news. The joy (and sorrow) appears to characterize the subject of being's passion, where realization *has taken place*. Sarah can thus rejoice that God has made her fertile. But at this moment she can also be looking forward to the birth of the child, although here the joy is anticipatory and inseparably connected with anxiety about how the realization of the remaining sub-processes in the course of events will fare. The joy can overwhelm her again when she feels the first signs of life, i.e. as a reaction to a realized sub-process. Finally there is the joy of having come through the birth and of the healthy child. Although one can look forward to something not yet realized, this anticipatory joy, which may well prove unfounded, must be distinguished from the actual joy caused by the accomplishment of a progression or protection process. Similarly, sorrows may be anticipated, but again the actual sorrow is caused by the accomplishment of a degression or repression process.

The Christian passion is the essence of Christian existence. The call to imitate (cf. 8,34ff), which involves persecution (13,9ff), encompasses suffering and death, but to the narrated persons as well as to the later Christians the passion is first and foremost zeal, an unceasing wavering between hope and fear, between joy and sorrow, which arises from the waiting period between promise and fulfilment. The presentic eschatology is founded on the Christian existence as *modal existence*.

b. Hope and Fear

The subject of being's affective frame of mind may be changed or preserved through influence. A subject of being which, for example, thinks that the actual state of being is satisfactory may be exposed to an influence, guiding or misguiding, which makes him change his perception. A subject of being which considers that he is in an unsatisfactory and hopeless situation (fatal repression or degression) may, through influence, be awakened to a hope that is either well-founded (veridiction) or unfounded (simulation).[35]

---

[35] Cf. *Logique du récit*, pp. 156.

Affective influence upon the subject of being will often involve the identification of a not-yet-realized state of being, as in Jesus' proclamation of the gospel of God. This virtual or actualized state of being is anticipated by the subject of being with positive or negative expectation ($\pi\rho\sigma\sigma\delta\sigma\kappa\acute{\iota}\alpha$). Either with *hope* ($\grave{\epsilon}\lambda\pi\acute{\iota}\varsigma$), if he anticipates a satisfaction, or with *fear* ($\phi\acute{o}\beta\sigma\varsigma$), if he anticipates an unsatisfactory state of being (if no indifference or ambivalence arises). According to the further circumstances, hope or fear is awakened, nourished, weakened or extinguished.[36]

Hope/fear may prove to be unfounded or well-founded. The narrative decides unappealably what has reason for being, and without discussion adjusts the subject of being's perception of reality, cf., for example, the rebuking of Peter.

The affective frames of mind, primarily hope and fear, refer to motives caused by outside events that have the form of influence. The narrative is sometimes content to establish a given attitude of the subject of being without explaining its origin, but it can also inform about the influence that leads to the conception of this motive. When it says of Joseph of Arimathea that he was waiting ($\pi\rho\sigma\sigma\delta\acute{\epsilon}\chi\sigma\mu\alpha\iota$) for "the kingdom of God" (15,43), the gospel narrative is content to establish his attitude; it gives no explicit explanation of how it was conceived. But on the basis of the hermeneutic context principle it is clear that his conviction results from the meeting with Jesus of Nazareth.

The hope of obtaining a satisfactory state of being constitutes, for example, the motive for the transition to action. In revealing the motive the narrative explains the action, but in revealing the presupposed influence it explains the motive. In the religious narrative every action is in principle meaningful, and therefore presupposes a motive (an objective, a purpose), which presupposes an influence.

It is clear that whoever desires a being does not at the same time fear the same being. The being desired by the narrative subject is indeed considered as Being, whereas the feared being is seen as Non-being. Whatever is of positive value to the subject cannot at the same time and in the same respect have negative value for the same subject. According to the bulistic modal system of being, a narrative subject can, if non-wanting is disregarded, either desire or fear a being X. A subject that desires being X can at the same time fear a second, a third, etc. being that is different from X, but this is literally another story. Because within an on-going narrative process fear seems only to apply to a being Y, which exactly appears as a correlate to being X, i.e. Y = non-X. Whoever is in extremis and fears death desires life. Whoever fears sickness desires health.

---

[36] Besides the thematic roles of doing the thematic roles of being can be distinguished, which may be referred to as *pathemic* roles, cf. $\pi\acute{\alpha}\theta\eta\mu\alpha$; *Sémiotique II*, art. "Pathémique (rôle -)". The states of mind are unstable and undergo changes which demand preservation initiatives. Besides factitive, cognitive and pragmatic processes pathemic processes may thus be expected, which for example revive the fainted hope.

Seducer and Intimidator

The influence directed against the subject's bulistic modalization appears, now as *seduction*, now as *intimidation*. Seduction refers to an influence that tries to evoke desire for a state of being (wanting-to-be) and the will to realize this (wanting-to-do). Intimidation is in turn an influence that tries to evoke fear of a state of being (wanting-not-to-be) and a reluctance to realize this (wanting-not-to-do). The subject of doing (the proclaimer) of the influence of the subject's wanting is referred to, now as *seducer*, now as *intimidator*. Here also a distinction may of course be made between reflexive/transitive and voluntary/involuntary influence.[37]

Desire and fear have a content that more specifically determines the influence. In its most general form, seduction (or intimidation) consists of evoking the anticipation of a satisfactory (or unsatisfactory) state of being with no further explanation of its possible realization.[38] In its more concrete form, the seduction, like any other influence, can be defined on the basis of a series of parameters: 1) the narrative process is a virtual, actualized or realized progression/protection; 2) the subject of being is the narrator, the narratee or a third person A; 3) the subject of doing is the narrator, the narratee the third person A or a fourth person B.

As proclaimer of the gospel of God, Jesus appears in the role of seducer, since he tries to evoke (or nourish) a desire for a state of being, the kingdom of God, and the will to realize or take part in this, cf. the call to repent. If the proclamation is groundless, if the proclaimer simulates, voluntarily or involuntarily, the seduction is a beguilement, a misguidance (ἀπατῶν - ἀπατάω - ἀπάτη; πλάνος - πλανάω - πλάνη); but if veridiction exists this is guidance (ἡγεμών/ἡγέομαι; ὁδηγός/ὁδηγέω; καθηγητής/καθηγέομαι). Without being quite identical therewith, the role of seducer may be said to correspond to the role of *the promising* (ἐπαγγέλλων - ἐπαγγέλλω - ἐπαγγελία). Jesus proclaims that God has passed to action, but he promises that the kingdom of God has come near and will see full realization within a foreseeable future.

Intimidation, however, corresponds to the proclamation of judgment. Here, the narratee is not interpellated on the desire for a satisfactory state of being but on the fear of an unsatisfactory state of being. Thus, John the Baptist's proclamation of repentance-baptism for the forgiveness of sins seem to stress the possibility of avoiding the wrath to come (cf. Mt 3,7f; Lk 3,7f): unless you repent you will be damned; on the contrary, Jesus' proclamation emphasizes God's love: if you repent you will share in the kingdom of God. This difference

---

[37] Cf. *Logique du récit*, pp. 264. "Seduction" is generally understood to mean leading astray, beguiling, i.e. an enticement to do something wrong (especially used about erotic relationships). Here, however, seduction refers to any guidance which is founded on the desire of the guided one.

[38] Cf. newspaper horoscopes of the type: "You have been low for a long time, but the wind is turning and you have every reason to be optimistic!".

is not unimportant, but it should be borne in mind that the Baptist's intimidating proclamation is nevertheless aimed at salvation and that Jesus' promising proclamation does not abolish the possibility of damnation.

John the Baptist

Information about John the Baptist is to be found in 1,1-15; 2,18; 6,14-29; 8,28; (9,12) and 11,30-32. The appellation of *baptist* (βαπτίζων, βαπτιστής) defines him on the basis of the thematic role:

$$βαπτιστής - βαπτίζω - βάπτισμα,$$

it is he that baptizes. The act of baptism, however, is the main act in a complex programme of action comprising several roles. He thus also appears in the role of prophet (cf. 11,32), i.e. as proclaimer: he proclaims "a baptism of repentance for the forgiveness of sins" and says that after him another will come who is more powerful, someone who will baptize not with water but with the Holy Spirit (1,4.8).

The expression "after me" (ὀπίσω μου) directly indicates a sequence in time, one thing follows another. First John appears, then Jesus appears. John prophesies about what is to occur in the immediate future. But there is reason to bear in mind that Jesus appears only at the moment when John has ceased to act. Only after the imprisonment of John (involving his death, cf. 6,14ff) does Jesus commence his public activity (1,14). The conclusion of the mission assigned to John coincides with the beginning of the mission assigned to Jesus. The asymmetric relative strengths between the two gave John a subordinate position relative to Jesus. His mission also became subordinate to the latter's.

But the gospel narrative contains no devaluating distancing from the baptism of John. On the contrary, it is emphasized that this baptism is "from heaven" (cf. 11,29ff), which singles out his work as an integrated part in an overarching action programme. It is true that relative to the final objective of this programme the baptism of John is in itself insufficient, but as a sub-mission it is nevertheless a necessary element in a complex of narrative processes. The task of narrative exegesis then becomes, on the basis of the rather scanty information the gospel narrative contains in this case, to carry out a *narrative reconstruction* of the baptism of John with a view to defining his narrative function, i.e. the significance of this act for the gospel narrative's further sequence of events.[39] So it is one of two: either the relationship between John and Jesus is merely of a chronological nature, the one coming before the other, and their missions are independent of each other; or there is a state of dependence between them, since

---

[39] It is *the narrative John*, the Baptist as a literary figure, who alone is concerned here, and not for example the relationship between the historical John and the Christian interpretation of him.

the realization of the first mission is the prerequisite for the commencement of the other one.

Also, the collage of quotations in 1,2f, which is attributed to Isaiah in its entirety but seems to be made up of Ex 23,20, Mal 3,1 and Isa 40,3, allows John to appear as a person whose mission has a positive function in the realization of God's action programme: he appears in accordance with the prophetic testimony. According to Mal 3,22 (LXX), John appears in the role of the prophet Elijah, who also appears at various places in the gospel narrative (6,15; 8,28; 9,4f; 9,11ff; 15,35f). In 6,15 the possibility is also mentioned that John is Elijah; in 8,28 that Jesus is perhaps this prophet. But interest is concentrated upon 9,11ff, where the reader is on the one hand informed about the aspect of God's salvation plan which says that Elijah must first come ('Ηλίαν δεῖ ἐλθεῖν πρῶτον) to restore (ἀποκαθίστημι) all things, and on the other hand hears that Elijah has already come and that they did to him whatever they pleased. Within the gospel narrative's context, therefore, John becomes singled out as Elijah: he came first, and they killed him (6,14ff). It is noteworthy here that Elijah comes first not only chronologically but that he has a necessary (cf. δεῖ) mission to perform: to restore all things. The realization of this clear protector mission is the presupposition that other, overarching narrative processes can be initiated.

In an attempt inferentially to reconstruct the work of John the Baptist, it is most appropriate to take as a point of reference the information that Elijah is to prepare the way for God, in that he makes the people return to the Lord so that the Lord can return to the people (Mal 3,1.7). The request: ἐπιστρέψατε πρός με, καὶ ἐπιστραφήσομαι πρὸς ὑμᾶς is a conditional promise: If X (the people return) then Y (the Lord will return), i.e. a promise that the covenant can be re-established and that the first step towards this has already been taken (cf. Zech 1,3; also Zech 13,9).

The verb ἐπιστρέφω means to turn, bring back onto the right road. It concerns a turn (ἐπιστροφή) from one diametric point to the other: for example, from idols to God, which presupposes movement from God to idols. The word ἐπιστρέφω is thus a parasynonym to μετανοέω (cf. Acts 3,19; 26,20); ἐπιστροφή is a parasynonym to μετάνοια (cf. Act 15,3; Mk 4,12). The repentance-baptism for the forgiveness of sins (βάπτισμα μετανοίας εἰς ἄφεσιν ἁμαρτιῶν) that John proclaims and practices is thus aimed at turning the people to God so that God may turn to the people.

It is this that the Luke narrative unfolds in 1,14ff, where it reads of John the Baptist that he will bring back (ἐπιστρέφω) many Israelites to the Lord their God. He (John) will go before him (God; not Jesus!) as a forerunner in Elijah's spirit and power, to turn (ἐπιστρέφω) the heart of the fathers to the children so that he can prepare (ἑτοιμάζω, cf. Mk 1,3) for the Lord a well-fitted (κατασκευάζω, cf. Mk 1,2) people. Here the narrative connection becomes clear: a well-fitted or well-adapted people is a people not only informed about, and as such prepared for, something that is to happen, but a people that has gone through a process (the repentance and the baptism), which qualifies it for what is to happen. Only when John has succeeded in turning the people to the Lord will the latter, according to the rules of the interactive exchange, i.e. the covenant, be able to turn to the people.

Against this background, it seems reasonable to infer that John the Baptist's mission within the gospel narrative was to fulfil a condition without which God would not be able to pass to action. In other words: John prepares the way for God's transition to action. His work to this end is an integrated factor in the complex of processes that are ultimately to lead to the realization of the kingdom of God.

The collage of quotations in 1,2f is in accordance therewith. It falls into three parts: a comment (v.2a), a first quotation (v. 2b) and a second quotation (v. 3), that itself consists of a quoted comment (v. 3a), and a quoted quotation (v. 3b). From the context, John may be he who cries in the wilderness (cf. v. 4).[40] His proclamation then contains the imperatives in v. 3b: "Prepare the way of the Lord, make his paths straight." But unless it is imagined that John cries out to remind himself of the mission assigned to him by God the narratee of this proclamation must be the people, who see themselves as singled out as the subject of doing in the role of road-maker (ὁδοποιός - ὁδοποιέω - ὁδοπιΐα; cf. 2,23). But John quotes only the command to which he himself is subject, and the impersonal voice thus also refers to the discursivator God. Both John and the people are road-makers in so far as an interaction is concerned: only if the people obey the call and turn to the Lord will the way be prepared for him (cf. Mal 3,1).

In his capacity of proclaiming road-maker, John must then be identified with the ἄγγελος referred to in v. 2b. It is God's speech that is quoted, it is he who sends the messenger, but it is not quite clear to whom he is speaking. It is, however, evident that it cannot be a matter of preparing the way for God. It is possible that God speaks to the Messiah.[41] In that event "the way of the Lord" in v. 3b is also the way of the Messiah. But there is also the possibility that God is speaking to the people. To prepare the way is to overcome obstacles, to open the closed road (ultimately to the kingdom of God, cf. Ex 23,20), and John prepares the way for the people, proclaiming the possibility of repentance.[42]

---

[40] Cf. Rudolf Pesch, *Das Markusevangelium, 1. Teil*, Freiburg 1980, p. 77.

[41] Cf. Rudolf Pesch, ibidem, p. 78.

[42] In a broader perspective, it is Jesus/the Messiah himself preparing the way to the kingdom of God, and he appears as such in the role of ἀρχηγός (a prime author), "der Anfänger, der als erster eine Reihe mit etwas beginnt und so den Anstoß dazu gibt", Walter Bauer, *Wörterbuch zum Neuen Testament*, Berlin 1971, p. 223; cf. Acts 2,15; Heb 2,10; 12.2. The final realization of the kingdom of God is preconditioned by the death of Jesus, and the Christians' resurrection is preconditioned by Jesus' resurrection. In the perspective of narration, Mark is the messenger sent by God who prepares the way for the reader.

1,2f is not merely a collage of quotations but also a condensed knot of signification that contains several - though compatible - interpretations. He who prepares the way for the Messiah also prepares the way for God, since God's transition to action consists in the anointing of Jesus of Nazareth (1,10f). And this event cannot be severed from the behaviour of the people. If the Baptist's proclamation had been ineffective, the heavens would have remained closed (cf. 1,10).

It then becomes clear that the difference between the Baptist's intimidating proclamation and Jesus' seductive proclamation is based upon no theological disparity. What is particular about the road-maker's proclamation is given by the moment at which it takes place in the total sequence. John proclaims *before*, whereas Jesus proclaims *after*, that God has turned to the people and has passed to action. He whom God elects and anoints with the Holy Spirit is a person of the new people (the baptized) whom the Baptist has prepared.

4. God's Commandment

The gospel of God is not only information about what is actually the case or a prophetic prediction of what will be the case. It is also - and more importantly - a message that gives information about God's commandment and thus reveals what should be the case. Through his gospel, God reveals a value perspective on the basis of which the existing world and the given existence see themselves disclosed and defined.

a. Deontic Modalities of Being

A given, i.e. ontic, existing state of being will, as already mentioned, be perceived by the subject of being involved as good (satisfactory) or bad (unsatisfactory) according to a subjective understanding of value. But the same subject of being already sees himself as unavoidably interpreted by the narrative's objective value system or axiology that is established according to being's *deontic* modal category (cf. δέον, δεῖ):[43]

---

[43] Cf. *Sémiotique*, art. "Aléthiques (modalités -)" and "Devoir". As already indicated, no distinction is made here between alethic and deontic modalities but between deontic modalities of being and of doing. Greimas gives a logical rather than a semiotic interpretation of this modal category when he calls the axis' terms necessity/impossibility, the sub-axis' terms possibility/contingence. These terms are also used about the dynamic modalities of being, cf. art. "Pouvoir" so that having-to-be corresponds to not-being-able-not-to-be; having-not-to-be to not-being-able-to-be; not-having-not-to-be to being-able-to-be; and finally not-having-to-be to being-able-not-to-be. A corresponding accord seems to exist between having-to-do and not-being-able-not-to-do, etc. The question is, however, whether this apparent affinity between having to and being able to rests on a delusion due to imprecise use of language. The Highway Code's command to drive on when the light is green is a having-to-do, whereas the prohibition against driving on when the light is red is a having-not-to-do. It is not meaningless to say: "According to the law, one cannot refrain (not-being-able-not-to-do) from driving on when the light becomes green!", or: "According to the Highway Code, one cannot (not-being-able-not-to-do) drive on when the light is red!", but it is imprecise because being able to is not always used as a transcription of having to. There is quite clearly an affinity

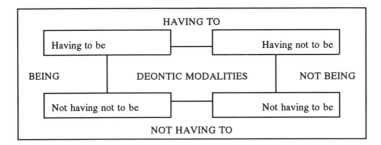

corresponding to:

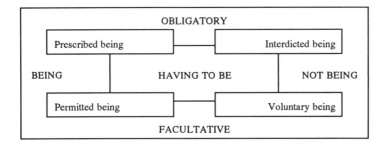

A given state of being is thus either valorized positively (prescription) or negatively (interdiction); or non-valorized positively (permitted) or negatively (voluntary).

The authority that establishes the being's value is referred to as *Destinator*. The authority for whom values are established is referred to as *Destinatee*.[44] The relationship between the Destinator and the Destinatee is asymmetrical, the former being superior, the latter inferior. Moreover, the relationship is structural, in that the two actants can be defined only in relation to one another. It is the Destinator's *wanting* (will, wish, desire) that appears to the Destinatee as *having to*. The designation "objective" must of course be understood in a relative sense.

---

between these modal categories, since the command gets a substantial part of its justification from the fact that the subject of doing can indeed refrain (being-able-not-to-do) from driving on. The prohibition is similarly founded - at least partly - on the fact that the subject of doing is able to drive on (being-able-to-do). Whatever the Highway Code says there is also the possibility that the brakes fail, so that the subject of doing cannot help driving on (not-being-able-not-to-do), the engine fails so that the subject of doing cannot (not-being-able-to-do) drive on. Considering the accidents caused by the discrepancy between having to and being able to, one can only regret that the affinity asserted by Greimas does not exist. On the other hand, it is precisely the intriguing world that occasions the narratives. As regards the relationship between the various modal categories, cf. A.J. Greimas, "Pour une théorie des modalités", *Du sens II*, Paris 1983, pp. 67. As regards the relationship between logical and semiotic interpretation, cf. "De la modalisation de l'être", ibidem, pp. 93.

[44] Cf. *Sémiotique*, art. "Destinateur/Destinataire".

The objective is not that which is independently given for any subject but that which has been established by the Destinator and to which the Destinatee is subjected. The objective is the given reality conjuncture in which the Destinatee sees himself as framed.

However paradoxical it may seem, the Destinator - that is to say, God in Christian discourses - cannot realize his desire without regard to the Destinatee, i.e. humankind. This bond to humankind is the precondition for the ability of the personified Destinator, God, to love, hate, rejoice and become angry. God has a part in humankind's project of being. Having-to-be refers to the desirable, the pleasant, that which is loved; having-not-to-be refers to the detestable, the abominable, that which is hated (the two other positions which both express a lack of interest concern the tolerable (not-having-not-to-be) and the unimportant (not-having-to-be).

The value perspectives of God and humankind can either be or not be in accord with one another. A distinction is made between two forms of compatibility and two forms of incompatibility:[45]

		Having to be $\equiv$
Compatibility	Complementarity	Wanting to be
	Conformity	Not wanting not to be
Incompatibility	Contrariety	Not wanting to be
	Contradiction	Wanting not to be

For example, the death on the cross is a provisional state of being prescribed by God (cf. 8,31). The Gethsemane scene (14,32ff) bears witness of the confrontation between the two value perspectives. The crisis consists of the discordance between what God wants (having-to-be) and what Jesus wants. The latter fears death (14,34), and is as such defined by wanting-not-to-be. Overcoming the crisis does not lead to full accord but to conformity between the two wantings: the death on the cross is endured (not-wanting-not-to-be).[46]

b. Narrative Ontology

In its capacity as objective system of value, axiology constitutes a νόμος on the basis of which judgment can be pronounced on the existing state of being: this is either as it should be, and in that case *nomie* is concerned; or it is as it should

---

[45] Cf. "Pour une théorie des modalités", ibidem, pp. 86.
[46] Cf. Chapter XI, C.2.b.

not be, and then *anomie* is concerned. That which is, the ontic, sees itself unavoidably interpreted and evaluated by this system of value that defines its ontological status.

In a process perspective the objective axiology exists as an objective *ideology*.[47] This prescribes the realization of that which should be, and thus demands a process of change. But it also prescribes that which should not be and in this way demands a preservation process. Ideology is therefore orientated towards a certain end, a τέλος; it is *teleological*.

It can now be clarified that it is on the basis of this telos that an ontic - and to this extent neutral as to value - process of change or preservation can be defined either as *progressive* (expedient, suitable, good) or as *degressive* (inexpedient, unsuitable, bad). Similarly, the final state of a process of change or preservation is either *acceptable* (favourable, good) or *unacceptable* (unfavourable, bad), and the subject of being is either *favoured* (winner, elevated, beneficiary) or *disfavoured* (loser, degraded, victim).

In the word εὐαγγέλιον, the prefix εὐ in the sense of good, positive, indicates that the message is good, that it tells of an on-going progressive event that is for the good of the recipient. In contrast to this is a *dysangelium* that tells of a possible or on-going degressive process of change, cf., for example, Gen 3,14ff. On the basis of the narrative's objective value-concept, an existing state of being is then characterized either by δυστυχία or by εὐτυχία.[48]

Ontological Modalities

The narrative's objective ideology is its foundation. This implies an *ontology*, in that the prescribed being, i.e. the state of being that the Destinator desires to be realized or preserved, is established by the narrative as *Being*: here the kingdom of God. The narrative's ideology designates an ideal being that either is or is not realized. The narrative ontology is a teaching about being in the sense that, on the basis of this ideal being, it can define a given state's status or mode of being in accordance with the ontological modal category:[49]

---

[47] Cf. *Sémiotique*, art. "Idéologie".

[48] Unhappy state versus happy state, formed by τυγχάνω, which figuratively means to reach one's goal, to realize one's intention, have luck on one's side; cf. also τύχη in the sense of lot, fate, luck or bad luck.

[49] Greimas does not operate with ontological modalities. The modalization of being is seen on the basis of the category *être vs. paraître* and is referred to as veridictory modalities belonging to the cognitive dimension. It is not unimportant to the understanding of this conception when Greimas emphasizes that the designations employed are semiotic and "sans aucun rapport avec les concepts ontologiques desquels ils peuvent être rapprochés", and that the category *vrai vs. faux* "se trouve située à l'intérieur du discours", "Pour une théorie des modalités", ibidem, pp. 72. The ontological modalities suggested here belong to the pragmatic dimension and are in no way an expression of a failure to appreciate the absence of the external referent. Even the category of *being vs. nothing* is given within the discourse. This does not concern the world's ontological nature but the narrative's implicit ontology. That the gospel narrative itself asserts that it speaks about the external world does not affect the ontological modalities' semiotic status. Neither is the veridictory modalities' status affected by the truth-claim of this narrative.

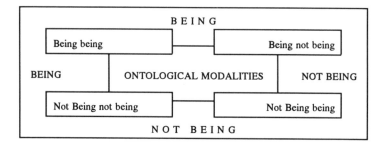

the positions of which may be referred to as:

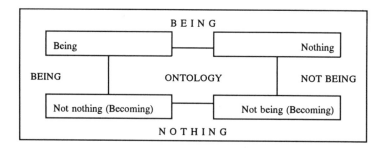

where Nothing, Not Being (degressive becoming) and Not Nothing (progressive becoming) see themselves defined as three *deficient* modes of being.

The relevant existing state of being is either in accordance with or in contrast to the established deontic Being:

		The ontic being $\equiv$
Compatibility	Complementarity	Having to be
	Conformity	Not having not to be
Incompatibility	Contrariety	Not having to be
	Contradiction	Having not to be

In the Christian narrative, the existing world, this world, is signified as a place where something is lacking: Being is deficient. There is discordance between what is and what ought to be. But this Being, the kingdom of God, Definitive cosmos, may exist as deficient in three different modes:

a) Conformal deficiency: Provisional chaos   ≅ Non-Nothing
b) Contrary deficiency: Provisional cosmos   ≅ Non-Being
c) Contradictory deficiency: Definitive chaos   ≅ Nothing

The existing world can of course be identified as neither definitive nor provisional chaos but only as provisional cosmos. In the first moment (before the anointing of Jesus) this is thus characterized by degressive becoming, in that Non-Being is orientated towards Nothing (cf., for example, Gen. 6,7: "So the Lord said: 'I will blot out from the earth the human beings I have created ..., For I am sorry that I have made them'."). Such a situation must be set against the moment where the ontically given exists as provisional chaos, a mode which is characterized by a progressive becoming, in that Non-Nothing is orientated towards Being (cf. Mk 13).

In accordance with this, the religious narratives fall into two basic forms (narrative genres): a) degressive narratives that tell about processes of change involving a loss of being, i.e. processes of decline or fall (κατάβασις, πτῶσις) orientated towards Nothing; b) progressive narratives that tell about processes of change involving the acquisition of being, i.e. processes of rising and raising (ἀνάβασις, ἀνάστασις) orientated towards Being. Within the Christian narratives these two basic forms are to be found in the Story of the Fall (Gen 2,4b-3,24) and the Gospel narrative.

Dynamic Cosmology

The four cosmological modes of being, which are all defined on the basis of Being, can be further defined modally in a dynamic and processual perspective.

The kingdom of God, Being/Definitive cosmos, is the state of being in which Being is *realized*. In accordance with the simple VAR structure, the kingdom of God must have been virtual (possible) and actualized before this moment, but the matter is more complex and can be described only on the basis of a more complex VAR structure that includes all the dynamic modalities and not only the possibility.[50]

There are also moments in which the kingdom of God's modal existence is characterized by impossibility (before the anointing of Jesus) or by inevitability (after the death on the cross).

In the case of Nothing/Definitive chaos Being is *virtualized*. Within the complex VAR structure this mode of being has a special status, in that it is as *amodal* as the realized Being mode of being.

---

[50] The simple VAR structure known from the wonder narrative's main act, for example virtual (1,30), actualised (1,31a) and realised (1,31b) healing, includes an incomplex narrative act, healing, which requires a single subject of doing, the healer. The complex VAR structure includes several connected narrative acts that refer to the interaction between two subjects of doing, the Destinator and the Destinatee.

In a creation perspective, virtualization, or rather virtuality, corresponds here to a state characterized by formlessness and void, i.e. an absolute beginning in which the divine relationship, the God-humankind relationship, without which any talk of world in the most literal sense is meaningless, is not yet established.

In an annihilation perspective, virtualization corresponds to destruction of this relationship. Realized Being and virtualized Being, Being and Nothing, thus exist as amodal terminals, in that each realization involves a demodalization. At the moment in which the kingdom of God is realized, it is no longer meaningful to inquire about its dynamic modalization; hence the designation *definitive*.

Being modes Non-Being and Non-Nothing, however, exist dynamically modalized. In the first case the kingdom of God is *semi-virtualized*, in the second *semi-realized*. Two forms of becoming are concerned here, both of which are determined, i.e. modalized by not-being-able-to: that Being in the state of Non-Being is semi-virtualized is to say that Nothing is inevitable (not-being-able-not-to-be; fatal degression); that Being in the state of Non-Nothing is semi-realized is to say that Nothing is impossible (not-being-able-to-be; fatal protection). The contractually controlled exchange between God and Jesus which conditions these modal situations is discussed in detail in Part 4, the Savior.

Here it may be emphasized that in the moment where Being is impossible Nothing is inevitable, and the kingdom of God's semi-virtualized existence is therefore characterized by a degressive becoming. In the moment where Being is inevitable Nothing is impossible, and the kingdom of God's semi-realized existence is therefore characterized by a progressive becoming. It can then be seen that the transition from degressive becoming to progressive becoming becomes a decisive point.

Yet another moment must be distinguished, in that Being may be *actualized*. In this moment the kingdom of God is at the same time possible and avoidable (being-able-to-be/being-able-not-to-be); it is not laid down which direction the process will take, but this undetermined becoming can go in both directions.

The following diagram shows processually the modes of being referred to:

	MODE OF BEING	MODALITY	ARTICULATION
I	Virtualized	-	Being (Nothing)
	Semi-virtualized	Impossible	Determined becoming ↑
II	Actualized	Possible/Evitable	Indetermined becoming ↕
III	Semi-realized	Inevitable	Determined becoming ↓
	Realized	-	Being

Within the complex VAR structure, phase II is a threshold that on the one hand marks the deactualization of Nothing (transition from impossible to evitable) and on the other hand states the actualization of Being (transition from impossible to possible).

It can now be clarified that the existing world as a provisional cosmos is in the first place characterized by degressive, determined becoming, since it is orientated towards Nothing: damnation is inevitable, salvation is impossible. Then comes a reversal (peripeteia), in that God passes to action and factitively makes the inevitable evitable and the impossible possible: the kingdom of God has come near. It is this joyful, factitive event that Jesus proclaims. Where annihilation has accomplished its project, there is ontological contradiction. But God's transition to action, which marks a resumption of the creation project, is directed towards ontological complementarity, where Being is being and the being is Being.

It is, however, Jesus of Nazareth who will be the subject of doing of the narrative, factitive process that is to effect the transition from possibility to inevitability.

c. Prescriptor and Interdictor

The influence that is directed towards the Destinator's deontic modalization appears, now as *prescription*, now as *interdiction*. In the light of the intended Being, any action therefore appears as resistance against or assistance to the realization of the kingdom of God. Prescription refers to the influence that attempts to evoke awareness of God's axiology and thus of a command that must be fulfilled. Interdiction for its part is an influence that refers to an axiologically founded prohibition which must be respected. In the capacity of subject of doing of the influence on the Destinator's having to, the proclaimer is referred to, now as *prescriptor*, now as *interdictor*.[51]

The prescription or interdiction that is announced has as its content the narrative (narrate) about a virtuality not yet realized but singled out by the prescriptor as a state of being determined by having-to-be, and by the interdictor as a state of being determined by having-not-to-be, now under any circumstances, now if certain conditions have been met.

Generally, the narratee for prescription/interdiction will at the same time be the virtual subject of doing for the realization of the command: he is prescribed/forbidden to accept a task that is either pragmatic (cf. the double command to love), factitive, or informative (cf. the command to secrecy, the command of mission) that concerns a subject of being that is either the person influenced, the influencer, or a third person. In those cases where prescription/interdiction is not categorical but conditional, a virtuality is concerned that comes

---

[51] Cf. *Logique du récit*, pp. 270; here prescriptor is used for *obligateur*. In these roles too a distinction can be made between reflexive/transitive and voluntary/involuntary influence.

into force only when certain conditions have been met, when a certain situation exists.[52]

The proclamation's disclosure of the nature of the world and God's desire will raise the question on the part of the recipient: "What am I to do?" (cf., for example, Acts 2,37). For whoever receives Jesus's proclamation of the gospel of God, the question concerns not what he is to do to realize the kingdom of God, but what he must do to obtain a share in this kingdom, to inherit eternal life (10,17). The imperative "repent, and believe in the good news" (1,15) is a prescription (an admonition) that anticipates this question.

---

[52] The conditional having to appears where a narrative process is to be realized through interaction, i.e. where the one subject's (for example, Jesus') doing depends upon the other subject's (for example, the sick person's) doing (pragmatic and/or cognitive-affective). With his knowledge of the nature of the world and God's desire, Jesus appears in the role of wonder-working savior. This doing can be considered as commanded, at least implicitly, since God's axiology selects, for example, sickness as an expression of ontological anomie. Whoever shares God's understanding of value, i.e. senses what God's is (φρονέω τὰ τοῦ θεοῦ, cf. 8,33), can only feel compassion for the victim; but the command to heal is not categorical. That Jesus can do no wonder-working in his native town (6,5) is not because of a momentary failure of ability, as if he suddenly saw himself as modalized by not-being-able-to-do; it is the conditions for transition to action which have not been met. The victim is thus not only a subject of being but must itself, as embedded subject of doing - where doing is necessary although insufficient -, contribute to the salvation. As wonder-worker Jesus presupposes the victim's faith, cf. 2,5; 5,34.36; 9,24;10,52. Unbelief (6,6) acts as self-repression, the transition from virtual to actualized/realized beneficiary is blocked. It is the role of virtually favoured alone that is given unconditionally. If the interactive relationship, the synergistic aspect, is abolished, a predestination theory which deletes the narrative articulation seems unavoidable.

D. God's Messenger

1. Apostle and Pseudo-Apostle

The roles of prescriptor and interdictor refer to the authority, God the Destinator, that is the source of prescription and interdiction. It is relative to this authority that the person called is responsible for his actions. It may be the prescriptor/interdictor himself who informs the subordinate, but it may also be left to a *messenger* (apostle) to inform about the authority's decisions. When a royal message is proclaimed in the market place, the messenger (emissary, apostle) who reads the command adopts the role of informator, whereas the sovereign who has caused it to be announced adopts the role of prescriptor/interdictor (Destinator).[53]

When Jesus proclaims the gospel of God, he proclaims the gospel from God and acts as such in the role of the delegated informator who proclaims what the authority, God the Destinator, has established. Whoever receives the proclamation thus does not receive Jesus but whoever sent him (cf. 9,37: ἀποστέλλω). Apostle is thus parasynonymous with prophet (Lk 1,49; Rev 18,20) and other thematic proclaimer roles.[54] The messenger (ἄγγελος) who is sent (ἀποστέλλω) is an envoy (ἀπόστολος), and apostle (ἀπόστολος) thus becomes parasynonymous with messenger (ἄγγελος), cf. 1,2 and Rev 1,1. It is in the capacity of delegated proclaimers that the disciples may be referred to as apostles (cf. 3,13ff; 6,7ff). But also Jesus himself is ἀπόστολος, God's messenger, cf. Heb 3,1.

A proclaiming person can however appear in the role of ψευδαπόστολος, voluntarily or involuntarily.[55] He pretends to be and considers himself to be spokesman for the Destinator (the discursivator as the foundation of truth), but represents in fact only himself. What he proclaims as having-to (truth; God's will and desire) is merely a simulated objectification of his own wanting-to, his own lie, wishful thinking, desire. In the Gospel of John, this general narratological issue is quite explicitly thematized, for example in 7,16ff and 8,44:

My teaching is not mine but his who sent me. Anyone who resolves to do the will of God will know whether the teaching is from God or whether I am speaking on my own. Those who speak on their own seek their own

---

[53] The herald is a universal figure of reference for the role κῆρυξ - κηρύσσω - κήρυγμα, cf. e.g. Logique du récit, p. 271; Rudolf Pesch, *Das Markusevangelium, 1. Teil*, p. 101; Walter Bauer, *Wörterbuch zum Neuen Testament*, p. 852; but this thematic role is only one among several proclaimer roles. Freed from its medieval connotations (court functionary; tournament leader), i.e. in the sense of *public* messenger, it can of course be employed.

[54] E.g. κῆρυξ (cf. 2 Pet 2,5) and διδάσκαλος, cf. 1 Tim 2,7; 2 Tim 1,11.

[55] Cf. 2 Cor 11,13; cf. also ψευδής (Rev 2,2; 21,8); ψευδοδιδάσκαλος (2 Pet 2,1); ψευδολόγος (1 Tim 4,2); ψευδοπροφήτης (13,22; Lk 6,26; Acts 13,6; 2 Pet 2,1; 1 Jn 4,1; Rev 16,13; 19,20 and 20,10); ψεύστης (Jn 8,44.55; Rom 3,4; 1 Tim 1,10; Titus 1,12; 1 Jn 1,10;2,4.22; 4,20; 5,10). Cf. also the role ψευδόμαρτυς - ψευδομαρτυρέω - ψευδομαρτυρία. As regards the relationship between the true and false prophet, cf. Klaus Berger, "Die königlichen Messiastraditionen des Neuen Testaments", *New Testament Studies 20*, Cambridge 1973, pp. 10.

glory; but the one who seeks the glory of him who sent him is true, and there is nothing false in him.

You are from your father the devil, and you choose to do your father's desires. He was a murderer from the beginning and does not stand in the truth, because there is no truth in him. When he lies, he speaks according to his own nature, for he is a liar and the father of lies.

Whoever speaks out of his own imagination lies; truth can come only from elsewhere than the speaker himself, from God only can it be given, cf. Ezek 13,1ff.

The proclaimer maintains that he speaks on behalf of the Destinator, on behalf of God. If he is in good faith, he will see himself as a voluntary revealator. If he is in bad faith, however, he sees himself as a voluntary deceptor. But the narrator's self-knowledge is one thing and what is in fact the case is another thing. Whoever sees himself as a voluntary revealator may be blind, wrapped in self-deception, and as such appear in the role of involuntary deceptor: he thinks he is speaking on God's behalf, but in fact speaks on his own behalf. The proclaimer's self-knowledge is one thing, his actual role another thing.

The narratee, appointed by the proclamation, must in turn evaluate whether the proclaimer appears on behalf of himself or of God. Perhaps he is blind, so that he considers the deceptor as the revealator or vice versa. Perhaps he is sufficiently clear-sighted to see through the deceptor and to recognize the revealator.

An acute dilemmatic situation exists if two messengers appear in the market place, each proclaiming his own message in the name of the same king. Who then is the true proclaimer, which message must the narratee follow? One deceives, the other reveals, but which? Assuming that the proclamation contains a command, the narratee must take a position on this forced choice, and by the choice obtain an unambiguity from the ambiguous situation. Not because it thereby becomes clear who is deceiving or revealing - that is still not certain - but because by his choice the narratee reveals what his position is. The dilemmatic choice has the nature of a projective test ($\pi\epsilon\iota\rho\alpha\sigma\mu\acute{o}\varsigma$), since the decision can only rest upon a projection of the narratee's own passion, his wishes, conflicts, attitudes and feelings. Conversely, it may be said that this difficulty of choice forces him to consider his identity. If he makes the wrong choice he has already condemned himself; cf. Jn 3,18.[56]

---

[56] The sanction which will be able to show whether the narratee made the right choice is eschatologically deferred. The *pragmatic* eschatology (the final realization of the kingdom of God) and the *cognitive* eschatology (when the narratee sees for himself, cf. Jn 20,29; or no longer recognizes partially but wholly, cf. 1 Cor 13,12) coincide but must be distinguished from one another. What is significant is that the narratee must choose *here and now*, and that his choice will have consequences for his actual life. Thus, in the cognitive-affective dimension one could seriously talk of a presentic eschatology, cf. 10,15.

The confrontation between Jesus and the Jewish authorities may be seen as a confrontation between two such messengers, each proclaiming his message in the name of the same Destinator, in the name of God. They are, however, not content with proclaiming, but act as subjects of doing on the basis of the commands contained in their respective proclamations. Thereby they inevitably appear as offenders in each others' eyes. In the following examination of the relationship between God's emissary and the Jewish authorities, the emphasis is on the proclaimer role, on the aspect that the proclaimer's cognitive doing is an attempt to influence virtual subjects of doing to carry out acts which are prohibited in the eyes of the other, and for this reason the act of proclamation itself appears as a transgression.

2. The Blasphemer

If 1,1-13 is distinguished as prologue and beginning, and 16,1-8 as epilogue and ending, one has a torso, 1,14-15,47, which has as its centre the story of the acting and suffering Jesus of Nazareth. From this centre it is possible to extract some relevant information on the Jewish leader's relationship with Jesus as regards the definition of the course of events that ends in their executing him as a violator of the law or a transgressor.[57]

Three main phases can be distinguished:

1) The offender is discovered and watched (2,6ff).
2) The offender is arrested, accused and condemned (14,43-52, 14,53-65; 15,1-15).
3) The offender is executed (15,16-37).

a. Discovery and Watching

If one disregards the dependence to which the Jewish authorities are subject relative to Pilate, then Jesus is put to death by the Sanhedrin as guilty of blasphemy. He blasphemes against God by pretending to be Christ, his delegated son, although he is only a carpenter of Nazareth. This is at least the official reason in which all other possible motives, such as "jealousy" (15,10: φθόνος, malice, hate), may find a footing. The legal proceedings are an expression of social justice, and as such are contrary to any possible self-constituted vengeance.[58]

---

[57] Cf. παραβάτης - παραβαίνω - παράβασις; παραπίπτων - παράπιπτω - παράπτωμα; cf.14,48; 15,(28); Lk 22,37, ἄνομος. Interest is concerned only with certain main features, and therefore "the scribes", "the elders", "the high priests", "the Pharisees", "the Sadducees" and "the Herodians" are considered as representatives of the Sanhedrin, which designates the Jewish authorities.

[58] Cf. Sémiotique, art. "Justice" and "Vengeance".

The account of the questioning by Pilate reads that the high priests accuse Jesus of many things (15,3), but the main accusation is blasphemy, which consists not only in offending God by distancing himself from him but is especially pernicious because Jesus makes himself equal to God, sets himself in God's place. Jesus is a deceptor who maintains that he represents God, but in reality speaks only for himself.

From the first time the scribes are mentioned (1,22), the polemic relationship between Jesus and the Jewish savants is indicated. People are astounded at Jesus' teaching, because he teaches them as one having authority (ἐξουσία: authority, power) and not as the scribes do; - who indeed also teach but obviously not with authority. By his teaching, Jesus thus contests the scribes' authority, those who decide what are the facts because they are thought to know, and people are plunged into an authority crisis, a choice between Jesus' teaching and the scribes' teaching, between one authority and another. Jesus' teaching is defined as "A new teaching (διδαχή) - with authority!" (1,27) i.e. a powerful teaching that in fact invokes a ready response from the recipients because its message speaks to them (at least sufficiently to create doubt, ἀπορία, cf. 6,20).

The conflict of interests is reflected not only as a discordance between doctrines. By his behaviour Jesus disregards the Jewish authorities' regulations: he eats with tax collectors and sinners (2,16f), he allows his disciples to pluck heads of grain although it is the sabbath (2,23f), he lets them eat with defiled hands (7,2f), and he heals on a sabbath (3,1f). Jesus not only contests Jewish authority but dethrones it, dissolves it, not by virtue of a desire to compete where the only purpose is to obtain power but in solidarity with the victims produced by Jewish teaching when it sets the teaching itself above the human life that it should serve. The teaching exists for the sake of humankind, and not humankind for the sake of the teaching; he who sets the teaching above humankind serves death, whereas he who sets humankind above the teaching serves life. He who in the name of the teaching fails to save life, kills (cf.3,4).

The power of the Jewish authorities depends upon acceptance by the people that the former are those who have the answers, those who know the truth. They therefore see in Jesus a demagogue who threatens to undermine their leadership. They cannot accept his teaching and power. On the other hand, they cannot convince him about their own teaching; they are even incapable of making him flee for fear of reprisals. Therefore only one final means remains to destroy the opponent: "The Pharisees went out and immediately conspired with the Herodians against him, how to destroy him", 3,6.

The Jewish authorities have in common with the demons that they are in no doubt about their identification of Jesus. They know for sure that he is an usurper, that he has unlawfully adopted an authority that is not only a revolt against them as leaders but a revolt against God. He claims to have the power (ἐξουσία) to forgive sins, although only God is entitled to do this (2,6f). Since the Jewish authorities know (or think they know) that it is impossible for Jesus of Nazareth to be God's delegated representative, his behaviour can be understood only as gross blasphemy (βλασφημία, cf. βλασφημέω, 2,7).

The scribes try to put him out of action by accusing him of being possessed by an evil spirit, 3,20ff. The Pharisees ask for a sign from heaven, set him a task he cannot solve to make him show the falsity of his claim that he is in fact who he pretends to be, 8,11f, and they set a trap for him, 10,1ff.

The confrontation between Jesus and the Jewish authorities comes to a head after the entry into Jerusalem, and culminates in the cleansing of the temple. This profaning act causes the high priests and the scribes to consider how to have him killed. The problem is pressing, because Jesus has succeeded in beguiling the whole crowd, which is spellbound by his teaching, 11,15ff.[59]

A person who thus, self-appointed, goes around acting on behalf of God must suffer from megalomania, he must have gone out of his mind, be beside himself (cf. 3,21: ἐξίστημι). Even those closest to him think this, and the scribes draw the consequence: "He has Beelzebul", the ruler of the demons, 3,22. In Jesus, one is confronted by not merely a demon but by the prince of the demons himself, Satan. Jesus is not only an opponent but the arch-opponent. He presents himself as God's representative, but he is in fact Satan's emissary; he acts as if endowed with holy, pure spirit, but he is in fact controlled by a profane, unclean spirit (3,29f).

Jesus replies by accusing the scribes of unforgivable blasphemy (3,29). It is the religious leaders who render God's word powerless, because they convey doctrines (διδασκαλία) that are only human precepts (7,7). They teach in the name of God and thereby wrongfully assume an authority, since in reality they speak only on their own. The religious leaders are self-appointed authorities, simulating what they are not and dissimulating what they are. They pretend to be one thing but are something different; their teaching is said to serve one thing but serves another: they are hypocrites (ὑποκριτής, 7,6).

The polemic relationship between Jesus and the religious authorities is a symmetrical rivalry, a dispute about who rightfully represents God and thus the truth. The symmetry exists between Jesus in the role of teacher, proclaimer, prophet, and the Jewish authorities in the form of scribes. They mutually accuse one another of being usurpers and blasphemers.

One step in the combat and controversy (συζήτησις, cf. συζητέω, 8,11, which refers to the work of interpretation as an exchange of arguments, cf. 1,27; 9,14.16; 12,28, a pensiveness, cf. 9,10) is the Pharisees' testing (πειράζω, 8,11)

---

[59] Whether or not the curse on the figtree (11,12-14.19-21) is understood symbolically as a judgment on Israel, Jerusalem and the temple, cf. Rudolf Pesch, *Das Markusevangelium, 2. Teil*, p. 195, the cleansing of the temple is an unambiguous expression of the gospel narrative's anti-Jewish attitude, cf. 13,1ff. This should not be suppressed, nor sought to be explained away. On the contrary, it must be emphasized that "the Jew" is an opponent role (antactant) that can be assumed by anyone, for example even by the denying Peter, and that therefore we are all Jews before the Lord.

of Jesus. The test has various aspects according to circumstances. It is a challenge, and as such refers to a combat aspect; it is for the test to show who is the stronger. It is part of an investigation, a re-examination, which is to impart on a basis of experience knowledge about something uncertain. The result of the test will render unambiguous the problem to be re-examined, either by verification, evidence, or by falsification, counter-evidence. But the word πειράζω may also contain the aspect of temptation (cf. 1,13) and thus refer to an attempt to beguile in which the test itself acts as a trap (cf. 10,2; 12,13.15). The intention is to get the dupe to reveal involuntarily who, in the opinion of the opponent, he in fact is.

The investigative aspect dominates; more specifically, the Pharisees seek, lack and demand (ζητέω) a sign (σημεῖον, mark, proof, omen) from heaven, 8,11. Jesus' reaction is significant; he "sighs" (ἀναστενάζω) in his spirit. He groans because he is burdened and frustrated, because the demand for a sign from heaven is a failure to appreciate that he himself is such a sign. He sighs because the situation borders on the intolerable. The Pharisees and other Jewish authorities have already had a sign from heaven in Jesus' proclamation, his words and his deeds, and the information thereby given is fully sufficient to pronounce the correct judgment on his identity. A quantitative increase in information changes nothing.

The demand for a sign that is to come not from Jesus but directly from heaven, i.e. from God, may perhaps be understood as a request for a definitive sign, i.e. an unambiguous sign that excludes any ambiguity and thereby differing interpretations. But such a definitive sign is out of the question, since it would then no longer be a sign but a direct vision, a peep into the ineffable. Jesus sighs because he is powerless. Although mastering language, he is reduced to indirect communication, calling for the recipient's trust and confidence. He has no power over his recipient's reception of the proclamation, but there is a slip between emission and reception that he cannot remedy, a distance he cannot do away with however much he may wish to do so. Jesus' rejection of the demand for a sign is thus twofold: he rejects the request for a definitive sign because such a sign cannot be given; he rejects the wish for a supplementary sign because such a sign is in vain. The demand is itself evidence of the futility of giving such a sign.

As witnesses to Jesus' offence against a religious law, the Jewish authorities, whose legitimate supremacy is itself thereby contested, become a possible subject of doing for a sanction. The discovery of the offender and his activities opens up a possible course of action which, by a sanction process, reaches its target: punishment of the offender. The discovery of the offence (2,6) leads to the decision *that* they will destroy the offender who appears as an enemy of society (3,6). The continuing conduct that culminates in the cleansing of the temple leads them to consider *how* they are to have him killed (11,18), how they are to seize him without the crowd knowing of it (12,12). Finally, they consider how they can arrest him by stealth (δόλος) and have him killed (14,1). But a favourable opportunity occurs (cf. εὔκαιρος 6,21; 14,11) when Judas Iscariot, one of the twelve, goes to the high priests and offers to betray him. Judas himself then seeks an opportunity to realize his project (14,11).

b. Capture, Accusation and Condemnation

Jesus is in no doubt that he is being conspired against by the Jewish authorities, that in their eyes he is a dangerous opponent. It has not escaped his attention that he is in danger.

A conflict between such partners can be nullified in two different ways.[60] One can, by negotiation and mutual acceptance, reach understanding and agreement by both parties showing a readiness to meet the other's demands. Jesus rejects this possibility; he does not wish to compromise. Or one can flee and so avoid imminent punishment, but Jesus also rejects this possibility; on the contrary, he seeks out and challenges his opponents in Jerusalem, in the temple, and later he allows himself to be seized, making no attempt to flee. Finally, one can try to eliminate one's opponent by use of force and violence, a possibility that might be relevant if the crowd were to rise up against its leaders. Jesus, however, makes no attempt to lead the crowd into rebellion; at his capture (14,43ff), all his disciples and companions take flight (14,50).

Despite his disregard of any attempt to protect himself, Jesus is nevertheless protected by the crowd, which is what the Jewish authorities fear. The Sanhedrin must therefore seize him covertly, as is recounted in 14,43ff.

When he is questioned by the high priest (14,53ff), Jesus is silent and makes no attempt to assert his innocence. Only to the question, whether he is Christ, the Son of the Blessed One, does Jesus reply: "I am." (14,61f). This reply is as an offence in itself equivalent to an admission, and all agree to the sentence: deserving of death (14,64).

The questioning by Pilate (15,1ff) plays no part in this context, where what is decisive is that the chief priests (15,3) succeed in implementing the Sanhedrin's plan, in that they make the crowd (15,11) and thereby Pilate (15,15) confirm the sentence. After this Jesus is handed over for crucifixion (15,15).

c. Execution

In this context, where the purpose is not an exhaustive analysis of the Passion but to bring to light as simply as possible the structure of the process of events that ends in the Jewish authorities' execution of Jesus as a criminal, it is sufficient to note that Jesus is executed and that the sanction process has thereby achieved its objective. The offender has been punished for his offence, and has now been

---

[60] Cf. Claude Bremond, "La logique des possibles narratifs", *Communications 8*, Paris 1966, p. 67.

eliminated. The Jewish leaders' view of the process of events may be summarized as follows: the guilty blasphemer has received his well-deserved punishment.

In the light of human experience, this process of events is quite probable. Nothing extraordinary about it springs to mind and arouses objection. The narrative verisimilitude, however, does not depend upon the fact that historically the process of events took this course, wholly or in part. It does not depend upon the fact that the narrative, although somewhat vague at the edges, has an historical core. But the important point is that what takes place during this process of events does not contradict the concept of reality which, for want of a better term, we call historical and which rests upon a foundation of experience. With the socially sanctioned knowledge we have of ourselves in the world, the process of events concerned appears to be realistic, but does not therefore have to be accepted - necessarily - as an historical account.

But it would be natural for an historian who regards the gospel narrative as a source illustrating what actually occurred to identify the verisimilitude of the narrative with whatever is historically probable, as if the latter follows from the former. In the section "Markus als Schriftsteller" WREDE rightly emphasizes that Mark, by his "Geschichtserzählung", does not provide a true picture of the life of the historical Jesus. Certain general historical concepts are however manifest. Among these WREDE includes, that Jesus comes up against the opposition of the Pharisees and the Jewish authorities, that these people persecute him and seek his downfall, that they finally succeed in this after he arrives in Jerusalem, that he suffers, is sentenced to death and executed, and that the Roman authorities participate in this.[61] WREDE thus fastens upon precisely those features that belong to the very process of events defined, from disclosure to execution, which may be called *the Jewish process of execution*.

In agreement with WREDE, however, it should be remembered that a process of events may be acknowledged as realistic without thereby taking a position on its value as historical truth: that something may be the case in a given world does not imply that it in fact is or has been the case. Nevertheless, what is crucial in this context is that the gospel narrative as a myth, i.e. as a narrative that recounts trans-empiric events, involves a process of events that is not in itself mythical, since it remains within an empiric frame of reference.[62]

3. Prophet's Destiny

Without prejudice to the process of events itself, it is possible for the narrative to provide an alternative understanding of the official Jewish perception of this. The Jewish authorities see Jesus as guilty, as an offender, but according to the narrative he is innocent, since he is in fact God's messenger. In their own self-

---

[61] W. Wrede, *Das Messiasgeheimnis in den Evangelien*, Göttingen 1901, pp.129.
[62] Cf. Chapter XVII.

awareness the Jews execute a criminal, but in fact they thereby involuntarily commit judicial murder.

In a different perspective, the sanction process whose three elements (VAR) may be defined as 1) injury to be inflicted (criminal to crucify), 2) aggression process (the crucifixion itself as execution) and 3) injury inflicted (crucifixion consummated, i.e. death on the cross) itself becomes a crime that includes the elements 1) misdeed to be committed (possible murder, cf. 3,6), 2) misdeed (the crucifixion as murder) and 3) misdeed committed.[63] If Jesus is guilty, the aggression of the law-enforcer is legal and the crucifixion an execution; if he is innocent, however, the aggression is illegal, since the law, which is based upon the objective axiology, cannot be enforced and the crucifixion is murder:

EXECUTION	vs.	MURDER
Injury to be inflicted	vs.	Misdeed to be committed
Aggression process	vs.	Misdeed
Injury inflicted	vs.	Misdeed committed

The execution is a sanction that ends the process of events. The misdeed committed, the murder, is however a manipulative act that opens the way to a possible sanction process aimed at punishing the murderers (cf. how the offences of the tenants of the vineyard raise the question: "What then will the owner of the vineyard do?", 12,9). But implementation of the sanction process requires power, and who has the power to punish the authorities in a world in which they have the power? If it is maintained that the authorities are wrong but admit no mistake, the question of the justification for the objection arises. But where is one to go with an accusation that will not be accepted, a perception that will not be enforced? Only a higher justice and the intervention of a higher law-enforcer will then be able to deliver justice.

It should be noted that Jesus is not innocent in the sense that someone is held liable for a misdeed performed by another. Jesus is responsible for his acts and is judged according to his acts. In the Jewish perspective he is indeed guilty. The problem is that according to the narrative the Jewish leaders do not know what they are doing (cf. Lk 23,34). This is not because of simple ignorance but because they are blind, victims of a reflexive simulation, a self-delusion. They believe that their value-concept is objective, that they represent God's commands,

---

[63] Cf. Claude Bremond, "La logique des possibles narratifs", ibidem, p. 62; *Logique du récit*, p. 132, fig. 3.

whereas in fact they represent only their own subjective value-concept and thus act according to human commands. This disbelief means that they see in Jesus a blasphemer, whereas in fact they are themselves denying God. They see Jesus' proclaimer act (ποιᾶ) as a misdeed (κακοποιᾶ), although in reality it is a good deed (ἀγαθοποιᾶ).

A general feature of the gospel narrative is that the difference between the intended result of the voluntary action (x) and the result obtained by the involuntary action (y) is structural, more specifically antithetic or oppositional (if x = progression, protection, information or persuasion, then y = degression, repression, dissimulation or dissuasion). The gospel narrative operates using perspective inversion, a renversement or reversal of values (anagnorisis) that turns right and wrong upside down.

·The Jewish authorities thus consider themselves to be performing a good deed (the execution of the deceptor), whereas they are in fact performing a misdeed (the murder of the revelator). The Jewish authorities' not-knowing may perhaps have been founded on a dissimulation, a suppression of the truth, but Jesus is judged precisely on the basis of his informative doing, which raises the question of his true identity: self-appointed proclaimer or God's messenger. The problem is the disbelief and hard-heartedness that may be perceived as self-repression founded on fear of loss of leadership if Jesus is right, i.e. fear of losing power, respect, and status.

Jesus' rhetorical question to the Jewish authorities: "Did the baptism of John come from heaven, or was it of human origin?" 11,30, formulates the basic problems that concern Jesus himself: is he from God or of human origin, has he divine authority to act as he does, or is he a self-appointed pseudo-prophet who prophesies as his own heart dictates (cf. for example Ezek 13,2; Jn 7,18)? The Jews are in no doubt that he is a deceptor (cf. Mt 27,63). But the narrative which sovereignly determines what is truth and what is a lie describes Jesus as sent by God, like John the Baptist.

The designation "Son of God" indicates that Jesus is sent by God, and thus acts with divine authority. The Roman centurion's admission: "Truly this man was God's Son!" (15,39), and the act of confession of Joseph (member of the Jewish council), manifested by the entombment of Jesus (15,42ff), each expresses in its own way but in parallel that even among the Roman and Jewish authorities, who jointly killed him, there were those who were convinced of his innocence, that he was from God.[64]

But the Roman centurion and the council member see death as the final event. The former admits that Jesus was (ἦν) the Son of God (but is now unfortunately dead), and thus acknowledges that the crucifixion is murder. The other shows his

---

[64] Cf. Lk 23,47, where δίκαιος states perhaps more unambiguously that Jesus is innocent, cf. Lk 23,4.14.22; and ὁ δίκαιος, Acts 3,14; 7,52; 22,14. The Jewish authorities consider Jesus to be ἄδικος.

recognition of the dead man by care for the body, which is laid in a tomb sealed with a stone. While death is perceived as the final point in the process of events, Jesus is assigned a prophet's destiny parallel to that which overtook John the Baptist.

John has been thrown into prison before Jesus begins his public activity, 1,14. The specific circumstances surrounding the forerunner's end are told in the interposed narrative 6,14-29. In the context of the gospel narrative, there are a number of similarities between the two processes: the arrest (6,17, cf. 14,46, but also 12,12; 14,1.44.46.49), the imprisonment (6,17, cf. 15,1), the opponent's wish to kill the prophet (6,19, cf. 3,6; 11,18 and 14,1), the fear expressed of the prophet and his followers (6,20, cf. 11,18.32; 12,12 and 14,2), and the disciples' (6,29) and a follower's entombment of the murdered man, cf. also 9,11ff.

John is an eschatological prophet sent by God as a forerunner to prepare the way for Jesus. As such he is identified with the prophet Elijah, whose reappearance heralds the messianic and thereby the eschatological time, cf. 9.11. But God's messenger is killed, like many prophets before him. The vineyard parable focuses on the destiny of the prophets. One after the other is put to death, even the last prophet is killed, 12,1ff. But God will come and destroy the murderers of the prophets, 12,9; cf. 14,65; cf. Lk 11,47ff.

The killing of John perceived as a misdeed opens the way to a possible process of sanction for which God is the subject. What is concerned here is the punishment of the murderers, as referred to in the vineyard parable. Only this process of sanction will show that John was right, that he truly was sent by God. As long as this process of sanction has not been realized John is contradicted by the given reality, where power is the law.

To summarize, then, it may be said that God's messenger to humankind is killed because he is not recognized as such by those he was sent to serve (cf. Jn 1,11). His identity remains hidden, and only retrospectively - by virtue of the resurrection - does it become evident (to his disciples) that he truly was God's delegated proclaimer, his eschatological prophet. However positive the Roman centurion's and the Jewish council member's confessions, they can be seen only as human confessions, i.e. statements of belief that may very well be based upon a deceit. Only the resurrection shows (in the narrated reality) that the crucifixion is the murder of God's delegated proclaimer, who was telling the truth.[65]

But if he was telling the truth, the content of his proclamation is true and the kingdom of God has really come near. And the question that arises is whether his death and resurrection alone on a cognitive level serve the proclamation that God has passed over to action, or whether these events refer to actions that contribute to the pragmatic realization of the kingdom of God.

---

[65] A distinction must be made between the two elements in the sanction process, on the one hand the punishment of the transgressor and on the other hand the restoration of the victim (the resurrection). Both these sub-processes may serve as evidence of who is speaking the truth.

In other words: does Jesus appear only in the role of informator and persuader, or does he also appear (apart from in the wonder narratives) in the role of progressor and/or protector in the process of realizing the kingdom of God? This question will be discussed below in Part 4, The Savior.

CHAPTER NINE

THE GOSPEL OF JESUS CHRIST

A. CONTENT OF THE GOSPEL

It may sometimes be expedient to ask quite elementary questions. For example, it is illuminating to consider who is really the principal character in the gospel narrative. Is it God, Jesus, or the disciples? The relevance of this question becomes clear when it is borne in mind that the proclamation of the gospel of God states that God has passed over to action and that the kingdom of God is thus being realized. It would therefore not be entirely wrong to maintain that the gospel narrative concerns God and his works. On the other hand, the disciples occupy a central position to the extent that the proclamation of the gospel rests on their belief in the resurrected one. The gospel narrative also specifically recounts the relationship between Jesus and his disciples, and it can be said with equal justification that it is concerned with these disciples. But the evangelist himself singles out Jesus Christ as the principal character (cf. 1,1).

One may therefore be tempted simply to declare that the gospel narrative is concerned with God, Jesus and the Disciples, but the task must consist in explaining in detail the relationships between the actors referred to in order thereby to clarify the evangelist's reasons for focusing upon Jesus of Nazareth.

1. Projects

It is reasonable to raise the matter of who is really the principal character, because the gospel narrative gives information on several independent but related narrative processes, each with its own responsible subject of doing. God is the responsible subject of doing for a project aimed at the realization of the kingdom of God. Jesus is the responsible subject of doing for a project that ends in death on the cross/resurrection; and the disciples are responsible for the progress of a project that ends in the proclamation of the gospel of Jesus Christ. The gospel narrative is concerned with the progress of these projects and their mutual interdependence.

It is fairly clear that the disciples' proclamation project presupposes the realization of the resurrection, and is as such of a subordinate nature. But it is less clear that Jesus' project which presupposes God's transition to action must first be realized, before God will be able to accomplish his project of the kingdom. As will be seen later in detail, this is nevertheless the case, and for this reason Jesus becomes the gospel narrative's principal character: the projects of both God and the disciples stand or fall on the realization of Jesus' project.

The gospel narrative's proclamation has a content, a narrate, which involves a composite narrative process (V, A, or R) that appears to the responsible subject of doing as a *mission* or a *project*. It is concerned on the one hand with changing and/or preserving the being of a subject, i.e. with a *pragmatic dimension*, and on the other hand with changing and/or preserving a subject of being's cognitive-affective perception of this being, i.e. with a *cognitive dimension*. In his capacity as mediator, Jesus participates as subject of doing in both dimensions.

Realization of the kingdom of God is a task that God has accepted with a view to consummating his creation. The superior pragmatic process then becomes God's re-creation, which is referred to as the gospel narrative's *creation project* (God as creator). Embedded in this process is a pragmatic sub-process for which Jesus is the responsible subject of doing. This is referred to as the gospel narrative's *salvation project* (Jesus as savior). Facing these two relatively independent but connected pragmatic processes are two, also relatively independent but connected, cognitive processes. Jesus' proclamation, of which the disciples are the privileged recipients, is in the nature of initiation and instruction, and for this reason it is referred to as the gospel narrative's *teaching project* (Jesus as teacher). The ultimate aim of this teaching is to qualify the disciples as apostles, i.e. delegated proclaimers, and therefore the gospel narrative's *proclamation project* (the disciples as apostles) is finally concerned here.

Some important aspects of the creation project (cf. Chapter VIII, B.2. and C.4.) have already been discussed, and the salvation project will be analyzed further below (in Part 4, The Savior). In what follows, however, attention will concentrate on the teaching and proclamation projects, which must themselves be seen in the light of the gospel narrative's proclaiming narration.

2. The Processes of Events

Considered collectively, Markan research to date appears to contain an inner tension reminding one most of a contradiction in terms. On the one hand, most exegetes will agree in defining the gospel as the apostolic message of salvation through Jesus Christ (cf. for example Rom 1,3ff; 1 Cor 15,3ff and Acts 10,37ff). The gospel is perceived as the proclamation's content, and this is a narrate that persuasively informs about pragmatic acts which have occurred and have effected a change in the nature of the world, so giving it a new direction. The gospel is concerned with salvation and creation.

On the other hand, Markan research has for nearly a hundred years primarily related to a complex of difficulties belonging to the gospel narrative's cognitive dimension, the question of the so-called *messianic secret*.[1] This is of course not in itself very remarkable, since the gospel narrative is in fact characterized in

---

[1] Cf. James L. Blevins, *The Messianic Secret in Markan Research 1901-1976*, Washington 1981.

general by a cognitive play between revelation and secrecy, information and dissimulation. But what is remarkable is that it has never been considered specifically whether the Christian gospel in fact embraces only the creation and salvation projects, or whether the information given by the gospel narrative on the relationship between Jesus and his disciples also forms part of it.

If the gospel's content is creation and salvation alone, then the account of the relationship between Jesus and the disciples is merely an irrelevance that the evangelist has for some reason taken the trouble to include. The gospel narrative consists, then, partly of the gospel of salvation through Jesus Christ and partly of a superfluous account of the relationship between Jesus and his disciples. This account could then be researched separately, with no need to bother about what is disclosed when the secret is revealed. Moreover, the question whether this information about the disciples may have a function in the context of the proclamation of the gospel can be disregarded.

But the point that Jesus is the Messiah has nothing to say unless this title is perceived as a reference to the complex of roles that defines Jesus within the creation and salvation projects. And as regards the function of the proclamation, it should be clear that if the subject of being which - apart from Jesus himself - is affected by the events that have occurred is not informed of this, then there is no gospel. Or, more fundamentally: if the pragmatic events that have occurred do not affect one subject of being that is different from Jesus himself, then there is no gospel. And, finally: if this subject of being, in its capacity of a virtual subject of doing, is not informed about what it must do (for example, repent and believe in the gospel), then there is no message of salvation.

By volume, the cognitive processes dominate in Mark's Gospel, and to this extent it is correct that Mark has written »ein Buch der geheimen Epiphanien«.[2] But nevertheless it is the pragmatic processes that make up the gospel narrative's foundation. Overstating the cognitive dimension constitutes a double danger: one overlooks on the one hand that the gospel narrative basically tells about salvation and creation, and on the other hand that the narrative about the disciples is a constitutive part of the Christian gospel.

The gospel narrative's four project sequences are connected in pairs. The creation and salvation projects belong to one common process that is referred to as the *gospel-constituting process of events*. The teaching and proclamation projects belong to one common process referred to as the *gospel-persisting process of events*. In this perspective, the gospel narrative is thus a *double narrative* that tells in part about the relationship between God and Jesus (constitution) and in part about the relationship between Jesus and the disciples (persistence). By this means, all other actors are given the status of extras and living setpieces.

---

[2] Martin Dibelius, *Die Formgeschichte des Evangeliums*, Tübingen (1919) 1971, p. 232.

When it is said that the gospel is to be proclaimed to "all nations" (13,10) "in the whole world" (14,9) then, does this message have the gospel-constituting events alone as its content or does it include the gospel-persisting events? In the opinion of narrative exegesis, there is an irrevocable connection between these two processes of events. From one viewpoint it is true that the persisting process of events is secondary, since it presupposes the constituting process and not vice versa. But from a different angle the constituting process presupposes the persisting process, since the transitive subject of being's possibility of relating itself to the change that has taken place is given only by virtue of the proclamation of this event. And in this context the detail in which the gospel narrative tells how this proclamation in fact came about is truly remarkable.

It can therefore be asserted that *the gospel is the gospel narrative* which tells of two relatively independent but connected processes, the constituting (or pragmatic) and the persisting (or cognitive) processes of events.[3] In the world of the narrate the cognitive presupposes the pragmatic, but in the world of the narration the situation is reversed, since the constituting events are available only as narrated in a persisting proclamation. The gospel narrative therefore emerges as self-dependent, characterized by an auto-genesis, in that these two worlds appear to relate to one another like the two sides of a *Möbius tape*.

---

[3] These problems should not be confused with the question of the relationship between the proclaiming and the proclaimed Jesus. What is concerned here is not whether the proclaimer of the gospel of God speaks in the gospel of the church (cf. Rudolf Pesch, *Das Markusevangelium, 1. Teil*, Freiburg 1980, pp. 106) but whether the gospel of the church includes both the constituting and the persisting events. If this is the case, it cannot be reduced to the message of Jesus' death and resurrection.

B. THE PROCLAMATION'S FOUNDATION

1. The Proclamation's Narrative

The gospel text begins with ἀρχή (1,1) and ends with γάρ (16,8).[4] The act of narration has the same beginning and the same ending. But the gospel narrative begins with an act, the Baptist's proclamation, which as execution of a commandment from God in turn presupposes a prophetic calling. This act has an initiating effect upon a project process aimed at the realization of the kingdom of God, and the gospel narrative can therefore be said to be completed only when this project sees its realization.

But the gospel narrative also includes another project that is initiated before, but realized only after, the narration's cessation. The proclamation project to be realized during the waiting period between the meeting with the risen one and his return at the parousia is an integral part of the gospel's content and an inseparable part of the narrative concerning the proclamation's foundation.

a. The Implicit Ending

In this connection, attention is concentrated on the ending of the gospel text, which is quite strange: "and they said nothing (οὐδέν) to anyone (οὐδενί), for they were afraid" (16,8). The women, "Mary Magdalene, and Mary the mother of James, and Salome" (16,1), are the first to receive the message that "Jesus of Nazareth, who was crucified" (16,6) has risen. And they are ordered to tell "his disciples and Peter" that he is going ahead of them (Peter, the disciples and the women) to Galilee; there they will see him, just as he told them (16,7; cf. 14,28).

How then is it to be understood that the women did not tell anyone?

It is natural to imagine that the women quite simply remained silent and preserved the resurrection message as a secret which they alone knew about. But in that case the gospel narrative contradicts itself, since how then could Mark narrate his narrative? There seems to be no way out of this. Either the women remained silent and the narrative contradicts itself, collapses into a subtle form of irony, or they passed on the message to the disciples and Peter as they were told to do.[5] As regards content, the brief postscript (16,9*) is thus congenial with

---

[4] The short ending (16,9*), the longer ending (16,9-20), and the so-called Freer logion (cf. *Novum Testamentum Graece*, 26. Auflage, Stuttgart 1983, p. 148) are secondary additions. According to the textual tradition's original form, the Markan text ends with 16,8, as is clearly evidenced by the two oldest manuscripts of the New Testament, Codex Sinaiticus and Codex Vaticanus; cf. Søren Giversen, *Det ny Testamentes Teksthistorie* (The Textual History of New Testament), København 1978; and Rudolf Pesch, *Das Markusevangelium, 1. Teil*, pp. 40; *2. Teil*, pp. 540. The problem is not to recognize the secondary nature of these endings but to explain the Markan text's abrupt ending, cf. below.

[5] The narrative cannot be made completely unambiguous; one must choose between a reading according to which the narrate disclaims the narration (the women's absolute silence contradicts the narrator's discourse) and a reading which allows the narration to disclaim the narrate (the narrator's discourse contradicts the women's silence).

the gospel narrative when it reads laconically: "And all that had been commanded them they told briefly to those around Peter.".

It has of course been considered whether an original ending may have been lost. There is no epilogue, such as is known from other gospel manuscripts. But, Mk 16,1-8 can, despite its open-endedness, be considered a "satisfactory closure" from a literary aspect, as has been shown in particular detail by J.LEE MAGNESS.[6]

He writes in his conclusion:

> Whether the women reported the news and the disciples gathered with Jesus to become eyewitnesses of the resurrection (as I think Mark implies) or not, the fact that their response is unnarrated concretizes the options available to those who have been told that Jesus arose from the dead. The options include appropriate action, inappropriate action, and inaction; proclamation, indiscriminate communication, and a total lack of communication; and obedient following, passive acceptance, and rejection. The suspension creates the necessity of choosing among these various options, of providing a resolution to the story in the experience of the reader rather than in the text. The emphasis of the Gospel thus shifts from past history to present proclamation, (...).[7]

It will be seen that here the ending is considered in the light of the narration, which concerns the relationship between narrator and reader.

It is possible that the solution of the story is more likely to occur within the reader than in the text, but the crucial point is that the supplementing interpretation is far from fortuitous but is governed by the narrated information, 1,1-16,5 in general, and 16,6-8 in particular.[8] The reader/exegete is subjected to a semiotic constraint that makes it possible inferentially to reconstruct with great certainty a *narrative ending* on the basis of the gospel text's information, which could be referred to as the gospel narrative's *implicit ending*.[9]

First, the women must tell Peter and the disciples what they have seen and heard. Either the women said nothing to anyone (the disciples) until they had regained their composure, or they said nothing to anyone apart from Peter and the disciples.

---

[6] J. Lee Magness, *Sense and Absence. Structure and Suspension in the Ending of Mark's Gospel*, Atlanta 1986, p. 119.

[7] J. Lee Magness, ibidem, p. 124.

[8] Magness concedes that Mark indicates that "The women pass on the confirming and guiding words of the angel. The disciples follow their instructions and are reunited with Jesus. They are renewed in their relationship and recommissioned for ministry."; ibidem, pp. 121.

[9] This is not a matter of an historical reconstruction; but neither is it an uncritical reading which allows itself to be fixed by the narrator's narrated world. The interest concerns exclusively the narrative's inherent probability structure, its possibility of substantiating its narration in the narrated events.

In the light of the role played by predictions and their fulfilment, it then becomes clear that the risen one appears to the disciples and the women of Galilee just as he had said (14,27ff).[10]

This meeting cannot be identified with the coming of the Son of Man (13,26), which presupposes inter alia that the gospel was initially proclaimed to all nations (13,10; cf. 14,9). But the meeting with the risen one is the precondition for the proclamation of the gospel, which has been placed as a mission in the hands of the disciples under Peter's leadership. The scattered sheep (14,27) know only silence, muteness, since they saw in the death of Jesus the dissolution of the foundation of every proclamation. Peter's denial of Jesus is also the denial of his proclamation. Jesus' resurrection involves for its part a re-awakening of the proclamation, a revival of his relationship with the disciples and Peter. The meeting with the risen one is the precondition for the resumption of the discipleship, which is itself the precondition for the realization of the evangelical proclamation. If the women do not tell the disciples and Peter what they have seen and heard, and if Peter and the disciples do not meet the risen one in Galilee, no proclamation will be heard, no gospel narrative will exist. It can then be seen clearly that *the gospel narrative is also the narrative of its own foundation as a proclamation.*

There is thus an inherent narrative constraint that obliges the exegete to thematize, in the implicit Markan ending, a resumption of the disciples' proclamation project in the light of the new proclamation basis constituted by the resurrection. The meeting with the risen one that re-establishes the ruptured discipleship must end in a re-delegation of the disciples as apostles equipped with the new perception in which every earlier proclamation recognizes its own explanation and clarification. Passages such as in 13,11 and 14,9 presuppose such a re-commissioning, *but to the narratee Mark's Gospel is itself the clearest evidence of this proclamation.*

It is not therefore surprising that the gospel manuscripts end in a thematization of the proclamation as a project. This occurs both in the detailed postscript to Mark's Gospel: "Go into all the world and proclaim the good news to the whole creation!" (16,15), and in its shorter postscript: "And afterwards Jesus himself sent out through them [those around Peter], from east to west, the sacred and imperishable proclamation of eternal salvation." (16,9*). There is a direct mission-command in Matthew's Gospel: "Go therefore and make disciples of all nations, ..." (28,19); in Luke's Gospel there is an indirect mission-command: "... and that repentance and forgiveness of sins is to be proclaimed in his name to all nations ..." (24,47); in John's Gospel, the mission is expressed when the disciples are referred to as those who have been sent into the world (17,18), and

---

[10] Cf. David Rhoads, Donald Michie, *Mark as Story. An Introduction to the Narrative of a Gospel*, Philadelphia 1982, pp. 96. These scholars, however, uphold the idea of the reader's uncertainty by virtue of the narrate's ambiguity.

when the object of the gospel is defined as that which will make the narratee believe (20,31; cf. also 20,19-23).

It is therefore possible to reconstruct an implicit narrative Markan ending that includes the following elements:

1)   The women tell Peter and the disciples what they have seen and heard.

2)   The women, the disciples and Peter meet and identify in Galilee "Jesus of Nazareth, who was crucified" as the risen one - as has been predicted.

3)   Jesus sends out the disciples as apostles to preach the gospel to all nations.

Yet another element should be included that thematizes the absence of the risen one during the period of proclamation ("the good news must first be proclaimed to all nations", 13,10), where false Messiahs and false prophets will try to lead the elect astray (13,21f). What is concerned is the vanishing (cf. Lk 24,31), but more permanently the ascension:

4)   Jesus is taken up (ἀναλαμβάνω), cf. 16,19, Acts 1,11) or lifted up (ἐπαίρω, Lk 24,51, Acts 1,9) into heaven (as regards the movement itself, the shift from one place to another, the journey, πορεύομαι is employed, Acts 1,10f).

This element is absent in Matthew, who however supplements with information on the place in Galilee to which Jesus had directed the eleven disciples (28,16), i.e. a mountain, as the place of revelation between heaven and earth, cf. 17,1ff.

This implicit ending is merely what narrative exegesis considers it possible to make explicit by a so-called catalysis procedure (by inference) as the necessary connection ("*the missing link*") between the gospel story's narration and narrate. The Markan narration presupposes this implicit ending *because it alone receives its authority and legitimacy from the events narrated.*

A possible objection might be that such a catalytic reconstruction is in reality merely a post-rationalization that uncritically records supplementary material obtained from the other gospel texts and Acts. But the need for a Markan ending is not because of a comparison with other gospel manuscripts; it is not because Matthew and Luke have an ending that it is necessary to reconstruct an implicit ending for Mark. The need is based on the Markan narrative itself, since the narrating of the narrative - the narration - can only base its legitimacy upon the events narrated. Without an implicit ending the narration would invalidate itself, since in that event it invalidates the relationship between the narration and the narrate. The reference to other manuscripts and parts of manuscripts is both legitimate and expedient, since these are themselves various attempts to meet the same semiotic requirement or constraint.

Another question that emerges is whether or not such narrative reconstruction unavoidably becomes the reconstruction of a formerly existing but lost Markan ending. But the answer to this must be in the negative. The point of reference is that 16,1-8 is the original ending of Mark's Gospel. The peculiar nature of this ending must give cause for interpretation and not the reconstruction of a lost text. But making the implicit Markan ending more explicit is not the reconstruction of a lost text but of the necessary, narrative connection between narration and narrate. Here the exegete does nothing more than undertake the interpretation which the text and the narration, with its abrupt ending in terms of content, foists on its implicit reader. Whoever disregards the narration and tries to interpret the women's silence within the narrated universe will be able only to achieve laboured constructions. The concept of the women's absolute silence remains meaningless. If one ties oneself to the assumption that it must nevertheless have a meaning, one abandons oneself to an unending search for a profundity which is as empty as the tomb.

b. The End of the Narration

Although it is possible (and necessary) to reconstruct a narrative ending, it remains to consider what is implied in Mark's ending his narration as he in fact does. The question contains many facets, but only those aspects of the matter that can be acknowledged on the basis of narrative exegesis are of interest here.

The point of reference is again the following model:

1) The narrator tries to convey to the narratee the concept of a virtual, actualized or realized state of being and/or process.

2) The subject of being for this state/process is the narratee, the narrator or a third person A.

3) The subject of doing responsible for this state/process is the narratee, the narrator, the third person A, or a fourth person B.

This includes several variables, and a large number of different combinations can therefore be predicted. If only items 2) and 3) are considered, a sub-division can be undertaken depending on whether the actant differs from or is identical with the narrator/narratee. This is what the linguist ÉMILE BENVENISTE does when he articulates the person-category in person/non-person. Where narrator/narratee appear in the narrate, the discourse (speech) is subjectivized and characterized by a person, 1st and 2nd person, I/you, for example a) "But after *I* am raised up, *I* will go before *you* to Galilee.", cf. 14,28; an *enunciative* narration may be concerned here.[11] Where these do not appear in the narrate, the discourse has been objectivized and characterized by non-person, third person, he, she, it; for example b) "But after *he* is raised, *he* will go before *them* to Galilee."; here an *utterative* narration may be concerned.[12]

The gospel narrative is characterized by an utterative narration - which is not of course contradicted by the fact that there are enunciative narrations embedded in the narrate, in that the narrate's utterative persons break into speech (transition from story into dialogue). For example, each time the narrated actor Jesus breaks into speech there is an embedded enunciative discourse. It is still far from clear which function this transition to speech has in the creation of signification, but it is at least possible to indicate the interesting feature that the embedded discourse takes on the nature of a *quotation*. The narrator (e.g. Mark) quotes *here and now* what the utterative subject (e.g. Jesus) said *at that time* (for example, "But after I am raised up, I will go before you to Galilee."), since the narrated has indeed taken place. But at the same time this speech is presented as direct speech, which can only be in the present. Mark is not content to say that Jesus said something: the reader hears precisely *his* speech that the narrator is quoting. It is as if the narrator has here vanished from his own discourse in order to give the floor to another.

But it must be said without evasion that this is an illusion. It is of course the narrator who is speaking although hiding behind a narrated figure, here the narrative Jesus. The narrative subjects, the narrative's actors, are like puppets that neither act nor speak unless there is a narrator behind them who pulls the strings and supplies the voice. Narrative exegesis therefore does not ask whether the narrator has quoted Jesus and the other persons correctly, since they say only what the narrator puts into their mouths. Even the fact that the narrative changes into dialogue is in no way remarkable. On the contrary, the transition to dialogue is one of the most elementary and well-known features of the narrative.[13]

Mark's Gospel is a narrative whose narrator and narratee do not appear on the stage of the narrated. One of the narrated persons is Jesus who sometimes breaks into enunciative speech, for example a controversy dialogue or an instruction to the disciples, but he may also break into utterative speech. This is what he is

---

[11] Émile Benveniste, *Problèmes de linguistique générale I*, Paris 1966, pp. 251. As regards the concepts of enunciative and utterative, cf. *Sémiotique*, art. "Localisation spatio-temporelle".

[12] Two further intermediate forms can be distinguished: the semi-enunciative narration, e.g. c) "But after *I* am raised up, *I* will go before *them* to Galilee"; and the semi-utterative narration, e.g. d) "But after *he* is raised up, *he* will go before *you* to Galilee."

[13] Cf. *Sémiotique*, art. "Débrayage". According to narrative exegesis, it is not possible to get back to the authentic words of Jesus. Everything that the narrative Jesus says refers back to the gospel narrative's enunciation alone.

doing when he tells a narrative, a parable, for example 12,1ff: "A man planted, etc.". But whether or not an embedded enunciative or utterative speech is concerned it is the narrator who supplies the voice. The relationship between narration and narrate cannot be abolished, which has important consequences for narrative exegesis.[14] However difficult it may be to analyze, a systematic connection must be reckoned with between the narration's actants and the narrated, narrative subjects. Where a narrated enunciative narration exists, the task of narrative exegesis is to explain the relationship between this and the superior narrative act, the narration. The question of the relationship between the proclaiming Jesus (narrated enunciative narration) and the proclaimed Jesus (narrating enunciative narration) is an expression of the recognition of such a connection. But where a narrated utterative narration exists it must try to explain the relationship between this local narrative (for example a parable) and the global narrative, the narrate (narrating utterative narration). The recognition of the similarity between the son's fate in the vineyard parable and the son's fate in the gospel narrative as a whole is also an expression of this connection.

It has been pointed out from various quarters that the gospel narrative does not end with a pragmatic act but with a cognitive act: verses 16,1-8, "offer *in discourse* the resurrection of Jesus".[15] Mark does not tell of the resurrection event but allows a narrated actor, the young man (16,5), to announce that it has taken place. This young man in his white robe is perhaps not an angel, but he is after all a messenger (ἄγγελος) who informs the women in an embedded narration.

In his capacity of narrator, he informs the women as narratee that Jesus has risen. The narrate, the content of the proclamation, is a realized state/process for which neither No nor Ne is the responsible subject of doing or the favoured subject of being. Neither the messenger nor the women are resurrecting or being resurrected. But then the messenger proclaims a narrative, and narrative exegesis must consider what relationship exists between this local narrative and the global narrative. Either the resurrection has nothing to do with baptism and death on the cross, or it must be seen as an event that belongs to the same process of action as baptism and death on the cross, cf. below in Part 4, The Savior.

Narrative exegesis must also, however, consider the relationship between this local narrative act and the global narrative act, i.e. what it means that the relationship between the messenger, the women and the resurrection message are isomorphous with the relationship between Mark, the readers and the gospel of Jesus Christ, because from a different perspective the messenger informs of a consummated process, the resurrection, for which God is the responsible subject of doing and the women are the favoured subject of being. Moreover, the

---

[14] Irrespective of how objectified the discourse appears, it is the result of a narration process whose subject of enunciation (ὁ λογοποιός), split into Narrator and Narratee, appears in disguise on the stage of the narrated.

[15] Cf. J. Lee Magness, ibidem, p. 115.

messenger acts as prescriptor, in that he informs them persuasively about a virtual process, the proclamation, for which the women are the responsible subject of doing, whereas the disciples are the favoured subject of being. Either the women believe the messenger and pass on the message, or they do not believe him. Either the readers believe Mark and proclaim the gospel to all nations (13,11; 14,9), or they do not believe him. Either the messenger is a revelator and his message is true, or he is a deceptor. Either Mark is God's messenger and his gospel is true, or he speaks for himself: he is a pseudo-apostle.

It may be said that the narration and narrate in 16,1-8 *tend* to merge, whereby the emphasis is shifted from narrated past to narrating present, "from past history to present proclamation". The message, "Jesus has risen", sounds almost the same to the women and the readers. By his abrupt ending, Mark then emphasizes that there is nothing more to say. Everything has been said. The rest is up to the reader, who cannot get the definitive sign he desires but must content himself with a message, a narrative. Not only the resurrection, of course, is absent. In the narration's perspective all events are absent, or present merely as narrated events in the discourse. Mark has seen nothing, but narrates what he has heard.

But only a tendency is concerned, since the narrative ending alone can establish the missing connection between the messenger and Mark via the women and the disciples.[16]

2. The Proclamation of the Narrative

Whoever narrates the narrative of the foundation of the gospel proclamation himself exercises a proclamation act, whose basis is to be found in the narrative message that is indeed being proclaimed. Although the narrator Mark does not appear among the narrated actors, an especially intimate relationship exists between his proclaimer project and the proclaimer mission to which the disciples see themselves as called under Peter's leadership.

---

[16] Although aware that the last sentence disclaims the narrative, Bas van Iersel insists that the women said nothing to anyone. It is by holding to this reading that the readers "realize that the message of the heavenly messenger in Mark is really not meant at all for the disciples and Peter, but for no one but the readers themselves", *Reading Mark*, Edinburgh 1989, p. 209. Through the messenger's words the narrator sets the reader in his own time, the time between resurrection and parousia, van Iersel believes (cf. ibidem, p. 206), but in that case the meeting with the resurrected one and the parousia merge. However, if the gospel narrative's realized proclamation is seen as evidence of the meeting with the resurrected one, then it is this proclamation which sets the reader in his own time not through an actantial identification (messenger = Mark; the women = the readers) but through a temporal identification, cf. below. If the merging between narration and narrate was to be more than a tendency, then text and narration would have to end as follows: [Do not be alarmed; you are looking for Jesus of Nazareth, who was crucified. He has been raised, he is not here. Look, there is the place they laid him. But go, tell his disciples and Peter that he is going ahead of you to Galilee; there you will see him, just as he told you. *This is my message for you* (or better: *Behold, now it has been told you!*).] (cf. Mt 28,5ff). The very last sentence must be "ἰδοὺ εἶπον ὑμῖν", Behold, now it has been told you!, which would refer at the same time to what the angel said to the women and what the narrator said (the gospel of Jesus Christ, 1,1) to the narratee; but this is (unfortunately) not the case.

Bishop Papias' strongly disputed note, according to which Mark, who had neither heard the Lord nor followed him, was Peter's interpreter, can at least be considered as expressing the later tradition's attempt to explicate the - semiotically - close connection existing between the narrated actor Peter and the anonymous narrator who was later given the name of Mark.[17] The concept of Mark as Peter's interpreter is the closest one can get in trying to construct a bridge to the circle of disciples and to overcome the dissonance that arises because Peter himself was after all in the better position to teil the story. The gospel narrative's linguistic form (third-person, objectivized discourse) indeed excludes the narrator's appearance on the stage of the narrated. But conversely Mark - and any other evangelist - must in the final analysis retell Peter's story.[18]

The reading, which involves a reconstruction of the gospel narrative's implicit, narrative ending, does not fail to observe the narration's character of presentic proclamation, but it shifts attention from the meeting with the risen one in Galilee to the eschatological Parousia. The question is whether Mark proclaims before or after this meeting in Galilee, and the reconstructed ending lets him proclaim after it.

Mark proclaims the gospel of Jesus Christ, which is characterized by an overarching action ending in the final realization of the kingdom of God. The subject of doing responsible for this process is neither Mark nor the reader but God. The favoured subject of being in the narrated world is neither Mark nor the reader but narrated persons (the baptized or the elect, cf. 13,20.22.27). Narrative in the true sense (*récit* vs. *discours*) is concerned only when the subject of doing and the subject of being are neither narrator nor narratee. The problem then is how the gospel narrative, which must indeed be defined as a narrative in this sense, i.e. as a discourse telling of objectivized, third-person subjects (God, Jesus, disciples, etc.), can become a proclamation understood as a personal address. As already mentioned, a number of scholars are seeking to lay bare the proclamation's presentic aspect by examining 16,1-8, but in what follows it will be attempted to show that the implicit reader's intuitive perception of a presentic proclamation is due to other semiotic properties of the gospel narrative's narration.

a. Deictic Semiotization

This concerns a pheno.nenon designated as *deictic semiotization*, which relates to the narration's person and/or place and/or time. The Danish children's song,

---

[17] Cf. Rudolf Pesch, *Das Markusevangelium, 1. Teil*, pp. 4; Walter Schmithals, *Einleitung in die drei ersten Evangelien*, Berlin 1985, pp. 30; Kurt Aland, *Synopsis Quattuor Evangeliorum*, Stuttgart 1986, pp. 531.

[18] Cf. the comprehensive literature on Peter within the apocryphal and pseudo-epigraphic texts; cf. Edgar Hennecke and Wilhelm Schneemelcher, *Neutestamentliche Apokryphen I/II*, Tübingen 1968.

"The chimney sweep went awalking", tells of a chimney sweep and a girl who elope and arrive in Africa. Here the girl first gives birth to twins, and then to a monkey (a fool). Having told this story (utterative narration), the narrator suddenly switches over to personal address in the last verse (enunciative narration): "The monkey (fool), that was you!", so that the chosen listener sees himself as semiotized by what is narrated. He or she is deictically semiotized as a fool, a bastard.[19] It could be said that the discourse interprets its presupposed reader as a fool, but this is too week a designation. The narration symbolizes or *semiotizes* its reader by attributing to him an identity and a being through the manner in which he is inscribed in and signified by what is narrated.

In other cases, there is not actantial but spatial semiotization, for example in etiological local legends. At Denmark's largest stone, Damestenen, which lies in the parish of Hesselager, East Funen, an information point has been set up from which something like the following can be read: "A giantess on Langeland took a dislike to the church of Svindinge. The high church tower was a thorn in her flesh. It was the first thing she saw when she got up in the morning, and every day she was thus reminded of Christendom's victory over paganism. At last it became too much for her. She took a large stone and threw it at the tower, but it reached no further than Hesselager where it can be seen to this very day." The legend is known in countless variations. What is important in this context is the legend's implicit reference: "Look, it was the very stone lying here!" corresponding to the song's reference, "The Monkey, that was you!".

In the case of the gospel narrative, however, attention is concentrated on the temporal semiotization. In the vineyard parable, 12,1ff, this phenomenon is particularly in evidence, and it is therefore appropriate first to take a closer look at this.

The parable narrative begins - as narratives often do - with a brief description of the situation: "A man planted a vineyard, put a fence around it, dug a pit for the wine press, and built a watchtower; then he leased it to tenants ($\gamma\epsilon\omega\rho\gamma\acute{o}\varsigma$; farmer, specified from the context as wine-growers) and went to another country.", 12,1 (cf. 13,34).

The owner of the vineyard is absent, the vineyard is in the care of the tenants, who have rights of use but not proprietary rights. When the time has come, the owner of the vineyard sends ($\mathring{\alpha}\pi o\sigma\tau\acute{\epsilon}\lambda\lambda\omega$, cf. 9,37) a servant ($\delta o\tilde{\upsilon}\lambda o\varsigma$, cf. 10,43ff) to the tenants to collect his part of the fruits of the vineyard. But they seize him, beat him ($\delta\acute{\epsilon}\rho\omega$; cf. 14,65) and send him away empty-handed. The owner sends another servant, but they hit him over the head and insult him ($\mathring{\alpha}\tau\iota\mu\acute{\alpha}\zeta\omega$; cf. 15,20.29.31.32). The next one they kill; those following are beaten or killed.

---

[19] The children's song is a dysangelium not unlike another dysangelium, the Fall myth, Gen 2,4b-3,24, where a man and a woman, through their transgression, validate themselves and their offspring, their descendants, not as fools but as sinners.

The owner of the vineyard is now left with only one, his beloved son (υἱὸς ἀγαπητός, cf. 1,1; 9,7). Finally he sends him to them, saying: "They will respect (ἐντρέπω, perhaps esteem) my son", 12,7. But the tenants see their chance; if they kill the heir (κληρονόμος), the inheritance will fall to them. So they seize him (λαμβάνω, cf. κρατέω 12,12; 14,2.46), kill him (ἀποκτείνω, cf. 8,31; 9,31; 10,34; 14,2; cf. ἀπόλλυμι, 3,6) and throw (ἐκβάλλω) the body out of the vineyard.

There is quite a lot to say about this parable, but what is concerned here is only the temporal semiotization, and first of all it must be emphasized that the parable narrative ends with 12,8. The remaining part of the pericope does not belong to the parable in a narrow sense, i.e. as an utterative narrative that concerns third-person subjects. At the same time everyone is aware that it has not ended, since the process of action it recounts is not concluded. The listener must indeed ask: "What then will the owner of the vineyard do?", i.e. the question Jesus himself rhetorically poses (12,9).

An obvious answer would then be: "Well now, listen: the owner of the vineyard *came* and *destroyed* the tenants and *gave* the vineyard to others!" The listeners ask in the future tense (ποιήσει) but the narrator answers in the past tense here. The future the listeners have in mind is, however, the utterative future, i.e. a future that applies only within what is narrated. Their question is identical with the question: "What happened then, *at the time* it happened that you now tell us about?" - an "at the time" which, it is worth noting, is not a chronologically defined point in time but a time set by the enunciation's "now". In relation to the enunciation's time, the enunciative time that constitutes *the narration's* presentic point of reference, a narrative will typically tell of events that *have* taken place, so that the narrative's time, the utterative time, emerges as past tense. There is no simultaneity between narrative and narration, since the narrative's process of events, quite independently of its internal temporalization, goes before and is considered as completed relative to the narration's here and now.

The parable's *narrative* pivotal point is the tenants' crime, which constitutes a presentic point of reference in relation to which something goes before (utterative "past"), the establishment of the vineyard and its transfer to their care, and something follows, the master's negative sanction in the form of the tenants' destruction and the re-transfer of the vineyard to others (utterative "future"). If it were an ordinary narrative, this temporalized process of events would thus be completed and past relative to the enunciative time of narration:

Utterative time:	Past ← Present → Future		
Enunciative time:	Past	← Present →	Future

What is significant, however, is that the two points of reference here tend to merge. This is most clearly to be seen in Jesus' use of the future forms: ποιήσει, ἐλεύσεται, ἀπολέσει and δώσει. A narrator can of course at a given time during the narrative interrupt the narration to ask his listeners what they think will happen. This could be a special way of holding their attention. But the future then concerned is the narrated future. The question: "What do you think will happen?" is identical here with the question: "What do you think happened then, *at the time?*"

But in this case the narrative's world merges with the narration's world: the utterative future is the enunciative future. It no longer concerns what is to happen in the narrative but what is to happen in the narrator's and the narratee's world, a reality that sees itself as semiotized by the narrative.

The parable's status as narrative presents itself with special clarity by virtue of its lack of historical anchorage. The parable narrative concerns a de-realized, narrated world that lacks indication of place (where was this vineyard located, where did the owner go when he went abroad?) and of time (when did these events occur?), and in which persons (the owner, the tenants, the servants and the son) appear without proper names.

The absence of anthroponyms (for example God, Jesus, John the Baptist), toponyms (for example Galilee, Jerusalem) and chrononyms (for example "In the days of King Herod (...)", Lk 1,5) which serve to evoke the signification effect of "reality" allows the narrative to appear as ahistorical, anonymized, dealing with an imagined or envisaged world that is nevertheless actorialized, since the persons appear designated by their roles (γεωργός, κύριος, υἱός, δοῦλος, κληρο-νόμος), spatialized, since it is possible to distinguish the vineyard's location from the owner's residence, and temporalized ("When the season came", τῷ καιρῷ; "What then will the owner of the vineyard do?", τί ποιήσει ὁ κύριος τοῦ ἀμπελῶ-νος).[20] By its ahistorical appearance, the parable narrative signals its status as analogy or metaphor. But at the same time, against this background the gospel narrative's intended historical appearance emerges all more clearly.

It tells therefore of a drama performed on another stage, of persons at a time and at a place different from those of the listeners. But only up to a certain point in the narration, when Jesus causes the two scenes to merge by his use of future-tense forms. The narrator allows his narrative to remain unfinished so that it can end not in an utterative future but in the enunciative future, in the narrator's and the narratee's future.

It is as if the narrated process of events grows straight out into the narrator's and the narratee's reality. By changing the grammatical time from aorist to the future, the narrative is referentialized, a deictic emphasis takes place which

---

[20] Cf. *Sémiotique*, art. "Ancrage", "Anthroponyme", "Chrononyme", "Localisation spatio-temporelle" and "Toponyme".

tendentiously abolishes the split between narrate and narration. Jesus does not say directly to his listeners: "The tenants, they are you.", but as can be seen from 12,12, they well understand that he tells this parable about them, and about himself.

The parable narrative is a third-person discourse, since neither Jesus nor his listeners appear in the narrative. If one focuses on the son/heir, then Jesus tries to impart to his listeners the concept of a consummated murder whose subject of being is the third person A (the son) and whose subject of doing is the fourth person B (the tenants). Within this aspect, it may be said that a *virtual* metaphorical relationship exists between the utterative and the enunciative actants. The term "metaphor" refers here to a *correlation*, i.e. a relation between relations: the relationship between "son" and "tenants" is homologous to the relationship between Jesus and the Jewish authorities:

Son : Tenants :: Jesus : Authorities

There is no metaphorical relationship between "the son" and Jesus but between the two relationships, which are characterized by similarity. The two sets of actants find themselves in situations that are homologous as regards narrative genre and role configuration.

But it is only the deictic semiotization of the narrator and/or the narratee that effectively turns the narrative into a parable, since the two worlds are hereby joined metonymically. As already pointed out, this may occur in relation to the person and location categories, but here it is the time category that serves this purpose, since the utterative and the enunciative futures merge. It is by virtue of this time-merger that the listeners understand the person-merger, that the parable he tells is about them. Or more correctly it is by virtue of this deictic designation that they see themselves as semiotized, unable to avoid interpretation. They are semiotized as tenants, prophet-murderers, and know very well that they have been struck a blow. In the action's first moment they appear as subjects of doing, but by virtue of this doing's nature of transgression they then become subjects of being, more specifically victims, since it is only a question of time before they are destroyed. To them the parable is a veritable dysangelium, a pronouncement of judgement.

b. Semiotization of the Narratee

An utterance, like "Jesus is risen!", which is given in a narrative where a narrated narrator (for example the messenger) informs a narrated narratee (for example the women/disciples), may be read on three different main levels.

The utterance informs about a narrative process, either degression or progression, which may be of significance to three persons:

a)   First, the resurrection is a progressive change in Jesus' fate and destiny. This aspect of the matter is all too often ignored, but it is quite crucial that Jesus is himself a favoured subject of being by virtue of this process.

b)   Second, the resurrection may be of significance to one or more actors who appear in the narrative, persons who are pleased about or are gripped by fear of this process, because it is of significance to their own fate and destiny. It is only at this level that one can raise the question of the significance of the resurrection, and thus the death on the cross, for many, cf. 10,45 and 14,24. But still only the narrative persons are concerned.

c)   Finally, the resurrection may be of significance to persons outside the narrative, the narrator (e.g. Mark) and/or the narratee (the implicit reader). But this significance is dependent upon the discourse's answer to a question, which the reader must always ask: "Why do you tell me this?"; - and here it is decisive that the narrated world and the reader's world are joined through the deictic semiotization.

If one considers the gospel narrative's creation project, Mark attempts to impart to his reader the concept of an on-going process for which God (the fourth person B) is the responsible subject of doing. But who is really the favoured subject of being for this process?

Initially, the answer must be: the third person A, i.e. a collective actor οἱ ἐκ-λεκτοί (13,20.22.27), who appears in the narrative. They will see the Son of Man coming in clouds with great power and glory (13,26). But precisely because this creation process has not yet been completed and will see its consummation not in the narrated future *but in the narrator's and narratee's future*, the gospel narrative's presupposed or implicit reader sees himself as deictically semiotized as subject of being (favoured or victim). Although he does not appear *in* the gospel narrative, the implicit reader nevertheless sees himself as inscribed in the narrated world and thus semiotized by the roles that constitute the Christian subject of being (who is at the same time a virtual subject of doing).

To be a Christian, then, means that one accepts the role-related identity, *the deferred eschatological identity* one might say, which the narrative establishes semiotically.

The implicit reader, or the reading person who undertakes this role, will understand that it is not only to him but also for him that Mark has told his narrative. Whatever attitude the reader may adopt, whether he believes in the gospel narrative, is in doubt about it, or is dismissive, he will be able to find his figure or type among the narrated actors, and thereby see himself identified as favoured or victim. It is in this sense that the gospel narrative as a whole may be seen as a parable, as dysangelium and evangelium at the same time.

In this connection it is expedient to distinguish between the modifying and the preserving proclamation. The modifying proclamation refers to a missionary proclamation directed at the non-informed and aimed at repentance. The preserving proclamation, however, aims to maintain or strengthen a Christian identity already achieved. The gospel narrative can and must of course serve both purposes.[21]

In another perspective in which the gospel narrative's proclamation project is central, it may be said that Mark tries to impart to his reader the concept of an on-going proclamation project for which the disciples, as apostles, are the responsible subjects of doing (proclaimers), whereas the subject of being is all nations, the whole world (13,10; 14,9).

Here also the narrative relates to the narrator's and narratee's world, in that Mark himself appears in the role of apostle, while the narratee sees himself defined as actualized disciple. The proclamation of the narrative is also the story of a proclamation project that sees its realization before the eyes of the reader here and now. The narration is the unmistakable testimony to the re-established discipleship and to the decisive transition from disciple to apostle. The Christian sees himself as subject to a proclamation command, and for this reason belief can be said to have been realized only when it expresses itself in a proclamation either in a missionizing project of change or in an edifying preservation project. Proclamation then obtains the nature of confession, and Mark's Gospel itself emerges as the visible testimony of the confession to Christ.

It is not clear whether "Ἀρχὴ τοῦ εὐαγγελίου Ἰησοῦ Χριστοῦ" (1,1) is to be perceived as a heading to the introduction (1,1-13) or to the entire text. If the evangelium is to be understood in a narrow sense as a narrate, the heading refers to the introduction that tells of the first events that began it all. But if the good news is understood as the existing discourse that includes narrate and narration, then what is concerned is a heading to the entire gospel narrative, since the gospel of Jesus Christ cannot be separated from the proclamation of this story.

The narrative analysis has shown that the main emphasis is on the heading as a definition of the gospel narrative as a whole.[22] The gospel proclamation's beginning and basis (ἀρχή) is what the gospel narrative recounts. It is true that it tells of future events that form part of the message's content, but the proclamation rests upon the events that have taken place. And here it is crucial to the understanding that one of these events is Jesus' sending out the disciples as proclaimers of an evangelium whose content includes the story of this sending out. The gospel of Jesus Christ is also the gospel of the proclamation of Jesus Christ.

---

[21] Rudolf Pesch draws attention to "Mission und Gemeindeunterweisung", ibidem 1. Teil, p. 75, i.e., the proclamation's persistence, but the Christian identity must be constantly preserved by reproductive (liturgical) practices. The Christian being is also unstable, seeing itself threatened by degressive and repressive processes; preservation initiatives are therefore always required.

[22] Cf. Rudolf Pesch, ibidem, Teil 1, pp. 74; and Vincent Taylor, ibidem, p. 153.

The proclamation's foundation is thus two-fold: it includes on the one hand the events forming part of the creation and salvation projects, and on the other hand the events forming part of the teaching and proclamation projects. The gospel of Jesus Christ is *the existing gospel narrative*, which also gives a detailed account of its own genesis as proclamation. By his heading, which lies somewhere between narration and narrate, Mark indicates the basis upon which his proclamation rests, a proclamation whose content is its own basis and its own foundation.

C. FROM DISCIPLE TO APOSTLE

Making explicit the implicit ending of Mark provides a narrative that concludes in the re-commissioning of the disciples as proclaimers of the gospel of Jesus Christ. As Mark's Gospel itself evidences, this proclamation takes the form of a proclaiming narrative that not only tells of the gospel-constituting events, Jesus' acts and God's acts, but also recounts the way in which the proclamation of these events came about.

The gospel narrative is also the story of the way in which the disciples became apostles. The gospel-persisting events are concerned here, since the proclamation of the good news would, as it were, have gone to the grave with Jesus had the disciples not taken upon themselves the duty of proclamation after the meeting with the risen one.

1. The Pre-Commissioning

According to the gospel narrative, part of Jesus' mission is to ensure the proclamation's persistence by initiating the disciples, who as apostles can proclaim to the whole world between ascension and parousia. It is not surprising therefore that the disciples - and here primarily Peter as *primus inter pares* - are the privileged recipients of Jesus' proclamation, his words and his acts.

The calling of the first disciples, Simon/Peter (cf. 1,17) and his brother Andrew, occurs by reference to a commission or task: "Follow me and I will make you fish for people." (1,17).[23] The calling of the other disciples (including James and John in 1,9; Levi in 2,14) ends in the selection and appointment of twelve disciples who are to be with Jesus and whom he will be able to send out "to proclaim the message, and to have authority to cast out demons" (3,13ff), i.e. equipped with a special knowledge and ability.

It is possible to recognize in this calling the narrative schema's first two phases, manipulation/persuasion and competence.[24] The calling is a manipulation that establishes the discipleship and nominates a task to be realized. Jesus (in the role of Destinator) transforms the disciples (in the role of Destinatee) to competent subjects of doing. The appointment is a factitive doing ($\pi o\iota \acute{\epsilon}\omega$, 3,14.16, cf. 1,17), a causing-to-do, partly in the form of prescriptions that legitimize the acts and partly in the form of a qualifying by knowing (proclamation) and by ability (being-able-to-do; capacity to carry out wonder-works).

---

[23] Now they are no longer to catch fish but people (cf. Lk 5,10). The role of fisher of men is a paradoxical figure comparing people with fish that involuntarily enter the fisherman's net or take the bait without seeing the hook. The fish caught moves from one element to another, through which it meets its death: capture and destruction. The person caught correspondingly moves from one element to another (the typology of conversion), but now to life: liberation and re-creation. The term is however quite pregnant, since in an introductory moment the virtual subject of being represents a resistance to conversion.

[24] Cf. *Sémiotique*, art. "Narratif (schéma -)".

The manipulation and competence phases are followed by the performance phase, where the virtual subject of doing passes over to action. The transition between the competence and performance phases is often characterized by a sending-out, in that the Destinatee effects the realization of his commission in the Destinator's absence. Jesus sends out (ἀποστέλλω) the disciples and thereby turns them into apostles (6,7). It is then told, in summary form, that they went out and proclaimed that all should repent, that they cast out many demons and anointed with oil many who were sick and cured them, 6,12f. Then follows the sanction phase where the Destinatee returns to the Destinator to submit his accounts and possibly receive a reward, at least in the form of honour and glory. Again in the form of a summary, it is then told that "the apostles" (οἱ ἀπόστολοι) gathered around Jesus and told him all they had done and taught (6,30). But nothing is said about Jesus' praising or rewarding his disciples in some way.

It should not be overlooked that the period of the first sending-out, however long it may be thought to have lasted, is restricted. No permanent sending-out is concerned but something more like a *pre-sending-out*. The reporting back to Jesus supports this view, as does the fact that the disciples do not again set out on a travelling mission. There seems to be only one possible explanation of this: their presence around Jesus is more important than their proclamation of repentance. Or in other words they are not yet fully-trained proclaimers, since the proclaiming mission proper lies beyond events that are themselves to be proclaimed but have not yet taken place.

It is noteworthy in this connection that nothing is said about what Jesus was doing during this period when he was without his disciples. Between sending-out and returning home there is the inserted story about the Baptist's execution (6,14-29). This is in turn scarcely fortuitous. The story of the Baptist's prophet-destiny is used by the narrator to introduce a subject that points ahead towards Jesus' suffering and death, a subject that contradicts the disciples' expectations and implies a dissolution of the relationship. Neither the mission itself, which is an imitation of Jesus in so far as the disciples proclaim the gospel of God (cf. 1,14f) and act as wonder-workers, nor the loyalty by which it is realized are of course unimportant. The pre-sending-out fulfils its own objective. But in a wider perspective only a preliminary test is concerned by which the disciples show themselves worthy of initiation into the discipleship itself.

2. The Initiation

In their capacity as privileged recipients of Jesus' proclamation that includes not only his words but also his acts, themselves full of significance, the disciples (all of them or some of them), following their calling/appointment, are constantly at Jesus' side as witnesses to his works. The gospel narrative tells of very few events at which the disciples are not observers, i.e. the events located before the calling (1,16) and after the flight (14,50). The disciples' presence is such a universal feature that the narrator has to emphasize their absence (1,35; 6,46; 14,35.39), and even after the flight it is recounted that Peter follows him at a distance right into the courtyard of the high priest (14,54).

The disciples are not observers of Jesus' death, but are represented by some women who looked on from a distance (15,40); among them were Mary Magdalene and Mary, the mother of James and Salome who also saw where the body was laid (15,47). It is these women who are the first to hear the message of his resurrection (16,6) whose actual recipients are the disciples and Peter: "But go, tell ..." (16,7).

The disciples are the privileged recipients of Jesus' proclamation because they have been singled out beforehand as privileged proclaimers of a gospel that includes his death and resurrection (the savior project). Their actual proclaimer mission can and must be carried out only after the resurrection. Where Jesus proclaims the gospel of God, whose content is that the kingdom of God has come near, he proclaims publically. But the proclamation that is specifically aimed at informing about his own role as jointly-responsible subject of doing for the realization of this creation project is reserved for the disciples. The proclamation is then given the character of *disciple instruction*, and this teaching project, which is aimed at qualifying the disciples as delegated proclaimers, establishes the true teacher/pupil relationship.

The relationship between the teacher and his chosen disciples should be seen in this light, and Jesus' relationship with other recipients and observers - the crowd, the sick and the possessed, the family, the religious and temporal leaders - is subordinate to this. All that Jesus says and does contains in this perspective a message to the disciples, whose task it is to interpret this message. Similarly, it is Jesus' task to teach them to undertake this interpretation by providing them with the *interpretant* (interpretation key) without which the message will be misunderstood or remain incomprehensible.

a. The Women at the Tomb

With a view to describing the processual basic-structure that seems to organize the gospel narrative's teaching project, it is appropriate to take as a point of reference the information process that characterizes the story of the women's meeting with a messenger inside the tomb (16,6f).

The messenger's speech to the women includes a number of remarkable facts that must first be differentiated and then connected.[25]

---

[25] The analysis of this discourse is strongly inspired by Per Aage Brandt's earlier (and unpublished) analyses of enunciation, later reformulated in a so-called theory of diegesis, cf. *Sandheden, sætningen og døden* (Truth, Sentence and Death), Århus 1983, note 280; also "Genese og diegese. Et problem i den almene narratologi" (Genesis and Diegesis. A Problem in General Narratology), *Religionsvidenskabeligt Tidsskrift 14* (Journal for the Science of Religion), Århus 1989, pp. 75.

The remark, "you are looking for Jesus of Nazareth, who was crucified", initially establishes the messenger as the subject of a knowing about a wanting, whose subject is the women:

Relation I: No knows that Ne wants Obj1.

The narrator (No) knows that the narratee (Ne) is looking for ($\zeta\eta\tau\acute{\epsilon}\omega$; also lacks, desires, wishes for) the crucified one, i.e. the dead Jesus, referred to as Obj1.

The messenger's next remark: "He has been raised, he is not here" is information about a fact he wishes the women to recognize. The messenger wants the women to know:

Relation II: No wants that Ne knows Obj2

It should be pointed out here that the object is not the women's Obj1 (the dead Jesus) but the messenger's Obj2, the Son of Man. The messenger does not inform the women that their dead Jesus is absent because he is lying in another tomb or has been stolen (cf. Mt 28,11ff). He informs them about the risen Jesus ("He has been raised") who is absent ("he is not here") in accordance with what he has said: "But after I am raised up, I will go before you to Galilee" (14,28). The messenger not only establishes a fact when he tells that Jesus is risen, since the resurrection cannot indeed be a fact to the women. At this moment the fact is the empty tomb only, which is because of either body-snatching or resurrection, depending on which interpretant forms the basis for interpreting the absence.

"He has been raised" therefore does not yet refer to the empirically accessible risen Jesus but to the Passion predictions that at the same time are resurrection predictions (8,31; 9,9; 9,31; 10,34). Note that Matthew adds by way of clarification that he has risen, "as he said" (Mt 28,6), and that Luke allows his messengers to draw attention to Jesus' prediction of death on the cross and resurrection (Lk 24,6ff). Mark refers explicitly to Jesus' speech only in 16,7, although an implicit reference is a possibility from the beginning. Without such a reference the messenger's speech is quite simply meaningless to the women. Jesus's teaching about the Son of Man, which the women have forgotten (cf. Lk 24,8), doubted or rejected, is the interpretant that alone will be able to interpret the empty tomb correctly.

Jesus taught that the Son of Man was to die but rise again three days later. This may be understood as a simple, prophetic prediction, but as will be shown in more detail later, it may also be understood as an initiation into a rule or legality. Jesus does not inform his disciples about a circumstance in the world, but initiates them meta-linguistically into a code or interpretant which makes it possible to interpret and understand the world, and it is this special form of *meta-proclamation*, or proclamation in this special function, that may be referred to as teaching or instruction (διδασκαλία).[26] The narrator then appears in the role of διδάσκαλος and the narratee in the role of μαθητής; but if the secrecy (μυστήριον) of the teaching is emphasized, then these appear as μυσταγωγός and μύστης.

Relation II then refers to the narratee's semiotic initiation (or re-initiation), since the women are on the one hand alienated in their desire - that which they are seeking they cannot get - and on the other hand are referred to the interpretant (predictions of suffering and resurrection), which signifies this absence. Jesus' absence is a sign to be interpreted on the basis of the interpretant, according to which absence signifies resurrection.

Only after this important element is the express relationship between narrator and narratee introduced. The latter is now referred to a different place, where the object can be seen: "he is going ahead of you to Galilee; there you will see him, just as he told you.". The actual information then appears in:

Relation III: No says that Ne will see Obj3

The object is now neither the women's dead Jesus of Nazareth (Obj1) nor the interpretant's Son of Man (Obj2) but the seen Obj3, Jesus of Nazareth/the Son of Man, who as visibly, empirically accessible is set as a presence deferred in space and time, but whose reappearance or coming will confirm the validity of the interpretant introduced. At the same time a social function is indicated, since Obj3 is made communicable or put into circulation in a certain community: "But go, tell his disciples and Peter,...". The narratee has been initiated as the coming narrator, as a messenger to the new recipients.

The processual connection through the process Obj1-Obj2-Obj3 thus corresponds to a movement whereby the subject is as a first step semiotically initiated and then socialized as proclaimer. If it is indeed the disciple-instruction's objective to turn the disciples into proclaimers, should they not likewise have to go through a semiotic initiation? Can Jesus' teaching of the disciples be seen as an initiation that involves a necessary alienation, because what must be recognized and experienced must initially appear to be incomprehensible, impossible, rejected by common sense? An answer to these questions will be sought below, but there is reason first to comment more specifically on the three relations.

The remark, "you are looking for Jesus of Nazareth, who was crucified", shows that the messenger knows what the women are looking for, i.e. the crucified one, the dead Jesus. The messenger thus knows the women's expectation, which is based upon a certain perception of the nature of the world: the

---

[26] Cf. Roman Jakobson, "Closing statement: Linguistics and Poetics", in T.A. Sebeok (ed.), *Style in Language*, New York 1960, pp. 350.

dead remain dead, since death is an irreparable state of being, characterized by a fatal preservation (repression). To be able to begin to speak, to be able to interpellate the narratee, the narrator must refer directly or indirectly to the narratee's *pre-understanding* of himself in the world. The messenger must thus add to the women's actual cognitive-affective situation, and it is this fact that the narrative makes more explicit by the introductory remark.

The women are in a cognitive space, a perception or intuition that points towards a collective universe that contains the narratively interpreted experience of the world and its nature. The women's perception that resurrection is impossible (not-being-able-to-be), because death is irreparable, is a conviction shared by others and has been recorded in this collective rationality's library of knowledge. By virtue of certain events (narrative processes) that can be thematized elsewhere in this library, the world exists in a specific nature.

As such, the world is established and founded by God (in the role of establisher and founder, θέτης, θεμελιῶν or θεσμοθέτης), and is characterized by predictability, either in the absolute sense, since certain processes are fatal, e.g. man will inevitably die, and the state of being thereby produced is irreparable; or in a relative sense (but tending towards the absolute), since certain processes - as a rule, i.e. because of having to - will take place: e.g. the just are rewarded but the unjust are punished. Having to is relative (regularity), because the process is dependent upon a responsible subject of doing that can both act and not act; but where God is the responsible subject of doing, having to tends to coincide with being able to (legality): what God has established that he himself ought to do, he will inevitably do. Man is living under such absolute and relative stipulations and regulations, and the knowledge of the world's processes and situations (including their modalization) is gathered in a narrative encyclopedia (for example, A Holy Scripture), a catalogue of knowledge of thematic and narrative roles that serves as an objective basis of reference, as an *interpretant*, for the cognitive subject's interpretation of phenomena and discourses.

Affectively, the women are linked to the dead Jesus in a relationship of desire (cf. ζητέω), their love and care is directed towards the deceased person (cf. 16,1), which represents an object of value. They understand themselves and their task relative to the dead Jesus, and their search is an expression of their passion. One can imagine the disappointment they will experience if the stone before the entrance to the tomb cannot be moved away (cf. 16,3), if they have mistaken where he was laid (cf. 15,47), if others have forestalled them, or if the tomb was quite simply empty. The desire to anoint the deceased (16,1) may perhaps be seen as an expression of the women's inadequate bond with the dead Jesus, a bond that is adequate according to their own perception of the nature of the world, but is in contrast to the perception they should have had.[27]

---

[27] The women's anointing project is a pseudo-project, even if the corpse is present in the tomb. They

The messenger's next remark, "He has been raised; he is not here. Look, there is the place they laid him", has three elements, the last of which positively identifies the tomb as the correct place; it was here he was laid. The second element, "he is not here", is a negation of the women's desire, the object of value they seek is gone. A kind of deprivation is concerned, an alienation, which casts the women into a serious affective and cognitive crisis, already begun by the meeting with the messenger (cf. 16,5f). The work of interpretation the women would be able to carry out at this moment in order to comprehend the absence of the dead man must take place within the framework of the cognitive space in which they initially find themselves, according to which death is characterized by fatal preservation. The most obvious explanation would then be that the body had been stolen away and removed in a direct sense (cf. Mt 28,11ff).

But the alienation of the women's desire is because of Jesus' absence by virtue of the resurrection, which refers to a different desire, God's desire. The fact that the Son of Man cannot be contained by death, that *the resurrection is inevitable*, is an expression of God's wanting, his establishment of a rule or legality, his re-creation. When God resurrects Jesus, he acts in accordance with a law or ordinance that he has himself established, and this regulation ($\theta\epsilon\mu\iota\varsigma$ or $\theta\epsilon\sigma\mu\acute{o}\varsigma$; $\delta\iota\kappa\alpha\acute{\iota}\omega\mu\alpha$) stands fast as an objective fact within the narrated world. The world has gone through a process of change, a re-creation, and its modal nature has become something different. It is this secret that Jesus has revealed through his proclamation and instruction of the disciples.

The third element, "He has been raised", refers the women to the interpretant which can explain Jesus' absence. It should be noted here that the physical absence (Jesus is elsewhere) is equivalent to the referent's absence in the collective library of knowledge to which reference is made. The individual actor, Jesus of Nazareth, does not appear in the narrative encyclopedia but only the "Son of Man" role into which Jesus is enrolled. It is not only the physically absent Jesus to which the messenger refers, but Jesus raised up in the "Son of Man" role, the point of which is that he must die but rise again three days later. The messenger does not refer simply to empirical facts but to the divine ordinance or regulation that determines these facts.

---

arrive too late, and also Jesus has already been anointed (14,3.8); cf. Rudolf Pesch, *Das Markusevange- lium, 2. Teil*, p. 530. The women appear in the role of involuntary subjects of doing, cf. *Logique du récit*, pp. 233. They seek *X* but find *Y*; they seek the dead Jesus but find, although indeed deferred, the living Jesus. One may discuss what the rhetorical effect of the difference between X and Y is in this case. On the one hand there is a clear difference, in that the women are seeking the dead but find the living; but on the other hand there is also a clear similarity, since the modest satisfaction the women long for is replaced by a great satisfaction. The narrator, who permits the proclamation project and thus God's entire project to depend upon these women, who act completely irrationally, shows two things. On the one hand, it is shown that although left to frail humans the gospel fights its way through. In the same way the narration is a disavowal of the women's silence. On the other hand, it is shown that the Christian gospel is incredibly vulnerable; the reality to which it refers stands or falls with its proclaimers. In this perspective, the women's silence is a disavowal of the narration.

The women's affective bond to the dead Jesus is in accordance with the perception that death is irretrievable, and therefore represents a rejection of Jesus' proclamation. However positive the women's bond to the dead Jesus may be, it represents a cognitive position that is false according to the narrative. The women are victims of a successful simulation, a delusion, which refers back to a narrator who speaks for himself. However paradoxical it may seem, the narrative defines the women's opinion as a subjective perception that refers to the subject's wanting, its desire, and it is this desire that is alienated by God's desire.

If the women act on the basis of the rule that death is irretrievable, then they act on the basis of a rule that they themselves or their pseudo-informator have invented. It is true that this rule was valid until recently, but it is now abolished and replaced by another. What the women consider to be an evident truth, namely that resurrection is impossible, the narrative turns into a lie, since it is God who establishes what is true, what can happen in the world. The narrative's cognitive reversal (anagnorisis) thus turns upside down the women's and the reader's customary ideas.

But only the meeting with the resurrected one, i.e. Jesus as the finally-revealed Son of Man, can confirm this new rule for the disciples and the women, and only this experience-bearing, collective actor will be able to undertake the proclamation. For the reader, only the meeting with the Son of Man at the Parousia can confirm this proclamation.

b. The Teaching of the Son of Man

The question, then, is whether the disciples will be able to proclaim the gospel only when they have gone through a similar initiation process. In extension of the above analysis, the following would then have to be established as a hypothetical point of reference for a more detailed examination:

1)   To begin with, the disciples are characterized by the desire or wish for a Christ1. But their conception of Christ has the status of wishful thinking, their expectations are unrealistic.

2)   The disciples' subjective conceptions are negated, and their desire is inscribed into an objective interpretant that sets Christ as Christ2.

3)   The disciples are informed that they will see Christ again as the transfigured, epiphanous Christ3.

The Disciples Failure to Understand

The question is obviously linked to two well-known themes: the disciples failure to understand and the messianic secret.

The motif of the disciples failure to understand is universal: 4,13: they do not understand the parable of the sower; 4,40: they do not understand who Jesus is; 6,52: although they have witnessed a bread-miracle (6,34ff) they have not become wiser, but their hearts are hardened; 7,18: they do not understand his teaching, censure it as unwise; 8,17.21: they do not yet understand, do not comprehend; their hearts are hardened; they have eyes and fail to see, ears and fail to hear; they still understand nothing; 8,33: Peter does not understand Jesus' teaching about the Son of Man, he does not perceive what is God's but only what is Man's; 9,6: on the mountain of transfiguration, Peter does not know what to say; 9,10: on their way down from the mountain the disciples discuss among themselves what this rising from the dead could mean, because they do not understand it; 9,19: they belong to this faithless generation; 9,32: they do not understand Jesus' talk of the Son of Man; 9,33f: they discuss who is the greatest, which rests on a misunderstanding; 10,24.26: they are perplexed at his words, shaken, because they are taken by surprise; 10,35-45: they argue about the place of honour and thereby reveal their lack of insight; 14,10: one of the disciples betrays Jesus; 14,27.50: the others are shocked and flee; 14,29-31.54.66-72: Peter denies Jesus; 14,32f: they are incapable even of keeping awake.

The messianic secret is less extensively presented, in that it is understood to mean only the secret that concerns Jesus' being or identity, and is expressed in the commands for secrecy to the demons and disciples.[28] As regards the demons, cf. 1,25.34; 3,12; 5,7, it must be emphasized that the command is violated, or always comes too late. Whoever witnesses the exorcism thus learns that something which should have remained a secret is nevertheless revealed, because the demons say too much. They cannot help themselves, and as such represent the involuntary or forced speech whose diametrical opposite is the involuntary or forced silence, muteness.

The command for secrecy to the disciples is to be found in 8,30: "And he sternly ordered them not to tell anyone about him.", i.e. that he was Christ; 9,9: "As they were coming down the mountain, he ordered them to tell no one about what they had seen", i.e. the transfigured Jesus, "until after the Son of Man had risen from the dead." It seems most natural to see these commands for secrecy as motivated by the disciples' failure to understand. As disciples they are under training and are to undertake no form of proclaiming until they have understood what the matter is really about, which can happen only when the events they have been taught about have occurred. The motif of the disciples failure to understand, cf. 8,32 and 9,10, then becomes the central point as regards the messianic secret, since who Jesus really is remains a mystery to the disciples, although it is revealed to them. They know the secret but in a special way, in that despite the

---

[28] Cf. Heikki Räisänen, Das "Messiasgeheimnis" im Markusevangelium. Ein redaktionskritischer Versuch, Helsinki 1976, p. 159.

disclosures, Jesus remains an enigma to them. The demons are aware of the truth, although there is no revelation; the disciples know the secret but do not understand it.

The enigma Jesus presents by his very appearance in wisdom and power (cf. for example 6,2; 4,41) sets off an interpretation exercise, and an attempt is made to identify him on the basis of what is already known, i.e. a given interpretant. Some think he is Elijah, others that he is a prophet like the other prophets, while others again are convinced he is John the baptizer who has been raised from the dead (cf. 6,14ff). When Jesus asks his disciples who people say that he is, they indeed reply: "John the Baptist; and others, Elijah; and still others, one of the prophets." (8,27f). An opinion has been formed as regards who Jesus is, i.e. to which type ($\tau\acute{\upsilon}\pi o\varsigma$) he belongs. Identification of him must be on the basis of the marks, the features, or the signs that give grounds for any attempt at recognition. But a type or a model must be understood as a person who sees himself as determined on the basis of certain roles, e.g. baptist, prophet, savior, i.e. as a person with a definite mission. Identifying Jesus as a certain type involves, therefore, a quite definite expectation relative to him. When, therefore, Peter on behalf of the disciples tells Jesus that they think he is the Christ (8,29), then on the basis of this type - Messiah - they have some quite definite ideas about his mission and about the significance of this mission for them.

Peter's (the disciples') "Christ-confession" is true, in that he is not dissembling but openly acknowledging what he thinks. But his Christ-image is a phantom he is wrapped in a delusion. He sees himself as a voluntary revelator, but he is in fact an involuntary deceptor. Against this background, the command for secrecy (8,30) receives its narrative rationality. The act of confession reveals to Jesus what the disciples seek in him. When immediately afterwards he begins to teach the disciples, "....that the Son of Man must undergo great suffering, and be rejected by the elders, the chief priests, and the scribes, and be killed, and after three days rise again" (8,31), Peter takes him aside and begins to rebuke him. But Peter is himself rebuked with the words: "Get behind me, Satan! For you are setting your mind not on divine things but on human things" (8,33). Peter's act can be understood only as a reaction to the breach of expectations caused by Jesus' teaching. Whatever he seeks or desires is suddenly taken from him, he is negated or alienated.

The narrative is far from silent about the specific content of the disciples' expectations. First of all, it is clear that the idea of suffering and death causes indignation. But apart from this reference may be made within the narrative's universe to the impression Jesus must have made on his disciples by his behaviour until then: he is the authoritative and perceptive person who has the power, the right and the strength to forgive sinners, to restore the prostrate. As a wonder-worker he shows his extraordinary ability, that he is God's representative.

How was this image to tally with the concept of the Son of Man's suffering and death? Why must he who has the power to restore Jairus' dead daughter to life himself die and rise again?

For any reader of the narrative, there is a contradiction between the image it presents of Jesus in the first half (1,1-8,26) and the fate that overtakes him in the second half (8,27-16,8). Peter's "confession", which marks a turning point, is the place where the narrator himself thematizes this evident contradiction. It is not wrong to assert that Peter reacts as he does because he feels himself deceived.

The impression the disciples have of Jesus, and thus the expectations they have of him, is not then pure imagination, but is supported by the influence Jesus has exercised by his words and deeds. To this extent the disciples' perception is a result of Jesus' own doing and action.

But in that case Jesus appears as seducer in the first half of the narrative. However unfounded the calling may be in its presentation, the disciples' bond to Jesus can be understood only on the basis of their expectation that he will be able to realize what they desire. He interpellates the disciples on their desire, which recognizes itself in his appearance as wonder-worker and masterful proclaimer, as God's powerful representative, as Man of God (cf. LXX, Deut 33,1: Μωϋσῆς ἄνθρωπος τοῦ θεοῦ).[29]

It is this glorious expectation of gain, the hope of participating in the power and glory, that makes the disciples follow Jesus obediently. And it is this expectation that Jesus negates by referring to a different desire: there is one law (cf. δεῖ, i.e. a having to, which refers to God's desire), according to which the Son of Man must suffer. It is true that his resurrection is also promised, but this lies beyond the suffering, is overshadowed by the suffering, and can in no way hold the attention.

It may now seem natural to define the gospel narrative as a simple rejection of power and glory. But such a concept would rest upon a misunderstanding; the matter is far more complex. The power and the glory are negated only to appear on the scene later in transfigured form (cf. 8,38; 10,37; 13,26 and 14,62). The question of power (strength) and glory is a universal theme, and the contrast lies rather between the unjustified and the justified honour.

Against this background one is reminded of SIGMUND FREUD's observation, that the fantasy life (that reveals what people are passionately concerned about) is guided by wishes falling into two main groups: one relates to sexuality, which seems to be of no significance to the gospel narrative, while the other in fact

---

[29] Cf. Rudolf Pesch, *Das Markusevangelium, I. Teil*, p. 279: "Obwohl die Wundererzählungen manche Züge mit den hellenistischen Vorstellungen vom θεῖος ἀνήρ teilen, kann die in ihnen ausgedrückte Christologie nicht als eine θεῖος-ἀνήρ-Christologie klassifiziert (und als 'gefährlich' bewertet) werden; (...). Mit den Wundergeschichten wird christliche Mission getrieben, die Jesus als den Christus, den die Gottesmänner des AT überbietenden Gottesmann, den eschatologischen Propheten, den Sohn Gottes (3,11), in dem Jahve seine heilvolle Macht erweist, verkündigt.".

relates to ambition (the industrious, the vain, the rank-seeking, the aspiring, the power-thirsty and so on), cf. 10,35ff.[30]

The Son of Man

The problem of understanding the term "the Son of Man" is somewhat comprehensive, and in this context cannot be discussed in its entirety. Only certain aspects of the matter that are of importance to an understanding of the three predictions of suffering, death and resurrection (8,31f; 9,31f and 10,33f) will be considered here.

In his thesis, *Der Ausdruck »Menschensohn« in den Evangelien*, MOGENS MÜLLER concludes that the expression ὁ υἱὸς τοῦ ἀνθρώπου must primarily be understood as a transcription of the speaking person, and that an understanding of what the expression covers must therefore be sought in what is actually said about this person.[31] On the basis of other premises, MÜLLER thus arrives at an understanding congruent with the concept that characterizes narrative exegesis: what the expression "the Son of Man" means must be determined on the basis of the information (both discursive and narrative material) that the gospel narrative itself provides.

The hypothesis that the term "the Son of Man" must be understood as a transcription of the speaker appears to deserve special attention. It is true that MÜLLER acts tradition historically and emphasizes that the gospel tradition's expression ὁ υἱὸς τοῦ ἀνθρώπου has its origin in the Aramaic *bar nasch(a)* that has served the speaker as a transcription of himself, when for one reason or another he wished to indicate a distance from what was said.[32] Gospel tradition thus represents a developmental stage in which this expression exercises several functions, but here also it is clear and striking that Jesus speaks of himself in the third person as the Son of Man.

The study of the narrative Jesus must of course take as its point of reference the fact that with few exceptions he speaks Greek.[33] The question then becomes, why does the narrator permit his main character to refer to himself in the third

---

[30] "Man darf sagen, der Glückliche phantasiert nie, nur der Unbefriedigte. Unbefriedigte Wünsche sind die Triebkräfte der Phantasien und jede einzelne Phantasie ist eine Wunscherfüllung, eine Korrektur der unbefriedigenden Wirklichkeit. Die treibenden Wünsche sind verschieden je nach Geschlecht, Charakter und Lebensverhältnissen der phantasierenden Persönlichkeit; sie lassen sich aber ohne Zwang nach zwei Hauptrichtungen gruppieren. Es sind entweder ehrgeizige Wünsche, welche der Erhöhung der Persönlichkeit dienen, oder erotische." (pp. 173), Sigmund Freud, "Der Dichter und das Phantasieren", *Studienausgabe Band X. Bildende Kunst und Literatur*, Frankfurt am Main 1975, pp. 171.

[31] Mogens Müller, *Der Ausdruck "Menschensohn" in den Evangelien. Voraussetzungen und Bedeutung*, Leiden 1984, pp. 245.

[32] Mogens Müller, ibidem, p. 169 and pp. 219.

[33] On the development from *bar nasch(a)* to ὁ υἱὸς τοῦ ἀνθρώπου and the consequences this occasioned for tradition, cf. Maurice Casey, *Son of Man. The Interpretation and Influence of Daniel 7*, London 1979, pp. 224. The question of a possible connection between the gospel narrative and Dan 7 is not otherwise covered in this study.

person as the Son of Man? Or, formulated more narrative-internally, why does the narrative Jesus in this way indicate a distance from what he tells his disciples?

The transcription by means of the Son of Man must mean, then, that in those places where the expression occurs it should be possible to replace it with the personal pronoun "I", which is generally employed when the speaker refers to himself. But if one takes into consideration the speaker's wish to indicate a distance from what is said, then it seems more natural to replace it with "one". A person who declares "One can do what one wants to do!", making it clear in the given situation that he is speaking of himself as a virtual subject of doing for a certain act, refers to a general rule which says "A man can do what a man wants to do!", or "Man can do what man wants to do!", which is asserted to have validity for the speaker. But perhaps he is showing himself to be the exception that proves the rule, and it is therefore the tension between the generally formulated role and the individual actor's semiotization thereof that should attract attention.[34]

Proper Name and Common Name

Whereas a proper name has only one referent and lacks a descriptive content, a common name refers to a class and has a descriptive content. But there are intermediate forms, since a proper name (Galilee) may function as a common name ("Jesus was a Galilean"), and a common name (a baptist) as a proper name ("the Baptist was beheaded").

The expression "the Son of Man" appears to be such an intermediate form, a syncretism of proper name and common name. In its indefinite form, "a son of man" (υἱὸς ἀνθρώπου, cf. Heb 2,6), the word is a common name and thereby has a descriptive content made up of the two roles "man" and "son", the complementary roles of which are "father/mother" (a son of man is a son of a human being, e.g. Mary, or Mary and Joseph) and "God" (a son of man or a human child is simply a human being and as such a son of God the father).[35]

The distinctive grammatical feature of proper names in the true sense is that they are not inflected in number (*"Two Jesuses is one too many"), and also that they have no indefinite article (*"A Jesus entered Jerusalem").[36] The proper name refers to one definite individual, not to an indefinite member of a class. In its definite form, however, the expression "the Son of Man" shares these properties. A definite, individual and singular actor is concerned. Where in this

---

[34] What is concerned, for example, is that the "16.17 train from Århus" runs to Copenhagen. The individual actor, the MY234 locomotive, may be this train, but it may just as well be MY148 or quite a different one. It is true of MY234 that it runs to Copenhagen when it finds itself allocated the role of "16.17 from Århus".

[35] Cf. Lk 3,23ff: "Jesus was ..., son of Joseph, ..., son of David, ... son of Abraham, ..., son of Nahor, ..., son of Adam, ..., son of God.".

[36] For the anaphoric use of the article with proper names, cf. Friederich Blass, Albert Debrunner, *Grammatik des neutestamentlichen Griechisch*, Göttingen 1970, § 260.

way a common name incorporates the proper name's properties of individuation and determination, it adopts the character of a title referring to a role of doing, either explicitly through its descriptive content (cf. baptist) where the emphasis is on the common name, or implicitly if the expression predominantly acts as a proper name, i.e. an empty designation that receives its content from what the narrative predicates about the person to whom the designation applies. Cf. again, as mentioned above, that the narrative Jesus, whose proper name probably means "Yahweh is salvation" (Joshua, cf. Mt 1,21), is a subject that is determined as a person only through the role the narrative assigns to him.[37]

As a common name, the expression ὁ υἱὸς τοῦ ἀνθρώπου can be understood as a parasynomym of ὁ ἄνθρωπος, which has a double meaning: 1) individual: the known, defined, previously-mentioned human being, 2) generic: the human being as a species (for example οἱ ἄνθρωποι as opposed to τὰ ἄλλα ζῷα or θεός).[38] The first meaning is anaphoric, in that it refers back to what is known or presumably known. An expression such as ὁ προφήτης (Jn 1,21; 7,40) refers to a quite definite prophet who is already known or is presumably known (referred to in an earlier discourse).

But at the same time he appears as the prophet above all prophets, the true prophet, because the species prophet is here present in a single individual. Where common names are employed as personal designations, the individual and the generic merge and the title resulting therefrom comes close to the proper name. The expression ὁ κύριος thus refers to one, in its nature (generic) unique (individual), being. What is concerned here is a definite "Lord", not just any lord. In the same way, ὁ ἄνθρωπος as a personal designation is an expression that refers not only to a human being or the species man, but permits the generic human being to be present in one single individual: the human being above all human beings, the true human being (cf. also "ἡ ὁδὸς καὶ ἡ ἀλήθεια καὶ ἡ ζωή", Jn 14,6). To what extent this signification dimension, which cannot be separated from the descriptive content, is concerned in the gospel narrative's use of the expression "the Son of Man" is a separate question that will be discussed further below, cf. Chapter XIV.

Identity or Dissimilarity

The fact that in the gospels Jesus refers to himself in the third person as "the Son of Man" has caused interpreters to assume that the historical Jesus has proclaimed a coming "Son of Man" without identifying himself with this entity.[39]

---

[37] The role does not refer to a singular entity but to a class of entities which is generic. The name (or the individuated role) has a general, although empty, meaning, since it subordinates itself to all the roles the persons are given. The context makes it clear whether it concerns Jesus as wonder-worker, proclaimer, teacher or savior; but also whether it concerns Jesus before or after the baptism, before or after the death, before or after the resurrection.

[38] Cf. Friederich Blass, Albert Debrunner, ibidem, § 252.

[39] For example D.F. Strauss, D. Völter, and B.W. Bacon; cf. Mogens Müller, ibidem, pp. 163.

By thus moving the difficulty from the stage of the narrative to that of history, the unequivocalness is achieved that mind instinctively seeks. It would be possible to achieve a similar unambiguity within the framework of the narrative if one assumes that the narrative Jesus merely uses the expression "the Son of Man" pronominally as a paraphrase for himself, i.e. as an "I". He then speaks of himself, what he is saying concerns himself, and the expression "the Son of Man" then receives its descriptive content from the fate that overtakes him. According to MÜLLER, it therefore applies to Mk 2,10; 2,28, 8,31; 9,9.12; 9,31; 10,33-34; 10,45; 14,21 and 14,41 that "der 'Menschensohn' konsequent das Personalpronomen ersetzt".[40] These sayings may be understood as a manner of speaking in which the speaker, because of the statement's special nature, uses the expression "the Son of Man" as a paraphrase for his own person.

As indicated, this study is interested only in certain aspects of the matter, and these two perceptions have been juxtaposed since, because of these very aspects, they may be considered as two opposite perceptions. According to the first perception, Jesus speaks of a person other than himself, whereas the other perception permits him to speak of himself only. The narrative, however, displays the phenomenon, which is also the point of departure of the perceptions referred to, that Jesus speaks of both himself and another, or he speaks of another who is also himself. Both perceptions referred to have thus grasped aspects of the matter, but have a preference for isolating one aspect at the expense of the other. It does not seem possible to maintain the complexity without landing in a contradiction.

It is true that the pronominal understanding concedes that Jesus speaks of himself in the third person, but it is content to state that this is what a speaker does when he wishes to indicate a distance because of the nature of the utterance. If therefore the first perception may be said to isolate the distance and/or the difference (the Son of Man is someone other than Jesus), the other perception may be said to isolate the proximity or identity (the Son of Man is a term that has no status other than the pronominal "I", which as a deictic entity has no fixed referent but always refers to the speaker). Both perceptions therefore evade having to explain why the narrative Jesus wishes to indicate a distance. The remarkable phenomenon which, as a problem, initiated the discussion thus remains unresolved.

In a narrative perspective, the pronominal perception is clearly the most inspiring, since in a way it accords with the narrative itself. Indeed, anyone can see that within the narrative's framework Jesus is speaking of himself in the Son of Man sayings. But if one assumes that the historical Jesus had quite a different person in mind, then one has simply given up interpreting the narrative. An interpretation of the existing narrative is concerned only when the term "the Son

---

[40] Mogens Müller, ibidem, p. 187.

of Man" is made comprehensible on the basis of the narrative context in which it appears.[41]

But if this indication of distance is taken seriously it must be admitted that it is the very term "the Son of Man" that cannot be replaced by "I". Faced with the perception that "the Son of Man" is a person different from Jesus, there is certainly reason to insist on the term's pronominal function. But once it has become clear that Jesus is speaking of himself - and the narrative is really unambiguous on this point - the next step must then be to understand the phenomenon of the indication of distance itself. MÜLLER's contribution to an understanding of this phenomenon is sparing, although it points in the right direction. Without going into the detail of this, he observes that where the evangelist permits Jesus to speak "über seine Rolle", this occurs through the Son of Man sayings.[42] The important question for narrative exegesis is indeed whether the term "the Son of Man" can be analyzed as a role, perhaps as a complex of roles.

"The Son of Man" Role

Semiotically, the phenomenon can be defined as an actantial disengagement.[43] The utterance A) "But after I am raised up, I will go before you to Galilee." (14,28) shows an enunciative disengagement, an uttered enunciation, allowing the enunciation's actants to appear in the discourse ("I" = Jesus and "you" = the disciples). But an utterance of the type B) "But after the Son of Man is raised up, he will go before his disciples to Galilee." is characterized by an utterative disengagement, in that the persons concerned belong to the uttered utterance. In this hypothetical example, "the Son of Man" (and the disciples) appear as objectified third-person subjects who have the character of non-persons, since "the Son of Man" cannot be identified with the narrator nor the disciples with the narratee.

The paradoxical aspect of the Son of Man saying is thus that Jesus employs an utterative disengagement ("The Son of Man must undergo great suffering ...") where an enunciative disengagement must be expected ("I shall undergo great suffering ..."). The question then becomes whether the utterative disengagement should be understood merely as an enunciative disengagement (the pronominal perception) or whether, in this paradoxical manner of speech, Jesus has factual reasons for speaking as he does.

The perception according to which Jesus speaks of a different person is in fact more correct that one might believe at first sight. Taken literally, the Son of Man cannot be identified with Jesus. He in fact speaks not about himself but about an objectified third person. Nevertheless, the disciples and the reader understand well that Jesus speaks of himself when he speaks of the Son of Man, and the

---

[41] Cf. Mogens Müller, ibidem, p. 3.
[42] Mogens Müller, ibidem, p. 181.
[43] Cf. *Sémiotique*, art. "Débrayage"; cf. above, p. 176.

exegete wishes to know why he does so in this indirect way, why he switches to *narrative*.

It seems possible to give an explanation, if one sees in Jesus' discourse a complex utterance that represents a syncretism of two utterances, an enunciative and an utterative, each of which serves its own purpose. It should be said immediately that in both cases the disciples are the narratee. In the enunciative utterance, then, Jesus speaks of himself: "I must undergo great suffering, and be rejected by the elders ... and be killed, and after three days rise again ..." (cf. 8,31, given here by direct speech). This is quite simply a *prediction* of his death and resurrection, and one cannot indeed discount such a prophetic element. But it is clear that it is becoming more than difficult to include the crucial point concealed in the little word δεῖ, that it is necessary for him to undergo great suffering, etc. The necessity does not mean here that the sequence of events referred to will necessarily occur (Jesus can merely keep away from Jerusalem), but that the said sequence of events should occur, and that when it has thus occurred it occurred with a deontic (and not dynamic) necessity because only in this way was it possible to realize a certain mission.[44]

Avoiding a general comparison, the term "the Son of Man" may thus remind one of a term such as "hero". It is indeed characteristic of the hero that this is a role a person may attempt to adopt. If he lives up to the demands of the heroic deed he certainly becomes a hero, since he is signified by his actions which are themselves interpreted by a social value-system. A hero is not therefore something one simply is but something for which one must qualify by adopting and realizing an already selected mission that prescribes the actions and thus determines the role of hero. Whoever accepts the mission but cannot carry it out is no hero. Similarly, it may be said that whoever accepts the role of "the Son of Man" but cannot realize the project connected to this is no "Son of Man". Whether the hero is truly a hero, *in casu* Messiah, remains hidden and is, as it were, a secret - a messianic secret - until the mission has been realized and recognized as completed by the superior authority that sovereignly establishes the values. One can therefore be a hero only in an objective sense, i.e. on the basis of an objective value-system that prescribes what is required, what is indispensable, to achieve the status of hero.

"The Son of Man" is thus not another person to whom Jesus refers (in the same way as, for example, John refers to Jesus), but neither is this person Jesus. Between Jesus and the role of "the Son of Man" is an arbitrary relationship, since this role could in principle be adopted by anyone, provided - and here the

---

[44] In his article "Theologische Beobachtungen zu δεῖ", *Neutestamentliche Studien für Rudolf Bultmann*, Berlin 1954, pp. 228, Erich Fascher writes: "Ein δεῖ im AT als Ausdruck schicksalhafter Notwendigkeit ist nicht nur deshalb unmöglich, weil Gott persönlicher Wille ist, sondern weil Gottes Wille Reaktion auf Menschenwillen ist und Menschenwille Gottes Willen beeinflussen kann.", p. 231. The same perception characterizes Mark's Gospel, cf. 3,35 and 14,36, and it is this interplay between God and Man that characterizes and defines the covenant, cf. Part 4, The Savior.

element of content nevertheless occurs - this person is *a human being*. Why God chose precisely Jesus of Nazareth for this mission (1,11) remains a mystery. But one thing is certain: he *is* not simply "the Son of Man" but *becomes* this by adopting the role of "the Son of Man". In this perspective it becomes clear that the utterative utterance, "Then he began to teach them that the Son of Man must undergo great suffering (...) and be killed, and after three days rise again." (8,31), concerns the *generic* Son of Man without proper name, i.e. the role or the role complex that expresses the term "Son of Man".

It is true that in the predictions Jesus informs the disciples of his coming fate (the prophetic aspect), but this occurs in the form of an initiation into *the rule* applicable to "the Son of Man" role (the teaching aspect). This rule stems not from Jesus himself: he informs the disciples of God's will. It is in his capacity as God's representative that Jesus teaches the disciples, in that he initiates them into a secret about the world according to God: the fact about the Son of Man is that he is not held by death, his resurrection is inevitable. In this perspective, Jesus speaks neither of his own nor about himself, but informs about a universal fact (for the Son of Man, the rule applies that ...) that is raised above time, place and person.

c. The Disciples' Alienation and Initiation

It is now possible to take a closer look at the question of whether the disciples can proclaim the gospel of Jesus Christ only if they have gone through an initiation process of the same type as that preceding the women's induction as proclaimers.

This question must be answered on the basis of the teaching assembled in section 8,27-10,52, i.e. a collection of sequences whose information is altogether more comprehensive, complex and pluri-isotopic than that which characterizes the straightforward description in 16,6ff. These sequences can be divided into three groups, each containing its own prediction of suffering and resurrection: 8,27-9, 9,29,30-50 and 10,1-52; but here interest is concentrated on the first group, more specifically on 8,27-9,8, i.e. the sequences "Peter's confession" (8,27-30), "First prediction" (8,31-33), "On losing and gaining life" (8,34-9,1) and "The transfiguration on the mountain" (9,2-8).

Peter's Confession and the First Prediction

It is not difficult to retrieve the first two relations in the utterance's logic. Peter's "confession", which is the disciples' "confession", reveals to Jesus what it is the disciples seek in him.

What is crucial here is not that it is Peter who informs Jesus, but that matters are revealed, i.e. that Jesus (No) has knowledge of the disciples' (Ne) desire:

Relation I: No knows that Ne wants Christ1.

Jesus knows that the disciples desire a quite specific Christ, referred to as Christ1.

In another relation, No wishes that Ne shall know Christ2:

Relation II: No wants that Ne knows Christ2.

"Then he began to teach them that the Son of Man must undergo great suffering, and be rejected by the elders, the chief priests, and the scribes, and be killed, and after three days rise again." (8,31). The first prediction or initiation signifies the beginning of the gospel narrative's teaching project.

The change from "the Messiah/Christ" (8,29) to "the Son of Man" (8,31) implies no rejection of the term "the Messiah", cf. 1,1 and 14,61ff, where to the question: "Are you the Messiah, the Son of the Blessed One?", Jesus answers: "I am", and goes on to speak of the Son of Man. The two terms are parasynonymous, but by virtue of their terminological difference they can be employed to emphasize different perceptions of the term "the Messiah/Christ". By thus employing the term "the Son of Man", Jesus indicates to the disciples that a typos different from what they imagine is concerned. On the other hand, the teaching is christological: "the Son of Man" is none other than the Messiah/Christ, the one chosen and anointed by God (1,11). By changing the plane of expression, the content-related difference in the Messiah/Christ perceptions between the disciples' Christ1 and God's Christ2, i.e. the Son of Man, is emphasized. In the predictions, "the Messiah/Christ" can thus be substituted for "the Son of Man": "Then he began to teach them that the Messiah/Christ must undergo great suffering ...".

Relation II indicates the narratee's semiotic initiation, in that the disciples are on the one hand alienated in their desire: what they seek they cannot get, and what they have must be handed over (cf. $\pi\alpha\rho\alpha\delta\iota\delta\omega\mu\iota$ in 9,13; 10,33; the delivery involves a handing-over associated therewith), Jesus is not their Messiah/Christ; and they are on the other hand referred to the interpretant (the predictions revealing God's commandment) which signifies the following absence: the Christ of glory is absent according to a rule, a commandment, which refers to God's desire.

Peter's reproof of Jesus must be seen as a rejection of this alienation that enrolls the disciples' desire into God's desire, appearing as having to (deontic modality, cf. $\delta\epsilon\hat{\iota}$, 8,31). Jesus' reproof of Peter is in turn adherence to and emphasis of God's desire: "Get behind me, Satan! For you are setting your mind not on divine things [the Destinator's having to] but on human things [the Destinatee's wanting]." (8,33). The verb $\phi\rho\rho\nu\epsilon\omega$ has as its object here the substantivized article more specifically defined by the associated genitive, $\tau\grave{\alpha}$ $\tau\upsilon\hat{\upsilon}$ $\theta\epsilon\upsilon\hat{\upsilon}/\tau\grave{\alpha}$ $\tau\hat{\omega}\nu$ $\grave{\alpha}\nu\theta\rho\acute{\omega}\pi\omega\nu$. An alternative translation might read: "but you do not understand what God wants but only what human beings want", since Peter's frame of thought or attitude (φρόνημα) is guided by the desire, by the subjective wanting (incompatibility between the subjective and the objective axiology). What Jesus rejects is the disciples' wishful thinking. Their thinking is affective-cognitive, their reaction is due to the rejection of a hope, an expectation, in which as subjects of being they are passionately involved.

To lose life and to save life

The subsequent teaching, 8,34-9,1, includes a reference to the coming of the Son of Man and concludes: "Truly I tell you, there are some standing here who will not taste death until they see that the kingdom of God has come with power." (9,1). Relative to what precedes this (8,27-33) and the subsequent (9,2-8) teaching, the future perspective is expanded here. The coming of the kingdom of God, which cannot be isolated from the coming of the Son of Man, is here the primary horizon, not the resurrection. The parousia's dependence upon the resurrection is clarified in more detail below, but here one can provisionally observe the narrative's effortless transition from talk of resurrection to talk of parousia, a transition that also, however, involves a change in person, from Jesus/the Son of Man to the disciples/the imitators. Whereas the earlier concern was to teach the disciples the rule that applies to the role of "the Son of Man", what is now concerned is the rule that applies to the role of "imitator"/ "follower" (ἀκόλουθος - ἀκολουθέω - ἀκολουθία): if one wishes to follow the Son of Man one must deny oneself (ἀπαρνέομαι ἑαυτόν), take up one's cross and follow him.

This hypothetical injunction is based on a general rule: If P, then Q, according to rule R. This rule, which here is aimed at the imitators (and which Jesus informs about but is not destinator for) can be given a general form to make it plain that the Son of Man is himself subject to this: whoever wishes to save (σῴζω) his life (ψυχή) shall lose (ἀπόλλυμι) it; but whoever loses his life in the service of God shall save it. The Son of Man will be killed but will rise again three days later. He loses his earthly life in self-denying service to God and his neighbour, but will preserve it by virtue of the resurrection as a heavenly life (cf. Jn 12,25f). Opposed to this possible process there is another process in which one selfishly fights to preserve and protect the earthly life which will however be lost. But the loss is two-fold: one loses not only earthly life but also heavenly life. A man may gain (κερδαίνω; κέρδος: gain, earn) the whole world (ὁ κόσμος ὅλος) but must pay with (ζημιόω; ζημία: risk, lose) his life, the earthly and the heavenly. What therefore seems immediately to be an advantage or a gain (ὠφέλεια), something that supports and benefits (ὠφελέω, 8,36) the life-preservation project (progression/protection), in fact proves itself to involve loss (repression/degression).

Man has been enrolled into a fatal degression process aiming at death. By protection processes, man may try to postpone realization of this process, but it remains inevitable. The fatality means that the free exchange (cf. ἀλλαγή, ἀλλάσσω) between the parties to the implied covenant has ceased and only a forced exchange remains, in that man is to lose his life by virtue of a take. During this modalization, man has nothing to give that might annul the degression process; life cannot be redeemed by an equivalent: what can a person give in exchange for his life which is required of him, what can he give as ransom (ἀντάλλαγμα; ἀνταλλάσσω: exchange, barter; cf. ἀλλάσσω, ἀπ-, δι-, κατ-, μετ-, παρ-; cf. λύτρον) for his life? (8,37). The degression process is fatal, God cannot be bribed.

Although 8,34-9,1 is aimed at the imitator, the information in this sequence, which its placing also shows, is of great significance to understanding the preceding sequences 8,27-33. The two processes, one of which runs from gain/preservation to loss (whoever wishes to save his life must lose it), whereas the other runs from loss to gain/preservation (whoever loses his life shall save it), indeed refer to two different perceptions of the nature of the world, the world according to man and the world according to God. It is true that the matter is here described from the aspect of the revealing truth, but thereby indeed light is cast on the delusion according to which the objective is selfishly to save one's life and gain the whole world.

It is more than natural here to include Jesus' temptation according to Matthew and Luke, who both tell that the Devil/Satan tries to tempt Jesus by offering him "the whole world", or as it reads "all the kingdoms of the world and their splendor" (δόξα; Mt 4,8); "all the kingdoms of the world" and their "glory" (δόξα; Lk 4,5.6). If only Jesus will serve him, he will be given all the glory, i.e. the power (ἐξουσία, Lk 4,6) over it, so that he can realize his own total desire and sovereignly determine others' access to the coveted values. But Jesus answers: "Away with you, Satan (ὕπαγε, σατανᾶ)! for it is written 'Worship the Lord your God, and serve only him'." (Mt 4,10), a saying that is parallel to the rebuke of Peter in 8,33 (ὕπαγε ὀπίσω μου, σατανᾶ). Satan tried to tempt Jesus by appealing to his ambition; Jesus rejects Peter and because of his ambition: it is as *doxomaniacs* (δοξομανία, δοξοκοπία) that the disciples are admonished.

It also makes good sense in this connection to include the sequence's judgment theme: "Those who are ashamed (ἐπαισχύνομαι) of me and of my words in this adulterous and sinful generation, of them the Son of Man will also be ashamed when he comes in the glory (δόξα) of his Father with the holy angels." (8,38). Whoever is ashamed of Jesus (cf. αἰσχύνη, αἰσχύνομαι), distances himself from him, denies him, cf. Mt 10,32f and Lk 12,8ff where ὁμολογέω (admit, acknowledge; ὁμολογία) is contrasted with (ἀπ-) ἀρνέομαι (deny, not wanting to acknowledge, disown; ἄρνησις). Whoever is ashamed of Jesus is ashamed because his way of thinking and attitude is orientated towards the glory of this world. Peter rebukes Jesus because he is ashamed at having to be associated with a loser, and fears that he will be dragged down with him into humiliation. Jesus rebukes Peter because in his doxomania he is governed by a value-perception in which man seeks himself. In contrast to this is a value-perception according to which what is essential is to serve God and one's neighbour.

On the one hand the anthropocentric view perceives the glory of this world as a *seeming* that bears witness to this world's glorious *being*, and on the other hand perceives this inglorious humiliation as a seeming that bears witness to a shameful being. But the theocentric view emphasizes the lack of accordance between seeming and being: the apparently glorious world is in fact empty, its glory is appearance and deception (the world simulates; or the world pretends; ὑποκρίνομαι). It is like a whitewashed tomb which on the outside (ἔξωθεν) looks beautiful (φαίνομαι ὡραῖος) but inside (ἔσωθεν) is full of bones of the dead. Contrasted with the outer positive appearance (φανέρωσις) is the inner negative being, cf. Mt 23,27f, which will be revealed; the apparently inglorious humiliation in turn hides a glorious being, as shall subsequently be revealed (God dissimulates). In other words: the glory appearing is delusion without being, whereas the humiliation refers to a concealed being of glory. The disciples and the Son of Man thus see themselves as confronted with the choice: to profess themselves to themselves and the world, i.e. to deny God; or to deny themselves and the world, i.e. to profess themselves to God. The world appears in glory but involves humiliation and damnation; God appears in humiliation, but involves exaltation and salvation.

It is as true of the world's empty being (Nothing) as of the kingdom of God's full being (Being) that it is absent at the moment of discourse. The revelation, partly the unmasking of the lie, partly the exposure of the secret, has in a way already taken place in the discourse. But this discourse might itself be a deception. It is different for the revelation that takes place when one sees it for oneself. It then becomes evident to all that the degradation and humiliation led to exaltation, whereas the self-exaltation led to degradation, as was predicted by reference to a divine rule (cf. Mt 23,11f: "The greatest among you will be your servant. All who exalt (ὑψόω) themselves will be humbled (ταπεινόω), and all who humble themselves will be exalted."; cf. Lk 14,11; 18,14; Mk 9,35).

The coming of the Son of Man is also the coming of the kingdom of God with power (ἐν δυνάμει; 9,1). The emphatic utterance that concludes the teaching: "Truly I tell you, there are some standing here who will not taste death until they see (ὁράω) that the kingdom of God has come with power" could just as well have had the coming of the Son of Man as its theme, since - anticipating events - he will be revealed for the disciples as such in the following transfiguration scene, cf. 9,9. Cf. also 13,26: "Then they will see (ὁράω) 'the Son of Man coming in clouds' with great power (δύναμις) and glory (δόξα). Then he will send out the angels, and gather his elect from the four winds, from the ends of the earth to the ends of heaven."; and 14,62: "you will see (ὁράω) the Son of Man seated at the right hand of the Power (δύναμις)" and "coming with the clouds of heaven.".

The use of the verb ὁράω is characteristic of these utterances. Jesus says that the narratee will see something that will confirm what he has said; on the one hand the discourse as prediction, on the other hand the discourse as initiation into the interpretant on which the prediction rests. Here the last relation of the information process is rediscovered:

Relation III: No says that Ne will see Christ3.

But, as referred to, 8,34-9,1 has the character of an insertion, because in relation to what precedes it and what follows it, a shift has occurred from the Son of Man to his imitators and from suffering/resurrection to parousia.

It is true that the prediction in 8,31 may be said to contain an implicit reference to a meeting with the resurrected one, in the same way as the reference to the parousia in 9,1 indeed preconditions the exaltation, but considering the clear presence of enunciation-logic's two first relations, a more developed thematization might be expected of the third relation, compared with which the two others are indeed merely preconditions. A thematization of Christ as Christ3 is lacking.

It is true that the Son of Man who comes in power and glory is this Christ, but as an extension of 8,31 (and in the light of 14,28 and 16,6f) the focus should be on the risen Christ.

The Transfiguration on the Mountain

And this is what the gospel narrative does. Although it does not at this point permit Jesus to tell the disciples that they shall see Christ in glory, it does something else: it permits the leading disciples to see already the glorified Christ - but only for a brief moment. They are allowed a glimpse of what they are to see: for the disciples, the transfiguration on the mountain (9,2-13) has the same function as the utterance that characterizes relation III.

Jesus' change or metamorphosis (μεταμορφόω, 9,3) is a change of Jesus' earthly figure into a heavenly figure, and must be seen as an anticipation of his resurrection. The white clothes thus radiate the glory of the resurrection.[45] To the disciples this is a proleptic revelation of Jesus as the resurrected one. They are shown the objective served by the suffering of the Son of Man.

There may be reason to emphasize that the change does not have the status of a transformation but of a transfiguration. The events on the mountain involve no change in Jesus' being. His relationship to God and thus his relationship to the mission he has been charged with is absolutely the same when he comes down as when he went up.

---

[45] Cf. Johannes M. Nützel, *Die Verklärungserzählung im Markusevangelium. Eine redaktionsgeschichtliche Untersuchung*, Würzburg 1973, pp. 96.

But what is concerned is a step in the teaching of the disciples, who are given additional help by this revelation ("This is my Son, the Beloved; listen to him!", 9,7). Jesus is not content to say that they will see the glorified Christ; he permits them to catch a glimpse of him in advance. Or by showing the glorified Christ God himself intervenes as convincingly as possible to initiate the disciples into the secret that they will see Christ in glory again beyond the suffering. To what extent the disciples are capable of retaining this insight, which is in the nature of a promise, is another matter.

That it concerns the glorified Christ is also to be seen from the fact that Jesus, on the way down from the mountain, speaks of the Son of Man's death and resurrection (9,9). Despite the revelation, the disciples' unwisdom is intact: they do not understand what it means to rise from the dead, they cannot think beyond the suffering. But - and this a crucial point - *they have now been initiated into the interpretant.* In the same way as the cockcrow makes Peter remember the words Jesus had said: "before the cock crows twice, you will deny me three times.", 14,30 (note that the "confession" in 8,29 is an involuntary deceit, whereas the denial is a voluntary deceit), the meeting with the resurrected one will therefore open their blind eyes and deaf ears so that they look and perceive, listen and understand (cf. 4,12).

Summary

The result of the analysis may then be summarized as follows:

In the first relation, Jesus is aware of the disciples' desire because Peter's "confession" reveals what they seek in him, i.e. Christ1, characterized by power and glory.

In the second relation, Jesus teaches the disciples that God desires Christ, that Christ2 belongs to him. The rule applies that Christ2, i.e. the Son of Man, is to suffer much. The disciples' expectation sees itself as negated here (cf. the mutual rebuke), and they are initiated into the interpretant, which foreshadows his return by virtue of the resurrection.

In the third relation, Christ returns from alienation and re-emerges for the subject of experience as found again in reality. Christ in power and glory must disappear according to God's desire. But then he must be found again marked by his disappearance (*stigmatized*, cf. Jn 20,19ff; or in clothes "dazzling white, such as no one on earth could bleach them", 9,3). A variant of Christ1, i.e. Christ3, is set before a subject consisting of the disciples addressed, which can be supplemented by other experience-bearers (cf., e.g., 1 Cor 15,3ff). Jesus tells his disciples that they and others will see Jesus again beyond suffering and death (resumed in 14,28). God is then the executant of reality, the one who allows to happen that which he himself has commanded, whereas Christ3 is the empirically existing, the resurrected, Jesus. In the same way as the meeting with the transformed Jesus on the mountain was preliminary and proleptic compared with the meeting with the resurrected Jesus, so is this second meeting itself preliminary and proleptic compared with the meeting with the Son of Man when he comes in power and glory. It is these socialized and experience-bearing disciples who will then be able to take upon themselves the Christian proclamation.

3. The Re-Commissioning

Following the pre-commissioning (the pre-sending-out), the disciples walk about and preach that all should repent (6,7.12). They preach what Jesus himself has publically proclaimed: "The time is fulfilled, and the kingdom of God has come near; repent, and believe in the good news!" (1,15). This proclamation tells that God has passed over to action, that the creation process aimed at the realization of the kingdom of God is in progress. But this does not inform specifically of the role Jesus of Nazareth has in this process. It is still hidden that the crux of the gospel of God will be the gospel of Jesus Christ.

It has been shown in the context of the reconstruction of the implicit ending of Mark that the meeting with the resurrected one must involve a renewed sending-out of the disciples, this time as proclaimers of the gospel of Jesus Christ. This proclaiming which is carried on between ascension and parousia corresponds to a doing that preconditions a motive which itself preconditions an influence.

The influence, which belongs to a manipulation phase, is itself the teaching of the disciples that takes place during the period between calling and flight. But it is important to distinguish two processes which lead to the disciples' being sent out as apostles. The pre-commissioning belongs to a process which itself includes manipulation, competence, performance and sanction. But the sanction phase which closes this first process functions simultaneously as the opening of the other process, as a manipulation phase.

Whether voluntarily or involuntarily, Jesus appears in this first process as a seducer who calls (first manipulation) the disciples on their subjective desire for power and glory (cf. the disciples' rank-complex, 9,34ff; 10,35ff). They are equipped with knowledge and ability (first competence) and sent out to work as apostles (first performance). But when they return home (first sanction) it is only to receive new teaching (second manipulation) which turns their self-knowledge upside down. The first manipulation awakens the desire for the glorious Christ1; the second manipulation negates this desire by enrolling it into God's desire that establishes the suffering Christ2. Through his teaching, which is partly cognitive (the predictions are informative narrates) and partly affective (the influence interferes with the narratee's horizon of expectation and causes a change in his passion, e.g. from hope to fear), Jesus tries to qualify the disciples as competent subjects, who - if the influence succeeds - will be able to undertake the proclaiming beyond death and resurrection.

If the disciples' competence is seen as a final, modal state of being, it may be said that the teaching makes them actualized apostles who become realized apostles only when the blindness and deafness ends. This competence is the precondition for the ending of muteness or silence in favour of the performed proclaiming. It is therefore only the meeting with the resurrected one that finally establishes the disciples as competent proclaimers.

The proclaiming's performance phase is the period between ascension and parousia, when the disciples are carrying out their role as apostles (the proclaiming project). In contrast to the process of pre-sending-out (the pre-commissioning), when the disciples leave their teacher to return to him subsequently, it is Jesus in the second process, the re-sending-out (the re-commissioning), who leaves the disciples (ascension) to return subsequently. In this process, the parousia corresponds to the sanction phase.

The command to proclaim is not the only command that Jesus imposes on his disciples, but it is the most important because any other prescription is explained by this proclamation. It should not be overlooked in this connection that the first step in the actual discipleship is the open proclaiming that coincides with the true confession to Christ. The Christian faith that exists as a reflexive confession has realized its full definition only when it exists as a transitive confession to God and Man. And the disciple who does not himself become an apostle (sent out narrator) must at least have the Gospel upon his lips as confession and praise (cf. Rom 10,9f; Phil 2,11).

The emphasis has been placed on the meeting with the resurrected one because, for the disciples, the resurrection becomes the prism through which they see the preceding events refracted and expounded, i.e. transfigured. The resurrection represents a knowing, since the seeing (vision) of the initiated involves an experience from which the mere believer is precluded; an experience that confirms Jesus' teaching.

But to the reader, the resurrection is given only as a narrated event in a narrative whose narrator perhaps simulates. The narrator says that the reader shall see the Son of Man coming in clouds. By his narrative he has negated his reader's desire, the dream of being able to preserve his life, and has enrolled this into God's desire expressed in the dual commandment of love (cf. 12,29ff). And he has initiated him into the fact that the life rendered in service to God and one's neighbour will be found again as eternal life.

But the reader only has his word for it; and the vision's day or hour is known to no-one, not even to the angels in heaven, indeed not even to the Son, but only to the Father (13,32).

4. The Disciples in Mark's Gospel

If one understands epistemological analysis as the critical examination of a given scientific methodology, its coherence and adequacy in relation to the subject under consideration, then C. CLIFTON BLACK's dissertation, *The Disciples in Mark. Markan Redaction in Current Debate*, is an epistemological analysis which assesses in detail the redaction-critical method and its results within Markan research.[46] In this context, it is important that BLACK compares the various redaction-critical investigations particularly with regard to their understanding of the disciples. By virtue of this analytic survey of research, it is possible within the framework of the present study to put into perspective narrative exegesis' understanding of the disciples' role, and thereby to define the distinctive features of the narrative method.

That the definition of the disciples' role in Mark's Gospel causes difficulty is not due to the New Testament exegetes. The gospel narrative's image of the twelve is truly complex and ambiguous, and in a way it is therefore not surprising that exegetes have arrived at different and contradictory interpretations. What is remarkable, however, is that the exercise of one and the same method, redaction criticism, has occasioned such differing interpretations as is in fact the case. In his systematic (and not simply chronological) survey of research, BLACK divides these differing interpretations into three groups, and in his heuristically based generalization he arrives at three types of interpretation.

Type I: the "conservative" position. This type has the following basic viewpoint: in accordance with ecclesiastical tradition and the historical facts, the theology of Mark's Gospel includes a largely positive assessment of the disciples. This viewpoint contains two parts; a tradition historical assessment according to which Mark's account is in accordance with historical fact and/or the early Christian tradition, and a theological assessment which emphasizes the disciples' positive role. This type is characterized by a predominantly positive understanding of Mark's attitude to history, tradition and the disciples' role.

BLACK now points to ROBERT PAUL MEYE's research as especially representative of this position. According to MEYE, the twelve are favoured by virtue of their special appointment through Jesus and because of his private and prolonged teaching of them. The disciples' answer to this is positive; they stay with Jesus until the end and remain incontestably obedient to his words. Briefly, as authoritative intermediaries of a messianic διδαχή, the disciples stand surety for the gospel. It is quite clear that Mark thus wishes to validate the existing tradition by showing that it originates from a group of witnesses who were specially selected and informed by Jesus himself. But MEYE does not conclude from this that the evangelist himself simply created this glorious image of the disciples. On the contrary, this positive description is an historically probable image fully in

---

[46] Sheffield 1989; Cf. *Sémiotique*, art. "Épistémologie".

accord with early Christian tradition as known from Papias, according to whom Mark's Gospel was created by Peter's interpreter.[47]

Type II: the "intermediate" position. The viewpoint here is that Mark's theology contains both a positive and a negative assessment of the disciples, and that he is probably indebted to ecclesiastical tradition and historical fact without being their slave. The evangelist has a positive, although considerably modified, attitude towards history, tradition and the disciples' role.

BLACK here draws attention to ERNEST BEST as particularly representative. According to BEST, Mark's Gospel is the result of a dialectic process in which the evangelist breaks with the traditions about the historical Jesus. Mark is not merely a collector of tradition but an author who makes use of the historical material, but in a theological interest. He is to some extent master of his material, which is arranged and modified, but he is also mastered by his material. The disciples are considered as examples of a discipleship characterized by imitation, suffering and persecution, but also mission. The negative tension arises from Mark's wish to use the disciples as a background. Their unwisdom gives Jesus the opportunity for further teaching; their fear gives Jesus an opportunity to show them the sources of placidity and courage; their rank-consciousness helps to emphasize the importance of the servant's task. The disciples' negative attitude and behaviour is countered by Jesus' positive teaching, which serves to reassure and encourage the reader. This position thus underlines the tension in the Markan image of the disciples, a tension encountered again in the Christian's existence between sin and forgiveness.[48]

Type III: the "liberal" position. Here the evangelist is considered as an almost autonomous author who is released from tradition and the historical facts. There are individual scholars within this category who perceive the disciples' role as positive, but this is done without asserting any continuity between the Markan text, the historical Jesus and the twelve. This category, however, is quite overwhelmingly represented by scholars who emphasize the discontinuity and the polemic relationship between Jesus and the disciples.

BLACK here draws attention to THEODORE JOHN WEEDEN as particularly representative of this type. He insists on a conflict relationship between Jesus and the disciples, which is asserted to correspond to the conflict relationship between Mark and his theological opponents. The disciples represent a *theologia gloriae*, a *theios aner* christology and a realized eschatology that characterize the theological opponents with whom Mark is in fact confronted, and they are therefore constantly attacked and discredited by the evangelist. Since the women never overcame their timorous silence, Peter and the disciples never receive the

---

[47] Cf. Robert Paul Meye, *Jesus and the Twelve: Discipleship and Revelation in Mark's Gospel*, Grand Rapids 1968; Black, ibidem, pp. 65.

[48] Cf. Ernest Best, *Disciples and Discipleship. Studies in the Gospel According to Mark*, Edinburgh 1986; Black, ibidem, pp. 99.

message about Jesus' parousia in Galilee. The evangelist thus deprives them of their apostolic legitimacy, in that he establishes that they were never reinstated after their defection.[49]

As is known, narrative exegesis makes no distinction between historical levels, levels of redaction, tradition and historicity, but between levels of signification, the occurrence-text, its narration and narrate. It is not therefore possible to establish a simple comparison between the results of redaction criticism and narrative exegesis. The questions raised by one method do not correspond to the other's answers. But by virtue of the methods' common third aspect, the gospel text, it is to some extent possible to put one reading into perspective against the background of the other.

If for example the "liberal" position regards Mark as an almost autonomous author, does not this correspond to narrative exegesis's assertion of an autonomous narrative? Perhaps this is so, but narrative exegesis insists on continuity between narrate and narration, because Mark can only legitimize his own proclaiming on the narrated events, whereas the "liberal" position asserts a discontinuity between redaction and tradition/historicity.

The narrative reading is thus also related to the "conservative" reading. The reconstruction of the implicit ending makes the disciples guarantors of the spread of the gospel; they see themselves reinstated as apostles after their defection. But this reconstruction is semiotic, not historic, and it by no means implies a failure to appreciate the conflict between Jesus and his disciples, which is however processually overcome.

The "intermediate" position notices the disciples' complexity, their negative and positive characteristics, but is sees the conflict relationship described between the disciples and Jesus as a didactic strategy on the part of Mark. For example, the call to the duty of servant emerges more clearly against the background of the disciples' ambition. The narrative reading does not assert that the disciples are either positive or negative, but stresses that as narrative subjects they participate in processes of change and preservation. The gospel narrative is in fact also the narrative of the gospel-persisting events, i.e. of the relationship between Jesus and his disciples, and like all other narrative processes this narrative is characterized by processual change and/or preservation initiatives.

Narrative analysis cannot merely consider the conflict relationship between Jesus and the disciples as a didactic device that refers to a specific communication strategy or rhetoric. In the narrated world, the disciples' failure to understand is by no means surprising. The conflict between Jesus as wonder-worker, i.e. Jesus in power and glory, and the suffering Jesus in powerlessness and ignominy does

---

[49] Cf. Theodore John Weeden, *Mark - Traditions in Conflict*, Philadelphia 1971; Black, ibidem, pp. 127.

not result from the disciples' unwisdom. They must necessarily be blind if their cognitive competence is taken into consideration.[50]

Jesus presents them with a new perception of the world, a world according to God, a perception that necessarily involves a negation of their view of the world to date. And here it is important to note that this does not concern a conflict between two religious opinions, between two epistemologically equal mythological universes, but between two epistemes, the world according to God and the world according to man. These do not have the same epistemological status, since the first perception, the world according to man (people die but do not rise again), *is confirmed* by empirical knowledge, whereas the other perception, the world according to God (people die but will rise again), *is denied* by this.

The disciples' failure to understand is constitutional and bears witness to the opposition with which the Christian proclamation has been confronted from the outset, and always will be confronted. It is not only modern man who cannot appreciate the necessity of the suffering and the possibility of the resurrection, but from the beginning this message has been an *epistemic scandal*. Mark knows that his narrative is unreasonable, and that its message cannot be proved unequivocally. From his own experience he knows only too well the opposition he is up against, and that the fate of the narrative depends upon the recipient's reaction.

The relationship between the narrated narrator, *Jesus*, and the narrated narratee, *the disciples*, is thus similar to the relationship between the narration's narrator and narratee, between *Mark* and *the reader*. Depending on the perspective, it can then be asserted that the narrative of Jesus and the disciples sets the scene for the processual relationship between the gospel story's narrator and narratee, or that the relationship between Mark and his presumed reader reflects the constitutional, but processually abolished, conflict between Jesus and his disciples.

---

[50] Hejne Simonsen emphasizes that the disciples *had to be* unappreciative until Jesus' death and resurrection had created the possibility of understanding; but he asserts at the same time that their failure to understand is *guilt*, cf. *Traditionssammenhæng og forkyndelsessigte i Markusevangeliets fortællestof* (Coherence of Tradition and Intention of Proclamation in the Narrative Material of the Gospel of Mark), København 1966, pp. 157. "Iøvrigt er det bemærkelsesværdigt (It is also remarkable)", he continues, "at den tilføjede uægte Mark.-slutning fortsætter med motivet om disciplenes uforstand og vantro også efter opstandelsen (16,11.13f) og hertil uformidlet føjer udsendelsesmotivet (16,15ff). Det synes at vise, hvorledes et motiv kan gå på egen hånd uden hensyn til dets oprindelige funktion, når det først er forhånden! (that the added artificial Markan ending continues with the motif of the disciples' failure to understand and disbelief, even after the resurrection (16,11.13f) and, unintegrated, adds the commissioning motif to this. It seems to show how a motif can work on its own, disregarding its original function, once it is to hand!"; p. 157). Simonsen here ignores that although Jesus' death and resurrection create the possibility of understanding it is only the meeting with the resurrected one that gives the insight. The eleven are reproached because they did not believe those who had seen the resurrected Jesus. The reproach then becomes paradigmatic of any situation in which the gospel of Jesus Christ is not believed, and is thus directed against the reader. The eleven are sent out as proclaimers because they have *now* themselves seen the resurrected one.

The fact should not be ignored that the gospel narrative interpellates its reader with the intention of making him (and then preserving him as) *Jesus' disciple*.[51]

---

[51] Cf. Robert C. Tannehill, "The Disciples in Mark: The Function of a Narrative Role", *The Journal of Religion 57*, Chicago 1977, pp. 386. As regards the relationship between viewpoint and reader identification, cf. Norman R. Petersen, "'Point of view' in Mark's Narrative", *Semeia 12*, Missoula 1978, pp. 97; Joanna Dewey, "Point of view and the Disciples in Mark", Kent Harold Richards (ed.), *Society of Biblical Literature 1982 Seminar Papers*, Chico 1982, pp. 97; Hans-Josef Klauck, "Die erzählerische Rolle der Jünger im Markusevangelium. Eine narrative Analyse", *Novum Testamentum 24. An International Quarterly for New Testament and Related Studies*, Leiden 1982, pp. 1.

PART FOUR
THE SAVIOR

CHAPTER TEN

SALVATION

A. Savior: Designation and Role

Several passages in the New Testament texts give Jesus the title of savior (σωτήρ), but as a christological title this designation is not nearly as preponderant as, for example, Son of Man, Son of God, Lord or Christ. Nevertheless it is Jesus in his capacity of savior who should, fundamentally, attract attention when determinating the roles which make up the narrative Jesus and the narrative genre that forms the gospel narrative.

Taken together, there are a number of explanatory features in the use of this *savior designation.*[1] First, it is often used about God (Lk 1,47; 1 Tim 1,1; 2,3 and 4,10; Titus 1,3; 2,10 and 3,4), but then usually in connection with a corresponding designation for Jesus (Lk 2,11; Titus 1,4; 3,6). Now God and now Jesus is the savior, with no contradiction arising here, cf. Jude 25: "the only God our Savior, through (διά) Jesus Christ our Lord".

Second, *savior* often appears together with *lord* (κύριος; Lk 2,11; Phil 3,20; 2 Pet 1,11; 2,20; 3,2 and 3,18), which emphasizes that the exalted Christ is referred to as savior and not just Jesus as wonder-worker (e.g. as healer). Third, most passages point to Jesus as the virtual savior who will intervene in the future, cf. especially Phil 3,20; "But our citizenship is in heaven, and it is from there that we are expecting a Savior, the Lord Jesus Christ.".

The designation *savior* is therefore frequently directed at Jesus in the role of the coming one, but this virtual future salvation act that is finally to realize the creation project refers back to a salvation act already realized, a consummated salvation project for which Jesus was the subject of doing. The connection between creation project and salvation project and thus the connection between the roles of doing of God and Jesus is to be the subject of investigation below.

In the synoptic gospels, the designation *savior* referring to Jesus occurs explicitly only in Lk 2,10f: "Do not be afraid; for see - I am bringing you good news of great joy for all the people: to you is born this day in the city of David a Savior, who is the Messiah, the Lord." (cf. also Jn 4,42). But Mt designates Jesus as savior when he allows the angel of the Lord to order Joseph to name the son Jesus (actually Joshua, which means "Yahweh is salvation"), "for he will save his people from their sins." (Mt 1,21). Here name and title merge ("Jesus", i.e. "he by whom God saves"), and the designation *savior* thereby becomes dominant.[2]

---

[1] Cf. Oscar Cullmann, *Die Christologie des Neuen Testaments*, Tübingen 1966, pp. 245.

[2] Cf. Acts 5,31 and 13,23.

The *savior designation* is absent in Mark's Gospel, but this does not prevent the presence of a *savior role*. The analysis of the wonder narrative's thematic roles (cf. Chapter V, B.3.) showed the presence of the protector role:

$$\sigma\omega\tau\acute{\eta}\rho - \sigma\acute{\omega}\zeta\omega - \sigma\omega\tau\eta\rho\acute{\iota}\alpha$$

(cf. 3,1ff; 5,21ff; 5,25ff; 6,56 and 10,46ff), whose corresponding degressor role is:

$$\dot{\alpha}\pi o\lambda\lambda\acute{\upsilon}\omega\nu - \dot{\alpha}\pi\acute{o}\lambda\lambda\upsilon\mu\iota - \dot{\alpha}\pi\acute{\omega}\lambda\epsilon\iota\alpha.$$

This is because the underlying contrast between the states of being of the victim and of the beneficiary is a contrast between death and life, corresponding to the contrast between degression and protection (to kill versus to save, cf. 3,1ff and 5,21ff).

The wonder narrative could then be defined as a Protection narrative genre, which includes the constituting narrative roles:

Degressor - Victim/Beneficiary - Protector,

and it was shown that the thematic roles:

$$\dot{\alpha}\pi o\lambda\lambda\acute{\upsilon}\omega\nu - \dot{\alpha}\pi o\lambda\lambda\acute{\upsilon}\mu\epsilon\nu o\varsigma/\sigma\omega\zeta\acute{o}\mu\epsilon\nu o\varsigma - \sigma\omega\tau\acute{\eta}\rho$$

were in their abstract indefiniteness identical therewith.[3] The disciples' instruction in 8,35ff, where $\dot{\alpha}\pi\acute{o}\lambda\lambda\upsilon\mu\iota$ is contrasted with $\sigma\acute{\omega}\zeta\omega$, can only confirm the assumption that the gospel narrative's basic thematics concerns life and death, salvation and damnation. But if Jesus appears as savior in a wider sense (outside the wonder narrative) then he must participate in an act whose narrative role configuration corresponds to the Protection genre. He must save someone who is victim of a threatening or on-going annihilation process. He may appear as

[3] Cf. Walter Bauer, *Wörterbuch zum Neuen Testament*, Berlin 1971, pp. 1584, who renders ὁ σωτήρ as "der Erretter, der Erhalter, der Bewahrer, der Befreier". Also *Theologisches Wörterbuch zum Neuen Testament*, (Gerhard Kittel, Gerhard Friedrich), VII. Band, Stuttgart 1966, pp. 966, confirms the narratological definition of the savior role. Conversely, it becomes clear that narrative exegesis could form the basis for a more methodical and systematic New Testament lexicography. In the weakly structured quantity of data on σωτήρ, which fills 58 pages, there is only a single pregnant general formulation, and this is very significantly fortuitous and restrictively classified under the section "C. Σῴζω und σωτηρία im Spätjudentum" (p. 981). This formulation, which could serve as point of reference for a restructuring of the σωτήρ role's semiotics, its syntactically organized semantics, deserves on the other hand to be quoted in full: "Die Einheit der vielfältigen Spezialbedeutungen der Wortgruppe σῴζω liegt in der Vorstellung von der Bewahrung oder Wiederherstellung der Integrität einer Person, Sache, eines wie auch immer beschaffenen Funktionszusammenhanges oder eines Zustandes. Dabei können Personen, Sachen und Umstände in gleicher Weise Subjekt oder Objekt des Vorganges sein.". The article is written by Werner Foerster and Georg Fohrer, but the lines quoted are by Albert Dihle.

savior in a narrow sense (e.g. as healer) or in a broader sense (as the one who saves his people from sin); but the roles of the narrative genre remain the same. Syntactically, it is impossible to distinguish one type of savior from another, but the difference between them must rest on a difference in semantic investment.

B. THE CONTENT OF SALVATION

1. Provisional Salvation

Protection has a dual aspect. Immediately, there is progression, a process of change from non-Y to Y, for example from sickness to health. However, this progression is embedded in a superior structure in which the degression phase concerned (sickness) is merely in advance, and in the final instance is aimed at non-X, death. The protection consists in neutralization of this degression process with a view to preserving the state of being X, life. The healer is not only progressor but protector, savior.

a. Salvation to Life

There is reason to emphasize that the salvation is pragmatic, that it concerns a change and/or preservation of *being*. As progression, healing is a factual change of a somatic nature (not only modal or cognitive/affective); it is concrete. When Jesus tells the healed person "your faith has made you well;" (5,34; 10,52), then a concrete and real salvation is concerned that consists in healing, and thus in neutralizing an on-going destruction process.[4]

The question then becomes, how does the restored state of being X, no longer threatened by an on-going degression process, see itself as modalized? In principle there are three possibilities: either the state of being non-X is thereafter impossible, i.e. life is maintained in a fatal preservation corresponding to a form of eternal life; 2) or it is possible/avoidable, i.e. life can be preserved, but can also be squandered; 3) or it is unavoidable, i.e. life is characterized by a fatal degression which, although it can be delayed, cannot be completely abolished. But only the fatal processes are significant here. To put the question differently: when Jesus restores Jairus' daughter to life (5,35ff), is she then given eternal life, or does the salvation consist in delaying destruction?

The question is illuminating. The gospel narrative's information gives no possibility of seeing this raising from the dead as a transition to eternal life. The salvation here consists in delaying destruction. But thereby the content of the narrow meaning of salvation becomes clear. In his capacity as wonder-worker,

---

[4] If the utterance extends beyond salvation to life, if it is also directed towards salvation for eternal life, then there is a dual function that merely urges the question of the relationship between these two forms of concrete salvation. On the wonder-work's possible baptism function, cf. Chapter XI, C.1.b.

Jesus carries out an act of salvation that occurs within the framework of a
modalization according to which death is fatal. Death can be resisted, but it is far
from being overcome: the salvation is *provisional*. On the other hand, the
struggle against death and destruction bears witness to an on-going process aimed
at a final confrontation and promising definitive victory.

In this sense, the wonder-works are a sign of the Kingdom's state of
becoming, partly as a premonition and partly as a pledge. As such they serve the
proclamation, but it would be wrong to see them merely as attention-seeking or
as a means of persuasion. The wonder-works have a salvation function in
themselves, they remedy a specific need whose redress is an aim in itself and
fully in accord with the proclamation's content. Jesus does not take the afflicted
hostage in the service of a different matter, he does not use his affliction as a
lever for a completely different project. It is true that the wonder-works point to
something beyond themselves, and to this extent they are also to be seen as a
kind of assisting act within a superior salvation project, but what is of overriding
importance is that there is a content-related correspondence between the wonder-
works' salvation and the superior salvation project. In both cases saving life is
concerned.

b. The Life/Death Isotopy

As states of being, Life and Death are *terminals*. A subject of being that
experiences an on-going degression process aimed at death finds itself somewhere
between these terminals, and a given moment can appear as a *transitional state*,
a subordinate state of being, where the process is temporarily interrupted or
merely maintained in its relative stability.

The Life/Death semantic category thus makes it possible to distinguish four
categorial terms: two mutually opposed liminal states of being which, despite
their relative stability, are orientated towards (↑) two mutually opposed terminal
states of being:

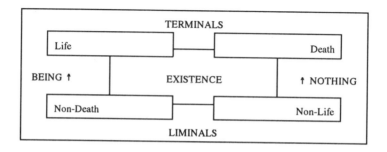

The state of sickness is such a transitional state, which can be designated as
Non-Life, i.e. neither Life nor Death but a negation of Life, since it is *orientated*

towards Death. The process of healing can likewise be maintained in a given moment between Life and Death, since e.g. the convalescent finds himself in a transitional state between the sickness itself and complete recovery, but thereby also in a transitional state between Death and Life. This liminal state of being can be designated as Non-Death, since the process is negatively turned against Death and *orientated* towards Life.

The four categorial terms are *isotopic* (belonging to the same location); they are to be found within one and the same semantic universe.[5] The wonder narrative appears as different variations of this universe, as specifications of the same thematic isotopy. The Life-Death isotopy is global, it is the leitmotif of all the wonder narratives. Irrespective of how expanded or condensed (cf. the summaries) a wonder narrative is, its semantic unity is given by virtue of this isotopy. And irrespective of how many wonder narratives may appear in the gospel narrative, they will never be able to go beyond this fundamental theme. The wonder narrative's semiotic universe can then be said to be constituted fundamentally of a *syntactic isotopy*, its narrative role configuration, and of a *semantic isotopy*, the Life/Death semantic category. It is death that Jesus negates in his wonder-works, a fact that emerges merely with particular clarity in the restorations to life.

2. Definitive Salvation

The question then becomes, when the gospel narrative speaks of "eternal life" and thus of salvation in a wider sense, how does this relate to the universe of provisional salvation?

a. Salvation to Eternal Life

The clearest information about salvation in a wider sense, i.e. final or *definitive salvation*, is to be found in 16,9*, which refers to "the sacred and imperishable proclamation of eternal salvation." (cf. Heb. 5,9), and in 16,16, which states that "The one who believes and is baptized will be saved; but the one who does not believe will be condemned.". These texts are, however, outside the field of investigation of this study. In Mk 1,1-16,8, interest is concentrated upon the following passages: 3,28f; 8,35ff; 9,43ff; 10,17ff; 13,13.20 and 15,29f.

Salvation is dependent upon an act, a doing, which changes and/or preserves a state of being. This act is immediately perceived as transitive; the subject of doing, the savior, is a different person from the subject of being, he who is saved. This transitive function is also indeed immediately recognizable in 10,45 and 14,24 (ἀντὶ/ὑπὲρ πολλῶν); but Jesus' salvation act also involves - and initially - a reflexive perspective.

---

[5] Cf. *Sémiotique*, art. "Isotopie".

A first evidence of this is the mockery in 15,29f: "Aha! You who would destroy the temple and build it in three days, save yourself (σῶσον σεαυτόν), and come down from the cross! He saved others; he cannot save himself (ἑαυτὸν οὐ δύναται σῶσαι).". This complex information, which in its own indirect or ironic way thematizes Jesus' reflexive salvation, gives reason to call attention to a number of significant facts:

1) Jesus does not save himself; he does not neutralize the on-going death process in order to save his life. The question is, then, how is this allowing-to modalized? According to the mockers, his not-doing is due to an inability, the powerlessness refers to his dynamic modalization (ἑαυτὸν οὐ δύναται σῶσαι, i.e. not-being-able-to-do). But another possibility is that his allowing-to is due to a deontic modalization, i.e. an interdiction against saving himself (having-not-to-do) and/or a command to sacrifice himself. In that case the dynamic modalization is being-able-to-do/being-able-not-to-do, and the observation of an interdiction/command emerges as obedience.

2) Jesus has saved others, cf. the wonder-works, and the narrator does not hesitate to allow the mockers to summarize his activity under the savior role. Not only for the narrated observers but for every reader there is a contrast between Jesus as savior and his apparent powerlessness on the cross; others he has saved, but himself he cannot save. This contrast, however, is given only where the salvation consists in preservation of this mundane life.

3) The resurrection may be seen as God's salvation. In that event, it must be stressed that Jesus does not save himself but is saved by God. It makes sense here to assert that Jesus cannot save himself, since he cannot raise himself.[6]

4) But in the case of the resurrection one must first appreciate the resurrection's status of progression. The transition from death on the cross to resurrected life is not the neutralization of an on-going death process with a view to preserving the mundane life, but a progression process that changes death into eternal life.

5) Next, it should be considered in what sense this progression process can be seen as a sub-process in a superior salvation project in which eternal life has the status of the initial state of being which, threatened by an on-going degression process, finds itself restored and preserved.

---

[6] In the enclosed tomb Jesus finds himself like the sheep in the ditch (Mt 12,11), which cannot get out on its own, cf. p. 53. 16,1-8 illustrates the resurrection as a liberation or door-opening miracle, cf. Acts 2,22ff; 5,17ff and 12,5ff; cf. also Rudolf Pesch, *Das Markusevangelium, II. Teil*, Freiburg 1980, pp. 522.

6) The question then becomes, what role has Jesus as a subject of doing in the complex process that leads to his own resurrection? If he has an integrated doing role in this salvation project, then he performs as savior of himself, and the mockers' scorn is given a further touch of tragedy: they do not see that death on the cross is the act through which Jesus saves himself.

7) Finally, it must be asked in what sense is Jesus' own resurrection a precondition for the resurrection of others to eternal life, i.e. how does Jesus' salvation project, which is initially of significance to his own salvation, extend beyond himself and become of significance to others? The mockers do not understand that Jesus' death on the cross is the precondition for his own resurrection, which is in turn the precondition for the salvation of others, for the coming of the kingdom of God.

To summarize, the problems presented may be stated as follows: what is the relationship between the mundane salvation where Jesus saves others but not himself, and the salvation hereafter where Jesus saves himself with a view to saving others? What is the relationship between God and Jesus in this process, which leads to Jesus' resurrection, and what is the relationship between Jesus' resurrection and the possible resurrection of others?

The answer to these contiguous and complex questions must be by stages. The first step is to emphasize the important but often ignored point that Jesus as savior saves in a wider sense above all himself, that the salvation project thus contains a reflexive perspective that gives the mockery in 15,30f its full tragic value, since it is the recognition of this reflexive function that makes it possible to define the isotopy to which the talk of "eternal life" refers. This isotopy must be defined by analysis of the process the narrative Jesus experiences in the capacity of *subject of being*.

b. The LIFE/DEATH Isotopy

When he is introduced in the gospel narrative (1,9), Jesus is a living person (Life^1). He dies on the cross (15,37), but becomes alive again by virtue of the resurrection (Life^2; cf. 16,6). The gospel story presents to its reader a simple narrative process:

$$\text{Life}^1 \rightarrow \text{Death} \rightarrow \text{Life}^2.$$

But what is decisive is the very fact that Life^1 and Life^2 are different. Before his death on the cross Jesus is mortal, but after his resurrection he is immortal. It is certainly not explicit that he acquires "eternal life" by virtue of the resurrection, but in view of the gospel narrative's other information about resurrection and eternal life any other interpretation appears to be excluded.[7] The narrative process thus displays a semantic system or universe of values:

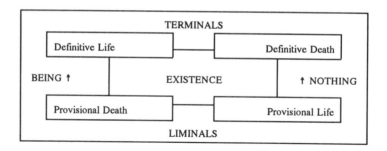

The life of the resurrected (Life[2]) is an eternal or definitive life, which cannot be changed through death (fatal protection). Life[1], however, is a provisional life that can be changed through death, as is of course shown by the death on the cross. Resurrection, on the other hand, shows that the death on the cross is a provisional death that can be changed into life, and opposed to this is a definitive death, i.e. an "eternal death" (cf. 3,29; 9,48) that cannot be changed through resurrection (fatal repression). These definitive and provisional states of being then correspond to:

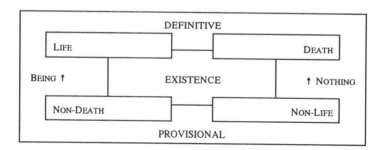

A universe is concerned here, since the four terms constitute all possible modes of existence. According to this axiology, therefore, four different modes of existence or states of being are to be found which a person - *in casu* Jesus - can occupy.

It is natural to perceive the matter as follows: before the resurrection, Jesus lives an earthly life and dies an earthly death. Only by virtue of the resurrection

---

[7] Cf. in particular 12,25ff. Jesus is the first to receive eternal life (10,17); he is the first to be saved (10,26).

does he enter into a non-earthly or mythical state of being. Up to and including the death on the cross, therefore, Jesus comes within an earthly sphere; only the resurrection makes him a mythical person. But such a perception introduces a break between death on the cross and resurrection which is alien to the gospel narrative. Narratively, the resurrection is the semiotic consequence of the death on the cross, which is because *the death on the cross itself already comes within a mythical dimension.*

The terms of axiology belong together, two-by-two, in a *positive deixis* (BEING) and a *negative deixis* (NOTHING). The negative deixis, which is dysphoric, is well-known. It is the earthly sphere in which one lives under the conditions of definitive death. The provisional life is orientated towards the definitive death, and these two states of being together constitute what one should refer to as *historical existence.* These states of being, the one characterized by fatal degression (death is unavoidable), the other by fatal repression (death is irreversible), are known from the empiric reality (the kingdom of death), which is the historical perception's frame of reference and fundamentally defines humankind's *historicity.*

It then becomes clear that the previously defined Life/Death isotopy which characterizes the wonder narratives and the provisional salvation can be more closely defined as the articulation of the *historical existence* whose terminals now see themselves as enrolled into a superior LIFE/DEATH isotopy (note the use of capitals) as negative deixis: Death $\cong$ DEATH; Life $\cong$ NON-LIFE, i.e. provisional life, the empirically-given life, which within the historical existence is part of the positive deixis, sees itself *revalorized* through this contextualization in a superior isotopy as a negative state of being that represents a negation of eternal life.

The positive deixis, which is euphoric, is characterized by mythical states of being, since they come within a transempiric reality. It is, however, of crucial importance to an understanding of the gospel narrative to appreciate that these mythical states of being come within the same universe as the historical states of being, and that the positive deixis (BEING) has ontological priority relative to the negative deixis (NOTHING). The Life/Death isotopy may be referred to as *historical existence*, whereas the LIFE/DEATH isotopy may be referred to as *mythical existence.* The important point is that the mythical existence includes and transcribes the historical existence (on this remarkable relationship between history and myth cf. also below, Chapter XVII).

If the four possible modes of existence in the mythical universe are isotopic, the immortal being that Jesus acquires by virtue of the resurrection cannot be in fundamental conflict with the being that characterizes the other states. They must all belong under one and the same anthropology. The structural inter-definition which applies to these categorical terms (they mutually define one another) must mean that not only do they differ from one another but that they are also linked with one another. There must at the same time be similarities and differences, i.e. structure. It is indeed one and the same *existence* which is articulated in four modes of existence or states of being.

Apparently two modes of life (definitive life and provisional life) and two modes of death (definitive death and provisional death) are given, but in an ontological perspective four modes of life are concerned, since DEATH (non-X) merely refers to absence of LIFE (X): death is the *deficient modus* of life. It is then possible to perceive the four modes of existence as four different constellations between one and the same subject of being, e.g. Jesus, and one and the same value *Life*, and to suggest the following interpretation of these states of being:

1) DEATH, Definitive death:
   Jesus does not have *Life*, but neither has he a right to it;[8]

2) NON-LIFE, Provisional life:
   Jesus has *Life*, but has no right to it;

3) NON-DEATH, Provisional death:
   Jesus does not have *Life*, but has a right to it;

4) LIFE, Definitive life:
   Jesus has *Life* rightfully.

The difference between the mundane, temporal life (2) and the hereafter, eternal life (4) does not fundamentally consist in a difference between life substances but between *life relations*. In both cases one has *Life*, but in the first case non-rightfully and in the other rightfully. The difference between eternal death (1) and provisional death (3) is likewise due to a difference in rightfulness.

The talk of rightful and non-rightful possession refers to an important aspect of the four modes of existence which has not as yet been included. The four states of being have been constituted not only by the relationship between Jesus and *Life* but also by the relationship between Jesus and God. The complexity of the God relationship will be explained below; here it will be mentioned merely provisionally that the complex, progressive process of change which Jesus experiences from provisional life via provisional death to definitive life is a salvation process which is negatively directed against the threat of damnation, definitive death. It should also be noted that the contrast between historical and mythical existence, and thus the tension between provisional and definitive salvation, is of a special nature, since the former sees itself processually *sublated and revalorized*

---

[8] This state of being is never realized, but omitted by the very project of salvation.

by the latter, a process that is wholly parallel to the teachings about the Son of Man through which the Christ designation is re-semantized.[9]

---

[9] The recognition of this peculiar tension between historical and mythical existence is also of importance to an understanding of the relationship between the wonder-worker and the savior, between salvation to Life and salvation to LIFE, and thus to the definition of the wonder narrative's christological function. Siegfried Schulz goes too far in maintaining that no such disparity exists between wonder narrative and passion narrative, *Die Stunde der Botschaft. Einführung in die Theologie der vier Evangelisten*, Hamburg 1967, p. 76. He identifies raising up to life with raising up to LIFE, but one must be content to establish that these two acts are solidary and conformal: the raising up to Life is a precursor of the raising up to LIFE. Dietrich-Alex Koch, however, goes to the opposite extreme when he over-emphasizes the discrepancy between the wonder-worker's and the savior's salvation act. "Die Christologie", he writes, "von der her Markus die Wundererzählungen aufgreift und interpretiert, ist diesen selbst fremd.", *Die Bedeutung der Wundererzählungen für die Christologie des Markusevangeliums*, Berlin 1975, p. 192; but thereby the wonder's positive function is reduced to being merely an attention-seeking factor, and in fact the wonder-worker takes the distressed person hostage. Faced with this opinion it should be stressed that the wonder has a positive function, since it bears unambiguous witness that the salvation is pragmatic, that the re-establishment of the created in its integrity is concerned.

CHAPTER ELEVEN

THE PROJECT OF SALVATION

The research procedure that basically characterizes the narrative method has been described above.[1] For clarity's sake, the analysis example was a brief basic sequence that primarily made it possible to consider the fundamental pragmatic process of change with its subjects of doing and of being.

The gospel text consists of such basic sequences; but the gospel narrative is constituted of narrative units, processes of change and/or preservation which are hierarchically and syntagmatically connected to one another.

It is characteristic of the wonder narrative that the basic sequence and the narrative process coincide. The basic sequence manifests an independent and completed narrative process and therefore appears as a relatively autonomous micro-narrative that may have a significance independently of the superior narrative of which it forms part.

When narrative exegesis inquires about the global narrative process which characterizes the gospel narrative as a whole, matters become more complicated, but the research procedure is in principle the same. The difference between the analysis of a single basic sequence and that of the gospel narrative as a whole is that the action isotopy, which constitutes the latter as one unity, has to be singled out among several narrative processes. It now no longer concerns a single narrative act but a series of narrative acts, i.e. an action, which constitute the overarching process.

The fundamental thesis of this study is that:

the gospel narrative's unity is constituted by a complex narrative process which includes the events of baptism/anointing, death and resurrection; this series of connected acts forms the process which constitutes the gospel narrative's unity-creating mythos, with beginning (baptism/anointing), middle (crucifixion) and ending (resurrection).

These vital events do not become coherent by virtue of their chronological sequence but by their relation to one and the same narrative process which concerns one and the same common person, Jesus of Nazareth in the main, but also God and the disciples. The events which take place are of significance to the person and his existential project.[2]

---

[1] Cf. Chapter III.

[2] Cf. Chapter I, B.2.

A division of the gospel text based on this perception will then be as follows:[3]

1)	1,1-13	Jesus' baptism/anointing
2)	1,14-15,47	Jesus' death
3)	16,1-8	Jesus' resurrection

Information on the individual event must of course be sought mainly in the relevant passage, but, as e.g. the suffering and resurrection predictions show, the individual main passage may very well contain information on the other events.

The division of the gospel text corresponds to the decomposition of the basic sequence into presentic narrative propositions which may be emphasized by the following re-formulation:

1)	Jesus is baptized/anointed
2)	Jesus is crucified
3)	Jesus is resurrected.

The pivotal point, which is defined as the act on the basis of which the other acts appear in retrospect as precondition and consequence, is the death on the cross, which thus becomes the central narrative act on which the analysis should be based.

---

[3] Cf. Chapter II, A.2.

A. The Death on the Cross

1. The Death on the Cross as a Take

Jesus' death on the cross is an ambiguous event, since in the narrative it finds itself framed by various cognitive spaces or worlds. As has been shown, it can thus be considered as either execution or murder.[4]

It is already inherent in the formulation "Jesus is crucified" that he is subject of being for a process whose subject of doing is a different actor. It is the Jewish leaders who condemn him to death (14,64), who must be identified as the responsible, voluntary subjects of doing of the process. Pilate is merely a possible obstacle to be overcome; the soldiers are merely functional henchmen. The Crucifixion is a pragmatic, transitive degression process that realizes its objective: the death on the cross (15,37). The Jewish leaders appear in the role of degressor; Jesus in the role of realized victim. In order to define this transitive degression process in more detail, it is expedient to look at the typology of elementary, narrative acts of which it forms a part.

a. The Narrative Act

The narrative act is a doing that causes something to be. Doing is the realization of a being that it serves; doing is a means, whereas being is an objective. The subject of doing must be distinguished from the subject of being, and two forms of change (progression and degression) must be distinguished and two forms of preservation (protection and repression). If the preservation aspect is disregarded, the narrative act (abbreviated to NA) may be considered as a narrative syntagm that consists of an utterance of doing governing an utterance of being and can be represented in two forms:

$$NA = [Sd \rightarrow (Sb \cap O)]$$
$$NA = [Sd \rightarrow (Sb \cup O)]$$

where Sd = subject of doing, Sb = subject of being, O = object, [ ] = utterance of doing, ( ) = utterance of being, $\rightarrow$ = function of act, and $\cap/\cup$ = junction (conjunction or disjunction indicating the final state, the consequences of the act).[5]

In a perspective of change, the narrative act will produce a state of being which is either X or non-X. The subject of being Sb will thus either see itself as in conjunction of Being, i.e. X = (Sb $\cap$ O) or in disjunction of Being, i.e. non-X = (Sb $\cup$ O). Since O is defined as the positive value X, the conjunction will correspond to progression, the disjunction to degression.

---

[4] Cf. Chapter VIII, D.3.
[5] Cf. *Sémiotique*, art. »Programme narratif« and »Jonction«.

These narrative acts may be further specified on the basis of whether they are reflexive or transitive and voluntary or involuntary. Here interest is concerned only with the voluntary acts that include four narrative types of act; two reflexive, in which the subject of being S1 is identical with the subject of doing S1, and two transitive, in which the subject of being S1 is different from the subject of doing S2. From the perspective of the subject of being S1, these four narrative types of act may be referred to in the following way:

A reflexive progression:

$$1) \quad [S1 \rightarrow (S1 \cap O)],$$

which may be defined as a taking or take ($\lambda\hat{\eta}\psi\iota\varsigma$); this narrative act is called *appropriation* (an usurpation, a pillage, a plundering).

A reflexive degression:

$$2) \quad [S1 \rightarrow (S1 \cup O)],$$

which may be defined as a giving or gift ($\delta\acute{o}\sigma\iota\varsigma$); this narrative act is called *renunciation* (a surrender, an offering).

A transitive progression:

$$3) \quad [S2 \rightarrow (S1 \cap O)],$$

which may be defined as a giving or gift; this narrative act is called *attribution* (a benefit, a gain, e.g. a reward).

A transitive degression:

$$4) \quad [S2 \rightarrow (S1 \cup O)],$$

which may be defined as a taking or take; this narrative act is called *dispossession* (divestment, deprivation, e.g. punishment).[6]

---

[6] Cf. A.J. Greimas, »Un problème de sémiotique narrative: les objets de valeur«, *Du sens II*, Paris 1983, pp. 19. Greimas distinguishes between *don*, which includes attribution and renunciation, and *épreuve*, which includes appropriation and dispossession (p. 39). But the term *épreuve* appears to be misleading, since both renunciation and appropriation of the object of value can have the character of a test, cf. *Sémiotique*, art. »Épreuve«. Here the terms giving/gift and taking/take are used (cf. *donner/don* and *prendre/prise*).

There are thus two forms of loss: renunciation and dispossession; and two forms of gain: attribution and appropriation. It then becomes clear that the crucifixion of Jesus is a take, more precisely a dispossession that forms part of a paradigmatic relation to other narrative acts. This insight is important to an understanding of the salvation project, but the typology shows generally that the narrative acts, reflexive and transitive progressions and degressions, may be perceived as a giving or taking that makes an object of value (O) circulate.

b. Execution

As execution, the crucifixion is placed in a wider context. The death penalty presupposes a crime, violation of an interdiction against blasphemy, which in turn presupposes the promulgation of this interdiction. The matter is in fact between the commander and the commanded, or more generally between a Destinator and a Destinatee or between a *covenantal lord* (κύριος - κυριεύω - κυριότης; δεσπό- της) and his *covenantal servant* (δοῦλος - δουλεύω - δουλεία; διάκονος - διακο- νέω - διακονία; παῖς).

The covenant, whose definition must be isolated step by step, is an arrange- ment according to which covenantal lord and covenantal servant are bound to one another by mutual obligation. In its conditional primary form, the covenant includes a prescription and an interdiction linked to a promise and a threat.[7] If the covenantal servant realizes the prescribed act, the covenantal lord will repay him with the promised reward. In its positive form, the reward is an attribution, which refers to the covenantal lord's doing; but it may have a negative form, which refers to the latter's allowing, since obedience to the prescription abolishes a threat of dispossession. If, however, the covenantal servant realizes the interdicted act, the covenantal lord will repay with the punishment announced. In its positive form, the punishment is a dispossession, but in its negative form it is an allowing, since the transgression of the interdiction abolishes a promise of attribution. There are no reward covenants or punishment covenants, but only covenants that include the dual possibility of reward or punishment.

The covenant frames a narrative process aimed at a covenantal objective, the state of being that according to the covenant's objective perception of value has been selected as Being. In the initial phase the covenantal lord appears as manipulator, in that he modally determines the covenantal servant as virtual beneficiary and virtual victim. After the manipulation phase follows the perform- ance phase in which the covenantal servant acts either by obeying the prescription or transgressing the interdiction. Finally there follows the sanction phase in which

---

[7] Cf. *Sémiotique*, art. »Contrat«; *Sémiotique II*, art. »Condition«. It is this contractually controlled narrative schema which is interpreted as a covenantal schema, cf. Ole Davidsen, »Bund. Ein religions- semiotischer Beitrag zur Definition der alttestamentlichen Bundesstruktur«, *Linguistica Biblica 48*, Bonn 1980, pp. 49; and *Le contrat réalisable. Contribution à l'élargissement et à la consolidation du concept de schéma narratif canonique*, Actes Sémiotiques/Documents 46, Paris 1983.

the covenantal lord appears in the role of sanctioner or retributor, now the rewarder, now the punisher.

The covenant's process schema can then be given as:

MANIPULATION → PERFORMANCE → SANCTION

and one perceives that the covenant schema is the overarching unity that gathers together the definitions of the narrative subject given above, and in which are distinguished an ontical and an ontological field of being, a field of influence (manipulation), a field of action (performance) and a field of retribution (sanction).[8]

At first, reward and punishment appear to be two processes of equal value; one is merely positive, whereas the other is negative. But a certain asymmetry asserts itself. Where the reward is aimed at preserving life (protection), the punishment aims at destroying life (degression). In addition, reward often involves a pecuniary change of status, i.e. a progression that takes place within the framework of life (for example from a life of poverty to a life of riches). It is true that punishment may also consist of a change in status (degression) within the framework of life (for example from rich to poor if the fine is large enough, or from freedom to imprisonment), but the punishment *par excellence* is the death penalty. *The object of value which is always at stake in the covenant is the covenantal servant's life.*[9]

In regard to Jesus, an initial state can be distinguished in which he has life (S1 ∩ O) rightfully. Transgression of the interdiction does not lead to his losing his life as a direct consequence, but in the covenant's perspective he does not now have his life rightfully, and therefore it must be lost (taken). After this intermediate state follows the final state, crucifixion, where he neither has life (S1 ∪ O) nor the right to it. To facilitate a distinction between these states of being they are noted as follows:

Initial state	(Sb ∩ (Sh ∩ O)	
	⇓	Transgression
Intermediate state	(Sb ∪ (Sh ∩ O)	
	⇓	Sanction
Final state	(Sb ∪ (Sh ∪ O)	

---

[8] Cf. Chapter I, B.2.

[9] 8,37 thematizes in its own way the fact that all the world's pecuniary objects of value will never be able to equal the special object of value which life constitutes.

where Sh = subject of having. The junction between the subject of having and the object concerns life (Sh ∩ O) and death (Sh ∪ O), whereas the junction between the subject of being and the embedded junction (O' = (Sh ∪/∩ O)) concerns its covenantal status of being, either protagonist (Sb ∩ O') or antagonist (Sb ∪ O').

The intermediate state results from a process of change for which Jesus himself is the subject of doing. It is by virtue of this demeriting act (blasphemy) that he is crucified. The acquisition of unworthiness logically precedes any award of punishment. The attainment of this negative state of worthiness is a first degression invoking another degression in the form of punishment that abolishes the imbalance caused by the violation.

It is not certain that the covenantal servant sees himself as a criminal. He may be wrapped in self-delusion and think that he carried out a prescribed (or permitted) task, whereas in reality he transgressed an interdiction (cf. Gen 2,4bff). It is a *judge* (κριτής - κρίνω - κρίσις/κρίμα; δικαστής) who decides, from a pleading of the covenant's objective perception of value, whether worthiness (τιμή) or unworthiness (ἀτιμία), righteousness (δικαιοσύνη; Jesus is righteous, δίκαιος, cf. Lk 23,47) or unrighteousness (ἀδικία; Jesus is unrighteous, ἄδικος) is at issue. This judge may himself be the victim of deception, but within the cognitive space that characterizes the Jewish leaders, Jesus is a criminal who deserves the death penalty and is therefore crucified.

c. The Death Penalty

To understand the punishment's semiotics, it is important to note that the relationship between the covenantal lord (God) and the covenantal servant (Man) before the establishment of the covenant is characterized by contradiction. They are each other's opponents, and the manipulation consists in these antagonists' being transformed into protagonists (synagonists). Here the asymmetric strength relationship between the parties is crucial. The covenantal lord is indeed defined as such because he has power to define and establish the covenantal servant's dynamic latitude (field of ability). As administrator of the covenantal servant's right to exist, the covenantal lord can sovereignly exercise the dynamic modalization and perhaps put him wholly out of action: the covenantal servant (Man) owes to the covenantal lord (God) his power to act or not to act.

The very first element of the manipulation must therefore be defined as the factitive act through which the covenantal lord (God) enables his virtual protagonist to act. This factitive act is a renunciation which for the covenantal lord involves a reflexive degression, a self-abasement, in that he renounces his omnipotence. The covenantal objective which the covenantal lord (God) must have set himself can accordingly only be realized with the participation of the covenantal servant. By allowing the covenantal servant (Man) to play an integrated role in the realization of his own destiny, the covenantal lord (God) has thus voluntarily assumed the powerlessness that results from his dependence upon this covenantal servant (this Man). It is this action-opening renunciation that forms the core of the gospel narrative's *incarnation concept*.

The covenantal lord's powerlessness is not of course the mere absence of being-able-to-do but the result of a self-elected deontic modalization of the sphere of action. According to the circumstances, there are acts he must carry out and acts he must not carry out. The situation is similar for the covenantal servant: there are acts he can carry out but may not carry out; and acts he can omit carrying out but must carry out. It may therefore be said that the covenantal lord's right restrictively to articulate the covenantal servant's dynamic sphere of possibility by prescribed and interdicted acts is given with his initiatory renunciation. To the extent that the covenantal servant (Man) attempts to realize his being outside the path indicated, the covenantal lord (God) will see therein a failure to appreciate the initial renunciation/attribution (gift) upon which the covenant rests. The covenantal servant (Man) acts as an equal, as if his power to act was attributable to himself. Transgression is a failure to appreciate the covenantal lord (God) as Destinator, and he repays by destroying the covenantal servant's latitude and thus the covenantal servant himself.

The initial confrontation between the two parties as antagonists may thus end either in a destruction of the virtual covenantal servant or in a validation of him as covenantal subject, protagonist. In fact, the inferior has no real choice: the only defence against destruction is to subject himself to the covenantal lord and his conditions.[10] But any attempt to evade the covenant's conditions makes the covenantal servant a covenant-breaker, an antagonist, who is liable to punishment. There are different forms of punishment, but they can all be considered as forms of loss of liberty (restriction of the sphere of being-able-to-do), e.g. imprisonment, which refers back to the covenant's foundation on the covenantal lord's setting the covenantal servant free to act. It should not therefore be surprising that the death penalty is the punishment *par excellence*. It is the execution of the destruction that the covenantal servant initially evaded by accepting the covenant. One then perceives that any other punishment is in fact only a suspended death penalty.

It also becomes clear why the covenant not only promisingly defines the covenantal servant as virtually favoured, but also threateningly defines him as virtual victim. The manipulator acts in the role of both seducer and intimidator. When one accepts that the covenantal servant's dynamic latitude is in a fundamental sense itself his power to exist, it finally becomes clear that what is at stake in the covenant is not only pecuniary objects of value. As the punishment shows, the covenantal servant acts at the risk of his life; this is a special form of

---

[10] Cf., for example, Gen 17, where the covenantal obligation initially consists in allowing oneself to be circumcised (17,10). He who does not allow himself to be circumcised will be exterminated, destroyed. (17,14).

object of value that can be given and taken. Acceptance of the covenant validates the covenantal servant as a subject that rightfully has its life: (Sb ∩ (Sh ∩ O). Violation of the covenant involves initially the realization of a state of unworthiness or unrighteousness in which the covenantal servant still has his life but is now no longer entitled to it: (Sb ∪ (Sh ∩ O). In a degressive perspective, this state of being is equivalent to the covenantal servant now no longer having his life as a gift but as stolen plunder, i.e. by virtue of a take. And the covenant's exchange logic is simple: in the same way as gift is repaid by gift, take is repaid by take. According to the covenant's ordinance, the covenantal lord is obliged under these circumstances to take the covenantal servant's life. From the covenantal servant's side, the carrying out of the death penalty is then a transitive take, a dispossession: (Sb ∪ (Sh ∪ O).

The execution of Jesus must be seen in this light. When the Jewish leaders pronounce the sentence on him, that he is deserving death (14,64), they act in the role of judges adhering to a law or covenant to which both they and Jesus are subject. The Jewish leaders are the representatives of the covenantal lord, whereas Jesus takes on the role of covenantal servant. The sanction includes two linked processes, on the one hand a cognitive process in which a judicial authority, invoking an objective perspective, establishes whether the accused is guilty (unrighteous) or innocent (righteous), i.e. pronounces judgment upon the state of worthiness of the person concerned, and on the other hand a pragmatic (and/or modal) process, the retribution process itself.

The blasphemy is a transgression that qualifies Jesus as unworthy, unrighteous. In the covenant's perspective, this violation is a reflexive degression through which Jesus changes his being from (Sb ∩ (Sh ∩ O), in which he has life rightfully, to (Sb ∪ (Sh ∩ O), in which he still has life but now unrightfully. The crucifixion is a punishment process in which the covenantal lord's representatives (S2) take Jesus' (S1) life: [S2 → (S1 ∪ O)]. By the realization of this state of being (Sb ∪ (Sh ∪ O) the imbalance introduced by the transgression is then abolished.

d. The Murder

This dispossession, however, is either legitimate or illegitimate. In the first case an execution is concerned, in the second case a murder. This contrast, execution versus murder, is not alien to the gospel narrative.[11] The parable of the vineyard in particular, 12,1ff, singles out the Jewish leaders as prophet murderers or apostle murderers. In this narrative, the homicide is thematized as an infringement that devalidates the acting parties and makes them liable to punishment, the death penalty: the owner of the vineyard will come and destroy (ἀπόλλυμι, 12,9) the tenants. Transferred to Jesus' crucifixion, this means that the Jewish leaders'

---

[11] Cf. Chapter VIII, D.3.

murder of the Son will be repaid by the Father. This could perhaps be thought to take place at the last judgment; but it is noteworthy that the gospel narrative does not primarily take the opportunity in the death of Jesus to tell of such a sanction process. The virtual retribution process that was to end in the destruction of the murderers is not actualized but is eschatologically postponed.

Instead, *God intervenes and raises the victim*, Jesus. It is true that this act may be said to confirm the perception (the cognitive space) according to which the crucifixion is murder, but the function of the resurrection is not merely to establish that the Jewish leaders were murderers. The acts of confession of the centurion (15,39) and Joseph of Arimathea (15,42ff) already show that there were those among the Romans and Jews for whom the crucifixion was murder. The resurrection cannot really be understood on the basis of the death on the cross as murder. What must be remembered is that whether or not the death on the cross is perceived as execution or murder, a dispossession is in both cases concerned, a transitive take in which life is taken. As such, the death on the cross cannot strictly be associated with baptism and resurrection.

The gospel narrative, however, contains another action isotopy according to which the death on the cross is not a transitive take but a reflexive renunciation, a gift. The overarching interpretation of Jesus' death here emerges that determines the gospel's narrative form and the message's content, and should therefore be given the greatest attention. The task of narrative exegesis then becomes not merely to resolve the "enigma of the cross" but to assist in clarifying the *narrative rationality* concerned in the gospel story's narrative interpretation.

2. THE DEATH ON THE CROSS AS A GIFT

The central text clarifying the gospel narrative's understanding of Jesus' death on the cross is 10,45: "For the Son of Man came not to be served but to serve ($\delta\iota\alpha\kappa o\nu\acute{e}\omega$), and to give ($\delta\acute{\iota}\delta\omega\mu\iota$) his life a ransom ($\lambda\acute{\upsilon}\tau\rho o\nu$) for many ($\grave{\alpha}\nu\tau\grave{\iota}$ $\pi o\lambda\lambda\hat{\omega}\nu$)." Here the death on the cross is unambiguously understood as a giving, a gift, not as a take.

As in 14,24, this information thematizes the significance of the death on the cross "for many". Through the death on the cross, this collective actor sees himself selected as a favoured subject of being. Jesus dies "for many", and in this perspective the cross event is a transitive progression, an attribution. But the narrative process within which this collective actor is the subject of being must be distinguished from the narrative process in which Jesus himself is the subject of being. One and the same event, the death on the cross, may have different functions within narrative processes, each with its own subject of being. This may be considered from different viewpoints, although the narrative can perhaps present only one of these.

Thus, the death on the cross may be considered as a narrative act whose subject of being is now the disciples (in a broad sense, i.e. the collective actor "many"), now Jesus, and now God. These viewpoints cannot be adopted simultaneously; each particular narrative process must be defined individually in order subsequently to see itself defined in its structural and integral relationship to the others.

In such a complex set of signification as is encompassed by the gospel narrative, it is important that exegesis should satisfy the pertinence principle.[12] Jesus' death is a pluri-isotopic event that can be understood now as a take and now as a gift, and exegesis must come to terms with the fact that analysis of such an ambiguous event calls for an ability to distinguish and extract only such features as are relevant to the chosen viewpoint. Among all the possible definitions of Jesus' death as are contained in the gospel narrative's information, exegesis must consider only such pertinent features as are necessary and sufficient for an exhaustive definition from the chosen viewpoint. What is concerned is the ability to separate the different levels of signification and to avoid the danger that threatens to overload the individual event with definitions which are relevant only to the analysis of another selected viewpoint.

10,45 and 14,24 state a viewpoint in which the disciples are the subject of being, but this in fact relates to only one of several possible viewpoints. The information can be analyzed on the basis of other viewpoints. Thus, 10,45 is not merely a text concerned with the disciples as subject of being, but also a text that - admittedly more indirectly - is concerned with Jesus (and God) as subject of being. This opportunity systematically to question on the basis of different viewpoints, which are restricted in number and mutually connected, gives narrative exegesis the ability optimally to utilize the narrative's information. It does not take one single basic sequence, which is then minutely commented upon verse by verse, but chooses a viewpoint, i.e. a narrative process, and then empties all relevant basic sequences for the pertinent information about this process.

a. Mark 10,45

What is concerned here is the information 10,45 gives about the narrative process in which Jesus himself is the subject of being for the act inherent in the death on the cross, and for this reason the disciples' role must be disregarded for the time being.

The verb δίδωμι defines Jesus in the role of giver:

$$δότης - δίδωμι - δόσις$$

---

[12] Cf. *Sémiotique*, art. "Pertinence".

cf. Gal 1,4; 1 Tim 2,6, Titus 2,14. The giver simultaneously exercises renunciation (he gives something away) and attribution (he gives something to someone), but it is not evident from this role whether the giving of the gift is a manipulation or a sanction (relative or absolute).

In the case of manipulation, the giving of the gift establishes an imbalance between the parties, in that the giver thereby validates himself as creditor (δανειστής - δανείζω - δάνειον) relative to the recipient, who becomes the debtor (ὀφειλέτης - ὀφείλω - ὀφειλή): the gift is a prepayment (πρόδοσις, προδίδωμι, cf. Rom 11,35), which calls for a gift in return.

In the case of sanction, the giving of a gift establishes a balance, in that the creditor/debtor relationship is abolished, i.e. the pre-established debtor relationship between giver and recipient: the gift is a repayment, a *quid pro quo* (ἀπόδοσις, ἀποδίδωμι).[13]

The giver role defines Jesus as the subject of doing for a narrative act. The formulation "Jesus is crucified" conceals this aspect, since it refers to the perspective in accordance with which the death on the cross is a transitive take (legitimate or illegitimate).[14]

Within the cognitive space in which the death on the cross is an event with Jesus as subject of doing, the act must therefore be indicated by the following presentic formulation: "Jesus gives his own life", i.e. Jesus (S1) gives (renunciation) the object of value, *Life*:

$$[S1 \rightarrow (S1 \cup O)].$$

In fact, only in this perspective is it possible to connect the death on the cross with baptism and resurrection.

The connection between death on the cross and resurrection is already evident when one perceives that "Jesus is risen" refers to an act in which Jesus receives

---

[13] The verb ἀποδίδωμι is used in the sense of paying what one owes, returning, repaying (retribution, also in the form of punishment cf., e.g., Mt 6,4; 16,27; Rom 2,6; 1 Cor 7,3), a meaning which is accentuated in the form ἀνταποδίδωμι (cf. Lk 14,14; Rom 11,35; 12,19; 2 Thess 1,6; ἀνταπόδομα, Lk 14,12; ἀνταπόδοσις, Col 3,24).

[14] The death on the cross is located in four different cognitive spaces. In the cognitive space of the Jewish authorities the crucifixion is a *legitimate take* (an execution), since Jesus is considered to be guilty. In the cognitive space of the centurion and Joseph it is an *illegitimate take* (a murder), since Jesus is regarded as innocent. It is open to discussion whether the murder should be conceived as a judicial or a ritual murder (scapegoating). In the superior cognitive space of the gospel narrative the death on the cross is interpreted as a *legitimate gift* (a sacrifice), since Jesus is perceived to be obliged to give his life. However, a fourth cognitive space may be identified in which this event is believed to be an *illegitimate gift*, since Jesus wastes his life in vain. The position concerned here can only be identified as suicide. When Peter rebukes Jesus (8,32) he attempts to dissuade him from going to Jerusalem. A well-intentioned warning may be concerned here, since Peter (cf. his denial) regards Jesus' conflict-seeking behaviour as ill-fated. He is convinced that it will be suicidal to go to Jerusalem. It is remarkable that Mark allows all four cognitive spaces to be presented by the narrative, which thereby gives the reading the status of a projective test. The reader himself is forced to interpret this relatively open structure and will thereby disclose the structuring principle of his own personality. "Tell me what you think is the correct interpretation of the death on the cross", says the narrative, "and I will tell you who you really are!".

the object of value, *Life*:

$$[S2 \rightarrow (S1 \cap O)].$$

The subject of doing for this transitive giving is God (S2), and the gift is either a manipulation that opens a narrative process or a sanction that closes a narrative process. Not just any process but a sequence in which Jesus is the subject of being and the object of value is *Life*.

God's raising of Jesus can thus only be a sanction, which closes a narrative process. Jesus' acquisition of a life that is eternal is the acquisition of a life that is no longer at stake. More specifically, this attribution is a reward. Jesus is the covenantal servant, Destinatee, God is the covenantal lord, Destinator. The resurrection is an ἀπόδοσις, God's positive retribution.

But in the same way as the punishment presupposes the transgression of an interdiction, the reward presupposes obedience to a prescription. This prescription in turn must itself be declared by a prescriptor. Here the covenant's schema is recognized, which - provided that the baptism (anointing) is on a par with death on the cross and resurrection - subjugates the gospel narrative's fundamental events:

MANIPULATION	PERFORMANCE	SANCTION
Baptism/Anointing	Death on the cross	Resurrection

The covenant is not only a matter between Jesus and God but is aimed at a collective actor, the new people of God, the disciples in a broad sense. In a wider perspective, Jesus' resurrection is merely the first element in a more comprehensive sanction process (judgment and retribution). The covenant, however, is *primarily* a matter between Jesus and God, and it is in this perspective that the story of the Last Supper, 14,22ff, must also initially be read.

b. Mark 14,24

In the context of the gospel narrative, the Last Supper is an event which takes place while Jesus is observing the Passover (τὸ πάσχα) with his disciples, 14,12ff. It is while they are eating their paschal supper that Jesus takes a loaf of bread, blesses it (εὐλογέω), breaks it (κλάω) and gives it to the twelve with the words: "Take; this is my body." (14,22; "λάβετε, τοῦτό ἐστιν τὸ σῶμά μου").

He then takes a cup, gives thanks and gives it to them to drink with the words: "This is my blood of the covenant, which is poured out for many.". (14,24; "τοῦτό ἐστιν τὸ αἷμα μου τῆς διαθήκης τὸ ἐκχυννόμενον ὑπὲρ πολλῶν").

Finally there follows a conclusion in which Jesus prophetically proclaims that he will never again drink of the fruit of the vine until that day when he drinks it new in the kingdom of God (14,25).

The parallelism between the bread act and the cup act is simply expressed in the identity between the two semiotizing interpretations: "this is my body" and "this is my blood". This identity makes it possible to explicate the two acts one from another.

The imperative "Take" (λάβετε) can be understood meaningfully only on the basis of an implicit imperative "eat" (cf. Mt 26,26, φάγετε). And when Jesus gives the cup it is because the disciples are to take it and drink from it. The situation contains a dual imperative: "Take; drink from it" (cf. Mt 26,27, πίετε). The information "all of them drank from it" (the one cup) corresponds to the implicit "and they all ate of it" (the one loaf of bread).

The development of this parallelism can be taken further:

"This is my blood of the covenant, which is poured out for many."

corresponds to:

"This is my body of the covenant, which is killed for many.".

The verb ἐκχέω means to shed, to pour out, but also to waste, to destroy. The term: to shed blood (αἶμα ἐκχέω; cf. Acts 22,20; Rom 3,15, Rev 16,6) is parasynonymous with: to murder, to kill, to destroy (cf. Mt 10,28: ἀποκτείνω, ἀπόλλυμι τὸ σῶμα). The two members thus refer parallelly to Jesus' death on the cross in which his body is killed and his blood shed. But it is quite important in this regard that Jesus is himself contained in "many". One may well say that Jesus dies so that "many" may live, but this is an ambiguous formulation, which encompasses the possibility of misunderstanding. Jesus does not die the definitive death (i.e. death as a punishment) so that the many may preserve their provisional life (i.e. avoid punishment, destruction). He dies a provisional death (a meritorious act) so that *he and the many* may receive definitive life (reward). The term "blood of the covenant" (cf. Ex 24,8) defines Jesus' death on the cross as a covenantal death, i.e. an event that receives its signification by being framed by the covenant's exchange structure. It is in obedience to the covenantal lord's prescription that Jesus suffered death on the cross. He therefore appears as a subject of doing, which gives its life to the covenantal lord, i.e. to God.[15]

---

[15] The commentators are more interested in discussing for whom life is given than to whom life is given. Ernst Lohmeyer, Rudolf Pesch, Vincent Taylor, and Eduard Schweizer silently ignore the question of the recipient. Walter Grundmann perhaps gives the explanation of this silence when he writes on 10,45: "Wem das Lösegeld gezahlt wird, danach darf man nicht fragen; ...", *Das Evangelium nach Markus*, Berlin 1971. In *Märtyrer und Gottesknecht. Untersuchungen zur urchristlichen Verkündigung vom Sühntod Jesu Christi*, Göttingen 1963, p. 121, Eduard Lohse points out that the question of to whom

The word διαθήκη is employed in LXX to translate the Hebrew *berit*, covenant. In classical Greek it means predominantly "testament", and is used as such in Heb 9,15ff. Otherwise it means covenant in the New Testament texts. That LXX uses διαθήκη rather than συνθήκη (agreement, contract) may be because the latter concept refers to an arrangement entered into between two equal parties. To translate *berit* by συνθήκη would then imply a failure to appreciate the asymmetric relationship that characterizes the covenant's parties. It is true that the covenant is an agreement, but its content has been established (διατίθημι) from on high by God's will (the covenantal lord in the role of θέτης - τίθημι - -θήκη).[16] The story of the Last Supper can thus only confirm the assumption that it is within the framework of a covenant that Jesus' death on the cross is to be understood as a gift.

The distinction introduced between subject of having and subject of being is important to the understanding of the gift's (and the take's) functional pluri-isotopy. The death on the cross as a gift involves a pragmatic loss (from having to non-having, Jesus gives his provisional life) but also a gain of worthiness (from non-being to being, Jesus obtains the right to a definitive life). The death on the cross is thus at one and the same time a degression and a progression, but of a different type. The degression concerns Jesus' pragmatic being, whereas the progression concerns his covenantal being or covenantal status. Alongside the pragmatic, cognitive-affective and modal states of being, *covenantal* states of being thus appear, which may themselves be an object of change and/or preservation (for example from righteous to sinner or vice versa).

---

the ransom is paid has caused "den Exegeten viel Kopfzerbrechen". Satan has been proposed, but this interpretation is contradicted by 8,33. The interpretation suggested here, which considers God as the recipient (e.g. on the basis of 8,33) is also rejected. Since the text gives no information on who receives the ransom, the question simply cannot be answered. Lohse concludes: "Eine konsequente Durchführung des Bildes - Gott als Empfänger eines unendlich wertvollen Lösegeldes - ist unmöglich, so daß die Satisfaktionstheorie nicht auf Mk. 10,45 angewendet werden darf. Gott ist der Stifter der Versöhnung, nicht ihr Empfänger. In dem Sterben Jesu vollendet und offenbart sich der unerforschliche Heilswille Gottes.", p. 121. But if one refrains from asking the question about the recipient because one is afraid of the answer, or because one finds it to be in vain, then one must give up trying to find the gospel story's narrative rationality. Ernest Best fully agrees with the gospel narrative's information when he writes in *The Temptation and the Passion: The Markan Soteriology*, Cambridge 1965, p. 144: "since in Mark the death of Jesus is a divine necessity it is probable that if he were pushed to the point of saying to whom the ransom was paid, he would say 'to God'.". The narrative Jesus cannot answer otherwise. But it cannot of course be excluded that W.G. Kümmel is right when he asserts: "von einer Einwirkung des Todes Jesu auf Gott kann Jesus nicht geredet haben", quoted by Lohse, ibidem, p. 121. Here Kümmel, however, speaks about what the reconstructed historical Jesus may have said.

[16] Cf. Vincent Taylor, *The Gospel According to St. Mark*, London 1959, p. 546.

B. THE RESURRECTION

It is characteristic of the covenantal schema that it consists of a number of linked narrative acts. Thus the resurrection is not merely an event that chronologically follows the death on the cross but an event that is connected, in a way which still remains to be disentangled, with this in a relationship of dependence.

1. The Narrative Trajectory

The complexity of the covenantal schema's course of action is due to the presence of several relatively autonomous narrative acts with different subjects of being and doing. It is the Destinator and the Destinatee, the covenantal lord and the covenantal servant, who take it in turns to adopt these roles. Thus, the death on the cross, seen as a gift, is a narrative act in which Jesus is the subject of doing and God the subject of being, while the resurrection is a narrative act in which God is the subject of doing and Jesus the subject of being.

a. The Dual Trajectory

The narrative events, here death on the cross and resurrection, do not obtain coherence by virtue of their chronological sequence but by being related to one and the same process of change concerned with one and the same subject of being.[17] But within the covenantal schema there are two processes, connected by interaction, each with its own subject of being. One process can be distinguished in which God is the subject of being and one in which Jesus is the subject of being.

The narrative cannot allow both these perspectives to be heard, but however concealed it may be, the narrative about the covenantal servant's fate is also the narrative about the covenantal lord's fate.[18] Both experience a process referred to as *a narrative trajectory*, and it is these two interwoven and correlated trajectories, this dual trajectory, which constitutes *the narrative covenantal schema*.[19] The events of baptism/anointing, death on the cross and resurrection provide direct access to the covenantal servant's (Jesus') narrative trajectory, from manipulation via performance to sanction, but principally it will be possible,

---

[17] Cf. Chapter I, B.2.

[18] Cf. *Sémiotique*, art. "Occultation". Greimas contrasts subject (S1) and anti-subject (S2), e.g. hero and villain, which refers to their individual contractually controlled project. The occultation concerns these inter-contractual subjects, but the same phenomenon can be recognized as regards the intra-contractual subjects, the Destinator (S2) and the Destinatee (S1).

[19] Cf. *Sémiotique*, art. "Narrativ (parcours -)" and "Narratif (schéma -)". Greimas distinguishes three autonomous segments within the narrative schema, the manipulator-Destinator's (manipulation), the performing subject's (performance) and the judicator-Destinator's (sanction) narrative trajectories, but such an opinion is untenable. Manipulator and judicator/sanctioner refer to one and the same Destinator authority; there are only two narrative trajectories which are interactionally connected, cf. Ole Davidsen, *Le contrat réalisable*, Paris 1983.

on the basis of this course of action, to obtain an analysis of the covenantal lord's (God's) correlative, narrative trajectory.[20]

b. The Covenantal Servant's Trajectory

The covenantal servant's narrative trajectory is a process that can be more specifically defined as an interactive progression process or as an interactive degression process. The covenant's dual possibility of punishment or reward defines the covenantal servant both as a virtual victim of a *negative* narrative trajectory and as virtually favoured by a *positive* narrative trajectory. These narrative trajectories can be seen as processes that gradually change the covenantal servant's being. He traverses an orientated series of states of being, which are merely a more complex version of the transition from $X = (S \cap O1)$ to non-X $= (S \cup O1)$, i.e. degression, or from non-Y $= (S \cup O2)$ to $Y = (S \cap O2)$, i.e. progression. The two possible trajectories can then be shown as:

PHASE/MOVE	NEGATIVE TRAJECTORY	POSITIVE TRAJECTORY
MANIPULATION ⇓ PERFORMANCE	$S \cap (S \cap O1)$ Transgression ⇓	$S \cup (S \cup O2)$ Obedience ⇓
⇓ SANCTION	$S \cup (S \cap O1)$ Punishment ⇓	$S \cap (S \cup O2)$ Reward ⇓
	$S \cup (S \cup O1)$	$S \cap (S \cap O2)$

Since these processes mutually exclude one another, a covenantal narrative will generally tell of either transgression of an interdiction (active disobedience, doing), which results in punishment (cf. the Fall myth, Gen 2,4b-3,24), or of

---

[20] Cf. Chapter XII, A.2.c.

obedience to a prescription (active obedience, doing), which results in a reward (the gospel narrative).

The narratives may, however, tell of covenantal servants who distinguish themselves by not infringing the interdiction (passive obedience; not doing), in that a *temptation* is overcome; or of covenantal servants who disqualify themselves by not adhering to the prescription (passive disobedience; not doing), in that they fail the *test*.[21] One then observes that the initial situation is preserved, now as protection of (S ∩ (S ∩ O1), now as repression of (S ∪ (S ∪ O2). The narrative can stop here, but it can also continue and allow the passive obedience to equal an active obedience, which results in a reward, or allow the passive disobedience to equal an active disobedience that results in punishment.

It can also tell of covenantal lords who fail to keep their obligations and thus occasion theodicy problems. Perhaps the obedient servant is punished, whereas the disobedient one is rewarded. But the lack of adherence to the prescription on punishment or reward is of special significance in this regard. If the reward is absent, the covenantal lord has failed the covenant and its servant, which threatens to abolish the confidence in the covenantal lord and thus the covenantal relationship itself. From the covenantal servant's side, this repressive situation is unambiguously negative.

If the punishment is absent, the covenantal lord has likewise failed to keep the covenant's conditions, but now to the advantage of the covenantal servant. The lack of negative sanction may bear witness to the collapse of the covenantal relationship, but may also be due to the covenantal lord's wish to protect his servant. The covenant's *raison d'être* is the positive covenantal objective (Being), and the covenantal lord may therefore show mercy, withhold punishment and offer the covenantal servant an opportunity to re-establish a positive covenantal relationship. As will be seen, the two narrative trajectories are thus given only in their most simple form.

2. The Covenantal Process

a. The Historical and the Mythical Covenantal Process

The distinction earlier introduced between historical and mythical existence makes it possible to distinguish an historical covenantal process from a mythical covenantal process.

In the historical covenantal process, the terminals are provisional life and definitive death; here the covenant recognizes only the preservation or destruction of the initial state, Life. But the punishment and the reward must first be

---

[21] The interdiction presupposes the covenantal servant's wanting-to-be; to overcome a temptation is to avoid realizing the interdicted but desired being. The prescription, on the other hand, presupposes the covenantal servant's wanting-not-to-be; to pass the test is to realize the prescribed but feared being. The Greek πειρασμός (πειράζω) can mean both temptation (cf. 1,13) and test (or trial, cf. 14,38).

considered within the framework of life as a worsening or improvement of living conditions. If the punishment is not a death penalty, what is concerned is merely a transition from abundance of being to lack of being (degression). The reward is similarly a transition from lack of being to abundance of being (progression):

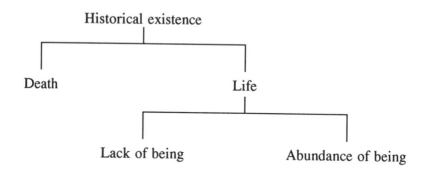

The lack of being and the abundance of being may concern all kinds of objects of value (wealth, power, honour, cattle, sons, women, etc.), but not life itself.

When the punishment is the death penalty the perspective is shifted from abundance/lack to Life/Death. In its basic form, the punishment process involves a change from life (X) to death (non-X); it is a degression. The malefaction involves the transition from life to death. But in this perspective, in which life is at stake as an object of value, the malefaction's degression cannot be paralleled with the benefaction's progression. The benefaction cannot involve the transition from death to life. One may then be tempted to permit the negative trajectory to relate to Life/Death and the positive trajectory to concern abundance/lack, but in such a case one ignores that both these trajectories can be defined in relation to both Life/Death and abundance/lack. The difficulty is because the punishment process is in both cases a degression, whereas the reward process is now progressive (from lack to abundance) and now protective.

The covenantal servant can obtain his unworthiness in two ways, either by infringing the interdiction (malefaction) or failing to adhere to the prescription (failed benefaction). The positive process is therefore also related to the covenantal servant's right to existence. In a situation in which the prescription must be met, the benefaction carried out, the covenantal servant sees himself as put to the test. If he carries out the prescribed task there is no change in his physical life: it is preserved. The covenantal servant's life is thus at stake in both narrative trajectories: infringement of the interdiction results in the loss of this life (degression); adherence to the prescription involves preservation of this life (protection). Quite independently of the pecuniary objects of value that may be concerned in the historical covenant's positive trajectory, the process of this covenant will result either in a change (death penalty) or in preservation (non-punishment) of the covenantal servant's life.[22]

In this perspective in which the covenant is defined on the basis of the object of value, *Life*, the negative narrative trajectory is a degression, while the positive narrative trajectory is a protection. Where the covenant's negative and positive trajectories are degression and progression, these trajectories' objects of value, the states of being concerned, cannot therefore be identical. Where the object of value is the same, e.g. *Life*, in both trajectories, the historical covenant's negative trajectory will be a degression, whereas its positive trajectory will a protection. In this covenant, the covenantal servant can either lose or preserve his provisional life; thus solely his historical existence is concerned. These observations are important in understanding the covenant between God and Jesus, since a covenant is involved here which is the systematic counterpart of the historical covenant. Now the positive trajectory serves not only the preservation of life but is a veritable progression process where life is an object of value (eternal life) that can be won. Thereby the negative trajectory sees itself defined as preservation in the sense of repression. If Jesus does not live up to the prescription's requirements (cf. 14,32ff), he will remain in the provisional life. Opposed to the historical or old covenant's degression/protection of *Life* is the new covenant's progression/repression of *Life*. This is thus characterized by its mythical covenantal process.

Perceived as a pragmatic sanction, God's raising of Jesus is an act that places him in the intended state of being: eternal life. For Jesus, it is thus possible to distinguish an initial state in which he neither has eternal life (O2) nor is entitled to it; an intermediate state in which he does not have eternal life, but is entitled to it; and a final state in which he rightfully has eternal life:

Manipulation		
Initial state	$(Sb \cup (Sh \cup O2)$	
Performance	$\Downarrow$	- Death on the cross
Intermediate state	$(Sb \cap (Sh \cup O2)$	
Sanction	$\Downarrow$	- Resurrection
Final state	$(Sb \cap (Sh \cap O2)$	

---

[22] Cf. also Gen 17. If Abraham does not allow himself to be circumcised, he will be destroyed (transition from life to death); the absent adherence to the prescription regarding circumcision here equates to the infringement of an interdiction, a malefaction. But adherence to this prescription acts as a benefaction which deserves reward, the transition from lack of being, in which Abraham and Sarah are without a son, to abundance of being, in which they have the promised son Isaac (O2), cf. 17,16.19. But by adhering to the prescription regarding circumcision, and in a wider perspective any prescription comprised by the covenant (cf. 17,1), Abraham preserves his life. This protective function relative to life, clearly thematized in Ex 4,24ff, must be distinguished from the circumcision's progressive function relative to the promised abundance of being (the country, the son, the offspring).

As covenantal servant, Jesus sees himself enrolled into a positive trajectory that is formally opposed to the punishment process. However, when the progression's object of value is not merely pecuniary but concerns the covenantal servant's life and death, the punishment process cannot be a degression but only a repression (non-reward). The semantics involved in this narrative syntax thus requires a differentiation between the two types of covenantal process, the historical and the mythical.

The above model (cf. p. 248), according to which the covenant contains the possibility of a degression (punishment) or progression (reward) is thus straightforward if it merely concerns two different objects of value in the two trajectories. But it conceals that both trajectories concern the covenantal servant's life, since in this perspective the degression does not correspond to a progression but to a protection. As model of a covenant in which the covenantal servant's life is at stake in a progression, it is also misleading, since the positive trajectory does not here correspond to a degression but to a repression.

If the model's two trajectories are then invested with the object of value life, now provisional (O1) and now definitive (O2), it becomes clear that two trajectories within one and the same covenant are no longer concerned, but a negative trajectory within a covenant A (from provisional life to definitive death) and a positive trajectory within another covenant B (from provisional life to definitive life):

TRAJECTORY COVENANT A		TRAJECTORY COVENANT B	
Negative	Positive	Negative	Positive
$(S \cap (S \cap O1)$	$(S \cap (S \cap O1)$	$(S \cup (S \cup O2)$	$(S \cup (S \cup O2)$
⇓			⇓
$(S \cup (S \cap O1)$	⇓	⇓	$(S \cap (S \cup O2)$
⇓			⇓
$(S \cup (S \cup O1)$	$(S \cap (S \cap O1)$	$(S \cup (S \cup O2)$	$(S \cap (S \cap O2)$
Degression	Protection	Repression	Progression

The covenant between God and Jesus is a new covenant B, which is characterized by its realized, positive trajectory. However, this can only be fully understood against the background of and within its integrated relationship to an old covenant A that is characterized by its actualized, negative trajectory. The remarkable fact manifests itself that the historical covenantal process A can exist without the mythical covenantal process B, but not vice versa. A superior viewpoint is thus present according to which these two simple covenantal processes obtain a status of narrative trajectories within one and the same complex covenantal process whose terminals become (S ∪ (S ∪ O), Definitive Death, corresponding to (S ∪ (S ∪ O1), and (S ∩ (S ∩ O), Definitive Life, corresponding to (S ∩ (S ∩ O2).

b. The Relation Between the Covenantal Processes

The integrated relationship between the historical and the mythical covenants can be recognized only if one keeps to the result of the semantic analysis and defines the object of value as *Life*. Quite independently of its figurative appearance (cf. the transfiguration), it has different values according to the state of being in which it finds itself. Thus, Definitive life can be defined as the state of being in which the covenantal servant has *Life* rightfully; Provisional life as the state of being in which he has *Life* unrightfully. But it is only the modal interpretation which can provide a clear recognition of this integrated relationship between the covenantal processes and their isotopic states of being.

Semantic Connection
The semantic universe:

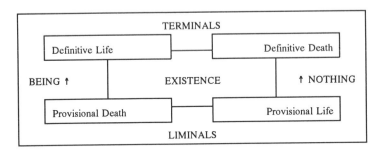

corresponds to:

Definitive Life	=	(Sb ∩ (Sh ∩ O)
Provisional Death	=	(Sb ∩ (Sh ∪ O)
Provisional Life	=	(Sb ∪ (Sh ∩ O)
Definitive Death	=	(Sb ∪ (Sh ∪ O)

There are two covenantal processes pointing in opposite directions:

$$\text{B} : (\text{Sb} \cap (\text{Sh} \cap \text{O})) \leftarrow (\text{Sb} \cap (\text{Sh} \cup \text{O})) \leftrightarrow (\text{Sb} \cup (\text{Sh} \cap \text{O})) \rightarrow (\text{Sb} \cup (\text{Sh} \cup \text{O})) : \text{A}$$

both of which include the covenantal servant's performance and the covenantal lord's sanction. The state of being (Sb ∪ (Sh ∩ O) is due to the transgression of an interdiction that makes the possession of *Life* equal to a take. According to the covenant's logic the covenantal lord answers take with take: (Sb ∪ (Sh ∪ O). The state of being (Sb ∩ (Sh ∪ O), however, is due to obedience to a prescription, the loss of *Life* is a gift that is answered with a gift: (Sb ∩ (Sh ∩ O). These two covenantal processes, the historical and the mythical, can be distinguished from one another, but they should be imagined as one superior narrative covenantal process. The gospel narrative's sublime semiotics is due to its ability effectively to hold together these two processes in a superior structure of unity.

Syntactic Connection
At a given moment, i.e. *before his baptism*, Jesus of Nazareth is in a Provisional life state of being (Sb ∪ (Sh ∩ O) which is orientated towards Definitive death (Sb ∪ (Sh ∪ O). The situation is fatal, destruction is unavoidable. At another moment, i.e. *by the death on the cross itself*, he finds himself in the Provisional death state of being (Sb ∩ (Sh ∪ O), which is orientated towards Definitive life (Sb ∩ (Sh ∩ O). Again the situation is fatal; resurrection is inevitable. But these moments are connected with one another: if Definitive death is unavoidable (not-being-able-not-to-be), Definitive life is impossible (not-being-able-to-be); if Definitive life is inevitable, Definitive death is impossible. It is one and the same being at work in both covenantal processes. It is therefore also possible to define the modal status of these categorial states of being on the basis of the ontologically defined Being, Definitive life.

It may now be said that Being in the Definitive life state of being has been *realized*, whereas in the Provisional death state of being it is *semi-realized*. In the Provisional life state of being, Being is *semi-virtualized*, whereas finally it is *virtualized* in the Definitive death state of being.[23] If Being is defined as Man's true existence, the four states of being may be stated as follows:

Definitive Life	=	Realized existence
Provisional Death	=	Semi-realized existence
Provisional Life	=	Semi-virtualized existence
Definitive Death	=	Virtualized existence

---

[23] Cf. Chapter VIII, C.4.b.

It is of course quite important to the syntactic and semantic connection between these covenantal processes that one and the same existence is concerned, which is to be found in four categorial modes of existence. Syntagmatically, a number of pragmatic states of being exist which, in their formal indefiniteness, may be orientated now degressively ($\Downarrow$), now progressively ($\Uparrow$):

DEGRESSION		PROGRESSION
Being	$(S \cap (S \cap O))$	Being
	$\Downarrow \quad \Uparrow$	
$\Downarrow$		$\Uparrow$
	$(S \cap (S \cup O))$	
Destruction	$\Downarrow \quad \Uparrow$	Creation
	$(S \cup (S \cap O))$	
$\Downarrow$		$\Uparrow$
	$\Downarrow \quad \Uparrow$	
Nothing	$(S \cup (S \cup O))$	Nothing

However, this series of states of being appears in the gospel narrative as determined. At the beginning it is degressively orientated, and as such bears witness to an on-going destruction process whose relative point of reference is Provisional life, but whose absolute point of reference is Definitive life. Provisional Life is thus merely an intermediate state on the path from Being to Nothing, in the same way as sickness is an intermediate state on the path from life to death. At the end it is progressively orientated, and as such bears witness to an on-going restoration process which is aimed at re-establishing the absolute point of reference, Definitive life. In the same way as healing, the progression is a process which is aimed at neutralizing the on-going destruction. In the overarching perspective of the covenantal process, therefore, a genuine Protection is concerned, i.e. an act of salvation.

3. Determinated Coming into Being

While the terminal states of being are characterized by a *stable* being, the liminal states of being are characterized by an *orientated coming into being*. Since this process of formation is fatal, in that the state of being towards which it is aimed is unavoidable, it may be said that a *determinated coming into being* is concerned here.

The relationship between the covenantal servant's performance and the covenantal lord's sanction has been noted as an implication relation: transgression/malefaction results in ($\Rightarrow$) punishment, obedience/benefaction (death on the cross) results in ($\Rightarrow$) reward (resurrection). In the same way, manipulation appears to result in performance, but this *covenantal rule* is a cultural law, not a natural law. The covenantal lord and the covenantal servant can both act and fail to act, and the covenantal process is therefore really open. It is the deontic modalization which introduces the compulsion that orientates the act.

The covenantal servant can carry out his performance, but he can also fail to do so. The prescribed act is at the same time modalized by having-to-do and by being-able-to-do/being-able-not-to-do. The interdicted act is at the same time modalized by having-not-to-do and by being-able-not-to-do/being-able-to-do. It is thus not certain that the covenantal servant passes over to action. But this reticence is in turn ambiguous. Relative to the interdiction it is affirmative, but relative to the prescription it is negative. According to the precise circumstances and conditions, this reticence can therefore result in a renversement in which the covenantal servant's lack of fulfilment of the prescription is now equated to an infringement of the interdiction that releases the sanction. Whatever the covenantal servant does or does not do, he must thus anticipate a sanction, positive or negative. He cannot avoid his covenantal lord's jurisdiction.

As regards the sanction, the covenantal lord finds himself in a similar situation. The punishment/reward is an act that has been prescribed if the transgression/obedience is performed; otherwise it is interdicted. But the covenantal lord is also a subject that may both act or fail to act. It is therefore not given that the punishment/reward will come. It depends on whether the covenantal lord lives up to his obligations, i.e. his covenantal fidelity. The covenantal servant and the covenantal lord are both weak links in the covenantal process' chain.

However, an asymmetry also seems to assert itself in a deontic perspective. Where the covenantal lord is God, the deontic modalization tends to merge with the dynamic modalization. God is sure to live up to his obligations, and disobedience/obedience therefore means that punishment/reward is unavoidable. One can count on God's covenantal fidelity; the truly weak link is the covenantal servant, Man. If, for example, the covenantal lord is obliged to punish the covenantal servant according to the covenant's ordinance, then the Definitive death is modalized by having-to-be, which equates to not-being-able-not-to-be. From a given moment, destruction is not only possible but fatal. The same applies to the reward. *The death on the cross as a gift is the fulfilment of a condition that obligates God to raise Jesus.* In this perspective it could be asserted that Jesus by his death on the cross buys out the God of Righteousness in order to release the God of Love.

As regards the covenantal servant, it may be said that he cannot violate the interdiction if he wishes to preserve his life; or that he cannot fail to observe the prescription if he wishes to realize the positive trajectory. Here, having-to-do seems equal to not-being-able-not-to-do and having-not-to-do equal to not-being-able-to-do. But there is reason to uphold the difference between having- to-do and being-able-to-do, despite this apparent equivalence. If one says: "The covenantal servant cannot transgress the interdiction", this is valid only if one adds: "if he wishes to preserve his life". What one says is thus merely that he cannot withdraw from the covenant's jurisdiction, that he cannot act without its having consequences. What is important, however, is that the covenantal servant may in fact transgress the interdiction, can in fact fail to observe the prescription. In this lies the whole misery of the plot of life.

To summarize, it may be said that the semi-virtualized Being (Provisional Life) is characterized by a degressive, determinated coming into being in which Definitive death is unavoidable and Definitive life is impossible. This is the situation in which Jesus of Nazareth initially finds himself. On the other hand, the semi-realized Being (Provisional death) is characterized by a progressive, determinated coming into being in which Definitive life is inevitable and Definitive death is impossible. This is the situation in which Jesus finds himself by virtue of the death on the cross. The resurrection is the consummation of this progressively determinated coming into being, the realization of Being, the intended covenantal objective, and as such is the diametric antithesis of the transition from provisional life to definitive death, which was not realized. The question is, then, what are the events that bring about this cosmic renversement from degressive to progressive coming into being, from destruction to re-creation?

C. The Baptism/The Anointing

In a preliminary form, the gospel narrative's mythos has been defined as a covenantal process B, which includes baptism/anointing (beginning), death on the cross (middle) and resurrection (ending). This covenantal process appears to be opposed to another covenantal process A, which involves the possibility of a death of damnation, a Definitive death. The two covenantal processes may be analyzed in their relative autonomy, but the gospel narrative also attempts to imagine them in their integral relationship to one another. The baptism event is the nodal or condensation point at which these two covenantal processes meet.

1. The Baptism of John

The gospel narrative's information on the baptism of John (cf. 11,30) is quite scanty. It is told that he preached a baptism of repentance for the forgiveness of sins, and that the whole Judean countryside and all the people of Jerusalem went out to him and were baptized by him in the river Jordan, confessing their sins (1,4f).

a. John - Elijah/Elisha

Of John himself, it says that he was clothed with camel's hair, with a leather belt around his waist, and he ate locusts and wild honey (1,6). He thus appears as an ascetic prophet-figure similar to Elijah who was "A hairy man, with a leather belt around his waist", 2 Kings 1,8.[24] However, if John is typologically associated with the Elijah figure he is at the same time associated with the Elisha figure. After Elijah has been taken up into heaven, Elisha takes over the prophet's mantle, and the spirit of the prophet rests on him, 2 Kings 2,13ff. It is the prophet role rather than the individuals Elisha and Elijah that should attract attention, and then the narrative of Elisha's healing of Naaman (2 Kings 5) becomes of particular interest as regards the baptism of John.[25]

Elisha heals Naaman of leprosy by making him bathe (LXX, $\lambda o \acute{u} \omega$), i.e. immerse himself ($\beta \alpha \pi \tau \acute{\iota} \zeta \omega$, 5,14) seven times in the Jordan, so that his flesh "was restored" ($\acute{\epsilon} \pi \iota \sigma \tau \rho \acute{\epsilon} \phi \omega$), i.e. returns to the preceding state of health and he becomes clean ($\kappa \alpha \theta \alpha \rho \acute{\iota} \zeta \omega$). There are a number of remarkable common features in the two acts: they concern baptism acts ($\beta \alpha \pi \tau \acute{\iota} \zeta \omega$), which take place in the river Jordan with a view to conversion ($\acute{\epsilon} \pi \iota \sigma \tau \rho \acute{\epsilon} \phi \omega$, $\mu \epsilon \tau \alpha \nu o \acute{\epsilon} \omega$); now somatic, now spiritual. But the difference between the pragmatic and the cognitive-affective conversions is by no means absolute. Naaman's healing is associated with

---

[24] Cf. Rudolf Pesch, *Das Markusevangelium, 1. Teil*, Freiburg 1980, p. 81: "der Text, der nun das Bild des Täufers überliefert, will ihn zweifellos durch Anspielung auf 2. Kön 1,8 und Sach 13,4 als prophetische Gestalt, womöglich als Elija, zeichnen". Cf. Chapter VIII, C.3.b.

[25] Cf. Chapter V, B.2.c. The narrative of Naaman is mentioned in Lk 4,27.

a spiritual conversion (cf. 5,15), and the baptism of John serves for its part a pragmatic salvation.

The term *typology* refers on the one hand to a viewpoint that establishes an inter-textual connection between persons and events, i.e. a narrative process, in the Old Testament and New Testament texts, and on the other hand to the result of this reading. Research thus speaks of an Adam-Christ typology which results from the comparative or typological reading undertaken by Paul when he compares and contrasts these figures. One may say that Paul interprets the Christ figure on the basis of the Adam figure, which has the status of a model, typos (cf. Rom 5,12ff; 1 Cor 15,45).

For narrative exegesis, however, typology is not merely a point of view that establishes typological relations. As interpretation, and in the context this means as creation of signification, the typological reading is an explication of the typologies that are already potentially given within the Christian universe of signification. For exegesis, this means primarily the canonical texts. The Adam-Christ typology is thus not merely the result of Paul's special viewpoint. He explicates only an inter-textual relationship that is already implicitly given as a semiotic fact in the Christian universe of signification.

The presence of a considerable quantity of as yet unheeded implicit typologies in the canonical text can be anticipated. This is by reason of the inter-textuality that characterizes the relationship between Old Testament and New Testament, but also the relationship between these books' own texts. Narratives (discourses) are not created out of the signification-creator's vision but on the basis of other narratives, which have formed and informed the narrator's narrative competence. It is therefore possible to speak of a narrative language that is, as a language system (*langue*), the precondition for the language processes (*parole*, speech; i.e. discourses, narratives) that appear in the canonical texts. Only because the narratives speak the same narrative language, i.e. belong to the same narratively organized universe of signification, are such typologies at the same time possible and unavoidable. This viewpoint, as yet only outlined here, implies that comparative analysis *does not* seek to demonstrate literary or linguistic dependence between texts, but inter-textual relations between narratives, their narrative and thematic role configurations.[26]

If one compares the baptism of John with the baptism of Elisha, it thus becomes clear that the two action processes belong to one and the same universe of signification. Both John and Elisha appear in the role of savior, and both narratives belong to the same Protection genre. The sick person (leper) is victim of an on-going destruction process directed towards death (cf. 5,7, in which the

---

[26] On the basis of a linguistic and literary analysis, Philipp Vielhauer believes he can show that John in his camelhair clothes did not wish to evoke Elijah associations, "Tracht und Speise Johannes des Täufers", *Aufsätze zum Neuen Testament*, München 1965, p. 47. Vielhauer is interested in the historical John, but the typology concerns the narrative John as *Elijah redivivus*.

life/death-isotopy is thematized). The healing is a progression that serves in a wider perspective to protect. Similarly, the baptism of John is initially a progression that involves the transition from sinner to righteous. The forgiveness of sins must mean that the sinner who finds himself in a state of unworthiness is restored to a former state of worthiness as sinless, i.e. righteous, cf. 2,17: "I have come to call not the righteous but sinners." (δίκαιος vs. ἁμαρτωλός). But in a wider perspective protection is concerned, since the sinner is a virtual victim of a virtual degression process, God's judgment, which is neutralized by virtue of the forgiveness.

However, the inter-textuality is due not only to this abstract syntactic and semantic identity but also to the specific figure-fellowship that characterizes the narratives: John is clothed like Elijah/Elisha; the action takes place in the river Jordan; both incidents concern "baptism" and "repentance"; and what is particularly important is that the two prophets have been sent by the same God. On the other hand, it must be emphasized that the "concepts", "ideas", "motifs" and the like cannot in themselves be typology-forming. It is the relationship between two sets of thematic and narrative role configurations that constitutes the typology, and in the individual cases one will be able to speak of typology between both subjects of doing and subjects of being.

b. Baptism and Healing

The Elijah/Elisha-John typology rests fundamentally upon the genre-fellowship that characterizes the role configuration: protection/salvation. As a correlation:

sick : well :: sinner : righteous

the typology opens up the possibility of metaphorizing, since baptism is regarded as a "healing", or healing is regarded as a "baptism". The phrase "Those who are well have no need of a physician, but those who are sick", which is correlated with "I have come to call not the righteous but sinners" (2,17), shows, independently of its context, an example of such imagery.

In view of the role baptism plays in the Christian tradition, already evidenced in New Testament, cf. in this connection Mk 16,16, "The one who believes and is baptized will be saved", it is remarkable that Jesus himself does not baptize. It is true of course that reference may be made to the baptism of John, and it may be said that this baptism, initially hidden, is a genuinely Christian baptism. But it is difficult to define precisely the soteriological function of the baptism of John, and no practice of baptism seems to have arisen in the period between the Baptist's death and Jesus' ascension. Within the narrative, it might be considered whether, for example, the paralytic, cf. 2,1ff, was baptized by John. If he was baptized, it becomes difficult to understand the difference between the forgiveness the baptism gives and the forgiveness Jesus gives, 2,5. If he was not baptized, then the promise, "Son! your sins are forgiven." receives the status of baptism.

If sickness and sin are connected as in this wonder narrative, the sickness can be regarded only as evidence of an already on-going destruction process that has God as its subject of doing, either in an active sense (degression: God punishes, doing) or a passive sense (repression: God does not save, allowing). It is the worthiness role of *sinner* (ἁμαρτωλός - ἁμαρτάνω - ἁμαρτία) that invokes the negative sanction. Jesus acts on behalf of God in the role of the forgiving one (ἀφίεις - ἀφίημι - ἄφεσις). By the ambiguous ἀφίημι, it is the significations of release, free, acquit, remit, reprieve, condone and forgive that are central here. In particular, there is reason to emphasize ἄφεσις in the sense of remission of guilt or punishment.

Punishment cannot be remitted without at the same time remitting guilt, and vice versa. The remission of punishment presupposes the remission of guilt, whereas remission of guilt involves remission of punishment. It is crucial that "the forgiveness of sins" is absolution, i.e. the change from a state of unworthiness to a state of worthiness, and that this process must imply the neutralization of an on-going or possible punishment process that must be defined more specifically as fatal: the sinner is lost.[27]

By his rhetorical question, whether it is the easier to say (do) "Your sins are forgiven," or "Stand up and take your mat and walk", 2.9, Jesus shows that forgiveness and healing are two aspects of the same matter. It is therefore also possible to be aware that on the basis of the healing the state of sin has been abolished, in the same way as one can perceive that, if Jesus has power to heal, this is because he has power to forgive. A promise of the forgiveness of the sins, i.e. abolition of the sinner's culpability, which is not followed - immediately or later - by an act neutralizing on-going punishment processes and/or restoring the injury caused (healing of the sickness), is to God a disgraceful insult to the victim. Neutralization of an on-going punishment process which does not rest on the forgiveness of sins is from the agent's side a disgraceful insult to God.

Forgiveness of sins should be understood as a re-manipulation, i.e. a factitive process, which involves a change in the Destinatee's covenantal status, from unworthy to worthy, from sinner to righteous. This process involves the Destinatee's reinstatement into his integrity as covenantal subject (protagonist), i.e. into a state of being in which Definitive death is no longer unavoidable, but only possible. For the subject of being which still possesses the provisional life in its integrity the baptism is only a modal transformation, but for the subject of being that is already marked by an on-going degression process (sickness), baptism must involve a restoration of this provisional life. Healing and the

---

[27] Occupies the role ὁ ἀπολλύμενος (versus ὁ σῳζόμενος), cf. 1 Cor 1,18; 2 Cor 2,15; 4.3; 2 Thess 2,10; also Lk 19,10.

baptism of John are thus two aspects of the same matter: the reinstatement of the Destinatee into his integrity, pragmatically and/or modally.

However, nothing is said to the effect that John heals. His baptism is not pragmatic but only modal. Jesus of Nazareth does not baptize, but his healings achieve a status of baptism because the restoration presupposes the forgiveness of sins. It seems that he can appear as a wonder-worker only by virtue of his possession of the Holy Spirit. When, therefore, John preaches that he baptized with water, whereas Jesus will baptize with the Holy Spirit (1,8), a designation of Jesus as a baptist in his capacity of wonder-worker may be inherent in this formulation.[28]

c. Jesus' Baptism

Jesus of Nazareth also is baptized by John in the Jordan, 1,9. Within the framework of the gospel narrative, this event is to be understood only against the background of the information in 1,4f. Jesus seeks out John on the strength of an impulse occasioned by John's persuasive proclamation. The motive can only be the wish for the forgiveness of sins, and the baptism act must have taken place because Jesus confessed his sins. It is only after this ordinary baptism of John has taken place that the heavens are torn apart and a new situation arises. If Jesus' receipt of the Holy Spirit is seen as a baptism, then consequently a sharp distinction must be made between his baptism of John and his Holy Spirit baptism. A distinction is made here between his *baptism* ($\beta\acute{\alpha}\pi\tau\iota\sigma\mu\alpha$, $-\mu\acute{o}\varsigma$) and his *anointing* ($\chi\rho\hat{\iota}\sigma\mu\alpha$, cf. 1 Jn 2,27).

Like any other subject of being, Jesus of Nazareth is a Destinatee who is defined in his relationship to the Destinator, God. As a sinner, he sees himself as enrolled into a negative trajectory that belongs under covenant A. He is in the life state of being, i.e. $X = (S \cap O1)$, which is fatally orientated towards death, i.e. non-$X = (S \cup O1)$. He has life (O1), but no longer has a right to it. Within a relative or embedded cognitive space whose boundaries are X and non-X, he therefore finds himself in a state of being $(S \cup (S \cap O1)$ which is orientated towards the state of being $(S \cup (S \cup O1)$ that is unavoidable. The baptism of John reinstates him in the state of being $(S \cap (S \cap O1)$ in which he has life rightfully. From an ontic perspective, however, there is no difference between $(S \cup (S \cap O1)$ and $(S \cap (S \cap O1)$; in both cases the subject of being has life. The rightfulness, which is relative, does not mean that life is possessed absolutely or definitively, but that death is now no longer unavoidable, merely avoidable/possible, i.e. conditioned by the Destinatee's doing and/or not doing. In the

---

[28] On the relationship between baptism and healing, cf. Sigfred Pedersen, "Dåbsteologien i Markusevangeliet" (The Baptism Theology in the Gospel of Mark), Sigfred Pedersen (red.), *Dåben i Ny Testamente* (Baptism in the New Testament), Århus 1982, pp. 49; and Christian Thodberg, "Perikopevalgets tekstforståelse og Ny Testamente med særligt henblik på dåben" (The Choice of Pericope's Textual Understanding and the New Testament, with Special Reference to the Baptism), ibidem, pp. 266.

initial state (S ∩ (S ∩ O1) the punishment of death is virtual; in the intermediate state (S ∪ (S ∩ O1) it is actualized; and in the final state (S ∪ (S ∪ O1) it is realized. By the forgiveness of sins, which reinstates the Destinatee in his integrity, the modally-considered on-going punishment process becomes neutralized.

However, if the perspective is expanded it becomes clear that the protective baptism does not really abolish destruction's unavoidability but merely postpones its realization. Yet this delay is significant in establishing the waiting period within which the readjustment from defensive to offensive can take place. The baptism of John stops the on-going degression process, which corresponds to a process of sickness being stopped at a given stage of development. This is of course an objective in itself, but in a wider perspective the intermediate state thereby established must then become the basis of a progression process that corresponds to healing. The forgiveness of sins therefore involves not only that the provisional life is relatively preserved, since the definitive death becomes avoidable, but also that the definitive life becomes possible.

However scanty the information about the baptism of John, it appears evident that the baptism act is a protection process aimed initially at preventing the threatening destruction. The baptism of John is protective. It was pointed out earlier that its aim is to turn the people to God so that God may turn to the people.[29] One may say that the people's conversion is a precondition for God's conversion. The baptism of John itself, however, is already evidence of compliance on God's part. God was turned from the people because of their sinfulness, and the threatened destruction was also the threat to abolish the covenantal relationship. But now God offers the people an opportunity to re-establish the broken covenantal relationship. The baptism of John is the first step on the part of God, which gives an opening for a restoration of a positive covenantal relationship: the forgiveness of sins is possible. But the restitution, which equates to the establishment of a new covenant, is an interactive process. If the people do not accept the offer, the progression process initiated stops and the degression process will be accomplished. Conversely, an acceptance on the part of the people can open up new initiatives on God's part.

By virtue of God's manipulative opening that enables John to baptize for the forgiveness of sins, a dynamic space exists in which protection is possible (modal transformation, from "Protection is impossible" to "Protection is possible"). This preservation of life is God's offer to Man. It is presented in the hope that Man has faith that God can and will forgive. When Man does a service to God, it is in the expectation that it is the service desired by God, which deserves as a benefaction a rewarding return from God, i.e. protection. What then is the service Man must perform for God in order to obtain salvation? It consists quite simply in the recognition of God and his covenant revealed by action. He who

---

[29] Cf. Chapter VIII, C.3.b.

allows himself to be baptized becomes a covenantal subject, Destinatee, i.e. a subject whose being and doing roles are defined by the covenant.[30]

The baptized are covenantal subjects who constitute God's covenantal people. Any talk of forgiveness is preconditioned by a command of the law that has been infringed or evaded. However, every command of the law is in turn preconditioned by a covenant that controls the interactional exchange between the two parties, God and Man. No God relationship exists for Man and no human relationship for God that is not contractually organized as a covenant.

Any restoration of the covenantal relationship between the creator and his creature is a repetition of the establishment of the covenant which for God involves a loss (self-abasement, renunciation) and for Man a gain (elevation, attribution), and can therefore only take place on God's supreme initiative. An opening, manipulative renunciation, which is not founded on a debtor relationship is an offering, an unconditional gift, χάρις, χάρισμα. The promise of forgiveness of sins restores the antagonist as synagonist, and thus merges with a restoration of the covenantal relationship without it thereby being given that the content of the covenant remains the same. The restoration can be connected with the introduction of a new covenantal content, and in that event it is meaningful to speak of a new covenant and of re-creation.

The restoration has the same form as the establishment. The virtual covenantal subject initially has a choice between accepting the covenant or dying: he who does not permit himself to be baptized remains in the covenantal state of sinner and is thereby lost. The confession of sins is also a confession to the covenantal lord and an acceptance of the role assigned of covenantal servant. However unfounded the forgiveness may be, it will be followed by a demand that the penitent must be willing to accept. In this perspective, the baptism is the act whereby the virtual covenantal subject obtains the status of a realized covenantal subject. But acceptance of the covenant is also an acceptance of the obligations the covenant implies, an acceptance of the covenant's project. Manipulation ends in the realization of the covenantal subject as regards its competence, but the covenantal being itself, the covenantal objective, thus becomes only a possibility, an imposed project, which is to be realized.

d. The Preparation

It is now possible to indicate the first elements of the gospel narrative's overarching narrative covenantal process, the *preparatory* process, which makes the way for the principal salvation project:

---

[30] To make the term covenantal subject unambiguous, it should be stressed that what is understood by this is a synagonist (actant) which is as such in contrast to an antagonist (antactant). In a certain sense both are covenantal subjects, since the antagonist can indeed break the covenant but cannot avoid its jurisdiction. Assuming that the breach of the covenant is premeditated, the antagonist will see himself as in opposition to the covenant and its lord (incongruity); but the synagonist or covenantal subject will in a real sense see himself as in congruity with the covenant.

1) Jesus of Nazareth is enrolled in an *absolute*, fatal degression process. The "Degression is avoidable/possible" modal state is from the Destinatee's point of view *impossible*; there is no way out.

2) Jesus of Nazareth is enrolled in a *relative*, fatal degression process, in that God, quite groundlessly, has opened an opportunity for the forgiveness of sins. The "Degression is avoidable/possible" modal state has now become *possible*, it exists virtually. The act that is to realize this modal state is the baptism of John, which as a narrative process itself exists as a virtual act.[31]

3) Jesus of Nazareth finds himself defined by a possible but also avoidable degression process after having been baptized for the forgiveness of sins. The "Degression is avoidable/possible" modal state has now become *realized*.

This sub-process in which John the Baptist plays the main role can on the one hand be seen as an independent process and on the other hand as a preparation for the superior narrative covenantal process. Enrolled in the life/death isotopy (Provisional life versus Definitive death), the preservation of life is an objective in itself, but in the light of the LIFE/DEATH isotopy (Definitive life versus Definitive death), Provisional life, even when rightfully possessed, is a degressive state of being, which still leaves much to be desired.

In the covenantal process' initial situation, Jesus has been placed between Being and Nothingness. The neutralization of the destruction process does not install him in the projected covenantal being, Definitive life, but establishes him competentially as virtual subject of doing and being for this Being. The baptism has thus a protective side and a progressive side. Functionally, John is associated with protection, whereas the progressive aspect of the baptism is connected with Jesus of Nazareth. In principle, it could be expected that *everyone* who is baptized by the baptism of John became a virtual covenantal subject for a

---

[31] One is baptized, i.e. undergoes as subject of being an act for which another actor is subject of doing. But baptism includes an action, a series of connected narrative acts. Here also an interactive process is concerned, since he who is to be baptized appears himself in the role of subject of doing. On the one hand it is he who is to be initiated who himself seeks out the baptist (in the same way as the sick person seeks out Jesus); on the other hand he has an active role to play in the confession of sins, which is at the same time a confession of faith, evidence of the confessor's faith or trust in God. But if a conversion is concerned, then the baptism is presupposed to be a transitive act, a change in the subject of being's self-knowledge. The subject must abandon an identity A to be able to acquire an identity B, and the affirmation of B presupposes the denial of A. It must as it were die away from A before being able to be reborn as B. The reflexive surrender of A (renunciation; a giving which correlates with a non-taking; cf. fasting and other forms of abstinence; confession of sins as self-denial) does not coincide with the acquisition of B (no more than Jesus' death on the cross coincides with his resurrection), but validates the subject of being to receive B as a transitive repayment (attributive sanction, bestowal of a status as covenantal subject).

covenantal project. However, God selects from the baptized *just one person* who is given the task of realizing this project.

2. The Anointing

The term *anointing* means the process by which Jesus of Nazareth is chosen, called and instituted as covenantal servant by the covenantal lord, God. On the basis of the information given about this covenantal relationship by the gospel narrative, narrative exegesis must try inferentially to reconstruct this *virtual* covenantal servant. The clearly manifested performance (death on the cross) and sanction (resurrection) raise the question of the latent but presupposed manipulation and its establishment of the covenantal servant's modal competence.[32]

a. Mark 1,10f

The story of Jesus's anointing with the Holy Spirit, 1,10f, is an epiphany narrative which includes a vision and an audition. Just as he is coming up out of the water, he sees the heavens torn apart and the Spirit descending like a dove on him. And a voice comes from heaven,

You are my Son, the Beloved; with you I am well pleased.

Epiphany, vision and audition are characteristic of biblical call narratives, which gives reason to consider whether Jesus' anointing is a call.[33] RUDOLF BULTMANN rejects this. Here the vision is not a subjective experience but a true revelation.[34] One hears nothing of Jesus' inner experience; nothing is said about the mission of the person called, nor about his answer to the call. One thus lacks important features, otherwise so typical of call stories. And, continues BULT-MANN, Jesus' actual mission is by no means concerned here, i.e. to proclaim God's gospel, but his Messiahship or status as Son of God, which cannot be described as a call.[35]

BULTMANN of course realizes that a vocation, i.e. a mission, presupposes a call and a commissioning. In his capacity as proclaimer, Jesus is thus both called and commissioned. He rejects that the anointing was supposed to be a call, because on the one hand this text (1,9ff) as text-genre does not meet the requirements of a call story, and because on the other hand he cannot recognize the

---

[32] Cf. *Sémiotique*, art. "Compétence".

[33] Cf., e.g., Isa 6,1-13; Jer 1,5-19; Ezra 1f; Acts 9,1-9; Lk 5,1-11; Rev 1,9-20.

[34] "Schilderung eines objektiven Geschehens", *Die Geschichte der synoptischen Tradition*, Göttingen 1970, p. 264; i.e. an event which is visible to others, e.g. John; cf. Mt 3,16ff and Lk 3,21ff.

[35] Cf. Rudolf Bultmann, ibidem, pp. 263.

mission to which Jesus is here supposed to be called. The initiation as Messiah ("der Messiasweihe") or Son of God gives Jesus a status of being but no mission.

This view, which relies on an exegetic understanding of the text that excludes the possibility of recognizing semantic and syntactic connections between different text-segments, shows that BULTMANN has abandoned any attempt to understand Jesus' anointing in the context of the gospel narrative. For him there is no objective connection between the baptism event and the other principal events (death on the cross and resurrection) of which the gospel narrative tells.[36]

From the perspective of narrative exegesis, however, the matter is viewed quite differently. Jesus is introduced in the gospel narrative as "Jesus ... from Nazareth of Galilee" (1,9), a human being of flesh and blood who has an occupation (6,3) and a family (3,21; 3,31ff; 6,1ff). He is the son of Mary (6,3), but through the anointing he becomes the "Son" of God (1,11). In the first case a simple kinship is concerned; in the second case a figurative kinship, since kinship terms are used metaphorically to express the relationship that character-izes Jesus and is *here and now established with God*:

Jesus : God :: Son : Father.

In contrast to the declaration at the transfiguration on the mountain (9,1ff), where the voice from the cloud, i.e. God, *speaks of* Jesus to a third party (the disciples, represented by Peter, James and John): "*This* is my Son ..." (9,7), the declaration at the anointing is an *address*: "*You* are my Son ..." (1,11). The voice from heaven, i.e. God, does not speak merely informatively here but also performatively. The announcement is a speech act; more specifically, a relation-establishing declaration: I hereby declare that "You are my Son,...".[37] Mary's son *is not, but becomes* the Son of God through the initiation that consists of the anointing. Why God casts his love precisely on Jesus of Nazareth (cf. ἀγαπητός, εὐδοκέω) remains a mystery. It can only be said that the next step in God's transition to action consists in selecting a Son from among the baptized.

The heavenly voice's discourse:

σὺ εἶ ὁ υἱός μου ὁ ἀγαπητός,
ἐν σοὶ εὐδόκησα

---

[36] Bultmann therefore sees a contrast between "die ältere Auffassung, daß Jesus nach Tod und Auferstehung zum Messias erhöht wurde" (Rom 1,3f) and the actual tradition, which has chosen Jesus' baptism as the hour of the Messiah initiation, ibidem p. 267.

[37] Jesus is instituted as son in the sense of covenantal servant. The father/son relationship was wide-spread in The Near East to figurativize the hierarchical relationship between the covenant's partners. The term *father* includes "originator, patron, master, guide, counsellor, protector, sustainer, etc." and implies "the idea of power and authority more than affection and benignity". The term *son* "stands for one who is intimately related to the other by means of submission, service, loyalty, trust, and reverential fear", Paul Kalluveettil, *Declaration and Covenant*, Rome 1982, pp. 130.

seems to refer to Ps 2,7:[38]

> I will tell of the decree of the Lord:
> He said to me, "You are my son;
> today I have begotten you."

LXX: διαγγέλλων τὸ πρόσταγμα κυρίου
                          Κύριος εἶπεν πρός με Υἱός μου εἶ σύ,
                          ἐγὼ σήμερον γεγέννηκά σε

and to Isa 42,1:

> Here is my servant, whom I uphold,
> my chosen, in whom my soul delights;
> I have put my spirit upon him;
> he will bring forth justice to the nations.

LXX: Ιακωβ ὁ παῖς μου, ἀντιλήμψομαι αὐτοῦ·
                          Ισραὴλ ὁ ἐκλεκτός μου, προσεδέξατο αὐτὸν ἡ ψυχή μου·
                          ἔδωκα τὸ πνεῦμά μου ἐπ᾽ αὐτόν,
                          κρίσιν τοῖς ἔθνεσιν ἐξοίσει.

Taking into account the differences, any literary relation between Mk 1,11 and the texts referred to cannot be unambiguously demonstrated. The question is whether the roles concerned have a typological status.[39]

---

[38] Cf. Lk 3,22, textcritical note. The term "Adoptionsformel" is frequently used, cf. Rudolf Bultmann, ibidem, p. 264. Others prefer "Legitimationsformel". The crucial point is, in relation to Ps 2,7, "daß der König von Israel nicht von Natur Sohn Gottes war. Sondern er bedurfte einer positiven Setzung Jahwes, um als solcher die Herrschaft über das Eigentumsvolk Gottes ausüben zu können, welches selbst 'Sohn' Jahwes genannt wurde.", Fritzleo Lentzen-Deis, *Die Taufe Jesu nach den Synoptikern. Literarkritische und gattungsgeschichtliche Untersuchungen*, Frankfurt am Main 1970, p. 185. Neither is the Christ King Son of God by nature in Mark's Gospel.

[39] The definition of the Marcan intertextuality, its connection with other texts, has traditionally been based on the demonstration of literary dependence. One has concentrated on explicit and implicit quotations, or one has gone so far as to identify individual themes and motifs or certain text genres. Fritzleo Lentzen-Deis stands firmly within this tradition. He can thus reject that there is literary dependence between Mark 1,11 and the passages referred to. First, in Psalm 2,7, the word order is reversed as regards the common choice of words (LXX: Υἱός μου εἶ σύ), and, second, there are clear differences between the predications' second member "today I have begotten you" and "the Beloved; with you I am well pleased". As concerns Isa 42,1, it is crucial that this text has "servant" (LXX: παῖς) rather than "son". Lentzen-Deis concedes, however, that "Jes 42,1 hört zu den wichtigsten Hintergrundtexten der Taufszene", ibidem, p. 158. But if there is no literary dependence, then what intertextual connection is concerned here? What is one really to understand by "background text"? The literary-critical analysis asks for literary dependence, recurrent language forms and text forms, but by thus allowing itself to be fixed by the occurrence-text, which is always unique and therefore always without

In Ps 2,7, Yahweh speaks to the king, his anointed (2,2; χριστός), whom he has installed (2,6; καθίστημι). The king is king by virtue of Yahweh's command or decree (πρόσταγμα), i.e. in accordance with his will, and it is his declaration that makes the person addressed king. The appointment to the new worthiness is an initiation that is figured as a birth.

The king-role's status of mediator between Yahweh and the people should be noted. He represents the people relative to Yahweh, and the covenant that applies between the king and Yahweh is at the same time the covenant between Yahweh and the people; but he also represents Yahweh relative to the people. This dual function involves his appearing now as subordinate, now as Yahweh's servant (cf., for example, 2 Sam 3,18: "Through my servant (δοῦλος) David I will save my people Israel;" 7,18ff), now as superior, now as the people's lord (cf., for example 2 Sam 9,11: "all that my lord (κύριος) the king commands his servant (δοῦλος), so your servant will do.").

A *king typology*, the correlation:

Jesus : God :: Son : Father :: King : Yahweh,

will then mean that, by his initiation, Jesus is appointed to a new worthiness as God's anointed. He becomes king of a people, God's people, in that he represents this people relative to God, but simultaneously represents God relative to this people. Expressed in another way: he becomes king (βασιλεύς) of the kingdom of God (βασιλεία τοῦ θεοῦ; cf. 11,1ff; 15,2.9.12.26.32).

The question of the Lord's servant is wide-ranging.[40] But in this context what is concerned is only to emphasize certain features of this servant-role. The word παῖς means child, more specifically son (ὁ παῖς) or daughter (ἡ παῖς) or servant, slave (δοῦλος). The words ὁ παῖς and ὁ υἱός may thus be considered as parasynonymous. In the "servant" meaning, παῖς is contrasted with lord (κύριος) and as such refers to a covenantal relationship. In Isa 42,1, the lord expresses his covenantal fidelity towards his chosen one (ὁ ἐκλεκτός), i.e. he with whom he has concluded his covenant. The servant has the task of propagating to the people that he is the covenantal servant of the covenantal lord, whose Spirit has been laid upon him: he is anointed as covenantal servant. It is unclear in the Masoretic text whether the servant is an individual or a collective person. LXX makes the

---

counterpart, it becomes blind to or unable to relate to the evident content-related narrative connection which the typology constitutes. The literary-critical approach also contains a special danger. Faced with the dual fact that on the one hand there is no literary dependence, while on the other hand there is a clear content-related similarity, individual scholars are tempted to correct the text, e.g. by asserting an earlier servant-christology, and "You are my Son" is then seen as a later replacement for "You are my servant". Lentzen-Deis can take the credit for having rejected these unnecessary speculations, cf. ibidem, pp. 186, unnecessary because the typology does not presuppose literary dependence.

[40] Cf. Herbert Haag, *Der Gottesknecht bei Deuterojesaja*, Darmstadt 1985.

text unambiguous by adding Jacob and Israel, which defines the servant as a collective covenantal subject.

A *servant typology*:

Jesus : God :: Servant : Lord

will then mean that, through the bestowal of the Holy Spirit, perceived as an anointing, Jesus sees himself as appointed covenantal servant with a view to realization of a mission.[41] One should be content to concentrate on these formal, typological features. What Jesus' mission involves in detail must be defined on the basis of an analysis of the gospel narrative.[42]

The ambivalence of the actor servant, now individual, now collective, should be kept in mind. The anointing is not merely a matter between Jesus and God but between God and his new people. In one movement Jesus is called and appointed a covenantal subject on a par with a David or an Abraham.[43] One may paraphrase what the voice from heaven says: "You are my son/servant, I have anointed you with the Holy Spirit, and by your hand shall I save my people, the true Israel." *The anointing is the restoration of a covenant between God and Jesus as representative of the new people of God.* And God is monogamous. He does not have more covenantal relationships with various groups: this people of God is his only such relationship. If on the other side there is only one God, then everyone will be thrown upon Jesus of Nazareth.

BULTMANN rejects that the anointing with the Holy Spirit was meant to be a call because, as he points out, nothing is said about Jesus' inner experience, about his mission, or about his reaction to the call. The anointing is not a call, since 1,9ff does not belong to the text-genre call narrative.

It is true that the text sequence is somewhat summary, but narrative exegesis can nevertheless recognize an *elliptic* call narrative in its narrate. And the motives BULTMANN lacks can even be narratively reconstructed on the basis of other information in the gospel narrative. Jesus has a mission to carry out which extends beyond the proclamation of God's gospel, and this mission can only have

---

[41] On anointing/spirit possession, cf., e.g., Isa 11,2; 61,1; PsSal 17,32.37.42; 18,5.7; 1 En 49,3; 62,1f; TestLevi 18; TestJuda 24; Acts 3,12ff, 4,23ff and 10,34ff.

[42] Cf. Fritzleo Lentzen-Deis: "Die Geistbegabung von Jes 42,1 sagt etwas über die Ausrüstung, noch nichts über das Schicksal des Ebed. Eine Zitation von Jes 42,1 ist noch nicht Hinweis auf Jes 53.", ibidem, p. 158. The question of the Lord's suffering servant has been disregarded in this study.

[43] The question of individual actor or collective actor is a genuinely semiotic question which can scarcely be raised or answered outside the covenant. In Gen 17, Abraham is an individual actor with whom Yahweh concludes a covenant (17,2); but at the same time the convenant is established with Abraham's entire offspring (17,9), i.e. Israel, which is a collective actor. The relationship between Jesus and his disciples, the elect, i.e. the church, displays the same features. The covenant which God establishes with the individual actor Jesus is also a covenant with the new people of God. Research has tried to combine the individual and collective aspects in the term *corporate personality*, cf. Herbert Haag, ibidem, pp. 134; and Mogens Müller, *Der Ausdruck "Menschensohn" in den Evangelien*, Leiden 1984, pp. 157.

been given by virtue of a manipulation. First, one can observe that the anointing is the opening act on the part of God, which occupies the manipulation's place in the covenantal schema. But in addition there is other information which thematizes the motives BULTMANN lacked. In 1,9ff these are present merely implicitly, but by means of an explicating procedure, referred to as *catalysis*, this call can be inferentially reconstructed.[44]

b. Mark 14,32ff

The important information is to be found in the story of Jesus' agony, 14,32ff. This sequence gives information on the relationship between Jesus and his disciples and on the relationship between Jesus and God, but only the latter relationship is of interest in this regard.

Jesus is at Gethsemane when he is overcome by fear of the coming suffering and death (14,33). This agony cannot arise because the situation takes him by surprise. As the predictions show, he has no doubt about the road he must tread, but now, with capture imminent, he is overcome by affliction. He is gripped by fear for his life and is thrown into a crisis situation. However, 14,32ff tells not only that Jesus is gripped by temptation and finds himself in a situation of crisis; this text also tells how the crisis is overcome by prayer.

The crisis must be understood as an involuntary *time out* in which the subject of doing temporarily suspends its doing with a view to reorganizing its competence. The crisis is a crisis in the subject's competential self-knowledge.

The cognitive-affective work initiated by the crisis can be considered as a dialogue, which is either reflexive (intrasubjective), in that the subject reflects within itself, and/or transitive, in that the subject's reflections (for or against) occur during discussion with another person. The prayer can be seen as an intermediate form in which the subject's inner reflexive dialogue is directed towards another person, God.

Viewed as reflections that must be brought to an end if the subject is to resume its role of acting, the dialogue (cf. διαλογίζομαι, διαλογισμός) is a discussion aimed at settlement, decision. The expression, "Enough!" (ἀπέχει, 14,41) marks the end of the temporary suspension of action. Jesus has overcome the crisis, has stabilized his competence and regained his composure. He is now ready to face his executioners.

If Jesus' death on the cross is considered as a giving, Jesus appears as a subject of doing for a mission, and 14,32ff becomes the central point of reference for the narrative reconstruction of this subject of doing's competence.

The prayer in 14,36 (which repeats parallelly the information in 14,35; cf. the corresponding parallelism between narrative and speech in 14,33ff): "Abba, Father, for you all things are possible; remove this cup from me; yet, not what

---

[44] Cf. *Sémiotique*, art. "Catalyse".

I want, but what you want" shows that Jesus' death on the cross is a matter of God's will: the mission Jesus is to realize is *prescribed*.

The death on the cross raises the question of Jesus' competence, his motive to act, but this competence in turn raises the question of a preceding process of influence.

As regards this process of influence, it cannot be referred to an individual text sequence in which God informs and influences Jesus. The gospel narrative lacks a developed call narrative, and the exegete must therefore reconstruct this narratively presupposed process on the basis of the factual information given about the relationship between Jesus and God.

From the context, it is clear that the manipulative process of influence must in this case aim at getting a virtual subject of doing to accept a task voluntarily. The covenantal servant's decision to accept the task may directly lead to a transition to action, and it then becomes an actualized subject of doing. But during the realization of the task the covenantal servant can stop at any moment to reassess his decision, and he then falls back into the role of virtual subject of doing.

Against this background, Jesus' overcoming of the crisis at Gethsemane is a confirmation of his earlier decision. The crisis itself, however, offers an insight into the situation preceding the decision. For this reason 14,32ff is of such importance to the possibility of reconstructing the presupposed process of influence and decision. This text contains what BULTMANN lacked: an insight into Jesus' spiritual life and a thematization of his mission and his reaction to the call.

To counter any misunderstanding, however, it should be stressed that this reconstruction in no way rests upon psychological empathy with the person of Jesus. The task of exegesis is only to explicate the roles that, according to the gospel narrative, constitute the narrative Jesus.

The basis of this is the following general narrative model:

a)   The commander orders a virtual subject of doing to accept a task, which includes:
b)   progression/protection and/or information/dissimulation and/or degression/repression of a subject of being,
c)   which is either the commander, the commanded or a third person.

It cannot be ignored that within the gospel narrative Jesus can be defined as progressor, protector, informator, dissimulator, degressor and repressor; but all these possible action isotopies must in this case be defined individually and then defined in their mutual hierarchal and syntagmatic relations of dependence. The establishment of a pertinence level is effected by eliminating the other parameters.

The model may be specified, for example, as:

a)   The covenantal lord orders a virtual covenantal servant to
      accept a task that includes:
b)   degression of a subject of being
c)   who is the covenantal servant himself;

for example, God orders Jesus to give his life.

The model gives the possibility of systematic questioning as regards a definition of a narrative's and/or an individual event's narrative rationality. It is thus possible to analyze the death on the cross by exhaustively considering all the constellations contained in the model.

For example, one may consider in which sense the death on the cross is to be seen as progression: 1) if Jesus is the subject of being (and, as shown, the death on the cross is a covenantal progression); 2) if the third person is the subject of being (cf. that Jesus dies "for many"); 3) if God is the subject of being (cf., for example, the classical satisfaction theory).

Constellation 3) is provisionally disregarded. 10,45 and 14,24 support constellation 2), but, as is emphasized, Jesus himself is raised as a consequence of his death on the cross. What is remarkable, in fact, is not that Jesus himself is saved but that the salvation of his people is postponed. The salvation process (the ecclesiocentric salvation) for which the many are the subject of being is connected with, but must be distinguished from, the salvation process (the christocentric salvation) for which Jesus is the subject of being. The death on the cross is only a sub-objective in a process that ends with the resurrection. In a wider perspective, the task God imposes on Jesus consists, therefore, in realizing eternal life, in overcoming death.

In this perspective, the death on the cross is not a degression but a progression, or is bifunctional in that the pragmatic degression from life to death is at the same time a covenantal progression that involves a transition from an indeterminated to a determinated state of becoming: eternal life is then inevitable.

It is thus possible to indicate a pertinence level, an action isotopy, in which Jesus as subject of doing has a mission to promote his own being:

a)   The covenantal lord orders a virtual covenantal servant to
      accept a task that includes:
b)   the progression of a subject of being
c)   that is the covenantal servant himself.

It is this specific (interactive) course of action which is called *the salvation project*.

3. The Covenantal Servant's Being-Able-to-Do

The covenant's prescription refers to God's restrictive modalization of Jesus' dynamic latitude. The prescription is meaningful only if the covenantal task can be solved. By way of introduction, narrative exegesis must therefore inquire about the dynamic modalization of the covenantal servant's doing.

It is true in general that the subject of doing is a virtual subject of being, since the (interactive) process in which it participates may result in an alteration or preservation of its own being. An actor's narrative trajectory will thus generally develop according to the schema: subject of being ($\simeq$ virtual subject of doing) $\rightarrow$ subject of doing ($\simeq$ virtual subject of being) $\rightarrow$ subject of being ($\simeq$ virtual subject of doing) etc.[45]

The pragmatic being is the narrative's basis, and the actor's process will therefore be seen as enrolled in a completed series, a mythos whose beginning and end consist of states of being. The end of one process (cf. the death on the cross as covenantal progression) will often form the beginning of a new process (cf. the resurrection as repayment), but in the extreme case one may encounter definitive ends (irreparable loss, for example definitive death, or inalienable abundance, for example definitive life).

However, one cannot have a doing that does not begin in a being-related starting point and ends in a being-related terminal point. The transition to action presupposes a preceding influence to which the act is the answer, and this itself necessarily implies one form or another of change in the subject of doing's own being.

The subject of doing is orientated towards an objective, the accomplishment of a task, the realization of a project. But the act may also entail a result different from that expected, and a distinction must therefore be made between the *voluntary* (in the sense of intended) and the *involuntary* (unintended) act. A *voluntary subject of doing* is then understood to mean any person who - having conceived or subscribed to a project to change the existing state of affairs - passes to action in order to realize this change.

However, it does not follow that the process of change (or process of preservation) is realizable. As is known, the acting subject is distinguished into three modes of existence: in the project phase it is a virtual, in the execution phase it is an actualized, and in the result phase it is a realized subject of doing, for example a progressor. In the designation of Jesus as a virtual progressor it is presumed that the progressive act is possible and thereby at the same time evitable (contingent), since the subject of doing is free to act (doing) or not to act (not-doing).

This freedom stands out in relief against the background of the dynamic modalities of doing:

---

[45] Cf. *Logique du récit*, pp. 174.

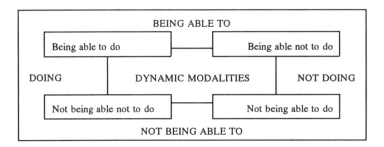

According to this modal category, doing may exist in four different dynamic modes (cf. δύναμαι, δύναμις):

it may be impossible, i.e. the subject of doing is *powerless*, unable to change the situation;

it may be inevitable, i.e. the subject of doing is *dependent*, unable to preserve the situation, forced to evoke the change;

it may be possible, i.e. the subject of doing is *powerful*, has power to change the situation;

it may be evitable, i.e. the subject of doing is *independent*, can refrain from acting and preserve the situation.

Two forms of bondage (δουλεία) can thus be distinguished: dependence, where the subject of doing cannot refrain from acting and thus appears as a puppet, an automaton, a robot, etc., perceiving itself as controlled by another will; powerlessness, where the subject of doing cannot act because its latitude is restricted.

In the case of bondage, it is of course meaningless to speak of a voluntary subject of doing.[46] The voluntary act presupposes that the subject of doing finds itself to be free, i.e. is modalized by being-able-to-do, which - and this is remarkable - implies the simultaneous presence of being-able-not-to-do.

Equipped with freedom (ἐλευθερία) of action, the subject of doing will then either pass to action (doing) or refrain from action (not-doing, allowing). If it passes to action, it will either obtain the being aimed at (successful doing) or it will have exerted its efforts in vain (failed doing, it came to nothing, i.e. not-being):

---

[46] The determinated doing, not-being-able-not-to-do, tends towards the impersonal, the automatic, cf. αὐτόματος 4,8.

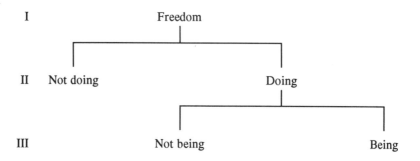

A detailed exposition of the subject of doing's roles can now follow this articulation. At the stage of establishment of the project (I), the subject of doing can be defined according to the influence (manipulation) that determines the decision to pass to or refrain from action. At the stage of execution of the action (II, performance), it can be defined according to the resistance and/or assistance it encounters. At the concluding stage (III), it can be defined according to the nature of the action result (failed or successful doing) and the consequences that follow from this (sanction).

It is clear that being-able-to-do does not necessarily lead to doing, and that doing does not necessarily lead to being. But a being presupposes a doing, which presupposes a being-able-to-do. The logic of presupposition that characterizes the narrative is orientated from the ending towards the beginning and not vice versa. We live forwards but perceive backwards, and this insight is significant to exegesis, which must analyze the narrative in reverse. An understanding of Jesus' anointing must thus be established on the basis of the orientated sequence of presupposition that characterizes the central events: the resurrection presupposes the death on the cross, which presupposes the baptism/anointing; - in the same way as the sanction presupposes the performance, which presupposes the manipulation.[47]

It has been shown that the baptism of John, which is orientated against destruction, involves a modal transformation, a factitive process of change, in that definitive death is thereafter no longer unavoidable but avoidable/possible. But the *evangelical reversal (peripeteia)* occurs only when it is no longer a matter of avoiding death but of realizing life, when the perspective is turned from destruction to creation.[48]

The establishment of the covenant between God and Jesus is the establishment of a covenantal project that must be realized. One can thus distinguish Jesus in

---

[47] Cf. *Sémiotique*, art. "Présupposition".

[48] Thereby the reader's perception of his actual world may change. The bondage of distrust and fear, which in any degressive and/or repressive process of life (hunger, sickness, death) recognizes a sign of the coming destruction, may be replaced by the freedom of trust and hope, which in any protective and/or progressive process of life will perceive an anticipation of the coming kingdom of God.

the role of virtual (by virtue of the anointing), actualized (by virtue of the death on the cross) and realized (by virtue of the resurrection) covenantal subject. He can reject or accept the covenant, but the initiative must come from God. However compelling it may be, the covenant is an offer preconditioned by a manipulation in the basic sense of this word, i.e. an act of creation that establishes a new order of existence. Here also a modal transformation is concerned, a factitive process of change that causes the transition from the "Definitive life is impossible" modal state to the "Definitive life is possible" modal state. That which was closed has now been opened; the kingdom of God has come near.

The anointing must be seen as a modal process of change that makes eternal life a possibility for Jesus, not only in the capacity of a virtual subject of being that will find itself favoured by another subject's doing, but as a virtual subject of doing that must itself contribute to the realization of this possibility. God establishes a liberty of action for his covenantal servant. It is natural in this connection to consider the attribution of the Holy Spirit as an equipping of the anointed. Jesus comes into possession of an extraordinary being-able-to-do (cf. the wonder-worker; and a remarkable knowledge, cf. the proclaimer, the teacher), but that being so it should be stressed that if this power is a necessary precondition for being able to realize the mission, it is in turn insufficient.[49] What is concerned is to avoid the reading that sees in Jesus an automaton, a robot, or a puppet, i.e. a mechanical doll characterized by not-being-able-not-to-do. He must be both able to act and able not to act, otherwise the temptation in the wilderness and the test at Gethsemane, indeed the entire salvation project, is meaningless.[50]

Before the baptism definitive death was unavoidable, afterwards it is avoidable/possible. Before the anointing definitive life was impossible, afterwards it is possible/avoidable. The baptism event's two acts, the baptism of John and the anointing, establish a liminal field in which both Definitive death and Definitive life are avoidable/possible. This situation is in itself untenable - the covenantal servant must make his choice, which is why an *indeterminated* coming into being can be referred to here in which Definitive life has been actualized (and Definitive death has been de-actualized).[51] By virtue of God's factitive change, it has become possible to realize eternal life/the kingdom of God. The question is whether the chosen covenantal servant will accept the project, and whether he has it in him to carry it out.

---

[49] Cf. below 9. The Anointed, p. 293, Note 67.

[50] Cf. Hans-Jörg Steichele, *Der leidende Sohn Gottes. Eine Untersuchung einiger alttestamentlicher Motive in der Christologie des Markusevangeliums*, Regensburg 1980, which emphasizes that according to Mark the Passion "- trotz der klar mit dem Tod rechnenden Leidensankündigungen und trotz der Entschlossenheit Jesu -" does not consummate itself "im Stile einer perfektionistisch ablaufenden heilsgeschichtlichen Automatik", p. 295.

[51] Cf. Chapter XII, A.1.

4. The Covenantal Servant's Knowing and Believing

The first condition that must be met before the virtual covenantal servant can pass to action consists in his being informed that the possibility exists of his undertaking a covenantal task. To the extent that the salvation project - ultimately the realization of the kingdom of God - requires active and voluntary participation on the part of Jesus, he must be informed that the opportunity is given, that he is in fact a virtual subject of doing for a possible act, a virtual covenantal servant for a salvation project, i.e. a virtual savior.

The gospel narrative does not include an account of whether God informs Jesus about the covenant's project, but such a process of information is nevertheless assumed. When, for example, Jesus teaches his disciples that the Son of Man must undergo great suffering, be rejected and killed, but after three days rise again (8,31), he either speaks of his own or he initiates the disciples into the knowledge he has himself received in the call. Narrative exegesis is not concerned with evoking a picture of how this information might historically have occurred, but is concerned exclusively - by inference - with explicating what is assumed by the narrative. Neither is it a matter of reconstructing the historical Jesus' self-awareness, but of reconstructing the process of influence which, by narratological necessity, precedes the narrative Jesus' self-awareness. There are only two possibilities: Jesus is either quite unaware of what he does and why he does it, or he is aware from the outset, from the anointing, of what is to happen and why.[52]

The information, which tells the subject of being that the opportunity is given to accept a task, and that it should therefore consider itself as a virtual covenantal servant for this task, may be true (veridiction) or false (simulation). One may thus distinguish the virtual subject of doing to whom the opportunity is really given from the virtual pseudo-subject of doing to whom the opportunity is not given. Jesus' self-awareness is not in itself proof of God's call, but may be the result of self-manipulation. Even if he is in good faith, he may very well be a pseudo-covenantal servant, a ψευδόχριστος (cf. 13,22), who merely does what he pleases. It is in this capacity that Jesus is crucified by the Jewish leaders.

The influence consists in persuading a subject either to act or to fail to act. An active aspect of the subject of being's role thus asserts itself, in that at any moment it allows itself to be seen as a virtual subject of doing. If Jesus is convinced that the salvation project is impossible, he cannot see that there is

---

[52] Cf. Klaus Berger, "Die königlichen Messiastraditionen des Neuen Testaments", *New Testament Studies 20*, Cambridge 1973, pp. 28: "Für die Taufe weisen alle formgeschichtlichen Parallelen darauf hin, daß es sich hier um einen Berufungsbericht handelt, nach dem das Verhältnis zwischen dem Vater und dem 'geliebten' Sohn konstitutiv dafür ist, daß der Sohn Erkenntnis und Offenbarung von Gott her empfangen hat. Auch der von Gott begabte Weise begründet seinen Anspruch auf Gottessohnschaft mit seiner Gnosis über Gott - und er versteht Gott als seinen Vater. Das weisheitliche Schema der Lehrübermittlung Vater-Sohn ist mit Elementen der prophetischen Berufungsvision verbunden worden, da hier der Vater Gott ist, der 'Weise' aber Gottes Sohn."

occasion to accept the assigned task. If, however, he believes in the possibility of the salvation project he will see that there is also occasion to pass to action. But the subject of doing that is in doubt will also be able to pass to action. The doubter who fluctuates between believing-to-be and believing-not-to-be, which on the basis of the narrative's veridictory modalities may be defined as belief (πίστις) and unbelief (ἀπιστία), may take a chance, as does the father in 9,14ff: "I believe; help my unbelief!", 9,24, cf. also 9,19.

It is illuminating to look more closely at veridiction and simulation. If Jesus is informed truthfully, he will either pass to action because he rightly thinks that the opportunity is given (successful veridiction), or refrain from action because he incorrectly thinks that the opportunity is not given (failed veridiction). If he passes to action, he will in retrospective appear as wise, clever, sensible (σοφός, φρόνιμος; cf. Mt. 7,24: ἀνὴρ φρόνιμος); but if he fails to act he will in hindsight appear as a ninny, a fool (μωρός), as unwise and silly (ἄφρων; cf. Mt. 7,26: ἀνὴρ μωρός).

If Jesus is fraudulently informed, he will similarly either pass to action because he incorrectly thinks that the opportunity is given (successful simulation), or fail to act because he correctly thinks that the opportunity is not given (failed simulation). In the first case he appears as a fool, in the latter as a wise man.

He who allows himself to be fooled by the simulation and he who does not allow himself to be convinced by the veridiction play the fool's role. He who allows himself to be convinced by the veridiction and he who does not allow himself to be deceived by the simulation play the role of a wise man. The same roles are concerned when other persons (the narrated actors or the readers) must decide for themselves whether Jesus is victim of a simulation or favoured by a veridiction.

The problem for Jesus is that *he cannot know whether the information is true or false*. If he makes an assessment on the basis of the prevalent episteme (the wisdom of this world) the answer is clear: the opportunity is not given, the salvation project is not possible. The information process thus contains a factitive element, since it sets a different episteme, a new perception of reality, which at the same time sets aside the old. Jesus finds himself in a dilemma: if he fails to act, he will thereby reveal either his wisdom or his folly; if he acts, he will thereby similarly reveal either his wisdom or his folly.

However, an asymmetry asserts itself: within the prevalent horizon of experience, Jesus will appear as a fool both in his own eyes and in the eyes of others if he passes to action on the basis of the information available, since this information is contrary to what one thinks he knows about the nature of the world. If he allows himself to be guided and instructed he will be seen as an abject fool, and excuses will be found for his affectively difficult situation; but if he persists in his opinion and moreover attempts to convince others of it, he will appear as someone out of his mind (cf. 3,20ff). His doing and allowing will thus experience interpretation by a censorious body which, on the basis of a given episteme, passes sentence on his behaviour. If he fails to act he is wise and worthy of praise because he confirms the prevalent perception of reality; if he passes to action he is a fool and worthy of rebuke (cf. 8,32), scorn, ridicule, etc. (cf. the mockery scenes of the Passion) because he fails to appreciate the prevalent perception of reality.

The first case concerns a progression that has the form of a reward; the second case concerns a degression that has the form of a punishment. Jesus can therefore be motivated to abstain from action for fear of scorn or ridicule. This fear cannot simply be annulled, but it can be overcome in the sense that other motives weigh more heavily. The virtual subject of doing's competence contains a complex of motives, which counteract and unbalance one another, motives whose relative strength can be changed (for example by temptation) or preserved (for example by prayer).

Jesus passes to action, he accepts the mission assigned, and in the gospel narrative the resurrection is evidence of his clear-sightedness and successful doing. But in the manipulation and performance phase he is cut off from knowing whether he is the victim of a simulation or is favoured by a veridiction. He must trust in God.

5. The Covenantal Servant's Wanting-to-Do

The mission's possibility is not sufficient reason for the virtual covenantal servant to decide to accept it. He must also be motivated to carry it out, and he is as such modalized by the bulistic modalities of doing:

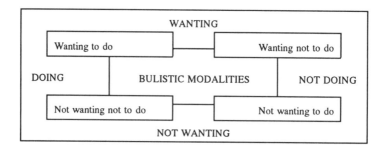

If the covenantal servant - in his capacity as a narrative subject that changes or preserves its own being - considers that the accomplishment of a task will effect an improvement in or consolidate its existence, it will be motivated to accept the covenant's task. But if on the other hand the accomplishment of a task seems to be leading to a worsening of its situation it can only be motivated to refrain from action. There are thus two fundamental *motives*:[53]

1)   the virtual subject of doing is motivated to accept the task in the hope of improving its existence (wanting-to-do; progression);

2)   the virtual subject of doing is motivated to refuse the task for fear that its situation will worsen (wanting-not-to-do; degression).

However, the following cases must be anticipated, where:

3)   the virtual subject of doing is motivated to accept the task for fear that its situation will worsen (not-wanting-not-to-do; protection);

4)   the virtual subject of doing is motivated to abstain from action in the hope of improving its situation (not-wanting-to-do; repression).

Jesus may thus be motivated to accept the task, on the one hand because he fears degression (Definitive death) and on the other hand because he hopes for progression (Definitive life).

One of the important questions is whether it is narratively meaningful to anticipate that actions will be carried out or not carried out in the absence of any kind of motive. The narrator can of course fail to narrate the motive and be content to name the subject's doing or not doing, or he may vaguely imply an unspecified hope of satisfaction or an unspecified fear of dissatisfaction. But this does not affect the motive itself. The problem only arises if one thinks, like BREMOND (although regarded as a borderline case), that one must employ an unfounded (*gratuit*) doing and not doing.[54] For in such a case the action becomes purposeless, the subject of doing may just as well accept the task as fail to do so. If one thinks that Jesus of Nazareth is above the question of motives, then his doing and not doing is meaningless. Unfounded actions are not included in the narrative rationality according to which any voluntary action is meaningful by virtue of its reason.

It is clear that the motive is closely associated with the expectation of the result of the action. The motive that impels the subject of doing to accept the task

---

[53] Cf. *Logique du récit*, p. 186.
[54] Cf. *Logique du récit*, p. 188.

anticipates a satisfactory result, whereas the motive that impels the subject of doing to refrain from action anticipates an unsatisfactory result. One can therefore characterize the motive on the basis of whether the associated expectation is well-founded or unfounded. The motive contains a promise or a threat that is either empty or means something, a promise (of eternal life) or a pronouncement of sentence (of eternal death), which is true or fraudulent, a prophecy (promising and/or condemning), which is either a genuine prophecy or a pseudo-prophecy.

Within the gospel narrative's universe, it is possible on the basis of the result of action to decide whether the expectation associated with the doing, i.e. death on the cross as a gift, was well-founded or unfounded. If Jesus failed to act because he considered it of no avail to do something about the situation, the narrator would only be able to disclose whether he was right in his assessment, since thereby Jesus would have precluded himself from gaining this experience. But if he passes to action and this brings about the expected result, the resurrection, then it becomes clear that the expectation was well-founded in the narrative world.

The analysis focuses deliberately upon Jesus and his destiny. Most exegetes would be content to concentrate on the salvation act's transitive aspect, which concerns the disciples in a broader sense. Jesus acts neither for the sake of God nor for his own sake but for the sake of the virtual disciples (cf. 10,45; 14,24). He is above selfishness, and is thus motivated to accept the task in the hope of improving not his own destiny but another subject of being's destiny. The question of motivation thereby receives an extra dimension, and one cannot indeed ignore the obvious possibility that consideration for this other subject of being, whose destiny Jesus holds in his hands (shepherd motif) becomes decisive to his decision to pass to action. Exegesis, however, must try to lay bare all the dimensions of signification at stake in the narrative, so helping to vary the image of the narrative Jesus.

A certain ambiguity asserts itself as concerns wanting-to-do. When the covenantal servant has accepted the covenant and thus decided to undertake the task, it may be said that he wants to carry out this task. But it is not certain whether he has a mind to do so. Perhaps he even detests the task, but nevertheless wants to carry it out. To understand this complexity, the modality of having-to-do must be introduced.

6. The Covenantal Servant's Having-to-Do

The gospel narrative's objective ideology prescribes the realization of what should be, i.e. Being. Any doing and not doing sees itself semiotized thereby and appears as either Progression, Protection, Degression or Repression, according to whether a realization of Being, a de-realization of Not-being, a realization of

Not-being or a de-realization of Being is concerned. Doing and not doing are modalized by the deontic modalities of doing:

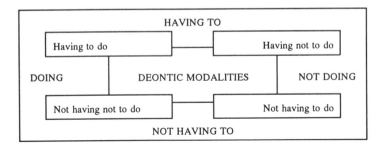

corresponding to:

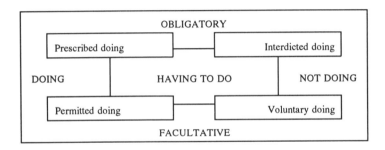

Within the scope of the covenant, the deontic modalities of doing seem to make unambiguous sense only on the basis of the dynamic modalities of doing. An interdicted doing is presupposed to be possible, a prescribed doing is presupposed to be avoidable. The interdiction affects what the covenantal servant can do but is not allowed to do; the prescription affects what the covenantal servant can fail to do but must do.

However, the deontic modalities also seem to be defined relative to the bulistic modalities. Here, the interdiction concerns what the covenantal servant wanted to do if he could decide for himself, whereas the prescription concerns what the covenantal servant did not want to do if he could decide for himself.

In the saying, "Whoever does the will of God (τὸ θέλημα τοῦ θεοῦ) is my brother and sister and mother." (3,35), Jesus indirectly defines himself as he who does the will of God. What God wants is what appears to Jesus as a having to: he does what is prescribed by God; he fails to do what is interdicted by God.

Whereas the term δύναμις falls under the dynamic modalities, the term ἐξουσία (cf. also ἔξεστιν) falls under the deontic modalities.

The objective value perspective (having to) refers to the covenantal lord (for example, God), whereas the subjective value perspective (wanting to) refers to the covenantal servant (for example Man). These value perspectives may either be compatible with or incompatible with one another, and the basis of the covenantal process is indeed characterized by incompatibility between covenantal lord and covenantal servant. The realization of the covenant then becomes a process through which this difference is turned into harmony, in that the covenantal servant subjects himself to the will of the covenantal lord.[55] It seems to be inevitable that this situation splits the covenantal servant into one part that identifies itself with the covenantal lord's wanting to and one part that remains in solidarity with the covenantal servant's own wanting to. Intra-subjectively, the covenantal servant will be split between obligation and inclination, and it is not given which part obtains control: the spirit is willing, but the flesh is weak (cf. 14,38).[56]

7. Flesh and Spirit

The call, which includes an initiation into the covenant's programme, throws the covenantal servant into a dilemmatic crisis. Relative to the project's final objective, the realization of eternal life/the kingdom of God, Jesus can be motivated to accept the task only since he desires this being. This is the fundamental wish that constitutes the basic impetus. Relative to the death on the cross, however, he can only be motivated to refrain from action. The decision to pass to action is the process by which the crisis is overcome, in that one motive comes to weigh more heavily than the other. But, as the Gethsemane scene shows, the weight distribution established can be de-stabilized at any moment, and the covenantal servant is then thrown into a new crisis.

The spirit (τὸ πνεῦμα), which understands that God's command serves the true life, is willing to accept the demand, but the flesh (ἡ σάρξ), which clings to the self-centred life, resists. Self-conquest, self-denial of the subject's own

---

[55] Cf. Gerhard Delling, *Der Kreuzestod Jesu in der urchristlichen Verkündigung*, Göttingen 1972: "Der gewaltsame Sterben Jesu ist im Gottes Willen eingeschlossen; im Kreuz erfüllt sich sein messianischer Auftrag (..)", p. 61; the keywords are "Gehorsam" and "Selbsthingabe", cf. pp. 71.

[56] Cf. Rudolf Pesch, *Das Markusevangelium, 2. Teil*, p. 393: "Auch die alt.-jüdische Überlieferung kennt seit Jes 31,3 den Gegensatz zwischen 'Geist' und 'Fleisch', aber nicht als Gegensatz innerhalb des Menschen. Mit den Essenern teilt Jesus die Auffassung, daß der Mensch zum Schauplatz des Kampfes zwischen Gott und Satan geworden ist. Gott schenkt den Menschen in der Endzeit, (...), seinen Geist, der die menschliche Schwachheit überwinden kann. Der Entscheidungscharakter menschlichen Lebens wird nicht autonom interpretiert, vielmehr die Angewiesenheit des Menschen im Glauben auf Gott herausgestellt.". This opinion, which reduces Man to a subject of being, cannot avoid landing in an inadequate predeterminism. It is true that it is God's command which splits Man, but if he, as created in the image of God, cannot recognize himself in the hope, then the fear of punishment becomes the only motivating factor.

wanting to, is necessary for the realization of God's command. The basic conflict is between wanting to and having to; the covenantal servant is split. He is tied to the flesh, but understands at the same time that the values sought by wanting to are empty and contrary to the ontological definition of existence. But God's will, his wanting to, which for Man appears as a having to, expresses the true values that are in accordance with creation's ontological order. The desire for eternal life bears witness to Man's sense of its true definition, its sense of life in its integrity. The incompatibility between the given world and the true Being is at the same time evidence of Man's frailty or weakness. Man's wanting to is directed towards the preservation of the provisional life which, like robbed booty, must be defended in constant anxiety about the lurking dangers, in the final instance death. God's will demands use, in the final instance renunciation of this life in obedience to the intention of creation.

Jesus' prayer to the Father: "for you all things are possible; remove this cup from me; yet, not what I want, but what you want" (14,36) witnesses the complexity that characterizes the covenantal servant's situation. Contradictory motives assert themselves simultaneously, ambivalence is the rule rather than the exception. The two general motives according to which the covenantal servant is motivated *either* to accept the task in the hope of progression *or* to refrain from the task for fear of degression are not sufficiently precise to explain his complex motivation.

BREMOND has attempted a further differentiation. He takes as his basis the general motives referred to, but also suggests a distinction between various forms of progression and degression, and thus between various forms of motive. However, the whole question of the subject of doing's motivation is quite extensive and complex, and his suggestion can be considered only as a possible basis for the preparation of a true *semiotics of passion*. But even in their preliminary form his thoughts are quite illuminating.

He gives the following example, which is not irrelevant in this context:

1) Socrate, joyeux convive, se plut à boire jusqu'à l'aube;
2) Socrate, malade, consentit à boire la purge prescrite pour retrouver la santé;
3) Socrate, condamné par les juges d'Athènes, voulut boire la ciguë plutôt que de s'enfuir au mépris des lois.[57]

In the first case, Socrates seeks no satisfaction other than that which he achieves through the accomplishment of the act itself. What is concerned here is to satisfy an inclination, a propensity, a desire. The subject of doing's accom-

---

[57] *Logique du récit*, pp. 187.

plishment of the task is similarly a progression of its own being. The motive is of a *hedonistic* order, it concerns a desired act that appears pleasant in itself.

In the second case, Socrates does not try to satisfy a wish to drink. On the contrary, drinking a laxative (for example, castor oil) is an unpleasant action that in itself can evoke only a negative motive of dislike and aversion. But to drink is after all a useful act if health is to be restored. The subject of doing sees the act as a means that must be undertaken to implement a different project (recovery of health). A motive of a *pragmatic* order is concerned here, a choice made on the basis of a favourable calculation ("par calcul favorable").[58]

In the third and last case, Socrates decides to drink the hemlock because it is his duty. He feels no pleasure in carrying out the act, he cannot hope for any reward in the other world or for a place of honour in people's memory. He simply wishes to fulfil what he considers an obligation. A motive of the *ethical* order is concerned here, a choice made on the basis of an awareness of a command.

Opposed to these action-promoting motives, which urge the virtual subject of doing to act, are the action-preventing motives, which similarly fall into three categories:

- in the hedonistic order, the wish corresponds to the aversion, which urges the virtual subject of doing to refrain from an act unpleasant in itself;
- in the pragmatic order, the favourable calculation corresponds to the unfavourable calculation, which envisages the unsuccessful consequences of the use of an unfavourable means;
- in the ethical order, the awareness of a prescription corresponds to an awareness of an interdiction that evokes fear of committing a guilty act.[59]

BREMOND's three orders seem to fall under a structure whose constituent poles are wanting to and having to, flesh and spirit. The hedonistic order appears as a wanting to with a tendency towards the exclusion of having to, and thus indicates a purely subjective value perspective. The ethical order, however, is a having to, an objective value perspective, which disregards completely the subject's self-interest. The hedonistic and ethical orders are the two extremes. The former knows of no objective perspective, the latter knows of no subjective perspective. The former is pure flesh, the latter pure spirit.

The pragmatic order, which is to be found somewhere in between, confronts the covenantal servant's wanting to with the covenantal lord's having to. As pointed out, the prescription is preconditioned by a wanting-not-to-do, the interdiction by a wanting-to-do. It is precisely this tension, this incongruity between the covenantal lord's and the covenantal servant's value perspectives, which gives the narrative and the life-intrigue its dynamics. As a project the

---

[58] Bremond's use of *pragmatic* should not be confused with the use of this term hitherto, cf. *Sémiotique*, art. "Pragmatique".

[59] Cf. *Logique du récit*, p. 188.

prescription means a *test* of the subject of doing, in that it must overcome its wanting-not-to-do, whereas the interdiction means a *temptation*, since the subject of doing must here overcome its wanting-to-do. In both cases, therefore, self-denial is concerned.

As an intermediate form, the pragmatic order is the most interesting because it thematizes the tension between covenantal servant and covenantal lord, which is presumably always in evidence. The three orders are perspectives which probably appear in any narrative act. There is no either/or, but motives from all three orders may play a promotive or an obstructive role in the decision whether to act or not to act.

BREMOND's example is particularly illustrative in this context, since the gospel narrative itself thematizes Jesus' principal act, the death on the cross, as *the drinking of a cup*, cf. 10,38ff and 14,36; also 14,23ff.[60] The prayer at Gethsemane (14,36) shows clearly that on the one hand Jesus does not want death but on the other hand wants what God wants. He is not hedonistically motivated to drink the cup, quite the contrary. The thought of death fills him with distress and agitation (14,33ff), aversion, and he can only be motivated to refrain from action. That he does not flee (like his disciples who cannot pass the test, cf. 14,31 and 14,50) but faces death must be because of pragmatic and/or ethical motives. The hedonistic order, however, is not absent but is in conflict with the ethical order.

If Jesus is ethically motivated he drinks the cup, the chalice of death, because it is his duty. He feels no enjoyment in carrying out the action, he has no hope of any reward in the other world but simply wants to fulfil what he regards as an obligation, God's will. The decision to carry out the task is then taken against the background of an awareness of prescription; he simply follows a categorical imperative.

The question is, however, whether or not such heroism ruptures, in strict terms, the narrative rationality. That God commands Jesus to drink the cup is because this act serves the realization of the Being aspired to, and not because he issues unfounded imperatives. It is of course possible that the subject of doing apprehends the prescription as meaningless or paradoxical because it conflicts with experience. But if he accepts the task, this can only be because he trusts that the fulfilment of God's prescription serves the realization of Being. Blind obedience, not exercised with confidence in God's promise, is demonic.

According to BREMOND's proposition, one may say that Jesus does not drink the bitter cup to quench his thirst, but because it is a useful action if he wishes to gain eternal life, to overcome death. The subject of doing sees the act (death

---

[60] The main emphasis is here given to the fact that Jesus himself is to drain the cup, which draws attention to him as subject of doing; in the death on the cross he gives his life. At the same time it should be remembered that although this cup is prescribed he can leave it be. On the interpretation of the cup in general, cf., e.g. Reinhard Feldmeier, *Die Krisis des Gottessohnes. Die Gethsemaneerzählung als Schlüssel der Markuspassion*, Tübingen 1987, pp. 176.

on the cross) as a means that must be implemented to accomplish another project (the resurrection). A motive of the pragmatic order is concerned here, a choice undertaken against the background of a favourable calculation.

Whereas the ethical order is categorical, the pragmatic order is conditional. He who informs about ethics is commanding, whereas he who informs about pragmatism is advisory. The advisor says: if you will achieve X, you must do Y; if you wish to regain your health, you must swallow the bitter pill. But at the very moment the subject of doing wishes to regain its health, the stipulation presents itself as a categorical demand. The pragmatic and the ethical are thus the same thing seen from two different angles. The pragmatic calculation, which must not be confused with opportunism, belongs to the considerations that precede the decision. It allows itself to contest or evaluate the objective. But when the objective has been fixed, when the subject of doing desires eternal life (wanting to), then the requirement of death on the cross manifests itself as a categorical prescription (having to). It must therefore be said that the narrative Jesus is both pragmatically and ethically motivated to accept the task. Acceptance of the covenant is given the nature of a promise through which the covenantal servant himself undertakes to realize the demand. It is given its character of a test (or a trial) by virtue of the very tension between wanting to and having to, between flesh and spirit.

It should also, however, be pointed out that in this case the calculation rests not upon positive knowledge, but upon faith. When BREMOND speaks of calculation he not only presupposes that the consequence is given by necessity, but also that the subject of doing has experience-based knowledge of this. For Jesus, such knowledge is not given. He cannot know whether death on the cross results in resurrection; this can only be believed, for which reason the relationship of trust in God becomes decisive. This cognitive test must also be taken into account.

BREMOND's proposition is illuminating, but still too imprecise. The so-called pragmatic order appears to be particularly unsatisfactory. Future attempts to establish the semiotics of passion may find inspiration in BREMOND, but they should avoid becoming fixated on his decontextualized examples, which are merely concise illustrations of a theoretical model that still leaves much to be desired.

8. The Temptation

In the very concise account, 1,12f, which is nevertheless capable of giving rise to many questions, only the temptation by Satan is of interest here.[61]

The location between call (1,11) and transition to action (1,14) should form the basis of the analysis, and the temptation must then consist in a request to

---

[61] Cf., e.g., Ernest Best, *The Temptation and the Passion. The Markan Soteriology*, Cambridge 1965.

break the covenant. What is important for Satan is to make Jesus do what is interdicted and/or fail to do what is prescribed.

Knowledge of the narrative organization's *polemical* principle makes it easy to single out Satan as an anti-subject and/or an anti-Destinator.[62] As influencing manipulator, what he says will be either a negative diction, which denies God's positive diction, i.e. veridiction versus negated veridiction (cf. Gen 3,1 "Did God say, 'You shall not eat from any tree in the garden'?", a feeble negative leading to the strong negative in 3,4, "You will not die "); or a positive diction that must itself be negated by a negative diction, i.e. simulation versus negated simulation.[63] In the case of positive diction, what Satan says will appear as a proposal to establish an alternative covenant; he is the covenantal lord, the beguiled covenantal servant as is known from, for example, Lk 4,5ff. Here also the covenant is conditional: if Jesus will worship Satan he will receive all the glories of the world and authority over them, i.e. a provisional life characterized by extreme fullness of being and an abundance of pecuniary values.

The confrontation between the two covenants bears witness to the polemical structure of the discourse and gives reason to speak of a dualistic articulation of the universe of signification.[64] But the term "dualism" is ambiguous. If the term is understood to mean *absolute* dualism, i.e. the presence of two opposing principles, two powers of being that cannot under any circumstances be abolished, then it is misleading to speak of a dualistic universe of signification. An opposition of the Being versus Nothing type can be described as dualistic, but in that case a *relative* dualism is concerned. Nothing is not a power of being but an absence of Being, which indicates an underlying monism. If it were a matter of absolute dualism both covenants would be true, but the gospel narrative knows only one truth.

The relative dualism, which refers to an underlying monism, bears witness to the polemical structures' semantic and syntactic isotopy. What is interdicted according to one covenant C1 will be prescribed or permitted according to another covenant C2. The prescription in C1 corresponds in the same way to the interdicted or facultative in C2. The death on the cross, which is prescribed according to God's covenant C1, will be interdicted or facultative in Satan's covenant C2. The earthly values of glory prescribed by C2 will be affected by an interdiction from C1 (cf. 10,21). Mark does not tell of what the temptation specifically consists, but it seems able to consist only in the offer of a covenant that makes the interdicted prescribed and the prescribed interdicted.

As pointed out earlier, the interdiction becomes meaningful only if the interdicted being X is desired by the covenantal servant. Otherwise the

---

[62] Cf. *Sémiotique*, art. "Anti-destinateur".

[63] Cf. Chapter VIII, A.2.a.

[64] Cf. *Sémiotique*, art. "Polémique".

interdiction is superfluous. Similarly, the prescription is meaningful only if the prescribed being Y is feared. Satan can therefore trade upon Jesus' desire and/or fear, his wanting-to-be and/or wanting-not-to-be. However, it is not Satan who establishes the conflict between the covenantal lord's having to and the covenantal servant's wanting to. This intra-contractual conflict is established by the incompatibility between God and Man, between the covenantal lord and the covenantal servant, a disparity that reflects the deficient nature of the existing world. The inter-contractual conflict between God's covenant and Satan's pseudo-covenant is merely a particular description of this intra-contractual conflict. This becomes clear when one considers that the pseudo-covenant's prescription is the command to seek the being X that the covenantal servant himself desires, whereas the interdiction affects the being Y that he himself fears. The pseudo-covenant is thus nothing other than an abolition of the covenantal relationship, the tension between having to and wanting to, i.e. a simple release of the subject's unrestricted desire. In this context, Satan is the representative of the subject's own wanting to, elevated to objective having to.

When Peter in his doxomania begins to reproach Jesus, thereby adopting (at least involuntarily) the role of tempter, he is rejected with the words: "Get behind me, Satan! For you are setting your mind not on divine things, but on human things!" Peter reacts to the teaching about the passion of the Son of God, i.e. the prescription of death on the cross, and thereby denies God's covenant. But at the same time he reveals his doxomania, a desire for glory and power, which characterizes the human thought process and value perception (wanting-to-be). By the words to Peter, the gospel narrative itself reveals that the God/Satan antithesis is a simulacrum that covers up the God/Man antithesis.

The gospel narrative says nothing about Jesus' acceptance of the covenant, and it is debatable whether Satan's temptation takes place before or after such an acceptance, whose existence is presupposed by Jesus' transition to action in 1,14. It is, however, natural to consider the forty days in the wilderness as a transitional period when it is still uncertain whether Jesus will arrive at the decision that is the precondition for transition to action. The covenant's first commandment is the prescription to accept the covenant and its action programme, and any call necessarily throws the one interpellated into a crisis. As the predictions show, Jesus is well-informed about the covenant's programme, and his acceptance has taken place in full awareness of this programme and its consequences. His transition to action is thus preconditioned by a promise given that he will realize the covenant's programme. Satan's temptation may be understood as an attempt to make him break this promise, but it may also be understood as an intervention into the decision-making process that leads to acceptance. Considering the temptation story's location before the transition to action, it is most natural to see Satan's intervention as an attempt to persuade Jesus to refrain from accepting God's covenant.

Assuming that Jesus is in any way affected by Satan's temptation, that he registers and reacts to the ambivalence established by the contrast between wanting to and having to, he will be put into a state of crisis, a spiritual struggle. Resisting the temptation consists in failing to realize the interdicted but desired being. A test has however been passed when the prescribed but feared being is realized.

But in the manipulation phase it is not the covenant's principal act that is concerned. What the covenantal servant must adopt a position on at this moment is whether he will accept or reject the covenant, and acceptance consists in giving a promise to meet the covenantal obligations. Jesus' resistance of Satan's temptation then coincides with his acceptance of the covenant and its action programme.[65]

However, Satan is not necessary for Jesus to feel resistance to the covenant. The objections are already known to him from himself *qua* a human being. The actual establishment of the covenant is a process in the nature of a test, in so far as the acceptance and its promise involves a self-denial. When the Spirit leads Jesus into the wilderness to be tempted by Satan, this corresponds to the conflict into which God necessarily throws his covenantal servant when he presents the covenant's programme to him. The prescription is structurally a negation of the subject's own wanting to, a matter that is merely radicalized when this negation affects not only pecuniary objects of value but life itself.

In 14,32 there is not one word about Satan. The crisis bears witness to a conflict between Man and God, between covenantal servant and covenantal lord, between Jesus and the Father. But this inter-subjective conflict is here presented as an intra-subjective conflict between the willing spirit and the weak flesh. The crisis can be dissolved only by self-conquest, which can be now strengthened by God when he speaks to the spirit and now weakened by Satan when he speaks to the flesh.

9. The Anointed

The gospel narrative's heading already designates Jesus of Nazareth as Christ. "Jesus Christ" is a double proper name, although Χριστός is in fact a title, the Greek translation of the Hebrew *masjiach*, which means "the anointed one". In other places in Mark this titular significance is clearly evidenced (8,29; 12,35; 13,21; 14,61; 15,32), ὁ χριστός is the Anointed, the anointed of God.

The role of the anointed may be compared with the role of the elected (ὁ ἐκλεκτός, cf. 13,20ff). Morphologically, substantivized verbal adjectives are concerned (χρίω, ἐκλέγω), but these roles describe he who has been anointed or

---

[65] The rejection of Peter (8,33) corresponds to a confirmation of this acceptance; but Jesus' own "confession" in 14,62 is the passage where his acceptance of the covenant is most clearly expressed.

elected, and semantically therefore they correspond to the past participle passive, cf. Lk 9,35 ὁ ἐκλελεγμένος = ὁ ἐκλεκτός.[66]

In contrast to the thematic roles of doing, defined by *nomen agentis* (savior/salvation, prophesy/prophet, teaching/ teacher, etc.) thematic roles of being are concerned here. But a special form of being is concerned, a modal being that refers to the subject of being's competence and thus its characteristic of virtual subject of doing. He who is anointed is anointed by someone (passive aspect), but is also anointed for something, a mission (active aspect). The worthiness cannot be separated from the function, the implicit role of doing, at which the anointing is directed. The anointed is inducted into his worthiness as subject of doing, for example king (βασιλεύς - βασιλεύω - βασιλεία).

On the basis of the role of being ὁ χριστός, it is impossible to recognize the content of the associated role of doing (or the role complex linked thereto). The title does not reveal the function, since the name Χριστός refers to *nomen est omen*, the name is a portent or an indication that implies a deeper significance, but this meaning must be sought in the context of the narrative. Only he who knows the narrative knows what "Christ" signifies. But *nomen et omen*, name and portent, applies to the name "Jesus", since the unity of name and signification here discloses the content of the thematic role of doing: Jesus is the savior. "Jesus Christ" then receives the meaning of "the savior chosen and anointed by God". It is, however, important to appreciate that the gospel story's narrative articulation is not abolished. By the anointing, God installs his covenantal servant in the role of *virtual savior*. If the emphasis is on "the anointed", then Jesus is a realized Christ, since the process of anointing has been accomplished; but if the emphasis is on "the savior", then before the transition to action he is still only a virtual Christ. More generally, Christ means the servant chosen by God, the servant with whom he has established his covenant. The content of the servant's mission may be more specifically defined on the basis of the events which in fact take place in the relationship between Jesus and God.

In this connection there is reason to look more closely at the two other titles which are used about the covenantal servant, "Son of God" and "Son of Man". Both are ambiguous and must be defined in more detail contextually. "Son of God" may be directly defined as a son role which is the counterpart to a father role (cf. 8,38; 11,25f; 13,32; 14,36), and this relationship is similar to the hierarchical relationship between lord and servant, Destinator and Destinatee:

Destinator : Destinatee :: Father : Son :: Lord : Servant.

---

[66] Note that Luke 9,35 has ἐκλελεγμένος instead of ἀγαπητός; cf., however, textcritical note; cf. Mark 9,7 and 1,11; cf. Jn 1,34 textcritical note. The term "ἐν σοὶ εὐδόκησα" (1,11) indicates "Gottes beschließende Wahl, nämlich die Erwählung des Sohnes, die einschließt Sendung und Bestimmung zum königlichen Messiasamt", cf. Gerhard Kittel and Gerhard Friedrich (eds.): *Theologisches Wörterbuch zum Neuen Testament*, Zweiter Band, Stuttgart (1935) 1960, p. 738.

In this perspective, the Destinatee is indeed the servant of the covenantal lord (cf. 10,18 and 13,32, which clearly mark the subordination relationship).

However, as the wonder-worker and preacher roles have shown, Jesus himself appears as covenantal lord relative to other covenantal servants in his capacity as God's representative. When, for example, Jesus calls his disciples he appears in the role of relation-establishing manipulator. In this perspective, "Son of God" indicates rather that Jesus is rightfully exercising his functions as inducted by God. He acts in the name of God (cf. 9,38), he is "the Holy One of God" (1,24), "Son of the Most High God" (5,7; cf. 3,11) who, equipped with extraordinary ability and knowledge, can appear in the role of Destinator, as lord (cf. 7,28).[67]

This dimension of signification is dominant, and the designation of "Son of God" thus becomes a sovereignty title, a king title, which defines Jesus of Nazareth as God's legitimate representative relative to Man. 9,7: "This is my Son, the Beloved; listen to him!" could be rendered as: "Jesus of Nazareth is my chosen and inducted representative; trust in him and obey him!" The high priest's question: "Are you the Messiah, the Son of the Blessed One?" (14,61) is a question about Jesus' authority, and could be rendered as: "Do you really maintain that you are God's legitimate and authorized representative?". It is Jesus' answer, "I am", to this question, which is interpreted as blasphemy. The centurion's "confession" in 15,39, "Truly this man was God's Son!" conveys that God's legitimate messenger has been murdered, cf. 12,1ff.

The "Son of Man" designation is also ambiguous. A "son" role is again concerned, which indicates a subordinate position, but the main disparity here is between God and Man. Fundamentally, "Son of Man" is an inferiority title. Only after the resurrection when the principal salvation project has been realized, does "the Son of Man" appear in power and glory, but then as subject of doing in a new project directed towards the final realization of the kingdom of God. The dominant dimension of signification concerns Jesus as Destinatee, as covenantal servant. "The Son of Man" is the representative of Man relative to God, chosen and recognized by God himself.[68] As Abraham, in Gen 17, represents Yahweh's people, so Jesus represents the new people of God. But the relationship between representative and represented is not organic, the representation relationship is not genetically established. It is true that in Gen 17 the covenant concerns Abraham's offspring, the virtual covenantal people is here a particular collective

---

[67] Cf. 1. Cor 1,24; also Klaus Berger, "Zum traditionsgeschichtlichen Hintergrund christologischer Hoheitstitel", *New Testament Studies 17*, Cambridge 1971, pp. 391: "Der Christos ist der mit heiligem Geist gesalbte endzeitliche Prophet. Salbung bedeutet Besitz der legitimen Lehre (Erkenntnis Gottes und Gebote); ..." (p. 400). As to the relationship between δύναμις and σοφία, cf. ibidem, pp. 398. Siegfried Schulz rightly states that only the Spirit as a baptismal gift "setz Jesus zu seinen Wundertaten instand", *Die Stunde der Botschaft. Einführung in die Theologie der vier Evangelisten*, Hamburg 1967, p. 73.

[68] Cf. Eduard Schweizer, *Erniedrigung und Erhöhung bei Jesus und seinen Nachfolgern*, Zürich 1962, pp. 62. Jack Dean Kingsbury, *The Christology of Mark's Gospel*, Philadelphia 1982, completely ignores this aspect of the matter and thus attributes to Mark a rather narrow christology.

actor, but only circumcision makes the individual a part of the covenantal people. In the new covenant the virtual covenantal people is "all nations" (13,10), i.e. a universal collective actor who can only take part in the covenant's promise by recognizing this representative, who thereby obtains the status of Destinator or lord: those who are ashamed of the Son of Man and his words, of them the Son of Man will also be ashamed when he comes in the glory of his Father, cf. 8,38.

The difficulties in defining the designations of "Son of God" and "Son of Man" are due not least to the fact that the gospel narrative uses these designations to serve various purposes. In some places "Son of Man" appears where "Son of God" might have been expected, cf. 2,10 and 2,28; in other places the narrative slides effortlessly from one designation to the other, cf. 9,7.9 and 14,61f. The complexity can scarcely be resolved; exegesis must content itself with indicating the dimensions that manifest themselves in this game of signification, merely emphasizing that the role complex, which defines the narrative Jesus is so complex that the titles' content of signification can never capture more than aspects of the matter, which is why they occasionally tend to appear as names. These names perhaps presage the nature of the matter, but they are given pregnant meaning only through the roles, the narrative processes, which they attempt to describe summarily and statically.

Christ the anointed is he with whom God has established his salvation covenant, and this covenantal subject, this *savior* - Jesus of Nazareth - appears now as representative of God relative to Man, i.e. as "Son of God", and now as Man's representative relative to God, i.e. as "Son of Man". This is the rule that all exceptions prove.

CHAPTER TWELVE

SOTERIOLOGY

The definition of the gospel story's narrative soteriology can profitably base itself on the well-known definition of narration:

1) The narrator (No) tries to convey to the narratee (Ne) the concept of a state of being and/or an action.
2) The subject of being for this state/action is No, Ne or a third person A.
3) The responsible subject of doing for this state/action is No, Ne, the third person A and/or a fourth person B.

A narrative in the narrower sense, i.e. an objectivized, third-person discourse, is concerned only when neither the subject of doing nor the subject of being is narrator or narratee, and it is on this aspect of the matter that attention will be concentrated.

As is known, the subject of being will be either victim of or favoured by the action concerned, and the discourse's information, its message, or angelium will thus be either a dys-angelium or an eu-angelium. As the name indicates, the gospel narrative designates its narratee as favoured by one action or another, but initially the subject of being must be sought among the narrated persons in the narrate. If the action, the narrative process, can be defined as a salvation act, who then is in fact the favoured subject of being for this process? And who is in fact the subject of doing? The answer to these questions is complicated by the fact that the gospel narrative includes several relatively autonomous but connected narrative processes. In addition, the third-person actors appear now as subjects of being and now as subjects of doing. However, in the light of the knowledge that doing serves being, these narrative processes can be defined on the basis of the pragmatic subject of being. It thus becomes possible to distinguish between a *local soteriology*, in which the subject of being is now Jesus and now God, and a *global soteriology* in which the subject of being is now the disciples and now the world.

A. LOCAL SOTERIOLOGY

The local soteriology concerns the salvation project, which sees itself realized in Jesus' resurrection. The accomplishment of this sub-project opens new possibilities, but exegesis must first define the local salvation project (the salvation project in its true sense) before the global salvation project (the creation project) can be considered.

If the action referred to in the above definition is the gospel narrative's inter-active salvation project, then Jesus allows himself to be nominated as the subject of doing and of being: in the death on the cross he gives life, but in the resurrection he receives life. In the same way God adopts both these roles: through the resurrection he gives life, through the death on the cross he receives life. But it is possible to isolate the covenantal lord's pragmatic trajectory from the covenantal servant's pragmatic trajectory. Both have a project aimed at realizing them as *sanctioned* subjects of being, i.e. they aim at a covenantal objective. The salvation project can therefore be considered now from Jesus' side, which gives cause to define a christological or *christocentric* soteriology, and now from God's side, which leads to the definition of a theological or *theocentric* soteriology.

1. Christocentric Soteriology

The gospel narrative's christocentric soteriology permits definition, in that exegesis disregards God as subject of being. The pertinence level thus established can then be given as follows:

1) Mark tries to convey to his reader the concept of a state of being (the resurrection) and of an interactive action (the salvation project).
2) The subject of being for this state/action is Jesus.
3) The responsible subject of doing for this state/action is Jesus and God.

This salvation project has been thoroughly analyzed above, but it still remains to summarize the results of the investigation.

As a human being, Jesus of Nazareth is initially found in the Provisional life state of being (Sb ∪ (Sh ∩ O) that is orientated towards Definitive death (Sb ∪ (Sh ∪ O). He is defined by a fatal degression process, and it is only a question of time before the negative sanction will take place. The punishment is preconditioned by guilt, a covenantal unworthiness (sinfulness), which itself refers back to a negative performance (malefaction; Adam's transgression).

At this moment, Jesus therefore sees himself as enrolled into an interactive degression process comprising the roles:

DEGRESSOR	VICTIM

Jesus is the victim of a degression process, which must in a superior perspective be seen as on-going. The degressor is God, but it should be noted that the degression is legitimate, and that it is released by the victim's own doing. The latter thus appears in the role of auxiliary degressor. It should also be noted that Jesus shares the fate of all other people. It is all of mankind that is the victim.

Opposed to this degression process is an interactive progression process comprising the following roles:

PROGRESSOR	BENEFICIARY

By virtue of the death on the cross, Jesus finds himself in the Provisional death state of being (Sb ∩ (Sh ∪ O) that is orientated towards Definitive life (Sb ∩ (Sh ∩ O). He now sees himself defined by a fatal progression process, and it is only a question of time (in this case from Friday to Sunday) before the positive sanction takes place. The reward is preconditioned by a covenantal worthiness (righteousness), which itself refers back to a positive performance (the death on the cross as benefaction).

Jesus is favoured by a progression process, and the progressor is God. But the reward is released by the favoured person's own doing, and he thus appears in the role of auxiliary progressor. It should be noted here that Jesus *does not* share the fate with all other people. The raising of Jesus is not the simultaneous raising of mankind or of the elect.

The four states of being, however, Definitive death, Provisional life, Provisional death and Definitive life, fall under one and the same semantic universe, the LIFE/DEATH isotopy. The degression process' relative point of reference is Provisional life, but its absolute point of reference is Definitive life. The Provisional life state of being should therefore be considered only as an intermediate state on the course from Being to Nothing. It can be compared as such with a state of sickness which, maintained in its relative stability, marks a stage on the path from life to death. If the sick person is clearly doomed, he can be categorized as half dead (ἡμιθανής, cf. Lk 10,30).

For example, a barrel filled with 1000 litres of water which is continuously being emptied with a spoon refers to a degression process that takes time. If the spoon is exchanged for a ladle it will be quicker, and if the bung is knocked out it will be rapid. A process can thus alter its pace, although this secondary aspect is disregarded here. The person emptying the barrel with a spoon will have reached the half-way stage at some time, but it is uncertain whether he considers it half empty when precisely 500 litres remain. If he becomes impatient he will begin to breathe more easily when 600 litres remain. Conversely, the patient individual will first take stock at the half-way stage when he has clearly removed more than half. Half-empty is a categorizing definition indicating a state fluctuating between 600 and 400 litres.

In its very simplicity, the example clarifies our understanding of the salvation project. The degression process that characterizes Jesus at the beginning of the gospel narrative does not take the 1000 litres as its point of reference, but the remaining 400 litres.

The baptism of John entails a neutralization of the emptying process, but by its definition the barrel must either be full or empty, so that this interruption can only be temporary and must be followed by a resumption of the emptying or by the initiation of an adversative filling process. Similarly, the healing of sickness can be seen in a dual perspective. It consists on the one hand in stopping the on-going destruction, and on the other hand in restoration of the absolute point of reference. The baptism of John thus becomes the preparation for the initiation of the true counteraction, the restoration of the absolute point of reference, the initial state of Being, or eternal life. It is the anointing that marks the evangelical reversal from destruction to creation, from degression to progression, from emptying to filling. This event does not consist of a pragmatic change in Jesus' being; the change is modal. After the anointing, Jesus is neither in Provisional life nor in Provisional death but somewhere in between, which can only be defined modally.

The four states of being can be regarded as four modes of being:

Definitive life	=	Realized Being	=	Being
Provisional death	=	Semi-realized Being	=	Non-Nothing
Provisional life	=	Semi-virtualized Being	=	Non-Being
Definitive death	=	Virtualized Being	=	Nothing

The Realized Being and Virtualized Being modes of being are both amodal. The Semi-realized and Semi-virtualized Being modes of being, however, are modalized. In the first case, Definitive life is inevitable and Definitive death is impossible. In the second case, Definitive life is impossible and Definitive death is inevitable.

The anointing, however, inducts Jesus into the Actualized Being mode of being, i.e. a modal state in which Being *is simultaneously possible and evitable*. The factitive establishment of this latitude of possibility is due to God, but it is for Jesus of Nazareth to realize this possibility. He is subject to a prescription to give his life, but at the same time he is free to comply with or fail to comply with the covenantal obligation. At the very moment when Jesus realizes the prescribed performance, God becomes obliged, according to the covenant he has himself established and of which he is himself guarantor, to raise him. Since God's covenantal fidelity is unswerving, Definitive life will thereby see itself modalized as inevitable.

It is therefore possible to define the modes of being below for the narrative Jesus:

	MODE OF BEING	MODALITY	ARTICULATION
I	Virtualized	Life (Death)	Being (Nothingness)
	Semi-virtualized	Impossible	Determined becoming ↑
II	Actualized	Possible/Evitable	Indetermined becoming ↕
III	Semi-realized	Inevitable	Determined becoming ↓
	Realized	Life	Being

in which it is the central events that determine the transition from one mode of being to another:

Virtualized existence

Semi-virtualized existence   - (Destruction)

Actualized existence   - Baptism/Anointing

Semi-realized existence   - Death on the cross

Realized existence   - Resurrection

If the connection does not require any more detailed specification, one could by way of simplification speak of the narrative Jesus' three phases of being:

I)   Virtual existence;
II)   Actualized existence;
III) Realized existence.

If one remembers that the progression process from Provisional life to Definitive life is aimed at the restoration of Being, then it becomes clear that from a superior point of view the salvation project is a veritable protection process that encompasses the roles:

DEGRESSOR	VICTIM	BENEFICIARY	PROTECTOR

Jesus is a victim in his virtual existence, but already in his actualized existence he finds himself chosen as favoured by virtue of God's factitive intervention. In his realized existence, he is inducted by God into the Definitive life state of being by the resurrection, and it is thus God who occupies the role of Protector. God is the savior, Jesus the saved.

However, Jesus is raised by virtue of his own doing, and in this perspective he is at least an auxiliary protector. One can therefore, in such an inter-active process, emphasize different passages, but if it is remembered that the salvation project is here to be defined on the basis of Jesus as a sanctioned subject of being, then it is God who is the savior. Jesus of Nazareth is the first to be saved, and the gospel narrative's information on this salvation may be designated as *christocentric soteriology*. Only when one raises the question of the significance Jesus' death on the cross has for the salvation of others, does he himself appear clearly as the savior.[1]

2. Theocentric Soteriology

The gospel narrative's theocentric soteriology can be determined, in that in the local salvation project exegesis disregards Jesus as subject of being. The pertinence level thereby established can then be given:

1)   Mark tries to convey to his reader the concept of a state of being (reconciliation) and of an inter-active course of action (salvation project).
2)   The subject of being for this state/action is God.
3)   The responsible subject of doing for this state/action is God and Jesus.

Unless exegesis is content to consider God as a functionary, i.e. as a circumstantial subject of doing that merely carries out its prescribed actions without otherwise being a party to the matter, exegesis must raise the question of the narrative's image of God's being. It is true that this image is almost completely concealed, and that therefore the formulation "Mark tries to convey to his reader the concept of..." may seem exaggerated here.

The concealment is not, however, conditioned by the narrator's wish to conceal something, but is an effect of the constraint arising from the fact that two parallel narrative trajectories cannot be manifested simultaneously by the discourse. One trajectory remains latent, without the semiotic relation according to which the two trajectories mutually define and precondition one another therefore being annulled.

---

[1] Dialectically, also as the savior of himself, cf. 15,32.

The covenantal lord's narrative trajectory is not simply absent but merely latently present, and must be arrived at by analysis of the covenantal servant's systematically correlated narrative trajectory.[2] The connection between these two trajectories becomes clear when the covenantal relationship is considered in detail.

a. The Covenant's Structure of Exchange

To be able to establish a contractual relationship, the covenantal lord must carry out a bulistic modalization. He must be able to evoke in the covenantal servant the desire for a state of being and the will to realize this. It is important here to be aware of the covenant's conditional interaction structure. The covenantal lord (abbreviated to Cl) must offer X to the covenantal servant (abbreviated to Cs), but at the same time he must want Y from him; the covenantal servant must be willing to offer the covenantal lord Y because he himself wants X. The covenant may be said to have been entered into when both parties agree to meet each other's desires, to annul one another's lack of being, now non-X, now non-Y. The covenant's conditional structure can then be given:

The covenantal lord establishes:

If S1 gives O1 to S2, then S2 must give O2 to S1.

Here the covenantal lord appears in the role of legislator. But he may also be a contracting party, now as S1, now as S2:

The covenantal lord establishes:

If Cl gives X1 to Cs, then Cs must give Y1 to Cl;
if Cs gives Y2 to Cl, then Cl must give X2 to Cs.

X and Y are *services*, either progression or protection (turned against a degression or against a repression of progression). What the covenantal lord establishes may be described as an obligation: if a given condition is met, S2 (Cl or Cs) is prescribed to carry out an attribution/renunciation.

When the covenantal lord as a contracting party accepts the covenant, he gives the conditioned *promise* that if Cs gives Y2 to Cl, then Cl will give X2 to Cs. The covenantal servant's acceptance is a corresponding promise to give Y1 to Cl if the latter gives X1 to Cs.

The covenantal lord also establishes:

If S1 takes O2 from S2, then S2 must take O1 from S1.

---

[2] Cf. *Sémiotique*, art. "Occultation".

I.e. the covenantal lord establishes:

> If Cl takes X1 from Cs, then Cs must take Y1 from Cl;
> if Cs takes Y2 from Cl, then Cl must take X2 from Cs.

X and Y are *injuries* (cf. to serve versus to injure), either degressions or repressions (turned against a progression or against a protection against degression): if a given condition has been met, S2 (Cl or Cs) is obliged to exercise a dispossession/appropriation.

If the covenantal lord as a contracting party accepts the covenant, he presents the conditional *threat* that if Cs takes Y2 from Cl, then Cl will take X2 from Cs. The covenantal servant's acceptance also involves a threat, but the question is of course whether seriously he will be able to exercise a degression or repression towards the covenantal lord. If the covenantal lord has committed himself to a project whose realization depends upon the covenantal servant's active participation, then he will be vulnerable to degression and repression. But if the covenantal lord renounces the covenant because the covenantal servant has nothing to offer that the covenantal lord desires, it is invalid: the covenantal relationship is asymmetrical.

The take is now degressive, now repressive: if S2 does not give O2 to S1, a repression is concerned in which S2 withholds O2 from S1. In the same way, the giving of a gift is now progressive and now protective: if S1 does not take O2 from S2 a protection is concerned in which S1 allows S2 to keep O2:

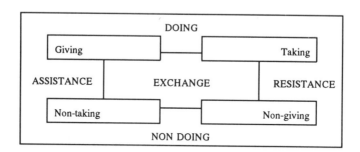

It is this *structure of exchange* that constitutes the covenant's innermost being.

a. Take versus Gift
The Take

The salvation project includes an exchange of services (mutual giving), but the take (mutual taking) is not merely included for the sake of the model's completeness.

This project's initial degression process clearly refers to this aspect of the covenant. But as pointed out, the covenant is asymmetrical, and there is only the one possibility:

If Cs takes Y2 from Cl, then Cl must take X2 from Cs

which seems to make sense.

The gospel narrative does not recount that Jesus takes something from God. But in the introductory degression phase God is nevertheless defined by having to take Jesus' life (transition from Provisional life to Definitive death, which does not, however, manage to become realized). And either this situation is unfounded, which annuls the story's narrative rationality, or God is obliged to destroy, because a certain condition has been met: Jesus has taken something from God. If it is borne in mind that in this phase Jesus shares the fate of the rest of mankind, "Jesus" is here merely a representative of the collective actor, Man. Although the gospel narrative does not itself recount the malefaction (take) Man has committed, it presupposes this act, which was either never recounted or is available as recounted in another narrative, for example Gen 2,4b-3,24, the narrative of Adam and Eve. The intertextual relationship between the gospel narrative and the Fall myth will be considered in detail below, cf. Chapter XIV.

The Gift

Recognition of the gospel narrative as a covenantal narrative requires the ability to indicate and retain a pertinent level of signification in which Jesus appears relative to God in the role of giver: death on the cross is a gift. Framed by the covenant's exchange structure, death on the cross and resurrection become interactively exchanged services whose narrative rationality is given by the following covenantal rules:

1)   if Cl gives X1 to Cs, then Cs must give Y1 to Cl;
2)   if Cs gives Y2 to Cl, then Cl must give X2 to Cs.

In a theocentric perspective, the question then becomes what in fact does Jesus give God in the death on the cross?

If Jesus gives his life (Y2) to God, then God gives eternal life (X2) to Jesus, according to covenantal rule 2). Jesus' performance (benefaction) is followed by God's sanction, which realizes for Jesus the state of being at which the covenant is aimed as far as he is concerned. The covenantal lord's sanction closes the covenantal servant's narrative trajectory. By virtue of the death on the cross, Jesus finds himself in a state of being in which he does not have eternal life but is entitled to it, because God, under the covenant he has himself established and of which he is himself the guarantor, owes it to him by virtue of the benefaction.

The death on the cross is in this perspective a prepayment by which God becomes indebted: he becomes the debtor. Jesus in turn becomes a creditor, and the resurrection is then the repayment that annuls the creditor/debtor relationship between covenantal servant and covenantal lord, but only in respect of the covenantal servant. Prior to this *christocentric reconciliation*, which satisfies the covenantal servant's desire, there is a theocentric reconciliation, which satisfies the covenantal lord's desire.

The death on the cross is bi-functional; it is at the same time prepayment (Y2) in regard to Jesus' being and repayment (Y1) in regard to God's being. Covenantal rule 1) is thus aimed at the covenantal lord's being, whereas covenantal rule 2) is aimed at the covenantal servant's being. Jesus owes to God his power to be able to act or to fail to act. By establishing the covenant, God has placed Jesus in a situation in which eternal life is possible and definitive death evitable. The anointing gives access to Definitive life and thus to the kingdom of God. At the same time, however, there is an opening from God's side involving the possibility of establishing an existence compatible with God's will (having to), which on the basis of the given incompatible existence means a *reconciliation*. The establishment of the covenant itself is the first step in the process that is to unite covenantal lord and covenantal servant, God and Man.

The anointing of Jesus of Nazareth is a renunciation, a sacrifice, which involves for God a reflexive degression, a self-abasement, in that he renounces his omnipotence. The covenantal objective he has set himself can then be realized only with Jesus' participation. By allowing Man in this way to play an integrated role in the realization of his own destiny, God has voluntarily accepted the impotence that results from his dependence on this human being. If it makes sense to speak of incarnation in Mark's Gospel, it is this action-opening declaration of love, this voluntarily accepted dependence relationship to Man, which constitutes the content of the term. God does not become Man, but factitively opens the way for the salvation and reconciliation project, which is to realize God and Man according to their true destiny, a destiny established since the days of the creation. God does not manage to hold on to his wrath, but is felled by love:

You are my Son, the Beloved; with you I am well pleased.

X1 is the covenantal servant's dynamic latitude of action or in its totality his modalized existence. Establishment of the covenant thus inducts Jesus as debtor, whereas God becomes creditor: Jesus owes it to God to observe the covenant in recognition of his merciful act, the anointing. When the covenantal servant accepts the covenant he accepts its obligations and thus his role as the debtor.

The obligation God imposes upon Jesus is that he must give his life. One might then be tempted to understand the matter in the sense that God is initially characterized by a disjunctive being S ∪ O, in which he does not have Jesus' life, and finally sees himself as determined by a conjunctive being S ∩ O, in which he has Jesus life. But God's being is not constituted by such pragmatic objects. What is important to Jesus is whether he has this life or not; his pragmatic being in fact undergoes a change in the death on the cross. But God does not desire Jesus' life in itself but as a pledge of love. He desires an obedient covenantal servant, but the covenantal lord is unable to fulfil this desire himself. He can achieve the coveted being only as a gift from his covenantal servant. When Jesus gives his life to God he gives himself (Y1) to the covenantal lord, who thus sees himself as rewarded for his merciful gift (X1). Jesus' self-denial is thus understood theocentrically as a sanction of God's being, the act that closes the covenantal lord's trajectory. When God subsequently repays this sanction by raising Jesus, a pragmatic process of change is again concerned as regards Jesus, but his acquisition of eternal life is not of course paralleled by a loss of being for God.

Within the theocentric soteriology it is Jesus who saves God, in that he fulfils or satisfies his desire. If narrative exegesis' definitions remind one of a classical satisfaction doctrine, this is only because it has been able to arrive at an analysis of the semiotic phenomena in the gospel narrative upon which such a doctrine presumably rests.[3]

3. The Trajectory of the Covenantal Lord

As already pointed out, the being that God has established as his own covenantal objective can be acquired only as a gift, not as a take. He desires an obedient covenantal servant, a human being, who senses what God thinks and does not merely follow his own wanting to. If one allows oneself to consider this covenantal servant (referred to as S for subject) as a kind of object of value, then the narrative trajectory that falls under the covenantal lord (referred to as A for *l'Autre*, the Other, i.e. a subject that is Destinator) can be defined by way of introduction as follows:

Manipulation

        Initial state $(Ab \cup (Ah \cup S)$

Performance   ⇓

        Intermediate state $(Ab \cap (Ah \cup S)$

Sanction   ⇓

        Final state $(Ab \cap (Ah \cap S)$

---

[3] On the satisfaction doctrine, cf., e.g., Albrecht Ritschl, *Die christliche Lehre von der Rechtfertigung und Versöhnung*, Bonn (1870) 1889, pp. 31.

Manipulation should here be understood as self-influencing, whereby God defines himself as a virtual subject of doing/being that lacks a being. Performance is an act whereby God qualifies himself as worthy to receive this being, i.e. an act that validates him as a creditor. Sanction is then a *quid pro quo* in which the covenantal servant gives himself and realizes the covenantal lord's being. In the covenantal lord's narrative trajectory, therefore, it is the covenantal servant who appears in the role of sanctioner or retributor.

The covenantal servant's performance is bi-functional in this perspective. The delivery of the object of value is a delivery of O as well as of S. Whether Jesus gives his life (O; 10.45) or himself (S; ἑαυτόν, cf. 1 Tim 2,6; also Gal 1,4; 2,20; Eph 5,2; Titus 2,14) seems to make no difference. It is, however, possible to distinguish this act as δόσις of O and as παράδοσις of S (cf. Gal 2,20; Eph 5,2). If God requires that Jesus give his life, this is because he requires a visible pledge of his obedience, an act that witnesses to his realized self-denial and self-abandonment.

As is known, any form of obedience to the covenant's requests (interdiction/ prescription) demands self-denial. The interdiction only makes sense if the covenantal servant wants what is interdicted; the prescription only makes sense if the covenantal servant does not want what is prescribed. The covenant thus always contains a self-denial requirement, and the realized covenantal process may be read as the process by which the introductory contradiction between the covenantal lord's having to and the covenantal servant's wanting to is annulled for the benefit of an agreement. This inter-subjective contrast will immediately be established as an intra-subjective contradiction in the covenantal servant himself, as a conflict between spirit and flesh. In this perspective, the covenantal process is an individuation process that establishes an equilibrium of the self. What is distinctive about the covenant between God and Jesus is the requirement's extremity; that it demands obedience (ὑπακοή) to the point of death (cf. Phil 2,8).

In his being, the covenantal servant S is double defined. One can distinguish the *including* being (S over O), where he is defined in relation to the object of being O (S ∪/∩ O), from the *included* being (A over S), where he himself is defined as object of value in relation to the covenantal lord A; (A ∪/∩ S). The death on the cross is a bi-functional act because it intervenes modifyingly into the including and included being. It not only establishes the (Sb ∩ (Sh ∪ O) state of being but also the (Ab ∩ (Ah ∩ S) state of being. In the covenantal servant's trajectory the death on the cross is a performance (renunciation), but in the covenantal lord's trajectory it is a sanction (attribution). Jn 19,30 "When Jesus had received the wine, he said, 'It is finished.' Then he bowed his head and gave up his spirit." emphasizes the sanction. In fact Jesus surrenders (παραδίδωμι) his spirit, i.e. his life, to God with the word τετέλεσται, it is finished, i.e. the prescribed act has now been realized, the task performed.[4] But in strict terms the objective of being has been reached only as concerns the covenantal lord. Only the resurrection will induct Jesus into Being. Narrative exegesis can now try inferentially to reconstruct the covenantal lord's narrative trajectory.

Manipulation. The reflexive manipulation splits the covenantal lord into a manipulating and a manipulated body (cf. the concept of βουλὴ τοῦ θεοῦ, for example Acts 13,36), and the first step must consist in a semiotization, which designates the manipulated as a subject characterized by an absence of being. This initial situation can be stated as follows:

$$A') \; Cl \cup (Ab \cap (Ah \cap S),$$

i.e. by disjunction the covenantal lord (Cl) God is related to an abundance of being. The established covenantal objective (Ab ∩ (Ah ∩ S), in which he will have his covenantal servant legitimately, is missing.

The next step must be the manipulated's acceptance of the designated role of being and the role of doing associated therewith, i.e. an acceptance of the covenant. This must accept the assigned being in an initial recognition of the manipulating:

$$B') \; Cl \cap (Ab \cup (Ah \cup S),$$

i.e. God has accepted the assigned being as his being and is now in conjunction with a specific lack of being. To God, the covenant's project is an annulment of this lack of being, but this can only happen with participation on the part of Jesus. The manipulation phase is concluded by this acceptance.

Performance. The next phase is the performance phase that appears to be particularly complex, since the first step here consists of the performance of a narrative act that can be understood only as a take. God appropriates the desired subject:

$$C') \; Cl \cap (Ab \cup (Ah \cap S),$$

---

[4] C.H. Dodd is uncertain "Whether the unusual phrase παρέδωκε τὸ πνεῦμα (...) is to be understood in the sense that Jesus in dying bequeathed the Holy Spirit to the world He was leaving, or whether it simply means that He surrendered the spirit (or vital principle) to God who gave it (...)", *The Interpretation of the Fourth Gospel*, Cambridge 1970, p. 428. In a note, he comments that "ἀποδοῦναι is the proper verb for restoring a gift to the giver, or delivering property to its rightful owner". But παραδοῦναι is "more often used of 'handing on' a piece of property (or a piece of information, or the like) to a successor; yet it is quite properly used of 'surrendering' (a city, ship, or person, for example) to a superior; and that is not far from a sense which would be quite appropriate here". That Dodd is in doubt and finds ἀφῆκε τὸ πνεῦμα (cf. Mt 27,50) "more natural" may be because he does not appreciate the function of the death on the cross in the covenantal exchange between God and Jesus. The interpretation that in death Jesus surrenders the Holy Spirit to the world he is leaving seems quite unfounded. In the light of Gal 2,20, Eph 5,2 and also Acts 15,26, there should be no doubt that Jesus delivers up the spirit/himself to God.

which is now possessed, although unrightfully. This take is the manipulation of the covenantal servant, who is apprehended by force.

The subject called is established as virtual covenantal servant, but if it does not accept the covenant it must die. Covenantal servant or death, this is the alternative, and so during this phase the covenantal lord thus acts quite intimidatingly.

The manipulation includes an interpellation (call in the sense of invocation), in that the covenantal lord intervenes without warning in the subject's world (for example in the form of an epiphany) and holds this in a double grip, partly by virtue of the intimidation associated with the virtual covenantal servant's fear of destruction, partly by virtue of the seduction associated with his desire for a certain state of being.

It also includes an alienation, in that the covenantal lord shows the covenantal servant who is master of the coveted objects and the coveted subjects. Finally, the manipulation includes a semiotization, in that the covenantal lord initiates the covenantal servant into the rule that applies to the legitimate acquisition of the coveted being. The covenantal servant thus sees himself as fatally in disjunction of the coveted abundance of being:

A) $Cs \cup (Sb \cap (Sh \cap O)$.

But this state of being can be achieved if the covenantal servant accepts the covenant:

B) $Cs \cap (Sb \cup (Sh \cup O)$;

and accepts the assigned lack of being, a role of being with associated role of doing. Failing this, he will be destroyed. The manipulation is a take, the covenantal servant is really in the hands of the covenantal lord. As far as Jesus is concerned, the fact is that a rejection of the covenant involves the realization of the destruction. Acceptance, on the other hand, means that the provisional life is tolerated as starting point for a progressive process:

C) $Cs \cap (Sb \cup (Sh \cap O)$.

It should be noted here that the $Cs \cap (Sb \cup (Sh \cup O)$ state of being, where Jesus does not have *Life*, but neither is he entitled to it, coincides with the $Cs \cap (Sb \cup (Sh \cap O)$ state of being, where Jesus has *Life*, but unrightfully. It is given by *Life*'s semantics that the starting point must be that the covenantal servant is alive. A living person can give his life, but a dead person cannot take his life. But if Jesus has *Life* unrightfully, this is equivalent to his having it as the result of a take, cf. Gen 2,4b-3,24.

The next step in the covenantal lord's performance is a renunciation, a giving. The covenantal servant is. released:

$$\text{D') } Cl \cap (Ab \cap (Ah \cup S),$$

and by this action the covenantal lord qualifies himself as worthy of reward, sanction. It is the sending. Like Jesus being driven out ($\dot\epsilon\kappa\beta\dot\alpha\lambda\lambda\omega$, 1,12) into the wilderness to be tempted by Satan, he is driven out in a confrontation with the mission he has been set to realize.

God withdraws, the heavens close, and the covenantal servant is left to his own devices. The words on the cross, "My God, my God, why have you forsaken me?" bear witness to the covenantal servant's unprotected freedom (cf. how Adam's/Eve's malefaction is similarly preconditioned by God's absence).

Sanction. The death on the cross is a performance, which for Jesus brings about a change of both being (from negative to positive deixis) and having:

$$\text{D) } Cs \cap (Sb \cap (Sh \cup O).$$

For God, however, a sanction is concerned, in that Jesus gives himself to him:

$$\text{E') } Cl \cap (Ab \cap (Ah \cap S),$$

and thereby realizes his Being. This is the realized reconciliation, where Man abolishes the debtor relationship that it has inflicted upon itself by the original transgression in the garden of Eden. God is hereby free (realised) to complete his project, which consists initially in the resurrection of Jesus:

$$\text{E) } Cs \cap (Sb \cap (Sh \cap O).$$

The ascension is the spatial conjunction that indicates that the process of union (reconciliation) has been completed.

The covenantal lord's narrative trajectory can then be given as follows:

DOING		BEING
A' Manipulation/Cl	$\rightarrow$	$Cl \cup (Ab \cap (Ah \cap S)$
B' Qualifying performance/Cl	$\rightarrow$	$Cl \cap (Ab \cup (Ah \cup S)$
C' Principal performance/Cl	$\rightarrow$	$Cl \cap (Ab \cup (Ah \cap S)$
D' Glorifying performance/Cl	$\rightarrow$	$Cl \cap (Ab \cap (Ah \cup S)$
E' Sanction/Cs	$\rightarrow$	$Cl \cap (Ab \cap (Ah \cap S)$

The catalytic definition of the covenantal lord's narrative trajectory shows that Mark's Gospel includes the narrative, although hidden, of an inter-active action whose responsible subjects of doing are God (Cl) and Jesus (Cs), and whose favoured subject of being is God (Cl). The distinction introduced between christocentric and theocentric soteriology has shown its full justification, and it should also be noted that the reconciliation concept is not feasible without the idea of satisfaction of God's desire.

The covenantal servant's narrative trajectory has precisely the same form as that of the covenantal lord:

DOING		BEING
A Manipulation/Cl	→	$Cs \cup (Sb \cap (Sh \cap O)$
B Qualifying performance/Cs	→	$Cs \cap (Sb \cup (Sh \cup O)$
C Principal performance/Cs	→	$Cs \cap (Sb \cup (Sh \cap O)$
D Glorifying performance/Cs	→	$Cs \cap (Sb \cap (Sh \cup O)$
E Sanction/Cl	→	$Cs \cap (Sb \cap (Sh \cap O)$

In the gospel narrative, the manipulation is not specifically developed but is presupposed. Exegesis must infer Jesus' qualifying performance, his acceptance of the covenant, on the basis of his transition to action, but cf. 8,33 and 14,61. The principal performance is completely absent because it has already been realized.[5]

The starting point cannot be Definitive death but only Provisional life, which by the manipulation's semiotization sees itself defined as a state of being in which Jesus has *Life*, but unrightfully. The glorifying performance is the death on the cross, where he does not have *Life* but has a right to it, and the sanction is the resurrection, where he has *Life* rightfully, i.e. eternal life.

The covenant's exchange structure is clear in relations between these two trajectories. God's glorifying performance, i.e. the act through which he obtains worthiness of reward, is the release of Jesus, who now has his existence as a gift (prepayment). Jesus reciprocates this gift by giving himself (repayment) in the death on the cross, and thereby he sanctions God's being. But the death on the cross is at the same time Jesus' glorifying performance (prepayment), which

---

[5] The principal performance (the taking) should not be confused with the narrative's pivotal point, although there may be coincidences, e.g. in the folktale in which the hero takes the princess from the dragon. Thereby he comes to possess her, but illegitimately, and she must therefore be returned to the king (glorifying performance). Only from here can he receive her as a legitimate object of value by virtue of marriage (sanction). It is true that the death on the cross is a decisive performance, but the gospel narrative's pivotal point is nevertheless the glorifying performance, a giving.

invokes God's sanction (repayment) in the form of resurrection, i.e. acquisition of eternal life. It is the interaction between God's and Jesus' narrative trajectory that constitutes the salvation project's covenantal schema and defines the gospel narrative's principal mythos by its beginning (manipulation/anointing), middle (performance/death on the cross) and ending (sanction/resurrection).

B. GLOBAL SOTERIOLOGY

The global soteriology concerns the salvation project that is accomplished by virtue of Jesus' reappearance, his parousia. The realization of the local salvation project has (virtual, actualized or realized) consequences for mankind and for the world, which gives occasion to distinguish an *anthropocentric* and a *cosmocentric* soteriology in which the former can be defined more specifically as an *ecclesiocentric* soteriology.

1. Ecclesiocentric Soteriology

When Jesus appears in the role of the one who calls, ὁ καλῶν (cf. 1,20; 2,17), in the gospel narrative, he appears at the same time in the roles:

$$\text{ἐκκαλῶν - ἐκκαλέω - ἐκκλησία}$$
$$\text{ἐκλεκτικός - ἐκλέγω - ἐκλογή}$$

i.e. as he who calls and elects a new chosen people. In a broader sense, the disciples are those who are called (οἱ ἔκκλητοι = ἐκκλησία; cf. 2,17) and elected as a new people of God (οἱ ἐκλεκτοί; cf. 13,20.22.27; ἡ ἐκλογή, cf. Rom 11.7).

As apostles, the disciples' mission is to proclaim the gospel to all nations between ascension and parousia. But this proclamation project is not only to inform. The proclamation, which consists, basically, *in narrating the gospel story*, is a persuasive discourse that semiotizingly initiates the one called and enrolls him in the role of a subject of being whose existence is defined and interpreted by the events narrated. The proclamation is a call, a fishing for men, which establishes the one addressed as a virtual disciple, and he must now seek his own self-knowledge in the light of the roles that characterize the gospel narrative's disciples. The listener's question to the narrator, "Why do you tell me this?", must already have been answered by the gospel narrative itself, in that it thematizes the relationship between Jesus and his disciples in a soteriological perspective.

The main question is, what significance does Jesus' death on the cross have to the disciples' being? The gospel narrative's ecclesiocentric soteriology can therefore be defined, in that exegesis on the one hand disregards the local salvation project (God and Jesus as subjects of being) and on the other hand disregards the global salvation project's cosmocentric soteriology (the world as subject of being). The pertinence level thereby established can then be given as:

1)   Mark is trying to convey to his reader the concept of a state of being (eternal life/the kingdom of God) and of an interactive action (the creation project).
2)   The subject of being for this state/action is the disciples.
3)   The responsible subject of doing for this state/action is Jesus and the disciples.

The salvation project, which leads to Jesus' resurrection, and the creation project, which leads to the realization of the kingdom of God, are two connected processes within one and the same creation or salvation project. If one moves from the question of Jesus' salvation to the question of the disciples' or followers' salvation, it then becomes clear that the acquisition of eternal life coincides with the entry into the kingdom of God: to enter life ($\epsilon\iota\sigma\epsilon\rho\chi o\mu\alpha\iota$ $\epsilon\iota\varsigma$ $\tau\eta\nu$ $\zeta\omega\eta\nu$, 9,43.45) is to enter into the kingdom of God ($\epsilon\iota\sigma\epsilon\rho\chi o\mu\alpha\iota$ $\epsilon\iota\varsigma$ $\tau\eta\nu$ $\beta\alpha\sigma\iota\lambda\epsilon\iota\alpha\nu$ $\tau o\upsilon$ $\theta\epsilon o\upsilon$, 9,47; cf. 10,15.23f).

After resurrection and ascension, Jesus sits at the right hand of the Power. When the time is fulfilled, he will come in clouds and send out the angels, and gather his elect (13,26), and lead them into the kingdom of God to eternal life. In a cosmocentric perspective in which the world is subject of being the kingdom of God is defined by the Cosmos/Chaos isotopy, but in an anthropological perspective in which the subject of being is the individual, this is defined by the LIFE/DEATH isotopy. From various points of view one and the same phenomenon is concerned, and these isotopies are therefore also isomorphous and semantically homologous; definitive cosmos corresponds to definitive life.

However, in contrast to what might have been expected, namely that Jesus' resurrection and the final realization of the kingdom of God coincide, it is Jesus alone who is raised. Only later, in association with the parousia, are those who belong to him raised up. Paul speaks of Christ as having "been raised from the dead, the first fruits ($\alpha\pi\alpha\rho\chi\eta$) of those who have died" (1 Cor 15,20). A distinction must therefore be made between Jesus' *mythical and local salvation* and the elect's *ritual and global salvation*, in that a mythical act is here understood as an act that on the one hand establishes the potential condition for, and on the other hand prescribes, the content of a ritual act. The word "rite" is employed here in a broad sense, i.e. as a term for everything to do with the formation of a symbolic community and the life of that community. The adjective "ritual" refers to any act of worship that is founded on the mythical act.

The mythical salvation is a matter between God and Jesus. But the ritual salvation is a matter between Jesus and his elect, which opens the way to a sociological perspective of the kingdom of God. Between the individual perspective (LIFE/DEATH; my salvation) and the cosmocentric perspective (Cosmos/ Chaos; the world's salvation), is given a collective or ecclesiological perspective (our, i.e. the elect's salvation). It is as a member of a people, a community, that the individual can be saved. The raising of Jesus was the raising of one individual; the raising of the disciples becomes the raising of the community, i.e. a collective person.

a. The Redeemer

A central text in defining the gospel narrative's global soteriology is 10,45: "For the Son of Man came not to be served but to serve (διακονέω), and to give (δίδωμι) his life a ransom (λύτρον) for many (ἀντὶ πολλῶν)." In this perspective, interest is concentrated on the death on the cross as a ransom for many.

The term λύτρον (means of liberation, ransom; ἀντίλυτρον, cf. 1 Tim 2,6) defines Jesus by way of the thematic role:

$$\lambda \upsilon \tau \rho \omega \tau \acute{\eta} \varsigma - \lambda \upsilon \tau \rho o \hat{\upsilon} \mu \alpha \iota - \lambda \acute{\upsilon} \tau \rho \omega \sigma \iota \varsigma,$$

i.e. as deliverer or *redeemer* (cf. Acts 7,35; Lk 24,21; Titus 2,14; 1 Pet 1,18; Lk 1,68; 2,38; Heb 9,12). This savior role can be considered as hyposynonymous with the role:

$$\lambda \upsilon \tau \acute{\eta} \rho - \lambda \acute{\upsilon} \omega - \lambda \acute{\upsilon} \sigma \iota \varsigma,$$

i.e. the releaser, the liberator, since λύω is understood in the sense of: release, liberate, ransom, redeem, satisfy, atone, make good again (cf. Mt 16.19; 18,18; Jn 11,44; Rev 1,5); λύσις in the sense: release, redemption, liberation, discharge, payment of debt, release from guilt. Cf. the parasynonymous roles ἀπολύτηρ - ἀπολύω - ἀπόλυσις (cf. for example Mt 18,27; Mk 15,6; Lk 13,12; Acts 16,35; Heb 13,23) and ἀπολυτρωτής - ἀπολυτρόω - ἀπολύτρωσις (cf. Lk 21,28; Rom 3,24; 8,23; 1 Cor 1,30; Eph 1,7.14; 4,30; Col 1,14; Heb 9,15).

The term ἀντάλλαγμα, Mk 8,37, is parasynonymous with ἀντίλυτρον, ἄλλαγμα (cf. LXX, Isa 43,3) with λύτρον. What is concerned is means of exchange, what one receives or gives in return, ransom. 8,37 may be translated as: "Indeed, what can they give as ransom for their life?". The subject of being who has life unrightfully shall lose it. To be able to preserve his life, the subject of being must give compensation therefore, an equivalent, which then becomes a ransom. But Man has nothing to give as ransom for his life; he is powerless, and can only await the transitive take that realizes death.

The basic meaning of the verb ἀλλάσσω is to change something into something else, to exchange something with something else. It is in the changing, exchanging, sense that the word is of interest in this context, where it initially gives an opportunity to select two parasynonymous roles:

$$ἀλλάσσων - ἀλλάσσω - ἀλλαγή,$$
$$ἀνταλλάσσων - ἀνταλλάσσω - ἀνταλλαγή.$$

The composition of the verb with the preposition ἀπό also gives the role:

$$ἀπαλλάσσων - ἀπαλλάσσω - ἀπαλλαγή,$$

cf. Heb 2,15. One liberates oneself or others from something, an obligation, a creditor (with whom one reconciles). Finally there appears the role:

$$καταλλάσσων - καταλλάσσω - καταλλαγή,$$

where καταλλάσσω means 1) to exchange, to interchange, 2) redeem, reconcile; καταλλαγή means 1) an exchange, interchange, 2) redemption, reconciliation, cf. Rom 5,10 "For if ... we were reconciled to God through the death of his Son, much more surely, having been reconciled, will we be saved by his life."; also 2 Cor 5,18f; also ἀποκαταλλάσσω, Eph 2,16; Col 1,20.

What is remarkable is that the redemption and reconciliation are associated with an *exchange*, an *interchange*. This interactive act (an interchange calls for two parties) can take place only within the framework of a *covenant* that establishes the worth of the object of value being exchanged and interchanged. Cf. also ἱλαστήριον in the sense of a means of atonement (Rom 3,25); ἱλασμός (propitiation, expiation; atoning sacrifice, 1 Jn 2,2; 4,10); ἱλάσκομαι (to appease, to make a sacrifice of atonement for, Heb 2,17).

The liberation theme gives an opportunity to include meaningfully Zech 9,11 (cf. Zech 9,9 and Mk 11,1ff), in which the covenantal blood (LXX: τὸ αἷμα διαθήκης, cf. Mk 14,24) appears to be the ransom that liberates the prisoners from the waterless pit. The pit figure (LXX: λάκκος, cistern; cf. Mt 12,11: βόθυνος, pit; Lk 14,5: φρέαρ well, cistern) is a particularly compact image. Whether the subject of being is to be found in the well as a direct consequence of an error (the sheep that falls in), or as an indirect consequence of an offence (the well as a dungeon), its dynamic latitude will be so restricted that it cannot itself preserve its life.

A fatal repression or degression is concerned. Liberation is either direct (the sheep is pulled out), or indirect, in that the repressor releases his prisoners. The release takes place, for example, because someone other than the victim himself has paid the ransom, which the repressor has fixed as equivalent compensation for the injury it imposed upon him. The prisoners themselves are unable to remedy the injury suffered; they cannot pay their debt, and therefore they incur punishment. When the debt is paid their unworthiness is neutralized, the reasons for punishment are voided, and they are released.

The "many" subject of being are prisoners who cannot change their situation. They are threatened by a fatal degression process; they have life but have no right to it, and therefore it must be lost. They find themselves in the Provisional life state of being, which is fatally orientated towards the Definitive death state of being. For Jesus, the liberation or deliverance consists in paying the price necessary to make the repressor, in this case God, annul this situation. The death on the cross is the fixed price, the ransom is his life.

It should be noted that both the repression and the liberation have a dual perspective. The repression not only places the subject of being in a situation in which definitive death is inevitable, but also in a situation in which definitive life is impossible. Similarly, the liberation is on the one hand a liberation from a fatal degression (definitive death is inevitable), and on the other hand a liberation to a virtual progression (eternal life is possible). The term "ransom" should similarly be seen in a dual perspective. On the one hand what is concerned is a debt that has to be paid, a guilt that must be atoned for: here God is a creditor, the claimant, Jesus a debtor, the obligor, and the death on the cross then becomes the act by which the imbalance, the difference between the parties, is annulled, obliterated: it is the reconciliation between God and Man. But on the other hand the death on the cross makes Jesus a creditor and God a debtor. It is this evangelic reversal that makes an opening for the future-orientated eschatological being.

In the death on the cross Jesus gives his life as a ransom for many ($\dot{\alpha}\nu\tau\dot{\iota}$ $\pi o\lambda\lambda\hat{\omega}\nu$). The use of "many" does not exclude the meaning "all" but emphasizes the asymmetry between the one subject of doing and the many subjects of being who are benefited by the action.[6] This benefit, which can be understood only in relation to the kingdom of God and eternal life, is either a pragmatic, a covenantal or a modal progression.

A pragmatic progression would mean that this collective subject of being realized eternal life by virtue of the death on the cross, and this possibility is therefore excluded. A covenantal progression would be equivalent to this collective subject of being seeing itself as qualified by the death on the cross as worthy of eternal life (like Jesus himself), but neither is this situation present. There remains only the modal progression in which the death on the cross consist of a factitive change in the collective subject of being's dynamic modalization. The subject of being is benefited by Jesus' death on the cross, because this event involves a modal change: the subject of being that initially finds itself in a situation where salvation is impossible (eternal life is impossible) sees itself placed by Jesus' death on the cross in a new situation in which salvation is possible (eternal life is possible).

---

[6] Cf. Vincent Taylor, *The Gospel According to St. Mark*, London 1959, pp.444.

316 THE SAVIOR

In this perspective, liberation is not the neutralization of the threatening degression process but the annulment of repression. By the anointing, God opened the door to the kingdom of God to Jesus. But only as a possibility. By his covenantal obedience, Jesus opens the door to the kingdom of God for all others, but here also only a possibility is concerned. The question then becomes what the beneficiary as virtual subject of doing must do to realize this possibility.

b. The Heir and the Follower

At a given moment, *before the death on the cross*, which proves crucial to the understanding, the gospel narrative simply thematizes the question of what is to be done to qualify oneself as worthy of eternal life. This occurs in the basic sequence, "The rich man and eternal life", 10,17ff.

A rich man approaches Jesus and asks: "What must I do to inherit eternal life?". Jesus refers to the well-known commandments, but he has kept to these.[7] Jesus then says to him: "You lack one thing; go, sell what you own, and give the money to the poor, and you will have treasure in heaven; then come, follow me." (10,21). However, the rich man becomes uneasy at these words and goes away grieving; "for he had many possessions". Jesus then says to his disciples: "How hard it will be for those who have wealth to enter the kingdom of God!" (10,23). The disciples are perplexed, but Jesus begins to speak again: "Children, how hard it is to enter the kingdom of God! It is easier for a camel to go through the eye of a needle than for someone who is rich to enter the kingdom of God!" (10,24). These words astound the disciples even more, and in fear they ask: "Then who can be saved?".

The question, "What must I do to inherit eternal life?" is identical with the question, "What must I do to be saved?". But it is doubtful whether, in strict terms, this question can be answered without taking Jesus' death on the cross into consideration. Exegesis must be aware that the question is raised at a moment when the salvation project has not as yet been realized.

This world, which is contrasted with the world to come (cf. 10,30), may be considered as a kingdom (K1), which is contrasted with the kingdom of God (K2). To obtain citizenship ($\pi o\lambda\iota\tau\epsilon\iota\alpha$, $\pi o\lambda\iota\tau\epsilon\upsilon\mu\alpha$, cf. Phil 3,20) of the kingdom of God one must renounce citizenship of this kingdom. Entry into the kingdom of God thus presupposes egress from the other kingdom that must be left, given up. But $\dot{\epsilon}\xi o\delta o\varsigma$ and $\dot{\epsilon}\iota\sigma o\delta o\varsigma$ do not coincide. Between egress and entry there is a transitional phase in which the subject of being has already left K1 but not yet reached K2.

He who sells all and follows Jesus has cut himself off from this world and its values (treasures; esteem, power and glory) in favour of other values to be found elsewhere ("a treasure in heaven"). But thereby he has already achieved a diffe-

---

[7] Jesus refers to the Decalogue (Ex 20,1-17; Deut 5,6-21).

rent status, which will subsequently be finally accomplished. The rich man asked Jesus what he must do to inherit eternal life (ζωὴν αἰώνιον κληρονομέω), which is the same as asking what he must do to become *heir* (κληρονόμος) to eternal life, i.e. to obtain right of inheritance or of citizenship in the kingdom of God.[8]

An heir is a person who does not have a given value but has a right to this. As such, he is the antithesis of a thief, who has a given value but has no right to it. In both cases there is an imbalance or tension that is cancelled out only when the heir has his inheritance bestowed upon him as his lawful possession and the booty is taken from the thief (or he himself returns it).

One cannot get around the fact that the prescription to give all one owns refers to a perception of value according to which the wealth is owned unrightfully, i.e. as the result of a take. He who renounces the values of this world does not immediately receive eternal life but is given a right to it, receives the status of heir.

An interactive action is also concerned here, whose rationality is established by a covenantal relationship. To begin with, the inquirer is in a state of being in which he does not have eternal life, neither has he a right to it. He then inquires about the prescribed performance to be undertaken to achieve the status of heir to eternal life, i.e. achieve the worthiness that is rewarded by eternal life in a positive sanction.

A narrative trajectory can thus be envisaged:

Manipulation			
	Initial state	(Sb ∪ (Sh ∪ O)	
Performance		⇓	- Following
	Intermediate state	(Sb ∩ (Sh ∪ O)	
Sanction		⇓	- Resurrection
	Final state	(Sb ∩ (Sh ∩ O)	

The performance to qualify for the role of heir is initially a renunciation, a sacrifice, which consists in parting with all pecuniary objects of value. But then added to this comes the requirement of following that concerns life and death.

Jesus answers the rich man's question by referring him to the role of *follower*:

ἀκόλουθος - ἀκολουθέω - ἀκολουθία,

---

[8] Cf., e.g., Mt 19,29; 25,34; 1 Cor 6,9f; 15,50; Gal 5,21; Titus 3,7; Jas 2,5.

(cf. 1,18; 2,14f; 6,1; 8,34; 10,21.28; 14,54; also the role μιμητής - μιμέομαι - μίμησις, 1 Cor 4,16; 11,1; 1 Thess 1,6). However, he who wishes to follow in Jesus' footsteps must deny himself and take up his cross and follow him (8,34). In other words: the follower must follow Jesus unto death, drinking the cup that he must drink and being baptized with the baptism with which he was baptized (10,38). When Jesus asks the sons of Zebedee whether they are able to live up to this demand, they arrogantly reply, "We are able." (10,39). Later, all the disciples make a promise to accept the follower role and go with Jesus to death: "Even though I must die with you, I will not deny you.", says Peter, and "And all of them said the same." (14,31).

Before the death on the cross, the role of the follower can be defined as a role, which designates the narrative subject as a virtual subject of doing for a task that consists simply of sharing a common fate with Jesus. Jesus' narrative trajectory, in which the death on the cross is the meritorious performance, and the follower's narrative trajectory thereby become *identical*. The place of the death on the cross is taken by the imitation unto death, and the follower understands himself as imitator. The rich man turns sadly away, he considers himself unable to assume the role and task assigned. But the disciples, who have not yet realized the gravity and radicality of the requirement, arrogantly promise to accept the role and its project.

The question is, however, whether this task is in any way possible. One may observe that, if it is possible, then it will be possible for each individual disciple to accomplish precisely the same performance as Jesus realizes in the salvation project. Anyone will be able through his own pragmatic doing to qualify as worthy of eternal life. But in that event it becomes difficult to understand what the redemption and liberation of the many actually consists of. If the follower is to do precisely the same as Jesus, has to imitate him, then any talk of representation is meaningless. Also, it is remarkable that no one, not even Jesus' closest disciples, is actually able to follow him unto death. They all flee (14.50). It is true that Peter follows him at a distance right into the courtyard of the high priest (14,54), but only to deny him (14,66ff). The gospel narrative thus contradicts in various ways the idea that following in this straightforward (identical) sense should be possible. If the requirement of imitation is the prescribed performance that alone can qualify the disciples as heirs to eternal life, then none of them is saved. Jesus goes alone into death, he is the only human being who is able to deny himself and live up to God's demand. In this perspective the imitation requirement serves to disclose the disciples' impotence, but at the same time it emphasizes what is unique in Jesus' salvation act.

The disciples' question: "Then who can be saved?" is not quite unambiguous. Does the question refer only to the salvation of the rich or to the salvation of all? On the one hand, the text is clear; it speaks of those who have wealth (10,23). Even verse 24b, "Children, how hard it is to enter the kingdom of God!", which is of a general nature, is itemized by the subsequent sentence in verse 25, "It is easier for a camel to go through the eye of a needle than for someone who is rich to enter the kingdom of God!" On the other hand, the disciples' perplexity (10,24.26) expresses the fact that they see themselves as affected by the teaching. Either they over-react, since they are not themselves rich, or their reaction is adequate, since the role of "the rich" is equivocal and is in fact aimed also at them and everyone else.

Wealth is a relative concept, and contains both a quantitative and a qualitative aspect. This is thematized in the narrative of the poor widow's offering, 12,41. The rich people put *large* sums (quantitative aspect) into the treasury, the poor widow only *little* (quantitative aspect), two small coins. But the rich people only give *something* (qualitative aspect) of their surplus, whereas the widow gives *everything* she has to live on (qualitative aspect). When everything one owns is given, all are equally rich in a certain sense, since all indeed become equally poor. But in addition to this is the requirement of imitation, which no longer relates to the pecuniary objects of value but to life itself. The consequence is that the imitation requirement is a requirement to give one's life.

Does this mean that total sacrifice of this kind is the precondition for salvation? The frightened disciples hasten to remind Jesus that they have indeed left everything (πάντα) and followed him. And Jesus asserts that all who have at this time (νῦν ἐν τῷ καιρῷ = in this world) performed a sacrifice for his or the gospel's sake will receive eternal life in the world to come. RUDOLF PESCH stresses that here Jesus' speech does not formulate the conditions for achieving eternal life but promises reward for certain acts. This is a matter not of entry requirements but of a guarantee of reward.[9] The question is, however, whether this sympathetic reading may merely express an opinion based on dogma. PESCH must at the very least explain the presuppositions under which his reading is valid.

On one important point the text is quite unambiguous. It concerns what one must do to inherit eternal life, i.e. what one must do to achieve the state of worthiness that is rewarded by eternal life; that is, it concerns the requirements of entry into the kingdom of God. Any talk of payment or reward is narratively meaningless if it does not refer to a meritorious act (the sacrifice) which, according to an implicit or explicit agreement, inducts the subject of doing into a state of worthiness (heir) that gives a right to a *quid pro quo* (eternal life). If, relative to the disciples, Jesus is really speaking of a guarantee of reward, this can of course only mean that the sacrifices referred to are not an entry requirement. But it would be a striking misunderstanding if one were therefore to assume that any talk of entry requirements was meaningless or contra-evangelical.

---

[9] Rudolf Pesch, *Das Markusevangelium, 2. Teil*, Freiburg 1980, p. 145.

It is scarcely fortuitous that Mark permits Jesus to speak to his disciples in general terms. He does not speak specifically about Peter and the other disciples but generally about the disciple role and anyone who has accepted this role for his sake and for the gospel's sake. And the question is whether this speech is directed at the situation beyond death on the cross and resurrection, as the reference to persecutions seems to imply, cf. 13,1ff. The cryptic formulation, "But many who are first will be last, and the last will be first.", 10,31, is then turned against Peter and the other disciples. It is true that the thematization of wealth makes the point that whoever is rich on earth is poor in heaven, while he who is poor on earth has treasure in heaven. But if one bears in mind that in a wider perspective the teaching of the rich man serves to teach the disciples, then the word has a sting directed against their doxomania. It is true that they have left all (pecuniary objects of value) and followed Jesus, but only because they expect thereby to qualify themselves to take part in the power and the glory.

To the disciples' question: "Then who can be saved?", a question testifying to the disciples' fear of not having been already inducted as heirs (or at least as privileged virtual heirs) to the glory's salvation by virtue of their discipleship, Jesus replies, "For mortals it is impossible, but not for God; for God all things are possible." Here it is said plainly: it is not possible for Man to qualify himself as worthy of eternal life. The rich man's question could be re-formulated: "What is a man to do to inherit eternal life?". Jesus answers by making the demand to abandon the values of the world and enter into the following. The disciples, it is true, have left everything (the pecuniary values) and followed Jesus, but they have not yet become aware of the radicality of the imitation requirement. When they finally realize what following involves they flee.

c. Baptism and Eucharist

Narrative exegesis tries to emphasize the gospel story's narrative articulation, and so turns against tendencies that seek to disarticulate its signification universe and thus to hypostatize its persons. Hypostasis would consist, for example, in isolating a given role in a certain situation in order subsequently to generalize it in an overall perspective. An utterance of the type, "For mortals it is impossible, but not for God; for God all things are possible.", might tempt one to hypostatize God as subject of doing; it is he who saves, and Man as subject of being is the one who is saved. However, the simplism that the disarticulation seeks fails to appreciate the complexity that characterizes the narrative's interactive universe. When exegesis falls to temptation and hypostatizes, it also fails to appreciate its own task and tends to carry out a static and abstract-dogmatic discourse.

The temptation to disarticulate is particularly intense for exegesis when it is confronted with a narrative that is not only complex but also lacking in information. What it means when it says that God alone can save is unclear, and the exegete is therefore content to establish: "Das eschatologische Heil des Menschen, auch des Reiches, liegt in seiner Hand.".[10] But the task must consist in trying to explain in detail what is actually meant by this. Exegesis must consider how this utterance interprets and is itself interpreted by the narrative rationality.

The Christian Baptism

In Acts, Peter's discourse ends with the words: "Therefore let the entire house of Israel know with certainty that God has made him both Lord and Messiah." (Acts 2,36). The discourse cuts to the heart of the listeners, and they ask Peter and the other apostles: "Brothers, what should we do?" (2,37). This is a question that any subject of being cut to the heart by the gospel narrative's message will also ask. The subject of being interpellated, which in the light of the gospel sees itself as favoured, will immediately inquire, since the favour is modal and not pragmatic, about the content of the role of virtual subject of doing arising from this new being. Peter could have replied: "You can do nothing; salvation lies in God's hands!"; or, "You must do nothing, for whatever was to be done has already been done!" But he answers them: "Repent, and be baptized every one of you in the name of Jesus Christ so that your sins may be forgiven; and you will receive the gift of the Holy Spirit." Acts 2,38.

Mark's Gospel contains, at least implicitly, a mission command: the gospel must be preached (κηρύσσω) to all nations (13,10; cf. 16,15). This gospel is the gospel of Jesus Christ (1,1), i.e. the gospel narrative (cf. 14,9), which proclaims that the time is fulfilled and the kingdom of God has come near. Those interpellated are therefore required to repent and believe in this narrative's message. The narrated proclamation has become a narrating proclamation. The presumed reader well understands that the demand to repent and believe, which is presented in the narrate, has its counterpart in the narration. As regards the demand to repent, Mark's Gospel therefore accords with the semiotically established terms. A narrative that designates its presumed reader as favoured subject of being must contain certain information about what this virtual subject of doing is to do. If this reader is prevented from questioning the person who communicates the narrative (cf. the question to Peter), he must seek the answer in the narrative itself, i.e. from its narrator.

Mark's Gospel contains no explicit baptism command (cf. Mt 28.19). In the pre-commissioning (6,7ff), the disciples are sent to preach and to heal. The re-commissioning no doubt includes the mission to proclaim, but the healing might here have been overtaken by baptism activities. The question of baptism beyond death on the cross and resurrection, i.e. the Christian baptism (versus the baptism of John), must however be unravelled in another way.

---

[10] Rudolf Pesch, ibidem, p. 143.

It could be said that the demand for following (8,34ff), a demand that consists in taking up the cross and following Jesus unto death, replaces the baptism command in Mark's Gospel. It is not to be understood that the demand for following is established directly by the post-paschal proclamation, but that the Christian baptism receives its signification content from the remarkable fact that, as a ritual act, it is equivalent in a crucial respect to following. It is of course possible for exegesis to disregard the Christian baptism, since Mark's Gospel does not explicitly refer to this practice. It cannot even be shown unambiguously that such a baptism practice was known within the gospel narrative's community, although this is probable. That narrative exegesis nevertheless involves the question of this Christian baptism is because the gospel narrative itself demands it. In a narrative perspective, however, the emphasis is not on the fact that in certain passages the gospel narrative seems to assume such a practice but that *as a consequence of its proclamation it demands it*. Mk 16,16, "The one who believes and is baptized will be saved; ..." only serves to make this point more explicit.

Following means that the disciple, the follower, must on the one hand renounce the glory of this world, pecuniary objects of value (wealth, power and honour), and on the other hand give his life as a sacrifice. Following means following Jesus unto death. In 10,38 Jesus refers to his principal performance, the death on the cross, as an act that consists in drinking a cup (cf. 14,36) and allowing himself to be baptized. The demand for following unto death can thus be formulated as a demand to drain the cup Jesus is to drain, or to be baptized by the baptism with which Jesus is to be baptized. In the context of their wish to obtain the promise of places of honour at his side in glory, Jesus asks the sons of Zebedee whether they will be able to live up to this request (10,38), and they arrogantly reply, "We are able." (10,39). James and John, however, do not know what they are saying (cf. 10,38). Their arrogant reply, which may be read as a promise to follow Jesus unto death (cf. 14,31), is fantasy. When it comes to the crunch, they are, as the narrative shows, unable to drain the cup or allow themselves to be baptized, but flee like all the others.

Against this background, Jesus' words to James and John, "The cup that I drink you will drink; and with the baptism with which I am baptized, you will be baptized; ..." (10,39), become ambiguous. Jesus cannot expect the sons of Zebedee to accompany him unto death, since they take flight. It is perhaps not entirely impossible that what is concerned is a case of *vaticinium post eventum*, but the question is whether a reading that sees in these words a reference to these disciples' post-paschal martyrdom does justice to the gospel narrative.[11]

---

[11] Cf. Vincent Taylor, *The Gospel According to St. Mark*, London 1959, p.440; Aage Pilgaard rightly points out "at forudsætningen for overhovedet at få del i hans herlighedsfælleskab er delagtighed i hans lidelsesfælleskab" (that the precondition for obtaining any share at all in his community of glory is participation in his community of suffering), but he does not explain in detail how this community is to

Although the words are spoken to the sons of Zebedee, the demand for following applies to all disciples, and it must therefore apply to anyone, i.e. all who accept the role of disciple, that he must drain the cup and be baptized. In this perspective, Jesus' discourse seems to allude only to eucharist and baptism.

From the perspective of tradition history there is no connection between 10,38 and the concept of a baptism into Christ Jesus, into his death, as is known from Rom 6,3f, asserts RUDOLF PESCH.[12] He is possibly correct in his assertion, but this does not exclude that for factual reasons the gospel narrative contains concepts of a similar nature. Within the context of the gospel story, the cup and the baptism in 10,38 cannot avoid raising the question of the eucharist and the baptism as ritual acts that see themselves as substantiated by this very narrative. It is not unreasonable to assume that Mark allows Jesus to refer to his death as a baptism because the baptism, the Christian baptism beyond resurrection, is a baptism into his death.[13] The cup, which refers to the eucharist, has been similarly employed about his death, because this ritual also gives the agent a participation in his savior act, the death on the cross.

The connection between death on the cross and baptism is, in evangelical terms, crucial. It is true that one may be immediately inclined to fasten on the similarity between Jesus' baptism by John and the Christians' baptism. The Christians allowed themselves to be baptized because Jesus was baptized. But the question remains whether the Christian baptism corresponds to Jesus' baptism or Jesus' death on the cross. In the first instance, the Christian is established by the baptism in a modal state of being in which eternal life is possible, i.e. may be realized through the fulfilment of certain conditions, for example the demand for imitation. The Christian is then in the same situation as Jesus himself. By matching up to certain obligations, he can qualify himself as worthy, as heir to eternal life. But the gospel narrative not only shows that this project is impossible, since the disciples, those closest to Jesus, fail; it also states plainly: it is impossible for human beings to qualify themselves as heirs to eternal life.

Exegesis should not allow itself to be seduced by the discourse's doctrinaire utterances, but should hold to the story's narrative articulation. It should thus be emphasized that for one human being, Jesus of Nazareth, it was possible to qualify himself. The utterance that God alone can save mankind must be similarly modified. As has been shown, God's salvation plan stands and falls by Jesus' covenantal obedience. In the perspective of ecclesiological soteriology, it now

---

be established when imitation unto martyrdom is not a condition, *Kommentar til Markusevangeliet* (Commentary on the Gospel of Mark), Århus 1988, pp. 150; 271. Walter Schmithals rightly emphasizes that Jesus asks his disciples "ob sie die Nachfolge des *Glaubens* auf sich nehmen können, die das christliche Leben überhaupt bestimmt. (...) Das Martyrium ist nur letzter Ausdruck des 'Sterbens mit Christus'", *Das Evangelium nach Markus* 2, Würzburg 1979, p. 468.

[12] Rudolf Pesch, *Das Markusevangelium, 2. Teil*, Freiburg 1980, p. 158.

[13] Cf. Vincent Taylor, *The Gospel According to St. Mark*, London 1959, p. 441; B. Standaert, *L'Évangile selon Marc: composition et genre littéraire*, Brugge 1978, pp. 496.

becomes important to define the sense in which the many see themselves as favoured by Jesus' death on the cross. If, as is asserted, this performance involves for the many a factitive process of change, from eternal life is impossible to eternal life is possible, it has at least now become clear that their performance cannot consist in giving life in a pragmatic sense. If they must do something to participate in Jesus' savior act, it can only be a matter of allowing themselves to be baptized into his death.

What is remarkable about the Christian baptism is that it does not correspond to Jesus' baptism but to Jesus' death on the cross. As a ritual act, the baptism gives the individual the worthiness that Jesus obtained by virtue of his covenantal obedience. *By the very baptism, the Christian becomes heir to eternal life.* The Christian does not have to imitate Jesus, in that he himself prepares the way to the kingdom of God. His following consists in allowing himself to be baptized in order thereby to follow Jesus, who has already prepared the way to the kingdom of God. The Christian's narrative trajectory can then be given as follows:

Manipulation

         Initial state $(Sb \cup (Sh \cup O)$

Performance $\Downarrow$ - Baptism

         Intermediate state $(Sb \cap (Sh \cup O)$

Sanction $\Downarrow$ - Resurrection

         Final state $(Sb \cap (Sh \cap O)$

If this trajectory is compared with Jesus' trajectory, it becomes evident that Jesus' death on the cross stands in the place of the Christian's baptism. Any other demand that might be put to the Christian now sees itself substantiated in the existence that the baptism gives him: he is the realized heir to eternal life. Only in this perspective can PESCH be right, that in 10,29f Jesus speaks of a guarantee of reward and not of conditions of salvation.

It should, however, be emphasized that *baptism* thereafter appears as a condition for salvation. The proclamation of the gospel narrative receives the character of a manipulation that interpellates the listener and semiotizing establishes him as favoured. The gospel is a joyful message that tells the called that he finds himself in a new situation. What was impossible has become possible, the kingdom of God has come near. Through his covenantal obedience, Jesus of Nazareth has restored the broken covenantal relationship between God and Man. His death on the cross means that hereafter any human being sees himself designated as heir to eternal life.

Only virtually, however, since only he who, through repentance and baptism, *acknowledges this inheritance* becomes a realized heir.

The baptism is the Christian subject's performance that enrolls it into a fatal progression process orientated towards eternal life. The sanction takes place when the Son of Man comes to gather his elect, his community, the baptized, the heirs.

When Mark allows Jesus to refer to his death on the cross as a baptism, this is most probably because the Christian baptism is a baptism into his death on the cross. If one disregards the Christian baptism, it becomes not only difficult but quite impossible to explain of what the deliverance of the many was to consist. Only by drawing attention to the ritual act, the baptism, does it become possible to demonstrate the sense in which the gospel narrative is a joyful message for its recipient, since only thereby does it become clear how he can participate in the promise.

Even at this level of the overall project hierarchy the interaction between God and Man applies. The favoured is not hypostatized as subject of being, but must as subject of doing himself act.[14] The theological questions, which then emerge, for example, whether the worthiness as heir to eternal life acquired through baptism is a state of being that can be lost and therefore requires preservation initiatives, whether the baptism is not merely the necessary but also the sufficient condition for salvation, etc., are outside the scope of the gospel narrative and will not be pursued here.

The Eucharist

The story of the institution of the eucharist (14,22ff) confirms the reading that emphasizes the disciples' ritual salvation. If the individual among the many could qualify himself as worthy of eternal life, then he would be a covenantal servant who could of his own accord realize the true God-relationship. But this is impossible, and the individual must therefore be content with Jesus of Nazareth with whom God has established his covenant of salvation.

The relationship between the covenantal servant and the collective he represents may be of differing kinds. In the case of Adam (Gen 2,4b-3,24) the relationship is spontaneous, since all descendants (followers) are born into the state of being (provisional life orientated towards definitive death) that exists by virtue of the malefaction. But at the same time the relationship is inclusive, since everyone without exception sees himself defined in his being of this relationship.

---

[14] Where the practice of infant baptism exists there will be a tendency to hypostatize, since the child cannot act itself. On the other hand, the obligation here rests with the parents who must accept the act, in the same way as the relations who, in the wonder narratives, bear the sick persons before Jesus; cf. 10,15; Joachim Jeremias, *Die Kindertaufe in den ersten vier Jahrhunderten*, Göttingen 1958.

In the case of Abraham (Gen 17) the relationship is exclusive; the covenant applies to his descendants alone, and the genealogical feature points in the direction of spontaneity. Here it should be noted, however, that the requirement of circumcision tends to sever the representation from the kinship. It is the culturally symbolic marking through the circumcision ritual that inducts the individual as a participant in the covenant. He receives his participative covenantal identity, and thus a share in the promise, through this ritual.

In the case of Jesus, the relationship is in no way spontaneous. It is true that genealogical terms are used to define the relationship, but it is whoever does the will of God who is his brother and sister and mother (cf. 3,35). Moreover, the relationship is inclusive/universal (all nations of the world) and cultural/symbolic. All stand as virtual heirs to the kingdom of God by virtue of Jesus' death on the cross. This state of worthiness can be attained by everyone. All are called, all are addressed by the repentance proclamation, and all thus have an opportunity to become members of the society of heirs, i.e. the community. In this relationship baptism has the same function as circumcision, since it gives the virtual Christian his participative identity and being and initiates him as an actualized Christian, i.e. as heir to eternal life. It is the baptism that semiotizes or symbolizes the individual, in that it participatively enrolls him into a covenantal relationship with Jesus of Nazareth, i.e. a fellowship of suffering and a fellowship of glory.

The eucharistic act, the ingestion of bread and wine, body and blood, is similarly a ritual, a cult act, through which the ingestor receives communion and participates in Jesus' meritorious death on the cross. The covenantal blood and the covenantal body are the covenantal sacrifice in which the disciples receive a share through the ingestion.[15] This can be understood as a progressive process of change, in that the subject of being is thereby qualified as heir to eternal life (cf. Jn 6,54: "Those who eat my flesh and drink my blood have eternal life, and I will raise them up on the last day."). The eucharistic act is then perceived absolutely and becomes identical with the baptism act (cf. Rom 6,3ff).

However, a differentiation can be carried out. Aspectually, the baptism is a once-and-for-all event, which produces a lasting state of being (durativeness), whereas the eucharist is a continually repeated event (iterativeness), which brings about a state of being of limited duration. It is true that an anamnesis motif (cf. Lk 22,19; 1 Cor 11,24f) is lacking, but the figure of the ingestion itself indicates an iterative act, since satiety abates. It also indicates a preservation aspect, since

---

[15] The term τὸ αἷμά μου τῆς διαθήκης seems to refer to Ex 24,8, which occasions a covenantal blood typology. Hebrews 9,20f elaborates this typology, but even so an understanding of "covenantal blood" is not exclusively connected with Ex 24. What is crucial is that the term not only thematizes the concept of covenant and victim but also links them, and that the covenantal victim in the gospel narrative is the mediator himself. As has been shown, it is really within the framework of a covenant that Jesus' death on the cross and the ritual eucharist must be understood. The covenantal blood refers to Ex 24, and opens the way to a Moses-Christ typology, but the covenant itself refers to a large number of texts which give an opportunity for typologizations with other mediators, e.g. David, Abraham/Isaac and Adam (cf. Mt 1,1ff and Lk 3,23ff).

the ingestion serves to maintain a state of being, the Christian existence, which would otherwise perish (cf. hunger → sickness → death). The anamnesis serves not only to bring to mind Jesus, his words and acts, but equally to help the Christian cognitively-affectively to adhere to his being. The eucharist is thus recursively linked to baptism, which receives the status of an objective semiotization (continuous durativeness). In itself it is rather a subjective semiotization, which iteratively and recursively attaches the baptized to his baptism and Christian identity (discontinuous durativeness). The post-paschal eucharist act that presupposes baptism must therefore be seen in a preservation perspective in which what is concerned is to nourish and maintain the Christian existence and passion.

2. Cosmocentric Soteriology

The cosmocentric soteriology looks at the world as a subject of being. The pertinence level thus established can then be stated:

1) Mark tries to convey to his reader the concept of a state of being (the kingdom of God) and of an interactive action (the creation project).
2) The subject of being for this state/action is the world.
3) The responsible subject of doing for this state/action is God.

Important aspects of the gospel narrative's cosmocentric soteriology have already been described, but it remains to provide an overall survey.[16]

The initial situation is that the world is identified as a Provisional cosmos, which is fatally orientated towards Definitive chaos. Destruction is inevitable. The kingdom of God, which can be defined as Definitive cosmos, is impossible at this moment, modalized by not-being-able-to-be.

The anointing of Jesus marks the first turning point, in that thereby God has opened the way to an interactive project directed towards and able to lead to the kingdom of God's final realization. Directly after the anointing, Jesus can therefore proclaim that the kingdom of God, which was absent has now come near (1,15). At that moment, the world is in a transitional phase in which it is not yet clear whether the project will be realized. Jesus' being and the world's being are here characterized by an indeterminate state of becoming.

The death on the cross marks another turning point, in that the kingdom of God is from this moment characterized by a determined state of becoming: it has become inevitable. This situation means that the existing world, Provisional Cosmos, at first sees itself as unavoidably orientated towards Provisional Chaos.

---

[16] Cf. Chapter VIII, B.2.; C.4.

The cosmocentric consequences of the death on the cross can already be glimpsed at the moment of death: when it was noon, darkness came over the whole land until three in the afternoon (15,33), and the curtain of the temple was torn in two, from top to bottom (cf. 13,1f). The darkness of the hour of death is precursor of the darkness when the Son of Man will come to gather his elect (13,24ff), a darkness that is the culmination of the sufferings in the time of chaos (13,3ff). In those days heaven and earth will pass away (13,32), but about that day or hour no one knows, only the Father.

The elect are those who are heirs to eternal life. Their resurrection coincides with the cosmocentric creation process that finally realizes the kingdom of God. That the provisional chaos is marked by "suffering, such as has not been from the beginning of the creation that God created" (13,19) is because God's final realization of his salvation project is a sanction that takes the form of a re-creation through which the world is inducted into the state of being to which it was destined from the beginning.

In this perspective, it becomes clear that the overall salvation and creation project is a protection process directed towards a re-establishment (cf. 3,5; 8,25; 9,12) of the creator, the creature and the creation in their integrity.

PART FIVE
THE CHRIST MYTH

THE CHRIST MYTH

The overall task of exegesis can be formally identified as *description* and *interpretation* of the New Testament texts. The term "description" refers to an exegesis based on a theory and method aimed at reading and identifying the primary, discursive phenomena that contribute to the formation of signification (production and reception). The term "interpretation" refers to an exegesis based on a theory and method directed towards explaining the discourse's existence and characteristics as secondary phenomena, i.e. as an indication of something outside the discourse and the discursivity/narrativity itself.[1]

The work of description appears to encompass four principal sub-tasks. The point of reference is the actual discourse described in its relative autonomy. But it is then possible to project this discourse into an authorship, a literary period, or a genre.[2] The work of interpretation encompasses in this perception four correlated sub-tasks. The teleological interpretation inquires about the author's motivation, inspiration and intention, his purpose or volition in creating his discourse. The biographical interpretation relates the discourse to the author's life, whereas the sociological interpretation sees this as being conditioned by given social circumstances. Finally, the ontological interpretation considers the discourse as a manifestation of certain psychological, philosophical, theological or anthropological structures that are asserted to have general validity.[3]

---

[1] This distinction between two main types of *reading*, descriptive and interpretative, is attributable to Peter Brask, cf. *Tekst og tolkning. Første del. Bidrag til den litterære semantik* (Text and Interpretation. Part One. Contribution to Literary Semantics), København 1973, pp. 59.

[2] It is the encounter between empirical data and theoretical pre-conception that generates the autonomous discourse in the description of the available text. This description is intratextual and as such is contrasted with the other descriptions, which are intertextual. The authorship description will, for example, be possible in the Lucan and Pauline writings. The period description considers the individual discourse in relation to a literary period's total corpus, for example the religious discourses of Hellenistic Judaism. The genre description can, for example, be an investigation of apocalyptic discourse. The terms "period" and "genre" demand further definition, but this will not be pursued here. A good survey of the difficulties characterizing the attempt of exegesis to determine the gospel genre is to be found in Robert Guelich, "The Gospel Genre", Peter Stuhlmacher (ed.), *Das Evangelium und das Evangelien*, Tübingen 1983, pp. 183. Narrative exegesis' determination of the gospel narrative's covenantal schema makes it natural to take a look at the narrative competence characterizing the Jewish storytelling tradition. It is the Isaac-Christ typology in particular that demands attention, and it may be anticipated that narrative exegesis will be able to contribute substantially to an illustration of the inter-textuality that characterizes the relationship between Gen 22 (not least in its Jewish interpretation history such as *Akedah*) and the gospel narrative, cf., e.g., Robert J. Daly, *Christian Sacrifice. The Judaeo-Christian Background Before Origen*, Washington 1978, pp. 175. However, neither can this task be pursued in this context, cf. Ole Davidsen, "Bund. Ein religionssemiotischer Beitrag zur Definition der alttestamentlichen Bundesstruktur", *Linguistica Biblica 48*, Bonn 1980, pp. 49.

[3] The interpretations are extratextual. An interpretation that describes Mark's Gospel as the evangelist's confrontation with a heresy is an example of a teleological interpretation, cf. e.g. Theodore J. Weeden,

This model is merely a heuristic outline to serve as an initial localization of narrative exegesis within exegesis' overall sphere of work and horizon of inquiry. It still remains to prepare a more specific and well-founded model, which is severely lacking.

With the reservations which, in the nature of the matter, must be adopted relative to this provisional model, narrative exegesis can be identified as a method that first and foremost can contribute to the description of the existing discourse. It thus covers only part of exegesis' overall sphere of activity, and in a global perspective must be supplemented by other methods. Narrative exegesis is only one model among others. But on the other hand it occupies a somewhat special position according to this interpretation of the task of exegesis, since the description of the existing discourse must be the point of reference for any exegesis. Any further description and any interpretation presupposes - at least because of the scientific deontology to which the exegesis is also subject - description of the existing discourse. The other descriptions and possible interpretations are different forms of contextualization and relativization, and as such are secondary in relation thereto, although they may perhaps be of primary interest to the individual exegete.

The question of the anatomy of exegesis' overall sphere of activity and horizon of inquiry, including the question of narrative exegesis' placement therein, will not however be pursued here, where narrative exegesis will be outlined by considering perspectively a number of central theological subjects in continuation of the investigation's results.

Mark: Traditions in Conflict, Philadelphia 1971. A biographical interpretation of Mark's Gospel is naturally not attempted, but elements of such an interpretation are contained in, for example, Günther Bornkamm, *Paulus*, Stuttgart 1969. The sociological interpretation extends from considerations of the gospel narrative's *Sitz im Leben* to materialistic readings, cf. e.g. Fernando Belo, *Lecture matérialiste de l'évangile de Marc*, Paris 1976. Finally, Rudolf Bultmann's existential-philosophical exegesis can be seen as an example of the ontological interpretation, cf. e.g. "Neues Testament und Mythologie", Hans Werner Bartsch (ed.), *Kerygma und Mythos I*, Hamburg (1948) 1960, pp. 15, to which, for example, René Girard's cultural-anthropological theory also belongs, cf. e.g. *Des choses cachées depuis la fondation du monde*, Paris 1978. It is also noted that the descriptions and interpretations contained in the model would be able to take the reconstructed historical Jesus' proclamation as its subject; that the available exegetic investigations are never entirely pure but represent hybrid forms with a predominant main trend; and that the interpretations never manage to tear themselves away from their discourses, since the interpretation's revelation of the discourse's *secret* remains a revelation of the *discourse's* secret: discourse and interpretation signify each other in the fusion of meaning generated.

CHAPTER THIRTEEN

NARRATIVE CHRISTOLOGY

The term *narrative christology* refers to the gospel narrative's teaching on Christ, God's anointed, his person and his acts. This teaching is not given as a systematic, theological account, but must be reconstructed on the basis of a narrative analysis of the story's universe.

As indicated in the introduction, this study is based on the perception that, in answer to the question "Who is Jesus?", the first Christians replied with a *narrative*. In this perspective, the christological titles are designations that take their pregnant content from what the gospel story tells of the narrative Jesus. The entire narrative is a christological proclamation; all the information serves to define Jesus of Nazareth.[1]

By his narrative, the narrator Mark informs his narratee of what the unifying designation "Christ" (cf. 1,1) signifies, i.e. of the thematic and narrative roles that constitute this name's or this title's functional (doing) and ontological (being) content.

The narrative Jesus is an actor in a narrative. Who this person is can be determined only from the information contained in the narrative. This information relates to narrative processes whose associated roles define and predicate the proper name "Jesus of Nazareth". Who he is, is determined uniquely from the roles the narrator causes him to enter into. The narrative's "Jesus of Nazareth" is not a person existing independently of the story of whom the narrative relates, but an actor who exists only by virtue of the narrative.

In this perspective, Mark's Gospel is a report about a narrated person, "Jesus of Nazareth", and consequently the gospel narrative emerges directly as a narratively exposed teaching about Jesus. It would therefore be reasonable for exegesis to seize occasion to shirk the issue of using the dogmatically heavily charged term "christology". One might instead speak of a theology about Jesus (a "Jesus-logy"). But the term "christology" can and should be preserved, with the qualification, however, that what is concerned is a *narrative christology*.

The gospel narrative tells of Christ, God's anointed, who happens to be Jesus from Nazareth. In this perspective, it is not a Jesus narrative but a Christ narrative.

---

[1] Cf. Rudolf Pesch: "Die Christologie des Mk-Ev, die christologischen Traditionen der urkirchlichen Tradition vereinigt, nachzuzeichnen, sie aus dem Evangelienbuch zu exzerpieren und in eine abstraktere Begrifflichkeit zu überführen, widerspricht nahezu der narrativen Grundstruktur der Geschichtsdarstellung des Markus. Wer Jesus Christus ist, sagt seine Geschichte, sagt er selbst.", *Das Markusevangelium, 2. Teil*, Freiburg 1980, p. 43.

A. Processual Christology

Jesus of Nazareth becomes Christ by the very fact of the anointing in association with the baptism (1,11), and all that he does and says thereafter is in his capacity as Christ. The investigation has shown that his Christ-act is unified in three fundamental roles, the *wonder-worker*, the *proclaimer* and the *savior*. But it has also shown that the role of savior is the main role. Christology and soteriology are two sides of the same coin.

The basic narrative structure of Mark's Gospel is made up of the narrative process, the mythos, which includes Baptism/Anointing, Death on the cross and Resurrection. All other narrative processes, preceding (cf. the baptism of John) or subsequent (cf. the parousia), hierarchally superjacent (God's being) or subjacent (the disciples' being), receive their *raison d'être* from this. This mythos, which constitutes the gospel narrative's whole-constituting semiotic (syntactic and semantic) signification structure, may be referred to as *the kerygmatic schema*, because it encompasses the gospel proclamation's (the narration's) principal content. But this mythos, which concerns the salvation project's (the narrate's) principal action, can equally be referred to as the gospel narrative's *christological schema*.

The covenantal servant's, i.e. the anointed's, narrative trajectory is a process of change that cannot be christologically indifferent. On the contrary, this narrative process, which involves a realization of the true God-relationship between Jesus and God, is to be considered as the actual basic structure of the gospel story's narrative christology. The semiotic unity of the narrative means that Baptism/Anointing, Death on the cross and Resurrection cannot be considered as independent events isolated from one another that merely follow each other in time but as parts of an integrated structure, one process of event, which takes the form of a covenantal project.

These decisive events are not correlated by virtue of a chronological sequence but solely by their relation to one and the same process of change that concerns one and the same person: Christ. Because of the narrative's syntactic organization, the Resurrection presupposes the Death on the cross, which itself presupposes the establishment of the covenant by way of Baptism/Anointing, and it becomes evident that the narrative receives its integrated status from this narrative organization, which extends from beginning to end (compared with the narrative's syntactic organization, its temporality is an epiphenomenon).

Exegesis must however take into account not only the connection between the gospel-constituting events; it must also be able to maintain the christological schema's narrative articulation. The question of Jesus' being must be answered in different ways, according to the aspect involved. A process of change is concerned, and for this reason the being of the Anointed must be distinguished from the being of the Crucified, which must itself be distinguished from the being of the Resurrected.[2] Jesus' being is not substantial but relation-determined, partly in relation to God and partly in relation to the object of value, *Life*.

To ask the question of Jesus' (pragmatic, covenantal, and modal) being is therefore, fundamentally, to ask the question of his relationship to God. It will then be seen that the narrative's christological definition of Jesus is not static but *dynamic*. The narrative christology is a dynamic or *processual christology*. Christ is not something Jesus *is*, but something he *becomes*.

Fundamentally, a distinction must be made between Jesus as:

Virtual Christ;
Actualized Christ;
Realized Christ.

The complexity of the narrative process, as perceived, determines the aspects that this processual structure articulates.

In a progressive perspective, the christological schema is a narrative trajectory in which the baptism/anointing makes Jesus virtual Christ, the death on the cross makes him actualized Christ, and the resurrection makes him realized Christ. These *actantial christological roles* can be stated as:

Manipulation	$\Downarrow$	- Baptism/Anointing
Virtual Christ	$(Sb \cup (Sh \cup O))$	
Performance	$\Downarrow$	- Death on the cross
Actualized Christ	$(Sb \cap (Sh \cup O))$	
Sanction	$\Downarrow$	- Resurrection
Realized Christ	$(Sb \cap (Sh \cap O))$	

In this definition, it is the being of the resurrected one that is considered as the processually and interactively realized Christ-being. Only at the very moment that Jesus realizes the being prescribed by the covenant does he become, ontologically, Christ. Only the sanction, as an act of judgment and as execution of the judgment, i.e. at the same time recognition (of the death on the cross as a benefaction) and retribution (resurrection as repayment), is able to realize and guarantee Jesus' Christ-being.

---

[2] The roles of the anointed, the crucified and the resurrected refer to events that can be considered in their relative autonomy, but these roles also refer to the syntagmatic progression through which Jesus passes and thus reveal his actantial status at a given moment in the process. The events belong to one and the same process, which involves an accumulating realization of being: the anointed one is anointed; the crucified one is anointed and crucified; the resurrected one is anointed, crucified and resurrected; cf. *Sémiotique*, art. "Actantiel (rôle, statut -)".

But the articulating section can be placed in other positions in this composite Christ process. Before the anointing, Jesus is a virtual Christ who is actualized as such through God's transition to action. In this perspective, the anointing itself becomes the action that realizes him as Christ (Christ1).

However, what is concerned here is God's qualification of Jesus, a competencial (modal) being that on the one hand singles out Jesus as a virtual subject of a definitive Christ-being (Christ3) and on the other hand defines him as a virtual subject for a Christ-doing. Even if Jesus in one sense becomes the realized Christ (Christ1) by virtue of the anointing, he is in another sense merely already/not yet Christ (Christ3). This concerns the narrative sub-process that ends in the establishment of the main process' actantial christological role, *virtual Christ*.

The death on the cross can also be perceived as a consummation of the realized Christ role. Through the anointing, the covenantal servant sees himself semiotized as a virtual subject of doing for a covenantal task. The actualization is his transition to the act that is consummated by the very realization of the performance.

In this perspective, Jesus becomes realized Christ (Christ2) by the death on the cross itself; but again, in a wider perspective, it is only a matter of an already/not yet realized being (Christ3). Here also a narrative sub-process is concerned, which in this case ends in establishing the main process' actantial christological role of *actualized Christ*.

Whether Jesus is allowed to become Christ by the anointing (realized Christ1 – virtual Christ3), by the death on the cross (realized Christ2 = actualized Christ3) or by the resurrection (realized Christ3 = realized Christ3) therefore depends on which aspect in the christological schema, i.e. the actantial role, is in fact in focus.[3]

---

[3] According to Rudolf Bultmann, Jesus is installed by the baptism directly in the consummated messianic being. This misunderstanding subsequently occasions considerations of the disagreement thereby produced between the synoptic tradition and the tradition expressed in, for example, Rom 1,3f, a tradition, Bultmann maintains, according to which "Jesus nach Tod und Auferstehung zum Messias erhöht wurde", *Die Geschichte der synoptischen Tradition*, Göttingen 1970, p. 267. The question is, however, whether this asserted discrepancy is not due to a difference in focalizing. It is true that there is a moment where it is correct to maintain "dass der Beginn der Regentschaft des Gottessohnes (im Sinne von Ps. 2,7) in der Erhöhung an Ostern angesetzt wurde", Eduard Schweizer, *Erniedrigung und Erhöhung bei Jesus und seinen Nachfolgern*, Zürich 1962, p. 92. But the syntagmatic progression through which Jesus passes is one coherent *enthronization process*, beginning with the baptism/anointing, by which Jesus already/not yet becomes the Messiah. Note also that any interpretation that allows Jesus to receive his full Messiahship by virtue of the anointing is forced to consider the gospel narrative as the exclusive unfolding of a cognitive process that successively permits the realized but hidden being to be revealed. In the cases where Jesus is born as the Messiah, both baptism and anointing suffer a loss of signification since these events loose their narrative rationality. It becomes unclear why Jesus is to be baptized by John, cf. Mt 3,14f, and the anointing alone receives a cognitive function as the designation of Jesus for a third party (John), cf. Mt 3,16f; Mk 9,7 and Jo 1,32f. The attempt of exegesis to remedy this loss of meaning, involuntarily leads to dead ends, cf., e.g., Ernst Haenchen's unclear considerations in *Der Weg Jesu. Eine Erklärung des Markus-Evangeliums und der kanonischen Parallelen*, Berlin 1968, pp. 51.

In a protective perspective, the articulating section is finally placed in yet a different way. What is concerned here is the composite VAR structure that includes the semi-virtual and semi-realized phases. Before the anointing, Jesus is in an ontological perspective a virtual Christ, more precisely semi-virtual. The anointing makes him an actualized Christ, the death on the cross a semi-realized Christ, and the resurrection a realized Christ.

It is important functionally that the virtual Christ is here the role that Jesus adopts before the anointing. In this aspect he is not in a position to preach God's gospel (1,14), to heal the sick, or to predict his suffering and resurrection. He receives a capacity for this only as actualized Christ (= virtual Christ3), i.e. by the very act of anointing, which as a transference of the Spirit can be perceived as God's modal qualification of his covenantal servant, in part cognitive by way of knowing (the prophet) and in part pragmatic by way of ability (the wonder-worker; cf. e.g. 6,2). As realized Christ, Jesus is no longer functionally defined as wonder-worker and proclaimer. On the other hand, he is at this moment - and only now - in a position to attend to his assignment as eschatological judge (8,38; 13,26; 14,62). Different *thematic christological roles* (teacher, healer, prophet, shepherd, redeemer, deliverer, servant, judge, king, savior, etc.) thus correspond to different *actantial christological roles*.

The christological titles, primarily "Son of God", "Son of Man" and "Christ", do not refer to christological roles. In themselves, they seem to be in no way christologically pregnant, since they are employed - like the proper name Jesus - to describe the narrative Jesus in his adoption of different thematic and actantial roles. They are generally employed as para-synonyms to describe Jesus as he with whom God has entered into his covenant of salvation. Who Jesus is (cf. 8,27) and what "Christ" (cf. 8,29) and "Son of God" and "Son of Man" signify are answered by the gospel narrative as a whole.

The messianic secret of this narrative is a double mystery. It is not sufficient to reveal that Jesus of Nazareth is Christ (the first secret), but the story must disclose to his implied reader the actual meaning of "Christ" (the second secret). Thus, the role complex that the Christ designation encompasses is revealed only through the gospel narrative.

B. THEMATIC CHRISTOLOGY

It is illuminating to consider the gospel story's narrative christology against the background of a number of themes or thematic roles that characterize New Testament christology as a whole.[4]

---

[4] Cf. M. Eugene Boring, "The Christology of Mark: Hermeneutical Issues for Systematic Theology", *Semeia 30, Christology and Exegesis: New Approaches*, Missoula 1985, pp. 125.

For instance, the idea of a pre-existence (cf. Jn 1,1ff; 1 Cor 8,6; Phil 2,6f; Col 1,15f; Heb 1,2; Rev 3,14) is absent. Jesus of Nazareth has not existed from eternity. He has therefore played no part in the creation (cf. also Heb 11,3; Rev 19,13). The incarnation concept (Jn 1,14) is absent, and he has not emptied himself for divinity (Phil 2.7).

In Mark's Gospel, Christ has a creative function from the moment of anointing. The wonder-worker role shows that he has a part in God's creative power, since he not only neutralizes the annihilation in progress, but is able to restore the prostrate, and the salvation project's consummation (the death on the cross) is a prerequisite of God's final realization of his project of creation, the establishment of the Kingdom of God. Jesus' extraordinary ability stems from the possession of the spirit; he is filled with the Holy Spirit and thereby becomes a man of God (ἄνθρωπος τοῦ θεοῦ), more than an ordinary man but not a god.

Jesus of Nazareth has not become man by emptying himself of divinity, but he has become the Son of God by becoming filled with divine power and perception. In the gospel narrative it is God who abases himself, since he renounces his omnipotence and permits his project of salvation and creation to depend upon one single man, Jesus of Nazareth. The latter must for his part abase himself, renounce the use of the creative power of which he has received a share through the anointing (cf. 15,32) and then deny himself unto death.

Jesus of Nazareth is the son of Mary, and has brothers and sisters (cf. 3,31ff; 6,3). Neither his conception nor his birth distinguishes him from others; he is a quite ordinary man. In this capacity he comes to John to be baptized with his baptism of repentance for the forgiveness of sins (1,4.9). Jesus is not described as sinless; he is not made sinless through the baptism, since only the death on the cross qualifies him as righteous by virtue of atonement. Through the anointing he becomes the Son of God, Christ, and bearer of the Holy Spirit, the Spirit of God. As such he is not sinless, but modally liberated from the reign of sin. He is not Christ, but is made into Christ by an initiation process, which may be described as adoption.

By establishment of the covenant he became God's legitimate and authorized representative in relation to mankind, Son of God. He is sent by God, but not locatively from Heaven, and the Son is clearly subordinate to the Father (13,32). But at the same time he is appointed as the acknowledged representative of mankind in relation to God, the Son of Man, whose task it is to realize the covenant's principal demand in self-denying obedience unto death. He is, as will be shown more precisely below, the second Adam who is to deliver the captives from the toils of death (provisional life orientated towards definitive death). He does so by being the only person to realize God's demand, the condition for the reconciliation between God and mankind.

Christ is the wonder-worker who on behalf of God forgives and restores. He is the crucified who himself gives his life to God, and the resurrected who receives eternal life from God. He is the exalted who sits at God's right hand (14,62), but shall come again to gather his elect (13,27). Meanwhile, however, the elect are left to themselves and must watch out for the false Messiahs (13,6.21ff). The period between ascension and parousia is characterized by Christ's absence. The resurrected speaks only through the gospel narrative. However, the Holy Spirit (13,11) is present in this time.

The relationship to Christ becomes decisive at the eschatological judgment (8,38), but it is not thematized in the narrative in which this post-paschal relationship sees itself constituted. The Gospel of Jesus Christ (1,1) can only be proclaimed and received in faith after the death on the cross and resurrection (the gospel story's narration grows organically out of its narrate), and it is this proclamation that establishes the Christian discipleship.

A Christian life can only be contemplated beyond realization of the salvation project. But the question is whether this proclamation is feasible without a command to repent and be baptized (cf. 1,4 and 16,16). Christ is king of the true Israel (cf. 15,32), and these people consist of the elect, who must be perceived as the baptized, i.e. the Christians.

As already said, christology and soteriology are two aspects of the same matter. Christ is the Savior, a covenantal servant, who on his own behalf and that of others prepares the way to God's kingdom. Although σωτήρ does not appear as a Christ title in the gospel narrative, the salvation project is the central mission that must be resolved and is resolved. And all who would be saved are obliged to turn to the deed that Jesus of Nazareth has performed in his capacity of Christ, both Son of God and Son of Man.

CHAPTER FOURTEEN

NARRATIVE TYPOLOGY

The so-called *Fall myth*, Gen 2,4b-3,24, is a narrative that must be considered as the gospel story's implicit narrative precondition. Although the designation "the last Adam" (ὁ ἔσχατος Ἀδάμ, 1 Cor 15,45; cf. Rom 5,12ff) cannot be found in the gospel story, a narrative analysis shows that Christ appears here in the role of the last Adam, and as such must be perceived in the light of the first Adam (ὁ πρῶτος ἄνθρωπος Ἀδάμ, 1 Cor 15,45). Protology and eschatology belong together.

Trends towards an implicit Adam-Christ typology in Mark's Gospel have often been pointed out. Attention is given in particular to certain structural accordance (similarities and differences, typos and anti-typos) between the serpent's temptation of Adam/Eve and Satan's temptation of Christ.[1] RUDOLF PESCH concludes that the most plausible explanation of the brief and obscure story of the temptation is that Jesus is here represented as the new (last) Adam, who in contrast to the old (first) Adam resists the temptation. In resisting this temptation, he re-establishes the paradisiac condition, where the wild animals do not attack people (cf. ApMos 10ff; absence of violence and death) and where angels provide them with heavenly nourishment ("angels' food", cf. Vita 4).[2]

The typology, however, is not restricted to a syncretism between individual motifs or themes. If the gospel narrative contains an implicit Adam-Christ typology, this must be intertextually connected in a more comprehensive and integrated sense with the narrative in Gen 2,4b-3,24. The Fall myth and the Christ myth must be characterized (typologically and/or anti-typologically) by narrative genre-community and structural resemblance in terms of narrative and thematic role configuration.

A. THE FALL MYTH

The Fall myth is a veritable *dysangelium* recounting an evil deed, a taking - "she took of its fruit" (3,6) - occasioning a negative sanction. Although the word

---

[1] Cf. Ernest Best, *The Temptation and the Passion: The Markan Soteriology*, Cambridge 1965, pp. 6; Leonhard Goppelt, *Typos. Die typologische Deutung des Alten Testaments im Neuen*, Gütersloh 1939, pp. 116.

[2] *Das Markusevangelium, 1. Teil*, Freiburg 1980, p. 95. See "Life of Adam and Eve" in James H. Charlesworth (ed.), *The Old Testament Pseudepigrapha*, Vol 2, London 1985, pp. 249. This restoration can of course only be anticipating the final renewal at which the entire project of creation is aimed.

covenant (*berit*) does not appear in the text, it is none the less a covenantal narrative, i.e. a narrative about the covenantal relationship between God as covenantal lord and man as covenantal servant.[3]

The covenant narratives, which belong to the Degression (Repression) narrative genre, will generally tell of an abundance squandered because of the infringement of a prohibition. In this case, the covenant's threat is brought to the fore to the disregard of the promise. In the covenantal narratives that belong to the Progression (Protection) narrative genre, the main emphasis is however on the observation of a prescription, and therefore on the promise. Degression is set against Progression, as dysangelium (the narrative about the first Adam) is set against evangelium (the narrative about the last Adam).

In the Fall myth, the stipulated threat is clearly manifested: "of the tree of the knowledge of good and evil you shall not eat, for in the day that you eat of it you shall die." (2,17). The covenantal lord (Cl) has established:

If Cs takes Y2 from Cl, then Cl shall take X2 from Cs;

or in other words: if Adam/Eve take of the fruit of the Tree of Life then Yahweh shall take their life (O). Taking is answered by taking. The covenantal servant's narrative trajectory can then be stated as:

Manipulation

Initial state	$(Sb \cap (Sh \cap O)$	
Performance	$\Downarrow$	- Misdeed
Intermediate state	$(Sb \cup (Sh \cap O)$	
Sanction	$\Downarrow$	- Destruction
Final state	$(Sb \cup (Sh \cup O)$	

In the initial condition, Adam/Eve have life rightfully. The misdeed (performance) involves a covenantal degression, the covenantal servant becomes a sinner

---

[3] As is also made plain in the later Jewish tradition: cf. Leonhard Goppelt, ibidem pp. 34 and Fritzleo Lentzen-Deis, *Die Taufe Jesu nach den Synoptikern. Literarkritische und gattungsgeschichtliche Untersuchungen*, Frankfurt am Main 1970, pp. 228. "Die Vorstellung von der Restitution des alten Bundes war nicht geeignet, die universale Wirklichkeit des Christusgeschehens voll auszuschöpfen.", writes Egon Brandenburger. That is why Paul did not use this tradition in his mission to the gentiles, but choose to use "die gnostische Anthropos-Kategorie mit ihrer Zuordnung von εἰς ἄνθρωπος und πάντες ἄνθρωποι", *Adam und Christus. Exegetisch-religionsgeschichtliche Untersuchung zu Röm. 5,12-21 (1. Kor. 15)*, Neukirchen 1962, p. 240. He may be right, but we are nevertheless facing two arch-covenants in the Christian system of signification, and the idea of an Adam-covenant is known at least from ApMos 8,2 (cf. even 23,3 und Vita 26,2; 34,1). See *Life of Adam and Eve* in James H. Charlesworth (ed.): The Old Testament Pseudepigrapha, Vol. 2, London 1985, pp. 249.

and now has his life, but unrightfully, wherefore it must be lost, taken. The sanction ultimately involves realization of the final state, death.

This perception is not erroneous, but it must be given more shades of meaning. One notices, for example, that the death penalty is not carried out there and then but is postponed. Initially, the sanction only involves expulsion from the garden of Eden:

> Then the LORD God said, "See, the man has become like one of us, knowing good and evil; and now, he might reach out his hand and take also from the tree of life, and eat, and live forever" - therefore the LORD God sent him forth from the garden of Eden, to till the ground from which he was taken. He drove out the man; and at the east of the garden of Eden he placed the cherubim, and a sword flaming and turning to guard the way to the tree of life. (Gen 3,22ff).

The expulsion from the garden of Eden means that man now no longer has access to the Tree of Life. Expulsion therefore involves a factitive process of change, since the covenantal servant's field of ability is curtailed: that which was possible (Definitive life) has now become impossible; that which was evitable (Definitive death) has now become inevitable. As already said, the death penalty is not executed there and then; it is postponed. In fact, Adam's full lifetime is no less than 930 years (Gen 5,5). Nevertheless, he is a doomed man when he leaves the garden of Eden, for he enters into the Provisional life state of being, which is fatally orientated towards Definitive death. Whether he lives for a long time or a short time does not change this *modal* situation. The threat, "in the day that you eat of it you shall die" (2,17) does not, therefore, signify that Adam/Eve die the same day as they committed their misdeed, but that from this moment death becomes inevitable.[4]

After expulsion from the garden of Eden, man finds himself in the Provisional life state of being, i.e. in the Semi-virtualized Being mode, which fatally (determined state of becoming) is orientated towards Definitive death, i.e. the Virtualized Being mode (Nothingness). But before they enter into the Semi-virtualized Being mode they must find themselves in the Actualized Being mode, where Definitive death is evitable. In this mode of being they must have freedom to act, they must both be able to break the covenant and be able not to do so (indeterminated state of becoming).

---

[4] Cf. Claus Westermann: "Der Tod kann (...) nicht als direkte Folge des Essens gemeint sein. Das ist auch deswegen nicht möglich, weil die Formulierung eindeutig eine Strafbestimmung bezeichnet. Daß der Tod am gleichen Tage eintreffen müsse, ist also nicht gemeint.", *Genesis*, Neukirchen 1976, p. 305. He does not believe, however, that the punishment should consist of man's becoming mortal, but emphasizes - in continuation of Hermann Gunkel - that the threat of the death penalty is never effectuated. The question is, however, whether this opinion is not primarily evidence of exegesis' lack of knowledge of and familiarity with the modal properties of the narrative processes.

It then becomes unambiguously clear that man's initial state of being in the Fall myth is not Definitive life, that his initial mode of being is not Realized Being. Adam/Eve do not have eternal life, but the possibility of attaining it.[5]

On the other hand, the narrative is open to interpretation when precise definition of the relationship to the Tree of Life is concerned.

If Yahweh says; "now, he might reach out his hand and take also from the tree of life, and eat, and live for ever" (3,22), then it is unmistakable that eating of the Tree of Life gives eternal life. But it is unclear whether man must eat merely once of this tree to obtain eternal life, or whether eternal life consists of the possibility of preserving his life by constant recurrent eating that neutralizes an on-going death process, thematized as hunger.

In this reading, emphasis is given to the eating's once-and-for-all character, for in this way the story's narrative articulation, which is basically the same in both readings, becomes clearer.

It may be said, on the basis of God's command in 2,16: "You may freely eat of every tree of the garden", that it is permitted to take of the Tree of Life. But if it is borne in mind that the actualized mode of being is untenable, because the covenantal servant *must* act, then it is not absurd to assert that the eating of this tree is prescribed.

It should in this context be remembered that in the final instance the prescription takes its rationality from the ontology that determines the covenant's objective. Here, this can only be the realization of Definitive life, i.e. eternal life, which is characterized by fatal preservation: Realized Being.

On this basis, it may be said that the eating of the fruit of the Tree of Life, perceived as a positive performance, a good deed, will install man in the Semi-realized Being mode, where he not yet has eternal life but is entitled to it (determined state of becoming by reason of covenantal progression). In this mode of being, Definitive life would be inevitable, Definitive death impossible. God's positive sanction would then consist of an apotheosis, a glorification, which means the complete demodalization of the covenantal servant's (and, it may be said, of the covenantal lord's) being.[6]

This reading follows the narrative's inherent symmetry: man may eat of the Tree of Life (prescription) or the Tree of Knowledge (interdiction), and just as the eating of the Tree of Knowledge (or the Tree of Death) leads to Definitive

---

[5] Cf. J.G. Frazer's remarkable reading, *Folk-Lore in the Old Testament*, London 1923, p. 16: "The gist of the whole story of the fall appears to be an attempt to explain man's mortality, to set forth how death came into the world. It is true that man is not said to have been created immortal and to have lost his immortality through disobedience; but neither is he said to have been created mortal. Rather we are given to understand that the possibility alike of immortality and of mortality was open to him, and that it rested with him which he would choose; for the tree of life stood within his reach, its fruit was not forbidden to him, he had only to stretch out his hand, take of the fruit, and eating of it live for ever."

[6] When God is "all in all" ($\pi\acute{\alpha}\nu\tau\alpha$ $\dot{\epsilon}\nu$ $\pi\hat{\alpha}\sigma\iota\nu$, 1 Cor, 15,28) the apotheosis exists, the fully demodalized being.

death, so the eating of the Tree of Life leads to Definitive life, not of itself but by virtue of God's sanction, which is either punishment or reward.

It is consequently possible to determine the following modes of being for Adam/Eve, i.e. man:

	MODE OF BEING	MODALITY	ARTICULATION
I	Realized	Life	Being
	Semi-realized	Inevitable	Determined becoming ↑
II	Actualized	Possible/Evitable	Indetermined becoming ↕
III	Semi-virtualized	Impossible	Determined becoming ↓
	Virtualized	Life (Death)	Being (Nothingness)

The principal events that determine the transition from one mode of being to another can then be given:

Realized existence

Semi-realized existence   - (Apotheosis)

Actualized existence   - (Benefaction)

Semi-virtualized existence   - Misdeed

Virtualized existence   - Destruction

In the context of the dysangelium also, therefore, it is possible to distinguish between man's three narrative phases of being:

I)   Realized existence;
II)   Actualized existence;
III) Virtualized existence.

In view of the way it happened, there is of course no sense in speaking of soteriology within the dysangelium narrative's framework. On the contrary, we are here concerned with an *apollyology* (cf. ἀπολλύων; or with a *perditiology*), and the negatively sanctioned subject of being, which has received attention, is Adam/Eve, the covenantal servant. It is Yahweh who appears in the role of ἀπολλύων, the destructive degressor, whereas man is the victim. The punishment is released, however, by the victim's own doing, and this appears therefore in the role of auxiliary- or auto-degressor.

Confronted with the anthropocentric is the theocentric apollyology, which raises the question of what it actually is that God loses because of Adam/Eve's offence. It is also applicable here that either Yahweh is a functionary, whose being is not at stake in the narrative, or his fate is decided by the relationship to the covenantal servant.

Interest is initially concentrated on the fruit of the Tree of Knowledge, since it is this fruit that man lays hands upon. It might then be assumed that man receives knowledge, whereas Yahweh loses knowledge, but, if the object is knowledge, then a participative communication is concerned, even if this is unintentional.[7] The covenantal servant's appropriation does not correspond here to the covenantal lord's dispossession; Yahweh does not lose his knowledge but merely his monopoly of this knowledge. The question is, however, whether this violation is sufficient to explain the sentence of death, or whether the narrative contains a deeper conflict.

If Adam/Eve take of the fruit of the Tree of Life, this is directly concerned with a taking, but this figurative taking corresponds to a narrative giving. This becomes clear if the other side of the covenant is considered:

If Cl gives X1 to Cs, then Cs must give Y1 to Cl;
if Cs gives Y2 to Cl, then Cl must give X2 to Cs.

X1 can here be determined as the covenantal servant's dynamic scope, which may in turn be interpreted as the covenantal servant's existence. Man has received his life from the covenantal lord as creator, and by virtue of the right to exist the covenantal servant owes the covenantal lord obedience to the covenant's prescription.

The interdiction affects that which the covenantal servant wishes to do but may not. Observance of the covenant demands therefore a self-denial on the part of the covenantal servant, since he can of course infringe the interdiction. Transgression of the covenant's interdiction is equivalent, for its part, to abolition of the covenant, since the covenantal servant disregards the covenantal lord's having to in favour of his own wanting to. But the action cannot shirk a deontic interpretation, and for this reason the covenantal servant's wanting to now presents itself as a pseudo-having to. The covenantal servant has put himself in the covenantal lord's place, has to this extent, at least as he sees it himself, put Yahweh out of the running as Lord, which is equivalent to parricide. The servant/son acts in the role of parricide ($\pi\alpha\tau\rho o\lambda\tilde{\varphi}\alpha\varsigma$).

Observance of the covenant demands obedience, which involves self-denial. When the covenantal lord has given the covenantal servant life, then the latter is bound to give himself in obedience to the covenantal prescription. Y1 can be

---

[7] Cf. *Sémiotique*, art. "Communication".

interpreted as the recognition of the covenantal lord that the covenantal servant expresses when he takes of the Tree of Life, i.e. accepts the gift that was offered him. The rejection of this gift is equivalent to a taking, since the covenantal servant's doing what is interdicted corresponds to his not-doing what is prescribed. The self-denial consists in a non-taking, a non-doing of what is interdicted, which is equivalent to doing what is prescribed.

What is concerned, is a renunciation that affects a desired being (cf. 2,9; 3,6), in its uttermost consequence life itself. In this narrative, man is not to give his life but to renounce a pecuniary object of knowing and the being associated therewith. But what is concerned, is more than information and a monopoly of knowing. Whatever the pecuniary values at stake in the covenant, this always concerns the covenantal servant's existence.

The self-denial is a narrative act in which the covenantal servant gives himself (renunciation) to the covenantal lord (attribution), and it is this self-submission that Yahweh desires. Or in other words: Yahweh's being is not constituted of diverse pecuniary objects of value (fruits, knowledge) but of the relationship with the covenantal servant: Yahweh desires an obedient covenantal servant.

What is concerned at this level of pertinence, is a love relationship. The commandment in Deut 6,4f: "Hear, O Israel: The LORD is our God, the LORD alone. You shall love the LORD your God with all your heart, and with all your soul, and with all your might", discloses what Yahweh desires. And whoever loves him follows his commandment.

In the love relationship, the value is not an object but another subject, and the services exchanged are declarations of love. Observation of the commandment leads to reward, but self-denial is initially aimed at satisfying what the covenantal lord lacks. It is crucial that the covenantal lord does not himself have the power to satisfy this desire. Through the establishment of the covenant he has voluntarily made himself dependent upon the covenantal servant, who is at liberty to be able both to give and to withhold what is wished.

Yahweh/God can obtain the coveted being only as a gift from his covenantal servant.

If Adam/Eve take of the Tree of Life, then they give themselves to the covenantal lord, who thereby sees himself rewarded (obedience as repayment) for his merciful gift (life as prepayment) to the covenantal servant. His self-denial is then, in this theocentric perspective, a sanction of Yahweh's being, and it is this sanction which thereupon, in the anthropocentric register, redeems the positive sanction of the covenantal servant. If the covenantal servant gives Y2, i.e. himself, to the covenantal lord, then the covenantal lord must give X2, Definitive life, to the covenantal servant.

Y1 and Y2 are in this case the same value, but seen from two different viewpoints. Y1 is the obedience as sanction, which closes the covenantal lord's trajectory; Y2 is the obedience as a covenantal progression that causes the covenantal lord to incur a debt, in that he is thereafter obliged to close the covenantal servant's trajectory by his positive sanction. Incurring the debt reminds one of manipulation but must be differentiated from this, since here it is merely a matter of complying with a condition that the covenantal lord has himself, by manipulation, set and to which he has committed himself.

To God also, the Fall myth is a veritable dysangelium, his project misses its target. The mode of being that he not only desires but to which he is entitled by virtue of the covenant, and which the covenantal servant has, at least implicitly, promised him to procure, is never realized. The sanction, the recognition of the Creator evidenced through action, does not take place. If the image of the vessel full of water is again employed, then this, in the dysangelium, is at the outset being filled up and nearly full. The serpent's intervention stops this process, in that Adam/Eve are persuaded not to eat of the Tree of Life.

But thereupon an emptying process is initiated, in that man is persuaded to eat of the Tree of Knowledge or the Tree of Death. And the covenantal lord's degression proceeds in parallel with the covenantal servant's degression. The satisfaction the covenantal lord may have obtained by causing the covenantal servant an injury as penalty for the injury he has himself suffered, cannot invalidate the disappointment over the covenant's failed project. According to the covenant, God is indeed committed to expel man from the garden of Eden, but the question is whether he will abandon his creation project in earnest.

In a cosmological perspective, what God loses becomes perhaps still clearer. The dual sanction, of God's being through the performance of the obedient covenantal servant, of man's being through the retributive action of the obedient covenantal lord, would involve realization of Being or Definitive cosmos, elsewhere called the Kingdom of God. This mode of being is not however realized. But, and this may perhaps be surprising, neither is it realized from the very creation. From the Creator's hand the Kingdom of God exists only as a possibility, i.e. as a project that must be realized. The Kingdom of God is the objective of the covenant that the creation project is aiming to realize, i.e. the objective that has conditioned the Creator's transition to action. God had promised himself realization of this objective, which he will realize, should realize, and can realize. The problem is that he cannot realize it without man's active participation. If Adam/Eve fail, then Definitive cosmos becomes impossible, Definitive chaos inevitable. The world man enters into from the garden of Eden is a Provisional cosmos that is disastrously orientated towards annihilation, the creation project's definitive abolition.

B. THE ADAM/CHRIST MYTH

The question may be anticipated, whether the definition of Gen 2,4b-3,24 as the dysangelium that the gospel narrative presupposes is fortuitous. This narrative certainly plays an important role in Pauline and later Christian traditions, but what basis has narrative exegesis for asserting the presence of an intertextual relationship between the Fall myth and Mark's Gospel? The question is justified not least if narrative exegesis wishes to go so far as to maintain that the Christ myth can in fact be understood only in relation to the Fall myth.

The objection is justified that the Adam/Christ typology in Pauline and in later Christian traditions is not in itself an argument for an intertextual association between Gen 2,4b-3,24 and Mark's Gospel. However, narrative exegesis' demonstration of this intertextuality does not rest on the use of the Adam figure in these traditions. The fact must be borne in mind that whereas the Fall myth is concerned with the beginning, the gospel narrative is concerned with the end, and the question is whether this beginning and this end belong to one and the same process (the creation project) that concerns one and the same subject of being, humankind in its relationship with God the Creator.

The one prerequisite for this is that both these narratives are articulated on the basis of the same semantic universe. But this condition is precisely met in the present case, where both dysangelium and evangelium receive their semantic unity from the LIFE/DEATH isotopy, whose terminals are Definitive life and Definitive death.

Expressed another way, in both narratives it is eternal life (individual perspective) and the Kingdom of God (collective perspective) that are at stake. Both narratives are also concerned with how each individual person's act (misdeed or good deed) becomes significant to the existence of the rest of mankind, whose existence (this world, the provisional life) can be defined only as a deficient mode of being relative to this eternal life, this Kingdom of God.

The other prerequisite that must be met is that the annihilation is not fully realized. But on this point also the requirement is met. It is noteworthy that the annihilation is eschatologically postponed. Adam and Eve certainly die, but before that they succeed in reproducing themselves. The individuals die, but mankind preserves the provisional life. It should also be noted that the individual man is born into this provisional life, which is fatally orientated towards definitive death. The modalization that characterizes this man's existence is because of the misdeed that Adam/Eve performed. He is born unworthy, a sinner, because of the first men's sin, whether or not one speaks of an original sin.

In *Christology in the Making*, JAMES D.G. DUNN writes:

Adam plays a larger role in Paul's theology than is usually realized - and even when that role is taken into account it is often misunderstood. Adam is a key figure in Paul's attempt to express his understanding both of Christ and of man. Since soteriology and christology are closely connected in Paul's theology, it is necessary to trace the extent of the Adam motif in Paul if we are to appreciate the force of his Adam christology.[8]

But this perspective is too narrow. The Adam figure - or more correctly the *dysangelium*, Gen 2,4b-3,24 - plays a much greater part in the New Testament signification universe as a whole than is generally assumed, and is crucial to an understanding of the gospel narrative's christology.

What is concerned, however, is not an investigation of "the Adam motif". Narrative exegesis does not ask for motifs but for the structures of signification, the narrative forms of organization, whose role configurations decide which actors can be typologized. It is the common covenant schema in the narratives of Adam and Christ that is the semiotic prerequisite for the explicit typology in Pauline and later Christian traditions, as well as for the implicit typology in Mark.

Narrative exegesis does not read the theological perception of traditional interpretation into the gospel narrative, but lays bare the semiotic reason that has determined this tradition's reception and theological reasoning.

If the Fall myth is collated with the Christ myth as one single narrative, then the narrative process that extends from creation's beginning to creation's completion becomes an interactive matter between one single covenantal lord, God, and a single covenantal servant, Adam/Christ, i.e. man. This man is mankind's representative, and as such the intermediary between God and mankind. The covenantal servant is *the one* mythical man, i.e. *the Son of Man*, whose doings and acts become fatal for the existence of *the many*, now to fall, now to rise.[9]

The Adam/Christ myth, or the myth of the Son of Man, includes two moves, the dysangelical degression (the Fall) and the evangelical progression (the Rise). The christological schema, the evangelical covenantal servant's narrative trajectory, thus proves to be merely one half of a superior mythical schema that constitutes the Christian semiotics. The other, prerequired half is made up of the

---

[8] James D.G. Dunn, *Christology in the Making. A New Testament Inquiry into the Origins of the Doctrine of the Incarnation*, London 1980, p. 101. Dunn's analysis of "Paul's Adam christology" will not be considered in detail here. It should merely be noted that his understanding of Phil 2,6-11 as an expression of this Adam christology in a narrative perspective deserves all possible attention, and that the observation that "the last Adam by his 'superexaltation' ($\grave{v}\pi\epsilon\rho\acute{v}\psi\omega\sigma\epsilon\nu$) attains a far higher glory than the first Adam lost", ibidem, p. 118, confirms the present investigation, according to which man in the garden of Eden had not as yet realized Being.

[9] If the relationship between Adam and Christ is not only formally but objectively substantiated, then "the Son of Man" becomes a title that receives its essential signification content from this. Narrative exegesis shows this objective, intertextual connection, in this context without the inclusion of Hellenistic Judaism's Adam traditions but by going directly to Gen 2,4b-3,24. It thus bases itself on neither the assumption of the existence of a Near-Eastern primitive-man myth nor a gnostic deliverer myth, cf. Mogens Müller, *Der Ausdruck "Menschensohn" in den Evangelien*, Leiden 1984, pp. 46.

dysangelical covenantal servant's narrative trajectory. This Christian proclamation necessarily includes all of this narrative process, i.e. the Adam-Christ myth.

The Adam-Christ typology is indeed oppositional:

Temptation	vs.	Test (trial)
Misdeed (taking)	vs.	Good deed (gift)
Penalty (annihilation)	vs.	Reward (creation)

But the antithesis is given within one and the same creation project. The postponed annihilation renders restoration of the covenantal relationship between God and man possible, and thus permits a possible realization of the project towards which this covenant has been directed since the creation.

The counter-move must necessarily assume the form of a progression, which, it appears, can be of only one specific kind. If the dysangelium's covenantal servant infringes the covenant's interdiction by a blameworthy taking, a selfish appropriation, which implies a well-deserved penalty, then the evangelium's covenantal servant must observe the covenant's command through a praiseworthy giving, an unselfish renunciation, a sacrifice, that implies a well-deserved reward.[10] So it is if the evangelium is to match the dysangelium. There are good reasons to assume that whoever conceived the first image of the narrative Jesus was governed - consciously or unconsciously - by certain semiotic constraints given by the narrative genre of the dysangelium. Substantially, the genre of the gospel narrative is presumably formed as the contrasting counterpart to the Fall myth.

This is not only for the sake of formal symmetry but because the injury the first Adam inflicted on God through the misdeed can be atoned for and restored only through the last Adam's good deed, which invalidates the guilty-one's culpability. So we have:

DYSANGELIUM	EVANGELIUM
The first Adam/Christ	The last Adam/Christ
Damnation/Fall	Salvation/Restitution
Appropriation ⇒ Degression	Renunciation ⇒ Progression
Misdeed ⇒ Punishment	Good deed ⇒ Reward
Disobedience/Sinner	Obedience/Righteous

---

[10] Cf. Claude Bremond, "La logique des possibles narratifs", *Communications 8*, Paris 1966, pp. 74.

In the capacity of Progression, the Christ myth is not merely formally in opposition to the Fall myth as Degression. For the death on the cross is an act that intervenes in and modifies the same process to which the primal crime belongs. The first Adam was a degressor, since by his misdeed he put mankind into a degressive mode of being (Provisional life). But because the annihilation was postponed he appeared as repressor, he who had blocked the way to the garden of Eden. The last Adam is a progressor, since by his good deed he put mankind into a progressive mode of being. But the relationship to Christ is not spontaneous, as is the relationship to Adam. This progressive mode of being is merely possible. The last Adam appears therefore as protector, savior. He has neutralized the on-going annihilation process and reinstated mankind in a mode of being in which eternal life is possible, he has reopened the way to the garden of Eden, to the Kingdom of God.

CHAPTER FIFTEEN

NARRATIVE UNITY

The gospel narrative covers two composite courses of action, the *gospel-constituting* and the *gospel-persisting* processes of events. The constituting events establish a world (new creation). The persisting events, on the other hand, associate the creature with and keep his attention upon this world.

The gospel-constituting process of events that concerns the relationship between God and Jesus is composed of the acts that belong to the kerygmatic schema, whose double narrative trajectory (the covenantal lord's and the covenantal servant's) makes it possible to discern a theocentric and a christocentric soteriology. This salvation project finds its conclusion within the gospel story's narrate. The superior creation project in which this salvation project sees itself embedded will, however, see its consummation in the narration's, i.e. the narrator's and the narratee's, future.

The gospel-persisting process of events that concerns the relationship between Jesus and his disciples initially includes a teaching project that is completed within the narrated world. The encounter with the resurrected becomes the sign of anamnesis (remembrance; cf. 14,30.72; anagnorisis; cf. Lk 24,31) that in retrospect opens the door to a perception of the teaching already given. This reversal forms an opening for the disciples' preaching project, the proclamation of the gospel of Jesus Christ, a proclamation that has already been realized by virtue of the gospel narrative's own narration (cf. 1,1).

This proclamation singles out the narratee as a favoured subject of being, since the salvation project has made eternal life possible for him. The proclamation narrated: "The time is fulfilled, and the kingdom of God has come near; repent, and believe in the good news." (1,15) now becomes a narrating proclamation addressed to the reader, and herein it is not difficult to hear a command about a Christian baptism of repentance (cf. 1,4). The baptism takes place in the narratee's future, during the period between ascension and parousia, and whoever is baptized becomes Jesus Christ's disciple and thereby heir to eternal life, one of the elect.

The gospel-constituting process of events is dominated by a pragmatic dimension that implies a change in Jesus' somatic being and the modal structure associated therewith. The gospel-persisting process of events is dominated by a cognitive dimension centred on the questions, "Who is Jesus?", "What does 'Christ' mean?". The difficulties of understanding encountered by the disciples - the privileged cognitive actors - is fundamentally because what is to be recognized, Jesus' being, *is a being in the state of becoming*. An adequate understanding of who Jesus is and what Christ means is in fact only possible after the resurrection, when he has realized his christological being. It is therefore impossible to decide before the resurrection whether the death on the cross is a definitive death (Jewish perspective) or a provisional death (Christian perspective).

The predominant part of the gospel narrative's information concerns the gospel-persisting process of events, the relationship between Jesus and his disciples. But exegesis should not, because of this, allow itself to be inveigled into a biased definition of Mark's Gospel on the basis of its cognitive problems. Considered qualitatively, the information on the gospel-constitutive process of events, on the relationship between God and Jesus, is of greater significance, since persistence presupposes constitution.

The gospel-constituting process of events is articulated by the kerygmatic schema, the fundamental salvation project, which is to be proclaimed.

The interaction between the processes of events forms the gospel narrative, which informs about what is to be proclaimed as well as about the project of teaching that ends in the enlightenment and faith, which this proclamation presupposes. GERD THEIßEN is of a different opinion, which will be described and discussed below.

A. THE THREE ARCHES

From the fundamental assumption that "erst die übergreifende Komposition verleiht den Evangelien einheitliche Gestalt", THEIßEN asks about the sequences of events that form "Spannungsbögen", which include the whole gospel text.[1] He believes that he can identify three such arches in Mark's Gospel: the aretalogical, the mythical and the biographical.

The *aretalogical* arch (aretalogy: teaching about the gods' wonder-working) is defined by a search "nach Erkenntnis der wahren Würde Jesu".[2] In the first half of the gospel, the question is raised of who Jesus is, occasioned by his words and actions (cf. e.g. 6,1ff), but no unequivocal answer is given to this question, either from the listeners and onlookers or from those who are subject to his actions. In Peter's confession (8,29) an incipient awareness appears, but this confession is nevertheless not an expression of an adequate understanding, and the arch is still uncompleted. It is completed only by the centurion's confession at the cross (15,39): "Hier spricht zum ersten Mal ein Mensch aus, daß Jesus Sohn Gottes ist".[3] And when the curtain of the temple was torn in two immedi-

---

[1] Gerd Theißen, *Urchristliche Wundergeschichten. Ein Beitrag zur formgeschichtlichen Erforschung der synoptischen Evangelien*, Göttingen 1974, p. 211.

[2] Gerd Theißen, ibidem p. 212.

[3] Gerd Theißen, ibidem p. 213.

ately before this confession, then Mark suggests that thereby the secrecy which has characterized the narrative sequence hitherto has now become revealed to the narrated recipient: Jesus is the Son of God (the reader has known this from the outset).

The *mythical* arch, which is also called "das mytische Stufenschema", includes baptism, transfiguration and death on the cross, the same steps that PHILIPP VIELHAUER, in analogy with an ancient Egyptian enthronement ritual, has interpreted as an enthronization process.[4] But because of the predominant position the centurion's confession assumes in the context of the death on the cross, THEIßEN does not emphasize this mythical schema as "stufenweise Realisierung der Würde Jesu" but as "sukzessive Offenbarung und Anerkennung".[5] Jesus becomes Son of God in baptism (adoption), and God reveals him as such to the disciples in the transfiguration on the mountain. The death on the cross is then the moment when Jesus publically appears before the world for rejection or recognition. Both the aretalogical and the mythical arches are thus completed by the centurion's declaration. But the mythical arch is, in contrast to the aretalogical, unfinished. THEIßEN considers that a mythical pre-history is lacking, and only the parousia can bring the mythical sequence to its conclusion. Mark's Gospel, therefore, receives its unity from the aretalogical arch, and can consequently be defined as "eine aretalogische Evangelienkomposition".[6]

The *biographical* arch is present first and foremost in the Passion, but includes any biographical-chronological definition of Jesus. THEIßEN appears to have in mind here primarily the elementary point that Jesus of Nazareth lives and dies. But Mark's Gospel has no childhood history, no unified description of Jesus' life. Mark is not interested in Jesus' life as a unity but in the unity in the sequence of events that longs for recognition of Jesus as the Son of God. Also, the partially present biographical arch ends at the death on the cross. All three arches thus culminate in the centurion's confession, but the aretalogical, which is the only arch completed, is dominant.

B. THE TWO PROCESSES OF EVENTS

What is most striking about THEIßEN's interpretation is that the wonder of all wonders - the resurrection - is disregarded. This event appears in none of the three arches, and for this reason alone one is forced to be dismissive towards his hypothesis. But the Achilles' heel of the hypothesis is the interpretation of the

---

[4] Cf. Philipp Vielhauer, "Erwägungen zur Christologie des Markusevangeliums", *Aufsätze zum Neuen Testament*, München 1965, pp. 199.

[5] Gerd Theißen, ibidem p. 215.

[6] Gerd Theißen, ibidem p. 217.

centurion's confession that occurs in all three arches, which strictly speaking disclaims the relevance of a distinction between them. The weakness in THEIßEN's analysis is most clearly expressed in the mythical arch, in which the centurion's *declaration* enjoys the undeserved honour of being equated to God's declaration relating to baptism and transfiguration.

What is concerned here, however, is a striking confusion of categories. If the centurion's confession is to be juxtaposed with anything it is with Peter's confession, as this also occurs within the aretalogical arch. Both express an acknowledgment of Jesus as something special, but neither of them has grasped the true understanding of his being. Peter has not understood what "Christ" actually means (8,33); the centurion sees Jesus' way of death as a sign of his divine mission, the crucifixion as a murder of the prophet, a son of God, sent by God, but nothing indicates that he understands what "Son of God" in fact signifies. No Christian confession of faith is therefore concerned.[7]

To assert that the three arches conclude in the centurion's declaration is just as incorrect as to state that Jesus' life concludes in the death on the cross.

The aretalogical arch whose information belongs to the gospel-persisting process of events in no way concludes in any narrated confession. One can only say that if the women had not told the disciples and Peter that Jesus had arisen and preceded them to Galilee, as he had said (16,6;14,28), and if Jesus had not appeared to his disciples, then no recognition would have existed, no proclamation sounded. The implicit ending is the link between the gospel story's narrate and narration, and Mark's Gospel itself is thus the original, narrating confession.

The Markan gospel narrative takes its justification and authority from the processes of events narrated.[8]

The mythical arch is also in another way a confusion of incompatible material. Besides confusing the centurion's declaration with God's declarations, THEIßEN here confuses baptism and transfiguration, probably led astray by VIELHAUER, although the baptism concerns the relationship between God and Jesus, whereas the transfiguration relates to the relationship between Jesus and the disciples. Baptism forms part of the gospel-constituting process of events, whereas the transfiguration forms part of the gospel-persisting process of events. THEIßEN's mythical arch is an incorrect construction.

The biographical arch on the other hand is a futile construction. THEIßEN does not see that Jesus' death on the cross is mythical, but succumbs to the general assumption that the narrative Jesus lives and dies just like other men, so as to

[7] Cf. Rudolf Pesch: "Mit dem Präteritum "war" (ἦν) beurteilt er den Gestorbenen - er spricht kein christliches Bekenntnis zum Auferstandenen aus. Die nicht determinierte Wendung "Sohn Gottes" (υἱὸς θεοῦ) zählt Jesus zu den Söhnen Gottes (vgl. Weish 2,18; 5,5), er ist als Gerechter Gottes Sohn. Eine exklusiv titulare Interpretation ergibt sich erst in christlicher Perspektive, die dem Hauptmann noch nicht unterstellt ist.", *Das Markusevangelium, 2. Teil*, p. 500.

[8] The narrator Mark cannot of course found his proclamation upon the centurion's confession to the dead Jesus.

become - paradoxically - rehabilitated by God.[9]) But there is, as has been established, no contradiction, no breach, between death on the cross and resurrection in the gospel narrative.[10]

Moreover, it must once again be stressed that the gospel-constituting process of events, the kerygmatic or christological schema, is a *mythos* with a beginning (anointing, establishment of covenant), a middle (from anointing to death on the cross) and an end (resurrection, which installs Jesus in his full covenantal being).

However mythological parousia appears, it belongs to the gospel-persisting process of events, since this is aimed at the relationship between Jesus and his chosen disciples, his community.

Against this background, THEIßEN's hypothesis that Mark's Gospel is an aretalogical gospel composition is rejected. It is above all the gospel-constituting process of events that - precisely as a gradual realization of Jesus' being, but in a manner other than that perceived by VIELHAUER - establishes the gospel story's *narrative unity*, since the *persistence* presupposes the *constitution* (in the same way as the cognitive presupposes the pragmatic).

The Markan narrative is basically a christological gospel composition.

Bearing in mind that the gospel text manifests a double narrative about the covenant between God and Jesus and the covenant between Jesus and his disciples, it may, however, be conceded that the gospel story's narrative unity results from the interaction between two hierarchically linked unities, the gospel-constituting and the gospel-persisting processes of events:

	Constitution	Persistence
Covenantal lord (Superior)	GOD	JESUS
Covenantal servant (Inferior)	JESUS	DISCIPLES

---

[9] Cf. also Theißen's comments in Rudolf Bultmann, *Die Geschichte der synoptischen Tradition/Ergänzungsheft*, Göttingen 1971, p. 125: "Sobald eine noch so fragmentarische Erzählung vom Tod Jesu im Evangelium seinen Platz haben sollte, ist ein festes chronologisches Moment gegeben: der Tod ist nun einmal das Ende des Lebens und gehört auch literarisch ans Ende.". The point of the Christian proclamation, also in Mark's Gospel, is however that Jesus' death on the cross was precisely not "das Ende des Lebens".

[10] Death on the cross is a provisional death belonging to the mythic existence. This should not be taken to mean that Jesus was only apparently dead or the like. To this extent, the death on the cross is - physiologically - a quite ordinary death. What distinguishes this provisional death from the definitive death is its contractual or covenantal value. Both are deficient conditions of being, but provisional death is temporary and will inevitably lead to the acquisition of eternal life.

Jesus is now the servant (διάκονος, 10,45;Rom 15,8; παῖς, Mt 12,18; Acts 3,13.26; 4,27.30), now the lord (κύριος). As mediator (μεσίτης, cf. 1 Tim 2,5; Heb 8,6; 9,15; 12,24) he appears in both processes of events, which are thereby linked.[11]

---

[11] The demonstration of the superior and integrating covenantal structure makes it natural to compare the gospel narrative's christology with the Letter to the Hebrews' explicit covenantal theology, but such an investigation is beyond the limits of this work.

CHAPTER SIXTEEN

NARRATIVE EVANGELIUM

The Christian evangelium, the good news, is a narrative whose principal content (narrate) is a series of narrated events centred around Jesus Christ. As proclamation (narration), however, the gospel narrative combines in a special way this narrated world with the narrator's world.

A. Narrative Kerygma

PETER KEMP quotes in *Poétique de l'engagement* HEINRICH OTT, who quotes MARTIN HEIDEGGER:

> Chaque grand poète ne compose qu'à partir d'un seul Poème ... Ce Poème reste non prononcé (*ungesprochen*). Aucune des œuvres du poète, même pas leur ensemble, ne dit tout. Néanmoins, chaque œuvre parle à partir de la totalité du Poème unique et, chaque fois, c'est lui qui est dit.

OTT is then quoted from his own use of this quotation:

> L'Evangile unique est, en quelque sorte, le Poème non prononcé de tous les témoignages bibliques ou, du moins, néo-testamentaires, le Poème à partir duquel ils sont tous composés.

And KEMP concludes that this analogy between the Gospel and the Poem undoubtedly shows the path the theologian must take.[1]

For the very reason that one intuitively perceives the truth in this viewpoint, it might be interesting to see how narrative exegesis would be able to reformulate these somewhat cryptic versions so that this systematic insight were given an exegetic basis.

If one understands by "New Testament testimonies" the canonical texts, then this *corpus* will be characterized, in accordance with the mode of thought, by *semiotic unity*, and the viewpoint adopted will necessarily be *generalizing*.

In accordance with the semioticians' hypothetico-deductive procedure, the generalization takes the form of the construction of a model that is hierarchically superior and extends beyond the analyzed text, which is considered merely as a

---

[1] Peter Kemp, *Théorie de l'engagement/2. Poétique de l'engagement*, Paris 1973, p. 27.

variant thereof.[2] This model remains implicit. None of the individual variants (e.g. the synoptic gospels) says everything, not even all of them together. Nevertheless, each variant speaks on the basis of the one model's unity and enunciates this every time. The superior task of narrative exegesis is then to define the model that may explicate the semiotics of New Testament, i.e. the canonical texts perceived as an articulated set of hierarchically organized (paradigmatic and syntagmatic) signification.

This viewpoint does not imply a denial of the differences between the various testimonies; this is not a matter of taking a short cut in order to harmonize. But the differences are considered as structural differences, i.e. the differences can be defined as variations relative to the constant model, which functions as *tertium comparationis*.

It is obvious that narrative exegesis thus adopts an achronic viewpoint and does not question the age of the different texts or sub-texts. It will not therefore consider itself obliged to seek to define the model - "the Poem" or "the Christ Poem" - on the basis of a, from an historical viewpoint (presumably), particularly early text, such as e.g. the Christ hymn in Paul's letter to the Philippians (2,6-11).

In continuation of ERNST LOHMEYER's investigation, which emphasizes this hymn's pre-Pauline nature, KEMP believes that we have here an opportunity to "considérer le kérygme à l'état naissant, à savoir sous forme de mythe pur", and he assumes that "le mythe qui est à la base de l'hymne est le Poème chrétien, c'est-à-dire le kérygme lui-même".[3]

One detects an exegetic embarrassment in KEMP's use of LOHMEYER's historical analysis. The actual concept of the one Poem has indeed already left behind the historical viewpoint, but nevertheless the hymn of the Letter to the Philippians is emphasized, because historico-genetically it is regarded as particularly close to the Poem.

The achronic viewpoint cannot however argue with the historico-genetic. It does not call for layers of tradition and redaction but for *layers of signification*, and it is of course particularly anxious to determine the fundamental layer of signification in Christian semiotics.

The working hypothesis that the kerygmatic schema defined above shows *the narrative kerygma* which forms the fundamental layer of signification in Christian semiotics must therefore be suggested.

This layer of signification is not necessarily first in an historico-genetic sense but represents the signification hierarchy's cornerstone, the arch-layer established by methodical procedure.

---

[2] Cf. *Sémiotique*, art. "Généralisation".

[3] Peter Kemp, ibidem pp. 105 and 110. Ernst Lohmeyer, *Kyrios Jesus, Eine Untersuchung zu Phil 2,5-11*, Darmstadt (1927) 1961, pp. 73.

Two points should be taken into consideration:

1) The *narrative kerygma* is a mythos with a beginning, a middle and an end, and as such constitutes a unified structure. This whole can be defined only by the structural relations that exist between its integral parts, and each individual part (e.g. baptism/anointing, death on the cross and resurrection) is therefore of equal significance and of equal necessity. Each individual part has value by virtue of its function in the whole, and cannot therefore be considered in isolation therefrom.

2) The *narrative kerygma* is a semiotically constructed model that can be used to determine not just one existing Christian discourse (e.g. the Markan narrative) but every Christian discourse. It exists - and has never existed otherwise - only partially manifested as a variant, since no Christian discourse can manifest the whole of its signification potential. An existing discourse is, however, a *Christian discourse* only if it is founded on the narrative kerygma, and even the most partial manifestation presupposes this whole.

This viewpoint implies that the narrative kerygma's structure of signification has the status of a constant of which the existing Christian discourses are variants. For narrative exegesis, therefore, the synoptic gospels are three expanded variants, while the kerygmatic formulae, e.g. Rom 1,3f; 1 Cor 15,3-7 and Acts 10,37-41, are condensed variants of the narrative kerygma.[4] It may be anticipated that as a fully developed and canonized model the narrative kerygma will be able to function as an Archimedean point of reference for narrative exegesis' explanation of the unity and variability in the abundance of Christian discourses.[5]

B. Kerygmatic Narration

Important aspects of the gospel narrative's kerygmatic narration are discussed above, where it is emphasized that the narratee sees himself as having been selected as a favoured subject of being by virtue of the deictic semiotization that results from the merger between the narrate's and the narration's future. The

---

[4] Cf. the relationship between the condensed and expanded wonder narrative, Chapter VI, D.2. The narrator proclaiming Jesus Christ as Lord (cf. Rom 1,3) must be prepared for the questions: "Who is Jesus?", "Which Christ?". To be able to answer these questions, the narrator must preach God's gospel (cf. Rom 1,1), i.e., tell the gospel narrative about his son (cf. Rom 1,2).

[5] Narrative exegesis thus seems to be a particularly appropriate methodical basis for the establishment of a New Testament theology.

salvation and creation project that exists in narrated form will see its conclusion only in the narratee's future. By this deictic semiotization, the gospel narrative provides the narratee with his Christian identity or role, but only by way of the word, and the proclamation roles characterizing the narrate are now rediscovered in the narration.[6]

The narrator, Mark, appears in the role of informator and/or dissimulator, and his information is either veridiction or simulation. Mark is either a revealator or a (involuntary or voluntary) deceptor. The proclamation's veridictory status will be revealed only when the Son of Man comes with the clouds of heaven. Until then, the narratee must content himself with the narrative of Jesus Christ. No sign other than this semiotic, narrative sign, whose linguistic plane of expression refers to a linguistic plane of content, exists, and consequently the narratee is reduced to the narrative proclamation's veridictory ambiguity.

The kerygmatic narration is not only informative but also persuasive. The proclamation is not merely a conveyance of knowledge but a process of influencing that singles out the narratee as a virtual subject of doing for a mission. This mission may be described in general as *the Christian life* (life in Christ, cf. Rom 6,4; Col 2,6; 2 Tim 3,12), but it is characteristic that the gospel narratives contain only little information about this post-paschal and post-kerygmatic existence. Information on this must be sought in the other New Testament texts that may thus be said to presuppose the gospels, not necessarily as gospel texts but as gospel narratives.

From the gospel narrative alone, therefore, what narrative exegesis is able to say about the roles that describe the narratee in the performed, post-kerygmatic Christian life is limited. But it is at least possible to describe his competence, which exists as a result of the meeting with the kerygmatic narration and is the presupposition for the transition to action.

Whoever is not informed about Jesus' salvation action is for good reasons excluded from relating to the matter. The disciples are therefore subject to a prescription to proclaim the gospel to all peoples. He who is informed, on the other hand, must decide what he is to think and believe. If the narratee rejects the narrative, miscarried information is concerned. If he accepts the narration, then either a successful veridiction or a successful simulation is concerned. Whether the believer is clearsighted (favoured by a veridiction) or blind (victim of a simulation) is, so to speak, a secret that will be revealed only on the Day of Judgment.[7]

The proclamation must also be directed towards the narratee's bulistic modalization as seduction and/or intimidation. It must try to evoke the desire for and the hope of a state of being (eternal life) and the will to realize this. And/or

---

[6] Cf. Chapter VII, B.2; and Chapter IX, B.2.

[7] Cf. Chapter VIII, A; C.2.

it must try to evoke (or nourish) the fear of a state of being (eternal death) and aversion to the realization of this. In the gospel narrative, the promise of eternal life predominates, but only against the background of the possibility of an annihilating judgment.

In relation to the question of seduction/intimidation, it may be said that the relationship between the narration's narrator (Mark) and narratee (presupposed reader) is homologous to the relationship between the narrate's principal narrator (Jesus) and narratee (the disciples).

However paradoxical this may seem, the prophet Jesus is the evangelist's mouthpiece and not vice-versa, as one might be tempted to believe. When the narrative Jesus speaks it is Mark who speaks, hidden behind a narrated actor. When the disciples speak it is similarly Mark who speaks, hidden behind narrated actors.

Both narrator and narratee are therefore referring to one single instance of enunciation - λογοποιός - that through the act of enunciation sees itself articulated and decentralized. The conflict between Jesus and the disciples thus reflects the conflict in Mark himself. The gospel narrative exists as the result of a signification endeavour by which the evangelist attempts to formulate his understanding of himself in the world, stretched as he is between censorship and wishful thinking.

Although closer exploration of these aspects of the narration is still to be carried out, it is possible to assert that the image of the disciples reveals Mark's image of his presupposed reader. The latter is just as unwise and of just as little faith as the disciples. But the point is that Mark is aware of the resistance to the proclamation of the gospel primarily from the censorship in himself, and it is this resistance that on the narrated stage appears in the form of disciples. The presupposed reader undergoes a reading process, in that he is led through the process of the narrative, and this must be homologous to the cognitive-affective process that the disciples undergo.

Mark cannot interpellate and retain his reader by teaching about the Son of Man's suffering, but must establish the recognition on the narratee's desire for glory and power. It is asserted, therefore, that the gospel narrative can only capture its reader if it initially appeals to his doxomania and wishful thinking. Mark knows what the narratee desires, and must interpellate him on the powerful Christ (wonder-worker).

Only then can he lead his narratee through the alienation and semiotization process that reveals that the world of reality is bound up with suffering and death. The glory is absent, but will be encountered again in an eschatologically postponed future.[8]

---

[8] Cf. Chapter VIII, C.3; and Chapter IX, C.

Finally, the kerygmatic narration must involve a commandment (prescription or interdiction) initially concerning repentance and baptism. In the same way as the disciples are referred to Galilee (16,7), the narratee is referred to the Christian baptism, which is merely the baptism of John transfigured through the prism of resurrection.[9] The gospel narrative is otherwise silent about the rules characterizing Christian life.[10]

---

[9] Cf. Chapter VIII, C.4.c; and Chapter XII, B.1.c.

[10] In this perspective it can be maintained that the gospel narrative requires Acts and the epistolary literature.

CHAPTER SEVENTEEN

NARRATIVITY AND HISTORICITY

One of the theological objections that could be raised against the suggestion of a narrative exegesis might read: might not the definition of Mark's Gospel as a gospel narrative, a definition that disregards the gospel text as an historical source and thus shifts attention from the historical Jesus to the narrative Jesus, imply from its actual point of reference a failure to appreciate the historicity in the Christian proclamation: that Christ was Jesus of Nazareth?

As a conclusion, this is the central question to be clarified and answered.[1]

A. HISTORICAL TRUTH

As pointed out in the introduction, the gospel narrative remains itself, whatever its correspondence to historical reality. As a semiotic sign (connotation language), it says precisely the same, whether it is true or false historically. The narrative does not take its meaning from whether it is true or false, but it is this meaning in toto that in the form of an assertion may be historically true or false.

As long as narrative exegesis is engaged in reconstructing the narrate's meaning, it is justified in permitting itself to disregard the question of the gospel narrative's historical truth. But when the distinctive narration is concerned narrative exegesis must also relate to the proclamation's claim of truth, not to decide whether it is true or false but to illustrate how the gospel narrative is itself concerned with the question of its own truth.

Is, then, Mark's Gospel true or false? Is it an account of actual events or a fictional narrative? If one asks the gospel narrative itself, it is in no doubt: it is true. One might perhaps have anticipated that it was in no position at all to answer the question, since it merely gives information on what took place, and must therefore feel uncomfortable about the questioning of its evidence.

But this is far from the case. The gospel narrative is not only an informative discourse but also a persuasive discourse pervaded from beginning to end by an interest in its own truth. It is thus not content to inform about Jesus' words and deeds but tells at length about its own origin as narrative proclamation. Artfully, the gospel narrative presents itself as an unfailing sign of the fact that at least

---

[1] It is beyond the scope of this exegetic study to enter discussion with more systematic approaches. The results presented are, however, of systematic relevance and may for example provide us with a more adequate perception of mythos and emplotment, cf. Paul Ricoeur, *Time and Narrative*, Chicago 1984.

some of the disciples had come to believe that the crucified Jesus of Nazareth was really Christ, the Son of God, and the Son of Man who was raised up on the third day. For if this is not so, no narrative would have existed.

It is one matter that the gospel narrative claims to be true; it is quite another matter whether it actually is true. Can it, for example, withstand historical criticism that mercilessly adopts the task of assessing its credibility as a source of actual historical events? The answer here is clear: it cannot. From an historical viewpoint that remains true to itself, the gospel narrative as it directly appears, i.e. as a single coherent assertion, is of no value as a source for the events it recounts.

The historian has not, however, come to this result because he has examined the matter carefully, but it follows from his epistemic starting point, which implies an empirical understanding of reality that is contradicted by the gospel narrative's view of reality. Viewed in the light of the historian's empirical understanding of reality, the gospel narrative is pure fiction. However much he would like to do so, the historian is not in a position to confirm or render probable the gospel narrative. He cannot even curb a doubt that would be to the advantage of the accused. If asked, he is bound to answer: the gospel narrative is unhistorical; what it recounts never took place.

Against such radical historical scepticism, however, it might immediately be argued that the gospel narrative, despite its indisputable character of purposeful writing, nevertheless contains discursive and narrative material that could very well be historically credible sources to illustrate what has, at least in part, occurred. For example, there is historically no reason to doubt that the crucifixion of Jesus of Nazareth actually took place, and that the gospel narrative has therefore an historical core. So it is quite unjustified to assert that the information that the historical Jesus of Nazareth was executed must be historically untrustworthy, and that this event never took place.

The question here concerned is painful, since the problems touch on the fundamental principles upon which our historical knowledge, and thus our historical self-perception, rest.

However, it must be asked, where did this self-assuredness, with which we so categorically pass judgment on the historicity of the death on the cross, originate? An answer which immediately suggests itself would be that the crucifixion emerges as an unquestionable historical fact, since it has been so well documented as an historical event that it must rest with whoever contests the factuality to show that it is unhistorical. But considering the number of historically improbable events recounted in the gospel narrative, one may well be sceptical about whether the death on the cross is indeed as well documented as initially assumed. It must be faced that the gospel narrative as a whole bears witness to a world which the historian must reject. The transempirical events predominate and set the mythical sign that determines the historian's scepticism as regards any information the narrator may advance.[2]

The matter can, however, be questioned in another way. In a narrative perspective it can, with full justification, be asserted that the raising up of Jesus of Nazareth is an event as equally well documented in the gospel narrative as the death on the cross. If one believes that the death on the cross according to the gospel narrative is a well-documented fact, then the resurrection (and all the other transempirical events) is a well-documented fact according to the same gospel narrative. The card has been played, and one must admit that these transempirical events must be given the same historical status if the only question is the gospel narrative's representation. But it then becomes clear that it is indeed not a matter of documentation, and the question then becomes: where did the certainty about the historicity of the crucifixion have its source?

Strictly speaking, can the historian know with *absolute* certainty that Jesus of Nazareth was crucified? No, he cannot, but it seems to him so *probable* that he finds it not only unjustified to doubt it but positively accepts it as an historical fact. It is nevertheless a matter of faith, in so far as it concerns the confidence in the gospel narrative as an historical source. The historian has only the evangelist's words to rely on, and these he encounters with preconception of himself and his world, where some events seem probable while others seem improbable. If the historian does not doubt the historicity of the death on the cross, this is because the event seems to him so probable that he must attribute to it the status of an historical fact.

It is noteworthy that when the historian is faced with a source that itself claims to relate an historical event, he is forced to accept this source as credible unless it is 1) contradicted by other sources in which he has greater confidence or 2) contradicted by his understanding of reality. If no other sources are available and the source is historically probable, i.e. relates events and acts that can occur in the historian's empirical world, then he cannot do otherwise than believe in it. That the source is perhaps a falsification - the subsequent discovery of other sources may perhaps change the historian's opinion - alters nothing in this regard. The historian has no choice, but is subject in his interpretation to a compulsion of thought whose peculiarity indeed constitutes and validates his viewpoint as the historian's viewpoint.

If, then, the historian asserts with great confidence that the crucifixion of Jesus of Nazareth is an historical fact which no one can doubt without denying

---

[2] "Man kann das mythische Weltbild nur als ganzes annehmen oder verwerfen.", writes Rudolf Bultmann quite correctly, "Neues Testament und Mythologie", Hans Werner Bartsch (ed.) *Kerygma und Mythos I*, Hamburg (1948) 1960, pp. 21. But if the gospel text's mythical image of the world is dismissed, then the gospel text itself is rejected, and can thereafter be read only symptomatically. It is true that modern man whom Bultmann has in mind cannot accept the gospel text as historiography, but then this "modern man" must reject the gospel text entirely - or read it as a gospel narrative of which he never really knows whether it is fiction in disguise of reality or reality in disguise of fiction.

reality, this is because this event is objectively probable according to the given understanding of reality. This preconception may be referred to as the *historical* or *empirical interpretant*, meaning the sum of presuppositions, i.e. the *epistemic competence* that guides the execution of historical or empirical interpretation.

B. Narrative Truth

It is tempting for theology to press historical interpretation's subjective aspect and to emphasize that reconstruction of the historical reality is founded on faith and confidence. In this way the empirical understanding of reality is relativized, and is then merely to be considered as one possible understanding among others. The reality of history and of the narrative is then basically given the same status, and everyone is content in his belief.

But the disturbing factor is still present.

Even if one accepts that historiography is a reconstructive work of signification ending in narrativized discourses to the effect that both historical narrative and mythical narrative are linguistically interpreted reality, the difference remains because two different forms of construction of reality are concerned that cannot be allocated the same ontological status. The relationship of tension between history and myth cannot be abolished.

> Der Christus, der verkündigt wird, ist nicht der historische Jesus, sondern der Christus des Glaubens und des Kultes. (...) Das Christuskerygma ist also Kultuslegende, und die Evangelien sind erweiterte Kultuslegenden. (...) Mk hat diesen Typus des Evangeliums geschaffen; der Christusmythos gibt seinem Buch (...) eine zwar nicht biographische, aber eine im Mythos des Kerygmas begründete Einheit.[3]

So writes RUDOLF BULTMANN, and although one may not agree with his assumption that the gospel narrative is merely a secondary supplementation and illustration of a pre-existing primitive Christian-Hellenistic kerygma, his definition of this as "Christusmythos" cannot be ignored. The gospel narrative is a Christ myth, and the Christian belief has nothing other than this narrative foundation to follow. But in this way the question of the role of historicity has only been intensified, and the main theological problem is then to determine which historicity is to be followed if belief itself is not to fail to appreciate its foundation.

This definition can be approached on the basis of a more precise perception of what is meant by saying that the gospel narrative is a myth. It may be said

---

[3] Rudolf Bultmann, *Die Geschichte der synoptischen Tradition*, Göttingen 1970, p. 396.

provisionally that it is a myth, since it is concerned with man's historical reality. This definition may perhaps seem paradoxical, since myth is indeed often contrasted exclusively with history. The worlds of myth and history have nothing to do with one another, since the myth-narrative and the history-narrative contain aspects of reality that mutually exclude one another. But the Christian understanding of reality is indeed characterized by its indissoluble connection between myth and history.

The nature of the actual world defines this as the world of *historicity*, a special latitude in which man sees himself modalized. He is defined by certain boundaries within which he displays his creative activity. In this historical world man is equipped with dynamic, although restricted, competence. In this "possible world" he will see himself defined in terms of processes that are both possible and evitable at one and the same time. For example, he may take his own life (this is a possibility), but he may also refrain from this (there is of course no necessity here). But this also applies in relation to processes that are inevitable, since he unavoidably will die, and processes that are impossible, since he cannot live for ever.

The changes taking place in the historical world will intervene to change this historical competence, since acts and events open up new, and close off existing, possibilities. But an historical act will never be able to change the modalization that constitutes the historical competence as historical. This requires a mythical or transempirical act.

Such an act can be defined as an act that establishes or abolishes man's historical competence, his historicity. More precisely, it may be said that the myth concerns man's historical reality, because it is the narrative of an act which (protologically) establishes or (eschatologically) abolishes historicity.

It is inherent in the matter that the historical interpretant alone accepts as real the acts that belong to the historical competence. It must necessarily, therefore, come into conflict with a myth-narrative which recounts transempirical acts modifying this competence. The myth is therefore always historically false; it will never be able to stand when confronted with history's demand for truth. Nevertheless, it is concerned with history itself.

It is also clear that while the myth of the origin of history must necessarily recount acts that took place outside history (temporally: in "primordial times"), the myth about the abolition of history must recount with the same necessity acts that take place within history (temporally: in "historical times").

The gospel narrative is a myth in this sense, recounting an act, death on the cross, which abolishes history - even though the fatal, cosmological sanction is postponed. This act must necessarily take place in history, since Christianity's reality is one. The Christ myth does not concern the mythical severed from history; the historical has been let into a greater reality that the myth discloses. The truth it reveals can never be an historical truth, although it is the truth about history and man's historicity. But it is a mythical or narrative truth, i.e. a truth that exists only in the revelation of it by the narrative.

The myth reveals a secret that cannot be revealed under any terms other than those of the narrative.[4] In this perspective, the Christ myth is in all seriousness the revelation of a *messianic secret*, the secret of the kingdom of God, 4,11.

The Fall myth that few would consider an historical source of reliable information about what actually occurred is the account of the origin of history. In the beginning, Adam and Eve find themselves in the garden of Eden, a place that is pre-historical in so far as they are in fact not modalized as historical subjects. Death is not inevitable for them; but it is the very inevitability of death, i.e. the provisional life, which characterizes and constitutes man's historicity. After the crime, they are expelled from this ahistorical place and thereby undergo a modal change that places them as historical subjects. They become historical by virtue of their misdeed, and their descendants are unable to change the fact that death becomes a boundary - the cherubim bar the way.

However strange this may sound, after the expulsion from the garden of Eden, man is an historical person. But only narrative existence can be imputed to him, since he is just a narrated actor in a narrative. On the other hand - and this is crucial - an historical interpretation that deprives Adam and Eve of historical existence in no way contests the validity of their narrative historicity. It is, of course, in no way possible to contest the validity of this narrative historically.

The Christ myth is the account of an event that involves the abolition of history. In the nature of the matter, this event must necessarily take place in history if man - the Son of Man - is to continue to play an integrated role in the cosmic process of events. It is therefore natural to consider the gospel narrative as the mythical Christ-interpretation of an historical fact, the crucifixion of Jesus of Nazareth. The historical taking, execution or murder, is interpreted mythically as a gift.

But this concept is equivocal. Within the gospel narrative one can distinguish between the "earthly Jesus" and the "heavenly Christ", which is the same as distinguishing between the "earthly Jesus" and the "heavenly Jesus". The antitheses earth/heaven are employed rather than the historical Jesus and the mythical Jesus to avoid confusion. What would otherwise certainly occur is that "the historical Jesus" in one sense would be confused with "the historical Jesus" in another sense. The problem is that the contrast between myth and history is often seen as a contrast between narrative and reality.

One ignores that the contrast between myth and history already exists within the gospel narrative itself.

The earthly Jesus is historical in the same sense that Adam and Eve are historical after expulsion from the garden of Eden. As an actor in a narrative, the

---

[4] Cf. Johannes Sløk, Det religiøse sprog (The Language of Religion), Århus 1981, pp. 91.

earthly Jesus has been assigned an historical existence, but a narrative historicity is here concerned. It is *the narrative Jesus* who undergoes a process from earthly to heavenly, from historical to mythical, existence.

If the gospel narrative's mythical or transempirical material is parenthesized and the narrative's historical aspect is focused upon, will this give a picture of Jesus of Nazareth that the historian can accept as historically true? Put differently: is there a coincidence between narrative historicity and historical factuality? Is the coincidence of names a guarantee that the historical Jesus of Nazareth and the narrative Jesus of Nazareth are one and the same person?

There may be coincidence, but such coincidence does not follow from necessity. One cannot infer from narrative historicity to historical factuality, cf. the Fall myth. Even in a case where a coincidence exists, a break will be concerned, a discontinuity, since the linguistic construction can never be anything other than a representation, either in the form of a true revelation or an untrue simulation.

One cannot infer from this in itself that the narrative has been told, that whatever it tells is historically true.

Now there can be no doubt that the gospel narrative asserts an identity between its own actor "Jesus of Nazareth" and the historical Jesus of Nazareth. But this historical identification must be distinguished from the narrative identification, where the narrated Jesus of Nazareth - in the narrative - is united with the narrated "Christ".

The historical Jesus should not be contrasted with the mythical Christ but with the narrative Jesus, who in his turn can be articulated in the narrative-historical Jesus, the earthly or realistic (empirical) Jesus and the mythical (transempirical) Jesus:

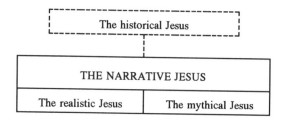

Strictly speaking, "the realistic Jesus" is the state of being the narrative Jesus occupies only until the anointing is accomplished. He already enters into the mythical sphere in his capacity of virtual Christ, and the death on the cross, which makes him the actualized Christ, is both a mythical and an historical event (provisional death). Only the resurrection makes him a fully realized mythical person. One can then see that the gospel narrative's events take place during a liminal period in which the narrative Jesus has left behind his historical existence but has not yet arrived at his mythical existence. Jesus thus appears in ambiguity, at the same time an historical and a mythical person. But both the historical and the mythical are a narrative existence, both the historical and the mythical are signification phenomena in the discourse.

Theologically, narrative exegesis builds upon the circumstance that the Christian faith has a narrative foundation and can never get behind the gospel narrative. But this point of reference in no way involves a failure to appreciate the belief's own foundation, i.e. that the Christ event is the union of history and myth. On the other hand, it is stressed *that this union has been established by the gospel narrative, which proclaims the narrative Jesus.*

It should of course be considered whether the myth/history dichotomy that is held to articulate the gospel narrative's content arises from an artificially introduced distinction which is in fact alien to the gospel. In that case this narrative would speak from an undivided understanding of reality, within which a distinction between mythical and historical existence would be meaningless. If one operates with such a distinction between myth and history, it could be objected that this is because one shares a split concept of reality which is alien to the gospel. The schism - as a result of an epistemological Fall - would then have had to occur somewhere between then and now and involve a replacement of the blind impotence of naivety by the delivering knowledge of experience. History has left myth behind, and the gospel narrative's mythical language must therefore be translated, perhaps demythologized.

Without failing to appreciate the differences that of course exist between the reception situation then and now, it is however possible to observe that the gospel narrative is not quite as mythologically simple as a self-overestimating exegesis would like to assert. When Jesus tells the mourners that Jairus' daughter is not dead but sleeping they laugh at him (5,39). His disciples do not understand what it means to rise from the dead (9,10). The Jewish leaders see Jesus as a blasphemer (14,64) and have him executed as such, but when he is hanging on the cross they ridicule him: "Let the Messiah, the King of Israel, come down from the cross now, so that we may see and believe." (15,32). The narrated opponents in fact do not reject Jesus on the basis of an alternative religious or mythological understanding of reality but from an ordinary, empirical concept of reality. There is here no mythological world image to demythologize.

This observation is important, since the narrated actors cognitive resistance is again found in the model reader's presupposed resistance to the narration. Mark knows, above all from within himself, that his message contradicts the narratee's empirical understanding of reality. The proclamation of Jesus' resurrection has from the outset encountered a resistance (cf. Mt 27,62ff; 28,11ff) which the proclamation of his death does not experience. The resistance to the gospel has manifested itself from the beginning, because this resistance is basically a structurally conditioned fact. In this connection one should not ignore that according to the gospel narrative itself - and not only to modern, historical criticism - the empirical concept of Jesus is the most probable. From this perspective, the difference between then and now is not so crucial; the basic difference between history and myth remains intact. And although the Christian message is open to any description or interpretation, it does not permit reformulation or translation once and for all into an anthropological or philosophical discourse.

Narrative exegesis may be said to *dehistorify* the gospel narrative, since it does not treat the existing discourse philologically and historically by placing it in an "original" context, but *decontextualizes* it and gives it the status of a virtual discourse that is initially its own context, but whose potential of signification is then actualized in the proclamation and realized in the reception.

Narrative exegesis has not thereby simply disposed of the question of historicity's role in the content of the Christian proclamation. The historical aspect appears, however, on the other scene that the narrative constitutes and demands all possible attention from the semiotic or narrative criticism, one of whose tasks is to explain in detail the extent to which the gospel of Jesus Christ symbolizes or semiotizes our historical reality.

God has revealed himself to his people through the *Word*, - *the story about the narrative Jesus*. But it remains a secret whether this narrative is true outside the narrated world. Neither is this generation to be given an unambiguous sign from Heaven; it must be content with an equivocal narrative. And no one who tells this narrative can guarantee its truth; - neither can Mark.

But behold, now it has been told you!

INDICES

INDEX OF SEQUENCES

A.

B.

INDEX OF TITLES AND ROLES

A.

ἀγαθοποιός 64, 67, 69
ἀγαπητός 181, 267, 292
ἄγγελος 107f, 145, 155, 177
ἄδικος 164, 238
αἱμορροῶν 73ff
ἀκάθαρτος 72, 76
ἀκόλουθος 206, 317
ἀλλάσσων 314
ἁμαρτωλός 260
ἄνθρωπος 200, 340
ἄνθρωπος τοῦ θεοῦ 197, 338
ἀνταλλάσσων 314
ἀπαλλάσσων 314
ἀπατῶν 116, 142
ἄπιστος 136
ἀποκαταστάτης 64f, 67, 70
ἀπολύτηρ 313
ἀπολλύων 84, 222, 344
ἀπολλυμένος 73, 75, 77, 84, 222
ἀπολυτρωτής 314
ἀπόστολος 155f
ἅρπαξ 66
ἄρρωστος 74ff
ἀρχηγός 145
ἀσθενής 74ff
ἀφίεις 261
ἄφρων 137, 279
βαπτίζων 143
βαπτιστής 143
βασιλεύς 269, 292
βλέπων 135
βοηθός 63f, 67, 69
γεωργός 180, 182
δαιμονιζόμενος 68, 73ff, 76
δανειστής 243
δεόμενος 78
δεσμεύων 66, 70

δεσμώτης 73f, 77
δεσπότης 236
διάκονος 236, 357
διασκορπιζόμενος 73, 75, 77
διδάσκαλος 88f, 107, 109, 155f, 191
δίκαιος 164, 238, 260
δικαστής 238
δότης 242
δοῦλος 180f, 236, 269f
ἐγείρων 53, 64ff, 70, 79
ἐκβάλλων 64f, 66
ἐκκαλῶν 311
ἐκλεκτικός 311
ἐκλεκτός 268, 292
ἐκλυόμενος 73, 77
ἐξορκιστής 66
ἐπαγγέλλων 142
ἐπιτακτήρ 71
ἐπιτιμητής 64f, 67, 71, 86
ἐσχάτως ἔχων 73f, 76
εὐαγγελιστής 107f
ἡγεμών 142
θαυματουργός 65
θεῖος ἀνήρ 197
θεμελιῶν 192
θεός 200
θεραπευτής 43ff, 64f, 66
θέτης 192, 246
ἰατρός 44, 64
ἰσχυρός 66, 77
καθαρτής 63, 66f
καθηγητής 142
κακῶς 74f, 76
καλῶν 311
κατακείμενος 72, 74f
καταλλάσσων 314

INDEX OF SUBJECTS

INDEX OF AUTHORS

BIBLIOGRAPHY

Achtemeier, P.J. "An Imperfect Union: Reflections on Gerd Theissen, Urchrist-liche Wundergeschichten", *Semeia 11, Early Christian Miracle Stories*, Missoula 1978, pp. 49.

Aland, K. "Bemerkungen zum Schluss des Markusevangeliums", E.E. Ellis and M. Wilcox (eds.), *Neotestamentica et Semitica*, Edinburgh 1969, pp. 157.

——, "Der Schluss des Markusevangeliums", M. Sabbe (ed.), *L'Évangile selon Marc*, Gembloux 1974, pp. 435.

——, (ed.), *Novum Testamentum Graece*, 26th edition, 7th print, Stuttgart 1983.

——, *Synopsis Quattuor Evangeliorum*, 13th revised edition, 2nd print, Stuttgart 1986.

Anselm of Canterbury *Hvorfor Gud blev menneske*, København 1978.

Aristotle *The Poetics*, The Loeb Classical Library, London 1965.

Baarlink, H. *Die Eschatologie der synoptischen Evangelien*, Stuttgart 1986.

Bauer, W. *Griechisch-Deutsches Wörterbuch zu den Schriften des Neuen Testaments und der übrigen urchristlichen Literatur*, Berlin 1971.

Belo, F. *Lecture matérialiste de l'évangile de Marc*, Paris 1976.

Benveniste, É. *Problèmes de linguistique générale I*, Paris 1966.

Berger, K. "Zum Traditionsgeschichtlichen Hintergrund christologischer Hoheits-titel", *New Testament Studies 17*, Cambridge 1971, pp. 391.

——, "Die königlichen Messiastradition des Neuen Testaments", *New Testament Studies 20*, Cambridge 1973, pp. 1.

Berger, P.L. *The Social Reality of Religion*, Harmondsworth 1973.

Best, E. *The Temptation and the Passion: The Markan Soteriology*, Cambridge 1965.

——, *Mark. The Gospel as Story*, Edinburgh 1983.

——, *Disciples and Discipleship. Studies in the Gospel According to Mark*, Edinburgh 1986.

Black, C.C. *The Disciples According to Mark. Markan Redaction in Current Debate*, Sheffield 1989.

Blass, F. and A. Debrunner, *Grammatik des neutestamentlichen Griechisch*, Göttingen 1970.

Blevins, J. L. *The Messianic Secret in Markan Research 1901-1976*, Washington 1981.

Boers, H. "Sisyphus and his Rock. Concerning Gerd Theissen Urchristliche Wundergeschichten", *Semeia 11, Early Christian Miracle Stories*, Missoula 1978, pp. 1.

Boring, M.E. "The Christology of Mark: Hermeneutical Issues for Systematic Theology", *Semeia 30, Christology and Exegesis: New Approaches*, Missoula 1985, pp. 125.

Bornkamm, G. *Paulus*, Stuttgart 1969.

Brandenburger, E. *Adam und Christus. Exegetisch-religionsgeschichtliche Untersuchung zu Röm. 5,12-21 (1. Kor. 15)*, Neukirchen 1962.

Brandt, P.Aa. *Sandheden, sætningen og døden. Semiotiske aspekter af kulturanalysen*, Århus, 1983.

——, "Genese og diegese. Et problem i den almene narratologi", *Religionsvidenskabeligt Tidsskrift 14*, Århus 1989, pp. 75.

Brask, P. *Tekst og tolkning. Første del. Bidrag til den litterære semantik*, København 1973.

Bremond, C. "La logique des possibles narratifs", *Communications 8, L'analyse structurale du récit*, Paris 1966.

——, *Logique du récit*, Paris 1973.

Bultmann, R. *Die Geschichte der synoptischen Tradition*, Göttingen (1921) 1970 (*The History of the Synoptic Tradition*, Oxford 1963).

——, "Neues Testament und Mythologie", Hans Werner Bartsch (ed.), *Kerygma und Mythos I*, Hamburg (1948) 1960, pp. 15.

——, *Theologie des Neuen Testaments*, Tübingen (1958) 1968 (*Theology of the New Testament*, London 1955).

Casey, M. *Son of Man. The Interpretation and Influence of Daniel 7*, London 1979.

Chabrol, C. and L. Marin, *Le récit évangélique*, Paris 1974.

Charles, R.H. (ed.). *The Apocrypha and Pseudepigrapha of the Old Testament*, Vol. II, Oxford (1913) 1969.

Charlesworth, J.H. (ed.) *The Old Testament Pseudepigrapha*, Vol. 2, London 1985.

Conzelmann, H. *Grundriß der Theologie des Neuen Testaments*, München 1968 (*An Outline of Theology of the New Testament*, London 1969).

Coquet, J.-C. (ed.), *Sémiotique. L'École de Paris*, Paris 1982

Courtés, J. *Introduction à la sémiotique narrative et discursive*, Paris 1976.

Cullmann, O. *Die Christologie des Neuen Testaments*, Tübingen 1966.

Daly, R.J. *Christian Sacrifice. The Judaeo-Christian Background Before Origen*, Washington, 1978.

Davidsen, O. "Bund. Ein religionssemiotischer Beitrag zur Definition der alttestamentlichen Bundesstruktur", *Linguistica Biblica 48*, Bonn 1980, pp. 49.

——, "Der Status der Religionssemiotik als autonome Wissenschaft", *Linguistica Biblica 49*, Bonn 1981, pp. 71.

——, *Le contrat réalisable. Contribution à l'élargissement et à la consolidation du concept de schéma narratif canonique*, Actes Sémiotiques/Documents 46, Paris 1983.

——, "Narrativité et existence. Sur une détermination du Jésus narratif dans l'évangile de Marc", *Sémiotique et Bible 48*, Lyon 1987, pp. 18.

Delling, G. *Der Kreuzetod Jesu in der urchristlichen Verkündigung*, Göttingen 1972.

Delorme, J. "Sémiotique du récit et récit de la Passion", *Revue des Sciences Religieuses 73*, Paris 1985, pp. 85.

Dewey, J. "Point of view and the Disciples in Mark", Kent Harold Richards (ed.), *Society of Biblical Literature 1982 Seminar Papers*, Chico 1982, pp. 97.

Dibelius, M. *Die Formgeschichte des Evangeliums*, Tübingen (1919) 1971.

Dodd, C.H. *The Interpretation of the Fourth Gospel*, Cambridge 1970.

Dokka, T.S. *Å gjenkjenne den ukjente. Om menneskers mulighet for å kjenne Gud - en studie basert på Johannes-evangeliets tegnstoff*, Oslo 1989.

Dunn, J.D.G. *Christology in the Making. A New Testament Inquiry into the Origins of the Doctrine of the Incarnation*, London 1980.

Eco, U. *The Role of the Reader. Explorations in the Semiotics of Texts*, London 1981.

Fascher, E. "Theologische Beobachtungen zu δεῖ", *Neutestamentliche Studien für Rudolf Bultmann*, Berlin 1954, pp. 228.

Feldmeier, R. *Die Krisis des Gottessohnes. Die Gethsemaneerzählung als Schlüssel der Markuspassion*, Tübingen 1987.

Frazer, J.G. *Folk-Lore in the Old Testament*, London 1923.

Frege, G. "Über Sinn und Bedeutung" (1892), G. Patzig (ed.), *Funktion, Begriff, Bedeutung. Fünf logische Studien*, Göttingen 1969.

Freud, S. "Der Dichter und das Phantasieren", *Studienausgabe Band X, Bildende Kunst und Literatur*, Frankfurt am Main 1975, pp. 171.

Frye, N. *The Great Code. The Bible and Literature*, London 1981.

Genest, O. *Le Christ de la Passion. Perspective structurale. Analyse de Marc 14,53-15,47, des parallèles bibliques et extra-bibliques*, Montréal 1978.

Girard, R. *Des choses cachées depuis la fondation du monde*, Paris 1978.

Giversen, S. *Det ny Testamentes Teksthistorie*, København 1978.

Goppelt, L. *Typos. Die typologische Deutung des Alten Testaments im Neuen*, Gütersloh, 1939.

Greimas, A.-J. *Sémantique structurale. Recherche de méthode*, Paris 1966 (*Structural Semantics*, London 1983).

——, *Du sens. Essais sémiotiques*, Paris 1970 (Cf. *On Meaning. Selected Writings in Semiotic Theory*, London 1987).

——, and J. Courtés, *Sémiotique. Dictionnaire raisonné de la théorie du langage*, Paris 1979 (*Semiotics and Language. An Analytical Dictionary*, Bloomington 1982).

——, *Du sens II. Essais Sémiotiques*, Paris 1983 (Cf. *On Meaning. Selected Writings in Semiotic Theory*, London 1987).

——, and J. Courtés (eds.), *Sémiotique. Dictionnaire raisonné de la théorie du langage. Tome 2*, Paris 1986.

Groupe d'Entrevernes. *Signes et paraboles. Sémiotique et texte évangélique*, Paris 1977.

Grundmann, W. *Das Evangelium nach Markus*, Berlin 1971.

Guelich, R. "The Gospel Genre", Peter Stuhlmacher (ed.), *Das Evangelium und die Evangelien*, Tübingen 1983, pp. 183.

Güttgemanns, E. *Offene Fragen zur Formgeschichte des Evangeliums*, München 1971.

Haag, H. *Der Gottesknecht bei Deuterojesaja*, Darmstadt 1985.

Haenchen, E. *Der Weg Jesu. Eine Erklärung des Markus-Evangeliums und der kanonischen Parallelen*, Berlin 1968.

Hahn, F. *Christologische Hoheitstitel. Ihre Geschichte im frühen Christentum*, Göttingen 1964 (*The Titles of Jesus in Christology*, London 1969).

Hallbäck, G. *Strukturalisme og eksegese*, København 1983.

Heine, G. *Synonymik des Neutestamentlichen Griechisch*, Leipzig 1898.

Hennecke, E. and W. Schneemelcher. *Neutestamentliche Apokryphen in deutscher Übersetzung I/II*. 4. Auflage, Tübingen 1968 (*New Testament Apocrypha*, London 1965).

Hjelmslev, L. *Omkring sprogteoriens grundlæggelse*, København 1943 (*Prolégomènes à une théorie du langage*, Paris 1968).

Holman, C.H. (ed.). *A Handbook to Literature*, New York 1972.

Hooker, M.D. *The Gospel According to St Mark*, London 1991.

Iersel, B. van *Reading Mark*, Edinburgh 1989.

Jakobson, R. "Closing statement: Linguistics and Poetics", Thomas A. Sebeok (ed.), *Style in Language*, New York 1960, ss. 350.

Jeremias, J. *Die Kindertaufe in den ersten vier Jahrhunderten*, Göttingen 1958.

Kalluveettil, P. *Declaration and Covenant*, Rome 1982.

Kelber, W.H. *The Kingdom in Mark. A New Place and a New Time*, Philadelphia 1974.

Kemp, P. *Théorie de l'engagement/2. Poétique de l'engagement*, Paris 1973.

Kermode, F. *The Genesis of Secrecy*, London 1979.

Kieffer, R. *Essais de métodologie néo-testamentaire*, Lund 1972.

Kingsbury, J.D. *The Christology of Mark's Gospel*, Philadelphia 1982.

Kittel, G. and G. Friedrich (eds.), *Theologisches Wörterbuch zum Neuen Testament*, Stuttgart, 1933f.

Kittel, R. (ed.). *Biblia Hebraica*, Stuttgart (1937) 1968.

Klauck, H.-J. "Die erzählerische Rolle der Jünger im Markusevangelium. Eine narrative Analyse", *Novum Testamentum 24. An International Quarterly for New Testament and Related Studies*, Leiden 1982, pp. 1.

Koch, D.-A. *Die Bedeutung der Wundererzählungen für die Christologie des Markusevangeliums*, Berlin 1975.

Konkordanz zum Novum Testamentum Graece edited by Institut für Neutestamentliche Textforschung og Rechenzentrum der Universität Münster, Berlin 1987.

Kümmel, W.G. *Einleitung in das Neue Testament*, Heidelberg 1970.

Kähler, M. *Der sogenannte historische Jesus und der geschichtliche, biblische Christus*, Leipzig 1892.

Lang, F.G. "Kompositionsanalyse des Markusevangeliums", *Zeitschrift für Theologie und Kirche*, 74. Jahrgang, Tübingen 1977, pp. 1.

Lentzen-Deis, F. *Die Taufe Jesu nach den Synoptikern. Literarkritische und gattungsgeschichtliche Untersuchungen*, Frankfurt am Main 1970.

Lidell, H.G. and R. Scott (eds.). *A Greek-English Lexicon*, Oxford 1966.

Linguistica Biblica. Interdisziplinäre Zeitschrift für Theologie und Linguistik, Bonn 1970ff.

Lohmeyer, E. *Kyrios Jesus, Eine Untersuchung zu Phil 2,5-11*, Darmstadt (1927) 1961.

——, *Das Evangelium des Markus*, Göttingen (1937) 1967.

Lohse, F. *Märtyrer und Gottesknecht. Untersuchungen zur urchristlichen Verkündigung vom Sühntod Jesu Christi*, Göttingen 1963.

Lührmann, D. *Das Markusevangelium*, Tübingen 1987.

Magness, J.L. *Sense and Absence. Structure and Suspension in the Ending of Mark's Gospel*, Atlanta 1986.

Marin, L. *Sémiotique de la Passion. Topiques et figures*, Paris 1971.

Marxsen, W. *Der Evangelist Markus. Studien zur Redaktionsgeschichte des Evangeliums*, Göttingen 1959 (*Mark the Evangelist*, Nashville 1969).

Metzger, B.M. and R.E. Murphy (eds.), *The New Oxford Annotated Bible with the Apocryphal/Deuterocanonical Books*, Oxford 1991.

Meye, R.P. *Jesus and the Twelve: Discipleship and Revelation in Mark's Gospel*, Grand Rapids 1968.

Müller, M. *Der Ausdruck "Menschensohn" in den Evangelien. Voraussetzungen und Bedeutung*, Leiden 1984.

Nef, F. (ed.), *Structures élémentaires de la signification*, Bruxelles 1976.

Noack, B. *Markusevangeliets lignelseskapitel*, København 1965.

Normann, F. *Christos Didaskalos. Die Vorstellung von Christus als Lehrer in der christlichen Literatur des ersten und zweiten Jahrhunderts*, Münster 1967.

Nützel, J.M. *Die Verklärungserzählung im Markusevangelium. Eine redaktions-geschichtliche Untersuchung*, Würzburg 1973.

Parret, H. and H.G. Ruprecht (eds.), *Exigences et perspectives de la sémiotique. Recueil d'hommage pour Algirdas Julien Greimas I/II*, New York 1985.

Patte, D. and A. Patte. *Structural Exegesis: From Theory to Practice. Exegesis of Mark 15 and 16. Hermeneutical Implications*, Philadelphia 1978.

Pedersen, S. "Dåbsteologien i Markusevangeliet", Sigfred Pedersen (red.), *Dåben i Ny Testamente*, Århus 1982, pp. 49.

Pesch, R. *Das Markusevangelium*, Freiburg 1980.

Petersen, N.R. "'Point of view' in Mark's Narrative", *Semeia 12, Rhetoric, Eschatology, and Ethics in the New Testament*, Missoula 1978, pp. 97.

Pilgaard, Aa. "Gudsrigebegrebet i Markusevangeliet", *Dansk Teologisk Tidsskrift 43. årg.*, København 1980, pp. 20.

——, *Jesus som undergører i Markusevangeliet*, København 1983.

——, *Kommentar til Markusevangeliet*, Århus 1988.

Pomerol, P.J. de. *Quand un évangile nous est conté. Analyse morphologique du récit de Matthieu*, Bruxelles 1980.

Prince, G. *A Dictionary of Narratology*, Aldershot 1988.

Propp, V. *Morphology of the Folktale*, Austin 1968.

Rahlfs, A. (ed.), *Septuaginta*, Stuttgart (1935) 1971.

Rhoads, D. and D. Michie. *Mark as Story. An Introduction to the Narrative of a Gospel*, Philadelphia 1982.

Ricoeur, P. *Temps et Récit*, Paris 1983 (*Time and Narrative*, Chicago 1984).

Ritschl, A. *Die christliche Lehre von der Rechtfertigung und Versöhnung*, Bonn 1870.

Räisänen, H. *Das "Messiasgeheimnis" im Markusevangelium. Ein redaktions-kritischer Versuch*, Helsinki 1976.

Saussure, F. de *Cours de linguistique générale*, Paris 1916.

Schmidt, K.L. *Der Rahmen der Geschichte Jesu*, Berlin 1919.

Schmithals, W. *Das Evangelium nach Markus*, Gütersloh 1979.

——, *Einleitung in die drei ersten Evangelien*, Berlin 1985.

Schulz, S. *Die Stunde der Botschaft. Einführung in die Theologie der vier Evangelisten*, Hamburg 1967.

Schweizer, E. *Erniedrigung und Erhöhung bei Jesus und seinen Nachfolgern*, Zürich 1962.

——, *Das Evangelium nach Markus*, Göttingen 1978.

Semeia. An experimental journal for biblical criticism, Missoula 1974ff.

Sémiotique et bible. Bulletin d'études et d'échanges publié par le centre pour l'analyse du discours religieux, Lyon 1975ff.

Simonsen, H. *Traditionssammenhæng og forkyndelsessigte i Markusevangeliets fortællestof*, København 1966.

——, "Messiashemmeligheden og Markusevangeliets struktur", *Svensk Exegetisk Årsbok 37-38*, Lund 1973, pp. 107.

Sløk, J. *Det religiøse sprog*, Århus 1981.

Standaert, B. *L'Évangile selon Marc: composition et genre littéraire*, Brugge 1978.

Steichele, H.-J. *Der leidende Sohn Gottes. Eine Untersuchung einiger alttestamentlicher Motive in der Christologie des Markusevangeliums*, Regensburg 1980.

Tannehill, R.C. "The Disciples in Mark: The Function of a Narrative Role", *The Journal of Religion 57*, Chicago 1977, s. 386.

——, "The Gospel of Mark as Narrative Christology", *Semeia 16, Perspectives on Mark's Gospel*, Missoula 1979, pp. 57.

Taylor, V. *The Gospel According to Mark*, London (1952) 1959.

Theißen, G. *Urchristliche Wundergeschichten. Ein Beitrag zur formgeschichtlichen Erforschung der synoptischen Evangelien*, Göttingen 1974 (*The Miracle Stories of the Early Christian Tradition*, Philadelphia 1983).

Thodberg, C. "Perikopevalgets tekstforståelse og Ny Testamente med særligt henblik på dåben", Sigfred Pedersen (red.), *Dåben i Ny Testamente*, Århus 1982, pp. 266.

Todorov, T. (ed.), *Langages 17, L'Enonciation*, Paris 1970.

Via, D.O. *Kerygma and Comedy in the New Testament. A Structuralist Approach to Hermeneutic*, Philadelphia 1975.

Vielhauer, P. *Aufsätze zum Neuen Testament*, München 1965.

Vorster, W. "Markus - Sammler, Redaktor, Autor oder Erzähler?", Ferdinand Hahn (ed.), *Der Erzähler des Evangeliums. Methodische Neuansätze in der Markusforschung*, Stuttgart 1985, pp. 11.

Weeden, T.J. *Mark: Traditions in Conflict*, Philadelphia 1971.

Westermann, C. *Genesis*, Neukirchen 1976.

Wilder, A.N. "Semeia, An Experimental Journal for Biblical Criticism: An Introduction", *Semeia 1, A Structuralist Approach to the Parables*, Missoula 1974, pp. 1.

Wrede, W. *Das Messiasgeheimnis ind den Evangelien. Zugleich ein Beitrag zum Verständnis des Markusevangeliums*, Göttingen 1901 (*The Messianic Secret*, London 1981).

Zimmermann, H. *Neutestamentliche Metodenlehre. Darstellung der historisch-kritischen Methode*, Stuttgart 1970.

DATE DUE

MAR 2 9 1995			
MAR 0 5 1998			
FEB 2 1 2005			
			Printed in USA